THE REAL ALL AMERICANS

THE REAL ALL AMERICANS

THE TEAM THAT CHANGED
A GAME, A PEOPLE, A NATION

SALLY JENKINS

Doubleday

New York London Toronto Sydney Auckland

For Nicky, who feels the drums . . .

PUBLISHED BY DOUBLEDAY

Copyright © 2007 by Sally Jenkins

All Rights Reserved

Published in the United States by Doubleday, an imprint of The Doubleday
Broadway Publishing Group, a division of Random House, Inc., New York.
www.doubleday.com

DOUBLEDAY and the portrayal of an anchor with a dolphin are registered
trademarks of Random House, Inc.

Book design by Chris Welch

Cataloging-in-Publication Data is on file with The Library of Congress.

ISBN: 978-0-385-51987-8

PRINTED IN THE UNITED STATES OF AMERICA

1 3 5 7 9 10 8 6 4 2

First Edition

Acknowledgments

First and most grateful thanks goes, as ever, to Esther Newberg of ICM for always thinking I can do it.

I'm indebted to Phyllis Grann of Doubleday for the opportunity, and her wise editing, and to Karyn Marcus for her aid in anything and everything.

Dave Meade's encouragement and his personal introductions at the U.S. Army War College made it immeasurably easier to start this book. His basic example of backbone made it impossible not to finish.

Anyone who looks into the Carlisle Indian Industrial School even briefly runs straight into the scholarship and the kindness of Barbara Landis and the staff at the Cumberland County Historical Society. It's the lucky writer-researcher who finds a path so clearly laid out. It's a luckier one who gets to sit in Barb's kitchen and sip a glass of wine, while absorbing her knowledge.

Pine Ridge, S.D., is a place of stirring beauty, awful instruction, and wonderful people. Joe American Horse shared his family history there, and Darlene Rooks did the same by phone. Tawa Ducheneaux of the Lakota-Oglala College gave invaluable help and advice.

Grace Thorpe's research on her father is essential reading, and she generously offers additional information to every caller and visitor, as does Mike Koehler with his own perspective and memories of his grandfather.

Fort Sill is not just home of the U.S. Army Field Artillery, it's also home to the Fort Sill National Historic Landmark, one of the great museums of the American West, through the efforts of curator Towana Spivey. He devoted the better part of a day to guiding me through the grounds and collection there, and tutoring me in local history.

The U.S. Army War College is one of the more remarkable places in this country, not least because the old Carlisle campus is hauntingly preserved there. A visitor can sleep in the old athletic dormitory, and jog around the field where Thorpe once ran. It's also home to the Military History Institute at the Army Heritage and Education Center, a treasure trove and a beautiful place to work.

The staff at the War College could not have been more hospitable, starting with Lt. Col. Merideth Bucher of public affairs, who was eloquent on the subject of "the thinking Army," and also offered a personal contact at Fort Sill. The Commandant of the War College, Maj. Gen. David H. Huntoon Jr., was an enthusiastic host and contributor of ideas, and Dr. Conrad Crane, director of the MHI, took time out from studying counterinsurgency to chat about the Army team of 1912, and to offer an elementary lesson in researching military history.

Each summer, the War College honors its past with a Jim Thorpe Sports Day, an uproarious and heated competition between the various service branch War Colleges. This country's most promising officers race across the field where Thorpe once ran. It's the last time they get to compete without consequence—most of them go hurrying back to Iraq or Afghanistan when their term of study is done. Thanks to the War College for allowing me to observe that extraordinary day.

It's hard to adequately thank all of the archivists who patiently answered questions. Most of the manuscript was researched and written in public buildings, from the National Archives to the MHI to the New York Public Library to the tiny John Jermain Library in Sag Harbor. Oddly enough, an old Carlisle benefactor built the latter.

Any book on Carlisle depends heavily on the work of David Wallace Adams. His book *Education for Extinction* is dazzling and indispensable, and he was kind enough to offer advice and to read parts of this manuscript. Thanks also to Michael Oriard, whose book *Reading Football, How the Popular Press Created an American Spectacle* reintroduced me to the Carlisle Indians as an adult, and was the initial inspiration, as well as a constant resource.

Finally, thanks to the ghosts and the doves.

CONTENTS

TWO FIELDS

THE GAME, LIKE the country in which it was invented, was a rough, bastardized thing that jumped up out of the mud. What was football but barely legalized fighting? On the raw autumn Saturday of November 9, 1912, it was no small reflection of the American character.

The coach of the Carlisle Indian School, Glenn Scobey "Pop" Warner, strode up and down the aisles of the locker room, a Turkish Trophy cigarette forked between his fingers. Warner, slab-faced and profane, wasn't one for speeches, unless cussing counted. But he was about to make an exception.

The twenty-two members of the Carlisle team sat, tense, on rows of wooden benches. Some of them laced up ankle-high leather cleats, thick-soled as jackboots. Others pulled up heavy football pants, which bagged around their thighs like shapeless quilts. They shrugged into bulky scarlet sweaters, with flannel stuffed in the shoulders for padding. Flap-eared leather helmets sat on the benches next to them, stiff as picnic baskets.

Often Warner was at a loss to inspire the Indians. He didn't claim to always understand their motives the way he did those of other college men, and he had put his boot in their backsides on more than one occasion. Jim Thorpe could be especially galling. The twenty-five-year-old Oklahoman from the Sauk and Fox tribe had a strange introverted disposition and a carelessness that baffled Warner. But on this occasion, Warner knew just how to reach Thorpe and his teammates. There was no question the players regarded this game dead seriously: Carlisle, the nation's flagship institution for Native Americans, was to meet the U.S. Military Academy in a game between two of the top teams in the country.

It was an exquisitely apt piece of national theater: a contest between Indians and soldiers. The scions of the armed forces, officers in training, represented a military legacy that taunted the Indians, Warner knew. The frontier battles between tribes and saber-waving U.S. Army "long knives" were fresh in their minds—he had been reminding them of the subject all week long.

"I shouldn't have to prepare you for this game," Warner told them. "Just go to your rooms and read your history books."[1]

The distance between battlefield and football field was not great that November afternoon. Just twenty-two years earlier, on December 29, 1890, the U.S. Army had met Big Foot's band at Wounded Knee in the last large-scale confrontation between the military and American Indians. Feelings between the Army and Carlisle ran so high that this was only the second time government authorities had allowed the two parties to meet on an athletic field. "When Indian outbreaks in the West were frequent Government officials thought it unwise to have the aborigines and future officers combat in athletics," the *New York Times* reported.[2]

To both sides, football was more than a game. It was war without death. As audience and participants alike understood it, the gridiron was a training tool to prepare the best-bred young men in the country to wield power. Harvard football coach W. Cameron Forbes, the grandson of Ralph Waldo Emerson, in 1900 called the sport no less than "the ultimate expression of Anglo-Saxon superiority." It was a game of clout. It was about, among other things, authority.[3]

On the eve of the game, contention filled the air: just four days earlier, an old football man, Woodrow Wilson, had won the presidency in a bitterly disputed three-party election. The defeated "Bull Moose" Progressive, Teddy Roosevelt, another football man, was walking around with an angry lunatic's bullet in his side. Even nature seemed belligerent, sinking the *Titanic* with a punch from an iceberg the previous April. In music, Scott Joplin's jangling rag dueled with the first blues; in Europe, there was skirmishing in the Balkans; and in medicine, the Nobel Prize went to a surgeon for advances in, fittingly, sutures.

In New York City, twenty thousand suffragists marched down Fifth Avenue that Friday night in a torchlight parade. "The fairest fighters," as the *New York Herald* called them, strode four abreast and were accompanied by twenty female trumpeters blasting horns. But Fifth Avenue society was less preoccupied by thousands of suffragists than by one round-collared, gangly young Harvard student, Vincent Astor, due to attain his majority that weekend and come into the fortune left by his father, John Jacob Astor IV, the hotelier, soldier, inventor, and slumlord, who had been crushed by a falling smokestack aboard the *Titanic*. Yet amid all this roil, Americans were transfixed by football. Holding place with these momentous topics in the headlines was the impending contest on the banks of the Hudson River. "Indians to Battle with Soldiers," the *New York Times* announced, as if spectators could miss the point, or the fraught nature of the contest.

Under a cold, slate-colored sky, five thousand observers filled the grandstands that ringed Army Field. Among them was the silver-mustached Walter Camp, the sport's eminence and arbiter of all-Americans, who had come to witness the affair firsthand. Correspondents from the *New York Tribune, New York Times*, and *New York Herald* scribbled bad Indian metaphors in their notebooks. Braid-shouldered officers and cadets in high-necked tunics stood erect in the bleachers, eager to see Army defend its honor. Sporty young men came from Manhattan in three-button sack suits with fashionably cuffed pants, to follow the result of their wagers. Ladies in organdy moved through the crowd, their enormous-brimmed hats floating in the air like boats.

It was an audience steeped in frontier lore, raised on bloodcurdling newspaper accounts of "hostiles," western dime novels like *Mustang Merle, the Boy Rancher*, and of course Buffalo Bill's Wild West Shows. The goateed huckster-showman William Cody was still performing in the fall of 1912, though he was aging, had gotten thick in the waist, and had sunk to endorsing leather halters to make an extra buck. Just a few months later, during a performance in Denver, his show would be seized for debts, and sold at auction.

The rising popularity of football had closely followed the ebbing of the frontier wars. It was as though America, at a loss for what to do with itself once the wilderness was subdued, had hit on football as an answer. Harvard, Princeton, Yale, and Columbia formed the Intercollegiate Football Association on November 23, 1876—just four months after the annihilation of George Armstrong Custer at Little Big Horn. By the 1890s, with the closing of the frontier, Victorian America was intensely preoccupied by the sport as a new male proving ground and a remedy for the neurasthenia of the age. On quadrangles across the country, collegians slammed into each other until the blood and spittle flew, and leviathan new stadiums were built to accommodate the growing pastime. The phenomenon was at least in part explained by the fear that a generation of Gilded Age young men was becoming soft and overcivilized, with nothing left to conquer, and too much time spent in parlors.[4]

One of the campuses most obsessed with football was West Point. Some form of participation in it was almost a requirement for the truly aspiring officer—the Army locker room contained no fewer than *nine* future generals. Their emotional investment in the game reached such a fevered pitch that the editors of that year's class yearbook, *The Howitzer*, pleaded for some perspective. "Football is not life and death. Football is a sport. Sport is chance. And chance can never be courted with other bait than chance . . . Then why not, you who are going to be here, why not play the game with that viewpoint? Why make it more serious than a religion?"

But the cadets didn't just love the game; they loved the most bullying physical form of it. They were a squad of imposing brawn: their captain, Leland Devore, stood six foot six and weighed 240 pounds. In their backfield was an iron-legged young halfback named Dwight David Eisenhower, known for punishing opponents.

The coach of the 1912 Army squad was Ernest "Pot" Graves, a beef-faced martinet whose notion of strategy was straight-ahead battering. Earlier that autumn, Graves had been sitting in the officers' club one day when someone asked him why he employed such a bruising style of play. Outside, a steamroller happened to be parked in front of the club.

"There," Graves said, "is my idea of football."[5]

In Carlisle, Army met its philosophic and stylistic opposite. The two teams could not have been more different. The Indian players who sat in the visitors' locker room were significantly smaller in size, but they were renowned for their dazzling sleight of hand and the breathtaking Olympian speed of their star runner, Thorpe. Under Warner's creative tutelage, they had an astounding array of trick plays, reverses, end-arounds, flea flickers, and spirals through the air. The talent for deception was partly out of necessity: with a student body of just one thousand or so, ranging in age from twelve to twenty-five, Carlisle was perpetually outmanned and undersized. But given a choice between power football and a piece of misdirection, they invariably chose the latter. They were a complicated team psychologically, a bunch of showboats and carousers with uproarious senses of humor, but also a keen sense of wrongs at the hands of the U.S. government. "Nothing delighted them more than to outsmart the pale faces," Warner observed. "There was never a time when they wouldn't rather have won by an eyelash with some wily stratagem than by a large score with straight football."[6]

Ironically, it was a soldier who had founded Carlisle. Richard Henry Pratt, a cavalry officer and veteran of the frontier wars, established the school in an old Army barracks in Pennsylvania in 1879 for the purpose of "civilizing" Indian children. On the exterior Carlisle looked like any other gracious old boarding institution. A series of cream-colored clapboard dormitories lined a quadrangle, where footpaths converged at a Victorian bandstand. But within the walls, Pratt directed a violent social experiment. As Pratt liked to declaim: *"Kill the Indian, save the man."*

On Carlisle's athletic green, however, an altogether different experiment took place, this one conducted by the pupils. The rankings and the record books couldn't convey just how experimental, and influential, the Indians were on the football field. Every time a quarterback feigned a handoff or reared back to throw, a debt was owed to the Carlisle Indians. Before Carlisle, football was a dull and brutal game, wedges of men pushing around in the mud. The Indians found new ways to win, and in the process they transformed the game into the thrilling high-speed chase it became.

They didn't just change football. They changed prevailing ideas about Indians. Carlisle flourished against a backdrop of trauma and dislocation for all Indians, of land swindles, scouring disease, and continual attempts by the federal government to acculturate them with failed policy experiments. To well-meaning missionaries, land-grabbing politicians, and Wild West Show audiences alike, Indians were alternately heathenish, degraded, mentally inferior, or simply assigned by God to be victims. The Carlisle players were something different: they were winners.

But against Army, just winning wasn't good enough. The Indians intended to win in a certain way. For the occasion, they had something planned: an extraordinary new offense, an exercise in sophisticated fakery, exact timing, artfully disguised ball handling, and, above all, speed.

It was Warner's most innovative scheme yet, and the Indians loved it. But they had intentionally held it under wraps, game after game, waiting for the opportunity to spring it on Army. When Warner asked the players which opponent they wanted to debut the new scheme against, they were unanimous.

"The soldiers," they said.[7]

As the Indians finished dressing, Warner surveyed the locker room. Their motives, tribes, and backgrounds were widely divergent, he knew. For some of them, football was an exercise in white acceptance; for others, resistance. There was quarterback Gus Welch, a Chippewa from Wisconsin, slightly built but with a conjuror's quickness of foot and hand, who had used Carlisle as a rescue from tuberculosis. There was Pete Calac, a Mission Indian from Fall Brook, California, who had lost two siblings to typhoid and come east on the Union Pacific with only a third-grade education. Then there was Thorpe, son of a roistering bootlegger, sleepy-eyed yet with his buried intensity. But for all of them, the reward was the same.

Warner took a few minutes to review the new game plan with his players. Then, when he was sure they understood their assignments, he turned to the front of the room to address them all.

"Your fathers and your grandfathers," Warner began, "are the ones who fought their fathers. These men playing against you today are soldiers. They are the Long Knives. You are Indians. Tonight, we will know if you are warriors."[8]

What happened next, as the Indians took Army Field, was a response to generations of hardship and defeat. Years later, Warner would remember it this way: "Carlisle had no traditions, but what the Indians did have was a real race pride and a fierce determination to show the palefaces what they could do when the odds were even," he observed. "It was not that they felt any definite bitterness against the conquering white, or against the government for years of unfair treatment. But rather they believed the armed contests between the red man and the white had never been waged on equal terms."[9]

1

THE REAL FIELD

December 21, 1866, Dakota Territory

T HE HILLSIDE ON which the Sioux, Cheyenne, and Arapaho were about to make such a grisly fool of Lieutenant Colonel William J. Fetterman was dun-colored and bare, with no cover save for some broken rocks that looked as if they had been thrown down by a short-tempered God. There was just one other visible thing on the expanse, the faint double track of the Bozeman Trail, heading off into the immensity that would become Wyoming. The trail sketched westward along a ridge, ragged but decipherable, its ruts worn into the ground by a succession of iron-rimmed wheels bearing the weight of American ambition.

Fetterman and his command of eighty men pushed over the hill and fanned out, barely holding their formation as they chased a handful of Lakota warriors mounted on ponies just ahead, baiting them. The impatient cavalrymen surged forward on their chesty Army horses. Infantrymen grabbed at their stirrups and ran along, trying to keep up.

The braves drawing the soldiers on had been chosen to lead the attack for their exceptional bravery and fighting skills. One of them was Crazy Horse, not yet famous. Another was a patrician twenty-six-year-old Oglala-Lakota named American Horse, a burgeoning leader who was participating in one of the many conflicts with whites that would engage him for the rest of his life.[1]

American Horse and his fellow decoys beckoned the soldiers with a variety of ruses. They galloped back and forth on ponies, screeching insults and firing occasional shots. They waved blankets at the cavalry horses, hoping to frighten them into bolting. Every now and then, one of the Indians would appear to tire. He would slow and walk his pony, seeming fatigued. This was another feint, perhaps the most tempting of all. The bluecoats hurried after them, down the Bozeman Trail.

Below, hidden in hollows and gullies on either side of the trail, fully two thousand Oglala, Cheyenne, and Arapaho warriors awaited the soldiers. They crouched in long grasses, wallows, and swales, holding the lariats of their ponies. Strapped to their bodies were a variety of knives, hatchets, bows, and brilliantly painted shields. They clenched war clubs made of rough triangular rocks bound to heavy wood handles. A few of them had rifles, but mainly they carried bows and arrows, thousands of arrows.[2]

The isolation and the unfamiliarity of the ground should have made Fetterman pause. The geography of the Dakota Territory alone was forbidding. It was just that—territory, not a state or a county, but an indistinct region where the Gilded Age stopped. It was a sun-burned and epic American Serengeti, a series of rolling mounds and weather-tortured prairie ridges that stretched as far as the eye could see, covered by scorched hay-colored grasses, only occasionally interrupted by weird rock outcroppings and misshapen trees. Out here, the world was still large and mysterious; not everything had been discovered, surveyed, charted, explained, and blueprinted.

It was a magnificent setting, but an austere one, and it provoked deep apprehension in one Army wife. The country was pervaded by "an almost overpowering sense of stillness," wrote Frances Grummond, whose husband, George, was a cavalry lieutenant riding with Fetterman, "especially at night when conversation could be heard and understood at a long distance." Frances had felt a deep sense of dread since her arrival just a few months earlier. Every cloud seemed to dim the entire landscape; every crack of a rifle in the night seemed to explode right by her bed. "Every sound exacted attention."[3]

The post that Fetterman and his men had ridden out from, Fort Phil Kearny, was hardly a stronghold. Rather, it was an unfinished, frighteningly remote stockade of newly hewn logs, just six months old, and it sat squarely alone in the middle of a six-hundred-mile tract of Lakota country. It was undermanned and underarmed, with just 640 troops, most of them inexperienced recruits. The nearest reinforcements could be summoned only with a four-day, death-defying gallop to Fort Laramie.

Fort Phil Kearny had been built in this forsaken locale to protect the Bozeman Trail, the hazardous new shortcut to the gold fields of Montana, forged by prospector John M. Bozeman in 1864 right through the heart of the Powder River country and Lakota hunting grounds. In just two years, the trail had become an enormously popular route west, with thousands of emigrants trekking along it, homesteaders bound for Oregon, gold seekers, fortune hunters, ranchers, farmers, and trappers. They all clamored for protection, and that spring the U.S. government acceded and sent a force under Colonel Henry B. Carrington to construct a series of garrisons to defend the route, one of them Fort Phil Kearny.

But in the brief life of the fort, there had already been terrible casualties. Men and livestock were lost almost daily to Lakota raiders, livid over the intrusion of the road and the new fortifications—in a six-month stretch of 1866 they would kill 154 settlers and soldiers.[4]

The post commander, Carrington, was increasingly anxious about his vulnerable position. When a woodcutting party was attacked that morning, Carrington issued cautious instructions: Fetterman and his men were to relieve the woodcutters but were not to pursue the Indians beyond the farthest visible ridge, called Lodge Trail.

Fetterman, however, was not inclined to obey anybody or anything except his own impulse toward bravery. Bristling with whiskers and decorations, he was a hugely confident officer who had been twice brevetted for gallantry in some of the worst fighting of the Civil War. He was the son and nephew of military careerists, with an eye on advancement, and it's likely he chafed at taking orders from Carrington, a painstaking administrative sort who had never been in a major battle. Carrington had been sent west for his efficiency in building forts, not for his fighting abilities. He was fine-bearded, sad-eyed, and hyperarticulate, and in Fetterman's view weak. "We are afflicted with an incompetent commanding officer, viz. Carrington," Fetterman complained in a letter to a friend.[5]

The mounted men chased the decoys down the slope and along a lengthy shoulder of parched yellow ground. The troops became strung out, their boots and their horses' hooves kicking up dust. Occasionally a cavalryman paused and fired a burst from his light carbine rifle.

Ahead, as the Indians raced across the prairie mounds, they did something curious. Two parties suddenly cut across each other's paths, riding toward each other, and then swerving away again.

This was the signal for attack.

On either side of the trail, the warriors rose from the golden brown prairie. It was as if the whole crust of the earth suddenly burst upward. Waves of arrows arced up from the gullies and draws. Pony hooves thrummed over rock and soil.

Months of preparation and pent-up aggression went into the attack. The battle plan was the work of Red Cloud, leader of the Oglala-Lakota.[6] For years, the Lakota had watched whites encroach on their hunting grounds, and they were furiously determined to shut down the new Bozeman passage. In 1840, the first small wagon train of settlers had crossed through to the Pacific. By 1848, huge lines of prairie schooners snaked westward, including Brigham Young's parade of 397 wagons. With them came a variety of pestilences, including Asiatic cholera, measles, and smallpox.[7]

Most important, they rousted the wildlife, particularly the all-providing buffalo, which gave the Lakota every element of their livelihoods. The Lakota, highly attuned naturalists, had a practical understanding of the famine that could result from the smallest disruption of their hunting patterns, one drought that came across the prairie as if blown from an eagle-bone whistle.

While American Horse couldn't have known the precise facts of white emigration, his own eyes told him that it was becoming a real threat to Lakota sustenance. He understood that, "unless the white people could be kept out of the buffalo country, they were doomed, so far as being a free and independent people was concerned. They would have a strange master to look to for existence," according to a white friend, the famed scout, cattleman, and sharpshooter James Cook.[8]

The Lakota in their dominant years were many things: hunters, natural philosophers, tireless orators, and seekers who felt that the ephemeral was graspable with deep concentration. But they were something else, too, when threatened: absolutely lethal combatants.

There was no better example than American Horse, the picture of flourishing Lakota male splendor. He was born in 1840, the son of a tribal leader named Sitting Bear, and he was of ancient stock, with a family winter count, the equivalent of a calendar, that went back five generations. His lineage showed in his handsome features, which exuded entitlement, vanity, and resolve. He was tall and deep-chested, with a face that looked as though it had been stroked with a knife out of wood. His mouth bowed downward, grim with purpose, and elongating his features were thick plaits falling over his shoulders, wrapped in cloth.

As a boy, he learned to hunt buffalo through the snow, on foot, with a bow and arrow. From the age of five or six years on, he played the Lakota war games that prepared braves for their adult responsibilities—games not unlike football. One of them was a harrowing contest called Throwing Them off Their Horses, a form of mock battle in which mounted boys lined up and charged at each other. As the ponies collided and floundered in a dust cloud, the riders seized each other, wrestling. They played until all of the men on one side were unhorsed.[9]

By the age of about fourteen, American Horse had fought victoriously against half a dozen enemy tribes. At eighteen, he earned his adult name of American Horse (Wasicu Tasunke) when he captured a large Army horse and rode it into battle and slew an enemy. In 1864, he was appointed a "shirt wearer," or leader, in the same ceremony with Crazy Horse. "The following are the names of the Indians I scalped and stole horses from: the Shoshonies, Arapahoes, Bannocks, Nez Perces, Blackfeet, Piegans, Assinaboines, Arikarees, Omahas, and white men," he said later in his life. "I defeated every tribe of the above named Indians that I came in contact with. That is what made me chief."[10]

By the time of the Fetterman battle in 1866, American Horse was a canny and commanding warrior, fully engaged in the campaign to drive out the whites. Just a few weeks earlier, in a similar ambush, American Horse had served as a deputy to Red Cloud in an attack on a train of forty wagons that killed fourteen emigrants. But they wanted larger prey: soldiers.

American Horse joined the frenzied battle. The air filled with the whine of arrows, black gunpowder, and dust. Horses wheeled, crazed, with arrows in their flanks. Infantrymen struggled clumsily to reload their outdated, single-shot, muzzle-loading Springfield rifles, pawing at the cartridge boxes at their waists as cold bit into their fingers. To a Lakota named Fire Thunder, the arrows slinging overhead from the gullies seemed "like a cloud of grasshoppers all above and around the soldiers."[11] Men staggered around with arrows in them. Others wobbled and fell down insensible, their heads crushed by blows from war clubs.

Fetterman and his men alternately fought and clambered back up the trail toward the split rocks that offered the only possible cover. Their belted greatcoats encumbered them, and their heavy Jefferson boots slipped on the icy ground, which became stained with sheets of red ice, blood freezing in rivulets down the hillside.

For a few minutes, Fetterman held together a band of soldiers among the rocks. But the boulders were only knee high, and the Indians steadily encircled, crawling toward them over the ground or galloping their ponies up the hill. The besieged soldiers fought with increasing terror and hopelessness. Combat became a horror, with men swinging gunstocks to fend off the hatchets, stone clubs, and thrusting knives.

There are conflicting accounts about what happened next. Carrington, who was not there and may have wished to perpetuate a noble story for the sake of the families, claimed Fetterman and Captain Fred Brown placed revolvers to each other's temples and pulled the triggers before the Indians could kill them. However, the report of the post surgeon who examined the bodies contradicted him. "Col. Fetterman's body showed his thorax to have been cut crosswise with a knife, deep into the viscera; his throat and entire neck were cut to the cervical spine, all around. I believe that mutilation to have caused his death."[12]

Years later, American Horse gave his own account of Fetterman's death. According to this version, American Horse and Fetterman, each the manful pride of his people, met on the hillside. The Lakota warrior galloped his mount toward the rocks, hurtled into the midst of the bluecoats, and ran his horse full speed at Fetterman, knocking him down. He then leaped from his horse, seized Fetterman around the neck, and slashed a knife across his throat—apparently with so much force that he almost beheaded him.[13]

It took only about ninety minutes from the time the first volley was fired until the last soldier died. Victorious, the Indians began to ritually mutilate the bodies, which they believed incapacitated their enemies in the afterlife. They stripped off overcoats and trousers, shook money and trinkets out of pockets, and kept what they liked. Then they sliced open arms, legs, and abdomens, pulled out muscles and organs, gouged out eyes, cut out tongues, and removed genitals. They cut the tops off skulls and removed the brains, and pulled arms out of sockets.

A soldier's dog darted from the rocks. One brave suggested that they let the dog run to the fort and carry the news of the battle. Another thought he was too sweet to shoot. Yet another said, "No, do not let even a dog get away."[14] They shot the animal full of arrows. The dog fell to the ground, one more dead thing on a field strewn for a mile with the corpses of Fetterman's command, as well as those of horses, shattered weapons, and an almost incredible number of arrows. One soldier's body had 165 arrows in it.[15]

A relief party of soldiers appeared on a high ridge to the east. The sharp, rapid volleys of fire had been clearly audible at the fort. As Captain Tenedor Ten Eyck stared down from the summit of the ridge at the valley below flooded with Indians, he could see no trace of the bluecoats.

But as the throngs of warriors began to recede from the valley, the battlefield gradually became visible. The soldiers spotted what at first looked like cottonwood limbs, stripped of bark. An infantryman suddenly called out.

"There are the men down there, they are all dead!" he said.

Chillingly, the Indians began to taunt this second group of soldiers to come down the hill. They catcalled, shrieked, showed their naked buttocks to the soldiers and slapped them. The soldiers did not dare move from the high ground.

Finally, the Indians withdrew. As they hurried back toward their camps, the temperature plunged. By nightfall, it would reach twenty-three below. When the soldiers came down to collect the bodies, there were entrails frozen in the grass. The scent of blood was so strong that the Army mules rebelled, overturning the wagons.

News of the Fetterman massacre reached Fort Laramie thanks to a perilous ride by scout John "Portuguese" Phillips, whose harrowing report interrupted heavy Christmas revelry. It traumatized officialdom.[16]

The Army immediately closed the Bozeman Trail to civilians, and by August it had withdrawn all of its soldiers from the area. The U.S. government decided the trail was simply too difficult and expensive to protect, and ordered the fort abandoned. As Carrington's men withdrew, the stockade was burned to the ground.

The Lakota had won their war—the only campaign ever lost by the U.S. Army to Indians. For American Horse, it must have been the triumph of his career as a warrior. This was no small raid on pioneers, but an orchestrated, large-scale campaign against a well-equipped force of U.S. regulars, and a total victory. He no doubt felt that the Lakota at that moment were the regnant, all-conquering tribe of the Great Plains, rulers of everything from Canada to Kansas. But he may have had a premonition, too, that the whites were an enemy that could not be permanently driven off.

In fact, it was a useless victory. Between 1860 and 1880, three and a half million Americans would move into the western states and territories, a human flood that slammed right into tribal homelands. The Great Plains area, that vast golden swath across the center of the continent, was overrun.

Stationed in southern Indian Territory, in what would later be Texas and Oklahoma, the young cavalryman Richard Henry Pratt watched firsthand as the buffalo literally vanished. The nomadic southern Plains tribes, the Kiowa, Comanche, southern Cheyenne, and Arapahoe, experienced the same fate as the Lakota to the north. They were increasingly hemmed in, their food and forage endangered by the massive surge of white settlements.

In 1868, the Lakota reached a compromise with the U.S. government and agreed to relocate to a Great Sioux Reservation in South Dakota, in exchange for their hunting grounds. They surrendered what they'd won—and would eventually lose more territory to emigrants, thieves, miners, and politicians. While there were more military confrontations still to come, such as Little Big Horn, the free wandering preeminence of the Lakota was over.

Instead, they faced another kind of battle: the long hard fight to survive engulfment by white America. "The white people are like ants," American Horse told his children.[17] American Horse would be at the forefront of this struggle, too. Before the turn of the century, he would be wearing a suit bought at the A. Saks department store. Seven of his sons and daughters would be enrolled at the new boarding institution in the East, the Carlisle Indian School.

2

PRATT

RICHARD HENRY PRATT was a hard-heeled, iron-assed cavalry-man. Whatever else he became, he was that first. He moved to the chink and rattle of his weaponry, an oil-black revolver at one hip, the fist-shaped brass handle of a saber gleaming at the other. Once, Pratt stabbed his sword straight through a book. The gesture was completely in keeping with his personality, the summary flourish of a soldier turned school founder.

Pratt was six feet two inches tall, and when mounted on a large military horse, he towered. He was on horseback when he saw the book, lying in a ransacked street in Nashville during the Civil War winter of 1862, as he entered the town with the first Union troops after the Confederates evacuated. It lay in a lane filled with the cast-off detritus of a vast Army abandonment: shattered wagons, scattered packs, gun carriages with broken spokes. As Pratt picked his way through the junk, he spotted the book, an illustrated volume of Bible stories, lying with its cover open. He leaned his height down from the horse and speared the book with the point of his blade. He lifted it up to his saddle and tucked it away as a souvenir. He kept it all his life—the saber cut unrepaired.[1]

Photographs of Pratt as a young man reflect a lean, clean-shaven face, a thatch of light brown hair combed straight over to the side, clipped sideburns, and a starch-stiff collar shooting up from his dark blue military jacket. His skin was pitted, the result of winning a bout with smallpox as a boy. His mouth was firm, his brow furrowed with opinions.

It was one of Pratt's opinions that he was a self-made man. But it was the U.S. Army that made him; without the intervention of the Civil War, he would probably have spent his life as a small-town clerk. The uniform of a cavalry officer gave Pratt stature and a path to importance. To it, he brought the belief that work was a moral value, and the dead certainty that it was a piece of jackpot-good luck to be born American. Pratt would attempt to pass on these convictions to his Indian students, with the same force that he used to stick a sword in a book.

"Stick-to-it-iveness," he called the quality.

Pratt was born in Allegheny County, New York, on December 6 in the clamorous, eventful year of 1840, the same year that American Horse was born in the West. He was the eldest child of a laborer who helped dig the Erie Canal, Richard Pratt, Sr., a dogged optimist and opportunist, "high spirited and direct in action," as Pratt's biographer described him.[2] The son would be much like him. Pratt's mother, Mary Herrick Pratt, was a "singing" Methodist, who gentled her husband and three sons with hymns and prayer.

Her voice was a counterpoint to the sound of whanging that filled the nation in 1840–41. It was an era of trial-and-error mechanization, of marvelous breakthroughs and giant mistakes. More than two hundred steamboats plowed up and down the Mississippi River, and the churn of wood paddle wheels would soon be replaced by screw propellers. More than two hundred railroads were in operation, but the chugging trip from New York to Philadelphia still took five hours—and could take several more if the Delaware River froze and passengers had to disembark from the train and walk across the ice.

Fanciful thoughts passed through American heads. James Fenimore Cooper published *The Pathfinder*, while Edgar Allan Poe was digging around in the dark basement of his mind with *Tales of the Grotesque and Arabesque.* Ballet dancer Fanny Eisler was introducing Americans to the Parisian sensation, the polka.

It was an age of fevers—land fevers, gold fevers, choleras, and poxes. Everyone seemed to be going somewhere; the U.S. population stood at seventeen million, but it was hardly worth counting, because over the next decade another 1.7 million immigrants would come streaming in. Secretary of State Daniel Webster estimated that there were thirty thousand to fifty thousand settlers west of Wisconsin—even though land wasn't yet for sale.

The Pratt family joined the throngs and moved westward to Logansport, Indiana, a trading center of raw lumber buildings that was built on the Wabash River and was teeming with newcomers, who traipsed through the mud of the booming young state seeking fresh prospects. In Logansport, Pratt contracted smallpox and fell so feverishly ill that his doctor sent for an undertaker. But when the undertaker arrived to measure the boy for his coffin, Pratt's father kicked the man from the doorstep.

"My son isn't dying," he announced.[3]

The younger Pratt survived, but the elder Pratt would shortly succumb to a deadly fever of a different sort: gold fever. Richard Senior was a forty-niner, one of those elated souls who got caught up in the Gold Rush of 1849. He joined a cross-country party to California and staked a claim on the Feather River, where he struck it rich. He wrote his family jubilantly declaring that they were fixed for life. No sooner had they gotten his letter than they received the news that he had been murdered for his stake.

In the space of a single fatal sentence, the Pratt family was emotionally and financially ruined. His mother's serene spirit somewhat softened the blow; she continued to sing hymns, quote texts, and lead the family in devotionals. But a lingering despair had been implanted in Pratt. One of his own daughters would say of him, "He could get the bluest blues of anyone I ever knew."[4]

At thirteen, Pratt left school and went to work full time to support his family. For the rest of his life, he grimly recalled the impoverished years after his father died. He ran errands for a railroad company that was building a bridge over the Wabash, and apprenticed as a printer's "devil" for a dollar and a half a week. In a tin shop, he learned to hammer out stovepipe and coffeepots. He hauled ice blocks on the town ice wagon, split rails, and sawed cordwood. When a local miller hired him to cut a pile of stove wood, the boy performed the chore with such desperate energy that the miller took pity on him and boarded him.

When Pratt bought himself a badly needed new pair of work boots, he was so conscious of the cost of shoe leather that he couldn't bear to wear them. Faced with a five-mile walk to his grandfather's house, he went barefoot. He tied the boots together and slung them around his neck to save wear on the soles.

The outbreak of the Civil War rescued Pratt. On April 18, 1861, eight days after the firing on Fort Sumter, and still shy of twenty-one, he enlisted with the Ninth Indiana Volunteers. By now, Pratt had reached his full height, and he had powerful shoulders from a youth spent swinging hammers and axes. He "seemed as if made for war," a boyhood acquaintance recalled.[5]

Fighting suited him. He made sergeant in the Eleventh Indiana Cavalry and cut a dashing, lofty figure as a trooper. He was a Bible-toting, rifle-waving idealist who believed, with his friends, that "a praying regiment . . . is worth ten times their number of stay-at-home Christians." He was certain that God would doom the Confederacy to an early defeat.

But when he arrived at Shiloh on April 7, 1862, all ideas of a short war for either side ended with 23,500 dead, the bloodiest battle in U.S. history up to that point. From there, Pratt campaigned through Tennessee, sometimes marching fifty-five miles in a single day, fighting for five and six hours at a time, from one battle to another, Stones River, Shelbyville.

At Chickamauga, September 18–20, 1863, he was nearly beheaded as he ran messages from the cavalry command to General Headquarters. Caught in the Confederate rear after James Longstreet launched a surprise assault through a breach in Union lines, a cannonball ricocheted toward him. Pratt's horse shied, and the ball shot between his head and the horse's neck before it spent itself at the bottom of a tree. "I certainly had a good horse that afternoon," he recalled.[6]

During a reprieve, back home in Indiana on recruiting duty, he met Anna Laura Mason, a well-off young woman from Jamestown, New York, who happened to be visiting her sister in Delphi. She was as imposing in her way as he was in his, a tiny but regal woman with waves of lustrous, upswept hair and a figure that managed to seem full even in a corset. Initially, she rebuffed him. Pratt, however, was determined, and his assertive style of courtship was evident in a letter he wrote to her on February 8, 1864, in which he underlined certain words forcefully: "You say you can never be _more_ to me than a _friend_. I do not ask you why, but it would add greatly to my happiness to know if _under some circumstances_ you would not _change your decisions_."

She responded composedly, in minute Victorian handwriting. "Mr. Pratt: As you requested an answer to your note of this morning I provide one, although I am at a loss to know what more it is necessary to say."

They were married a month later, in April 1864.[7]

Pratt immediately went back to the front line, and over the next year, he twice had horses shot from under him. He got just two weeks of leave, long enough to welcome a son, Mason, into the world. In September 1864, he was cited for gallantry and promoted to captain. He fought in the battles of Franklin and Nashville before he was finally mustered out on May 29, 1865.

The war was over, and Pratt was not yet twenty-five. He reunited with the young family he barely knew, and, perhaps for lack of any better idea, returned to Logansport, where he took up an ordinary life in the hardware business and settled down to clerking. But Pratt must have missed the Army almost immediately. He was presumably bored, and perhaps wished for his former sense of importance, because a year later, on April 5, 1867, Pratt was back in uniform again, a commissioned second lieutenant in the regular Army, with brevet ranks of first lieutenant and captain.

If Pratt was looking for something more adventurous than clerking in Logansport, he found it. He was assigned to the Tenth Cavalry, a newly formed regiment of former slaves, with white officers. The Tenth was going to Indian Territory, that vast tract of unsettled land that is now Oklahoma and northern Texas, where they would become known by a more famous name, given to them by the tribes they encountered there: the buffalo soldiers.

P RATT ARRIVED at Fort Gibson in Indian Territory in June 1867, with his character hardened into its permanent, if complicated, shape. The young soldier was personally warm and enthusiastic, with seemingly unlimited physical vigor. He was self-reliant, capable, a man with multiple aptitudes who could execute any task. He had survived his mean background and the cannon shot of the Civil War with valor, to acquire rank and status.

But he was also battle-coarsened and hardheaded, with a touch of the bully. He could be overwrought and sensitive to insults. He bore grudges. He was almost neurotically obsessed with physical and moral hygiene, despised alcohol, and was ashamed of his predilection for tobacco. He was a fervent idealist who read the Constitution literally and regarded it as a document of almost biblical authority. Above all, he did not tolerate ambiguity; he was a man who had to square every corner of an idea or argument. He had no questions. Frances E. Willard, the leader of the Women's Christian Temperance Union, once said of him, "His is the voice and gesture of a man who *knows*."[8]

What Pratt did have was immense will and force of personality. He would need both of those qualities in Indian Territory, where he would serve for eight hard years. Two things are noticeable in any survey of the action in Indian Territory during Pratt's time there, which encompassed the Plains Wars of 1868 and 1874–1875, and numerous small skirmishes in between. One is the amount of strain, and in some cases outright mental disorder, that occurred among Army officers. Another is the number of suicide attempts by Indian captives.

The men who served on the frontier for the rest of their lives considered it the toughest duty they ever had. Those who survived it with their bodies and brains intact confessed that Indian fighting was unlike anything they had faced in the Civil War. Even the general of the Army, William Tecumseh Sherman, called Indian campaigning the "hardest kind of war."[9]

In reality, it wasn't a conventional war, but rather a series of short, brutal military campaigns to suppress the sporadic "outbreaks" that occurred in various theaters. It was the army's job to move tribes out of the way of post–Civil War expansion, and the job was performed with merciless fighting energy under Lieutenant General Philip Sheridan, head of the so-called Department of the Missouri, who relentlessly campaigned from the Mississippi to the Rockies, often in winter. Sheridan was a hard-faced, short-necked combatant who had a special talent for laying waste, and he supposedly said, "The only good Indians I ever saw were dead." The warfare was guerrilla, on unfamiliar terrain against deadly adversaries who were brilliant horsemen and crack shots. Another general, George Crook, once observed that the Plains tribes were the finest light cavalry in the world.

The Tenth Cavalry when Pratt joined it in the summer of 1867 was engaged in the quixotic task of trying to restrain and pacify the agitated tribes of the southern plains, in the face of encroachments from white settlers and the track-by-track advance of the railroads. The question the U.S. government had to answer was how to clear these tribes out of the way of colonization while still calling itself a moral nation.[10]

Policy makers arrived at a solution that seemed both simple and virtuous: the Army would drive them to reservations, where missionaries would do them the favor of curing their barbarism and teach them to farm. The Bureau of Indian Affairs, the federal agency in charge of administering to the tribes, would "protect and subsist them until they can be taught to cultivate the soil and subsist themselves." This doctrine would be fully formalized in 1869, when President U. S. Grant enacted his "Peace Policy."[11]

But executing such a mishmash of moralizing, military strategy, and pseudo-altruism was not simple. The territory was populated by tribes with divergent rituals, customs, and languages. The Cherokee, Seminole, Creek, Chickasaw, and Choctaw were agrarian. But to the Kiowa or Comanche, tilling soil was an anathema. A Comanche chief said he "would rather stay out on the plains and eat dung than submit to such terms."[12]

One day the Army was supposed to fight the Indians, and the next day feed them. The government dealt falsely yet expected the soldiers to keep peace. Settlers made conscienceless land grabs and then howled when Indians attacked. Missionaries demanded Indians be forcibly civilized but scolded the Army when blood was shed.[13]

At the best of times, it was frustrating and ill-defined duty, with constantly dueling tensions. Above all, it was arduous, requiring hard days and nights on end in the saddle, pursuing tribes in all kinds of weather with no bed but the ground and no cover but what was on one's own back.

Pratt reported to Fort Gibson, which sat in the northeastern corner of what is now Oklahoma, completely unprepared for what he was about to face. He was summarily given command of a company of twenty black enlisted men, and with them twenty-five Cherokee scouts. They were the first Indians Pratt had ever seen. As he surveyed them, he received a small shock. They were clean and wore military garments and buckskins, and some of them even spoke a little English, learned at reservation schools. He had imagined Indians as primal subhumans. But these men were, well, men. "They had manly bearing and fine physiques," Pratt found. "Their intelligence, civilization, and common sense, was a revelation, because I had concluded that as an army officer I was there to deal with atrocious aborigines."[14]

Pratt hurried to organize and equip his men. Their gear had just come up by steamboat: uniforms, horses, saddles, blankets, bridles, lariats, carbines, sabers, and pistols. Pratt's first assignment was to escort the highly strung district commander, General John W. "Black Jack" Davidson, on an inspection tour to Fort Arbuckle, 225 miles away.[15]

As Pratt's troopers marched out of Fort Gibson, they fumbled with their weapons and struggled to control their horses. It suddenly dawned on Pratt that his men were untrained. Pratt had to halt to instruct them in basic horsemanship and cavalry principles: how to sit, how to move by twos, how to form columns, how to mount and dismount, and how to do so without accidentally discharging a pistol or stabbing oneself with one's own saber.

Pratt had some learning to do, too. On just the second night out, the cavalry horses stampeded because Pratt didn't know how to properly secure them in an open field—after assuring Davidson he did. The animals galloped through the camp and leaped over the sleeping men, dragging their lariat ropes. In a frantic scramble, the horses were recovered, and an exhausted Pratt finally chose a spot on the ground for his bed and laid his head down under a bush.

He had just fallen asleep when he felt something warm and heavy on his neck. He awoke, screaming, and clawed a thick snake from around his shoulders. Afterward, Pratt sat bolt upright, shuddering, unstrung, and unable to sleep. An Indian sergeant, sympathetic, came to sit by Pratt and quieted him by telling him of his own experiences with deadly rattlers.

Next, lightning streaked through the darkness. Dark clouds skidded low across the sky, and it began to pour. Pratt resignedly took cover in a tent with the other officers until the storm passed. But he was done sleeping. His new command was untried, he had almost lost his horses and nearly been strangled by a viper, and now he was soaked. This was his initiation to Indian Territory. The experiences of those first days and nights, Pratt wrote later, gave him "about as many sensations in as short a time as ever came into my long life."[16]

Pratt and his men continued on. As Pratt relaxed somewhat, he fell into an idle discussion with his quartermaster, Amos S. Kimball, a fellow Civil War veteran, about politics. They discussed the Fourteenth and Fifteenth Amendments to the Constitution, which concerned voting and citizenship rights. Something didn't sit right with Pratt as he mulled the subject. The men in his command were performing the highest service for a country—namely, risking their lives to defend it—yet they weren't even full citizens. The Negro men were not entitled to become officers. And the Indians had no rights at all.

This to Pratt was intolerable. The Declaration of Independence's statements included all men. He presumed the Constitution *"meant what it said."* He saw only one remedy: Negroes and Indians must "become equal and able to compete as citizens in all the opportunities of our American life." It was nothing less than a test of the nation's integrity.[17]

This firm opinion, formed when bleary-eyed on a hard ride, became the motivating force of Pratt's life. It seems no great insight now, but to view Indians as deserving of membership in American society was fairly extraordinary for a man of Pratt's generation. Congress wouldn't reach the same conclusion until 1924, when the Indian Citizenship Act finally passed. In Pratt's mind, all that was required for Indians to be naturalized was a little instruction. It would be several years before he could put his idea into action, but the thought never left him.

First, however, Pratt had to instruct his own men and learn the perils of the country. The hardships were constant. A cholera epidemic struck just as Pratt's family arrived. As he escorted his wife and young family to Fort Arbuckle they crossed the swollen, muddy Washita River, and the mules lost the bottom. The wagon began to drift. A wooden bucket that had been at the driver's feet floated past Anna Laura, headed downstream, and for a moment it seemed the whole wagon might follow. Finally, the animals regained their footing.

The Tenth Cavalry was ordered to a new post, deep in the heart of Kiowa and Comanche country, where Sherman wished to establish an "occupying force." This garrison, initially called Camp Wichita, would become Fort Sill, and it would be Pratt's home for much of his western service—if it could be called a home. The Pratts arrived to find nothing more than a series of white military tents atop a ridge. Pratt built their new residence himself, a cabin of rough, unpeeled bark logs, mud filler, and dirt floor. Anna Laura did what she could with it. She stretched white unbleached muslin over the walls, hung pieces of striped flannel at the windows, and for flooring covered the raw earth with corn sacks. Army life, Anna Laura discovered, was one of wearying "uniformity, of sameness whatever objects were in view."[18]

But it was a life of nearly constant anxiety too. Pratt's duties were a mix of arm-wearying labor and breakneck rides. During the day, there was the business of quarrying rock and hewing wood to build the new post. Pratt earned the nickname "Lieutenant Timbers" for his woodcutting ability. Gradually, an elegant cantonment took shape that is still visible today at Fort Sill, buildings of light gray stone with overhanging wood roofs, fronted by broad planked porches, arranged around a greensward of a parade ground.

At night, there were the constant alarms, reports of raids on settlers by Kiowa or Comanche, who seemed to Anna Laura to be frighteningly stealthy. "The hostile Indians seemed to be everywhere, without being anywhere," she recalled.[19] *Depredations*, the Indian raids were called. This meant kidnapping, burning, ravishing, plundering stock corrals or wagon trains, and then swift races back to the reservation. Between 1862 and 1870, General Sheridan estimated, at least eight hundred men, women, and children were murdered in the region "in the most fiendish manner."[20]

A shot would be fired as a warning, military drums would beat, and the Pratts would hear a rap at the door. "The Commanding Officer's compliments to Lt. Pratt, and desires him to report at once to his office with twenty men from company D and each with five days rations."

Pratt would roll out of bed and rush to the corral, where the muscular horses stood waiting for him. He would haul his large body into the saddle and rush off into the night, galloping along trails he could see only by moonlight or a flash of lightning, leaving his terrified young wife to contemplate the fact that the nearest railroad was five hundred miles away. Shortly, there would be another knock on the door. Anna Laura would open it to find a well-armed young Negro soldier, who touched his cap respectfully. "The captain ordered me to remain near your door until morning."[21]

But the local tribes weren't simply lawless marauders, Pratt quickly learned. They had deep grievances. After witnessing the wretched circumstances of Indian Territory firsthand, he realized that the tribes were "goaded" into raiding by treaty violations and inedible government rations. As General John Gibbon remarked, "The record of white treachery and hostility would force any man to fight: thus would the savage in us come to the surface under the oppression which we know the Indian suffers."[22]

At the government agency, meager allowances of foul-smelling or even diseased beef were doled out to the Indians. Some of the rations were simply nonsensical. The Kiowa didn't know how to use flour. They poured it out or fed it to their horses, and made summer leggings from the cotton sacks.

When the tribes rebelled and returned to hunting and roaming, they found the Army, as a matter of policy, was systematically destroying their game, so as to drive them back to reservations. Pratt could literally see the buffalo herds thinning, thanks to the new repeating rifles. All of this was "plainly portending disaster to them," Pratt observed.[23] So they raided.

"The white man did not keep his promises," Pratt wrote in his memoir years afterward. "Why should they keep theirs."[24]

If it was a misconception that Indians were naturally enraged savages, Pratt discovered, it was also a misconception that the military officers in Indian Territory were sadistic glory seekers who believed "the only good Indian was a dead one." Pratt's commanding officer at Fort Sill, Benjamin Grierson, was a dedicated abolitionist from Illinois who had personally organized the Tenth Cavalry and who believed he was in Indian Territory to seek peace, not war with the Indians. He fought as hard on behalf of the tribes as against them, and was so humane that it hurt his reputation.[25] Many officers, Pratt and Grierson among them, believed that most of the trouble would be solved if only the tribes were decently fed and dealt with straightforwardly.

But nothing was straightforward in Indian country. The Indian Bureau was a mess of fraud, mismanagement, and graft. White outlaws plagued the region. Horse thieves stole Indian mounts and sold them in Kansas and Missouri. Bootleggers ferried in drink on their packhorses, especially outraging the abstemious Pratt.

To make the whole job more difficult, there weren't enough troops to police the sprawling region. Pratt and his fellow frontier regulars may well have felt overworked and unappreciated back home.[26] It was impossible not to be angry—but it was difficult to know at what or whom. This combination of fear, sympathy, frustration, and anger smelted the innards. It worked on men in various ways. Some it hardened.

In the fall of 1868, Indian raiding became so aggressive that Sheridan ordered George Armstrong Custer to conduct a harsh campaign to curb it. On November 27, Custer fought his controversial so-called battle of the Washita, surprise-attacking a band of peaceable Cheyenne under Black Kettle at dawn on a snowbound morning. He burned the camp and deliberately butchered the Cheyenne's herd of eight hundred ponies, so that the survivors would be stranded and starved all winter. Even some of his own men were repulsed as Custer took up a carbine and began to shoot animals, intentionally dropping them near the terrified women and children he had taken as prisoners. He shot dogs as well as ponies, and laughed as he fired over the heads of his own men, startling them.[27]

Pratt, just sixty miles away at Fort Sill, no doubt heard a full account of the battle. At the end of his life, in his memoir *Battlefield and Classroom*, he was still ambivalent over it. It was the kind of war they were forced to make, Pratt states. There were atrocities on both sides. "It was perfectly human for the Indians to attempt to maintain their freedom and to hold on to their primitive life and resources when that was the only other door of escape available to them. . . . The righteousness of methods, multitude of acts, and their quantum of annihilation by either side were not materially different. General Sherman's 'War is Hell' applies."[28]

It was Pratt's duty to carry out policy, no matter what he thought of it. Ultimately, there was no question in his mind that American civilization was the superior one. The Army was on the frontier to clear the way so that the West could become a place where, as General Sherman put it, things could reassuringly "be counted, taxed and governed."[29] For Pratt to question that mission would have meant rounding a psychological bend, rejecting all of his schoolbook values, hymnal Christianity, and presumptions of American destiny. Pratt simply wasn't prepared to do that.[30]

IF INDIAN Territory was trying, it was also a place of shimmering newness and intensity, with exquisite interludes. Landscapes altered from month to month as if God had washed the palette and started over. In autumn, long grasses rippled like sheets in the wind. In winter, northers raked branches black and deadened the fields. In spring, wildly voluptuous pecan, cottonwood, and redbuds sank under the weight of foliage so glossy they seemed hung with tiny mirrors. In summer, creek beds became red-brown arroyos with alkaline trickles.

There were peaceable times, when the officers socialized with the local Kiowa, Cheyenne, and Comanche leaders over dinner, or watched a local tribal game called shinny, a cross between lacrosse, hockey, and football. Uniformed soldiers and wives mingled with the buckskin-clad tribes. A homemade ball was thrown into the field, and "Immediately there was rushing to and fro," Pratt reported. "Their grace and exceptional speed in getting over the field was a revelation. . . . Like our football and baseball, the fans were divided and vociferously applauded the success of their favorites."[31]

Pratt marveled at their physical skills. In the summer of 1870, Pratt and Grierson were escorting a large number of Kiowa back to the reservation when they came upon a herd of buffalo. Grierson's curiosity got the better of him. Turning to a Kiowa leader named Kicking Bird, he asked with the wonder of a small boy, "Can Indians really kill buffalo with bow and arrow?"

Kicking Bird assured him that they could. Would the general like to see how? Grierson, delighted, replied that he would.

The soldiers watched with fascination as Kicking Bird hopped off his horse, stripped himself of his clothing and accoutrements until he was practically nude, and bounded back onto the horse with only his bow and arrows in one hand. He galloped toward the herd and headed off a fat buffalo, nimbly dodging the beast. He deftly circled the animal, came up on its flank, and shot an arrow into its shoulder.

The buffalo stopped and stood perfectly still. After a moment, it tottered and fell dead. Kicking Bird motioned to the awestruck officers, and they came forward and examined the animal. Kicking Bird's arrow had knifed straight through its vitals. Pratt could see the point sticking out of its other side.[32]

The Pratts learned to love Indian Territory, and when Anna Laura decided to return back East for a visit, Pratt obtained a leave and took her on a sightseeing route through paradisiacal, unspoiled country populated only by buffalo. For two weeks, they traveled and camped entirely alone, without meeting another human. One evening they were mesmerized by a wild prairie fire that swept across the dry grass and popped like a thousand guns, at once "beautiful and fearful," she recalled. Pratt hunted buffalo, and when he felled an animal, he brought Anna Laura over to it so she could plunge her arms into the enormous rich brown coat, up to her elbows.

It wasn't until the fifteenth day of the journey that they saw their first sign of civilization. They gazed into a small valley where, behind a newly built rail fence, a farmer plowed a field. Smoke curled from the chimney of a new frame house. Anna Laura's eyes filmed over, and tears ran down her cheeks.

"Why are you crying?" Pratt asked.

But they both understood. She wept to see something so familiar again, but she also wept because soon other houses would be built next to the small homestead. Then there would be another settlement, and the country would be ruined.[33]

T HE PEACE was short-lived, however. In 1871, the Indian Bureau cut the tribes' already meager food allowance, and the Kiowa, fed up with the meat from diseased cattle and worm-ridden flour, revolted.

The Kiowa, as Pratt knew them, were militants. But they were also reverent, mystical people who believed they had been drawn into the world through a knothole in a tree and could hear messages in nature that floated on the seemingly silent air. They were independent, not easily united or subdued, and their leaders had indelible personalities, such as the famed warrior-speechmaker Satanta, the "orator of the plains."

In the spring of 1871, a war party of about 150 Kiowa set out with Satanta at its head. Satanta was a conspicuous figure, both physically hulking and loudly eloquent, who didn't do anything in a small way, and his gifts as a speaker were equaled by his pitilessness as combatant. As he headed toward Texas, he was looking to pillage.

General Sherman was also traveling the Texas border area. The Kiowa party and the general headed directly toward each other. Sherman had decided to investigate complaints of depredations coming from the Texas settlers; he wanted to judge for himself whether their grievances were real or exaggerated. On May 18, the general, with a small cavalry escort of about fifteen soldiers, traveled across a plain called Salt Creek Prairie. He was watched the entire time by the war party, hidden in the timber atop a ridge.

The Kiowa considered attacking the officers, but a wraithlike seer and medicine man named Mamanti advised them to wait for something larger. Sherman went on his way, unaware he had almost been waylaid.[34]

Shortly, the Kiowa were rewarded as a ten-wagon train piled with corn slowly wove along an old stagecoach track through the grass. This was a government-contracted train, fat with supplies, that was bound for Fort Griffin. The Kiowa swept down the hill and fell upon it. The teamsters tried to use grain sacks as barricades. Seven were quickly killed. Five men escaped into the wooded hills as the Kiowa hacked up everything they could find, inanimate or human.

The Kiowa made their way back across the Red River with forty-one loaded mules and seven white scalps. Meanwhile, the escaped teamsters arrived, bloody and in shock, at Fort Richardson, where Sherman had paused. He immediately ordered General Ranald S. MacKenzie of the Fourth Cavalry after the Kiowa. MacKenzie was another brilliant but high-strung officer, who would be wounded seven times before finally losing his mind while commanding in Texas in 1884.

MacKenzie and his troopers rode all night in a driving rainstorm and found the remains of the teamsters the next day, May 19. The ground was strewn with litter: grain sacks ripped open, scattered wagon parts, spent arrows, shredded harnesses. The bodies were lying in pools of water, swollen. They were riddled with bullets and covered with gashes, and their skulls were crushed. One of them had been chained to the tongue of a wagon and roasted, face-first, over a fire.

Sherman, by now arrived at Fort Sill, was determined to catch the killers. He didn't have to wait long. On ration day, Lawrie Tatum, the Quaker who served as Indian agent, summoned the chiefs to the council room and asked them what they knew of the attack. Satanta rose from the floor, jabbed himself in the chest with a finger, and began to talk, his agitated speech recorded by an interpreter. "Yes, I led that raid," he said. He listed the Kiowa's seething grievances, from the poor rations to the Army's refusal to give them weapons for hunting. Then he named some of the warriors who had raided with him, including a grizzled old warlord named Satank and a youngster named Big Tree. He bragged: "We went to Texas, where we captured a train not far from Fort Richardson, killed 7 of the men, & drove off about 41 mules. Three of my men were killed, but we are willing to call it even. We don't expect to do any raiding around here this summer, but we expect to raid in Texas. If any other Indian comes and claims the honor of leading the party he will be lying to you for I did it myself!"[35]

Tatum remained calm. He suggested the Indians take their grievances to the big soldier chief (Sherman) who happened to be visiting the fort. He then scribbled a note to Grierson and Sherman, informing them that the confessed raiders were on their way.

At Fort Sill, platoons of cavalrymen readied for their arrival. A squad hid in Grierson's house, behind shuttered windows, and more troops quietly prepared for trouble inside the stone corrals. Pratt, commanding Company D, was among these. It was an anxious moment for the young officer. Anna Laura was in their log home just six hundred yards away, eight months pregnant with their third child.

When about twenty Kiowa had gathered on the porch and another hundred were on the parade ground, Sherman stalked onto the porch and sharply asked the tribesmen, through an interpreter, which of them had been present at the wagon train killings. Satanta thumped his chest and said loudly, "I'm the man."

Sherman informed him that in that case, he and his accomplices were under arrest and would stand trial in Texas for murder. It was a cowardly thing for a hundred warriors to attack twelve teamsters, Sherman said, but if they wanted a real fight, the troops of Fort Sill would oblige them.

Satanta, enraged, threw back his blanket and grabbed for his pistol. Sherman barked a command and the shutters flew open to reveal the troopers at the windows, all leveling carbines.

"Don't shoot, don't shoot!" Satanta cried.

Kicking Bird turned to Sherman and tried to negotiate. He asked that the soldiers, in the interest of peace, not arrest the Kiowa chiefs. Sherman refused. "Today is my day, and what I say will have to go," the general said.

Kicking Bird grew agitated. "You have asked for those men to kill them," he said. "But they are my people, and I am not going to let you have them. You and I are going to die right here."

The Kiowa crowded together on the porch, furious. A bugle sounded, and the troopers moved out of the stone corral and formed two lines leading up to Grierson's porch, Pratt among them.

In the distance, standing on a hillside and watching the scene warily, was a Kiowa leader named Lone Wolf. He was an imposing man with a face as hard as an iron skillet, with agates for eyes. A contemporary newspaper report described him: "A rough, jagged face, with two keen, subtle black eyes, full of deceit, a form erect and about five feet eleven inches in height, broad shoulders, head thrown backwards and chest forwards, clad in an old soldiers' jacket."[36]

Lone Wolf was the closest thing the tribe had to an overlord, a member of the Kiowa nobility, and a leader of the rarefied Tsetanma warrior society. Although he was not insensible to peaceful overtures—he traveled to Washington in 1863 for a diplomatic conference—his instinct was to violently resist whites, and he didn't have much reason to like them. In 1868, when Lone Wolf and Satanta had tried to negotiate with Custer, the yellow-haired commander took them hostage and threatened to hang them. They hadn't forgotten it.

Kicking Bird spotted Lone Wolf on the hillside and in sign language asked him to come to the porch. Lone Wolf signed back in agreement.

Lone Wolf galloped into the yard, dismounted, and stalked toward the porch carrying two Spencer repeating rifles and a bow and arrows. He threw the bow to Stumbling Bear and tossed one of the carbines to another Kiowa.

"If anything happens, make it smoke," he said vehemently.

Lone Wolf cocked and brandished his rifle. The Kiowa pushed at the soldiers, shouting. Someone whooped shrilly.

Lone Wolf leveled his carbine in Sherman's face.

Grierson lunged, throwing himself at Lone Wolf's gun. Stumbling Bear drew his bow—but a soldier deflected his aim, and the arrow whirled away harmlessly. Grierson and Lone Wolf landed in a heap on the floor. Soldiers and Indians, both screaming, aimed guns at each other.

Amid all the shouting and cocking of triggers, Sherman somehow held his composure. Calmly, he ordered his men to lower their guns. After a moment, the soldiers obeyed. Grudgingly, the Indians also lowered theirs. With muzzles no longer pointing, both sides relaxed somewhat. Some of the Indians sat down again.

"It only needed the firing of a shot at that moment to have brought on a disaster in which probably the General of the Army, with General Grierson, and their staffs, as well as the Indians, would have perished," Pratt wrote in his memoirs.[37]

The Kiowa, outgunned, gave in to Sherman. Satanta as well as elderly Satank and young Big Tree were manacled and put in a cell under the barracks. On June 8, 1871, they were ordered transferred to Texas. Pratt was officer of the day, and he led them into the yard, where two wagons and a guard were assembled. They squinted in the sunlight. Satanta, realizing what was happening, broke down and appealed to Grierson. "My friend!" he said. "My friend!"[38]

As the prisoners were loaded into the hay-lined wagon beds, the aged Satank began to chant in a doleful, quavering, high-pitched voice. Horace Jones, the interpreter, said, "You had better watch that old Indian. He is singing his death song, and means to die."

The caravan started down the hill, past the corrals and barracks, on the road to Jacksboro, Texas. The wagons had just passed out of sight of the fort when the grizzled old Satank somehow pulled his hands free of the manacles, scraping the flesh off them, whipped out a concealed knife and stabbed a guard, and wrested his rifle away. But before the old man could work the lever, several troopers emptied their guns into him.

The troopers left Satank's body propped against a tree by the side of the road, blood still pouring from his mouth. He was buried in the post graveyard.

His son would be a student at Carlisle.

THE STRAIN of these events may have begun to tell on Pratt, or perhaps he began to resent his tedious duties. In any event, in the fall of 1871, he became insubordinate and was court-martialed.

It was a simple argument over an officer-of-the-day detail: Pratt, sensitive to matters of grade, insisted it was another officer's turn, and refused the duty. Pratt then went over Grierson's head with a petulant letter to the assistant adjutant general of the entire Department of the Missouri, complaining that he was "rendered dissatisfied."

I have long been annoyed with the way details are made, both for the routine garrison duty and detached service, and believe the facts can be satisfactorily proven, which will show they are conducted in a manner calculated to breed discontent, and injurious to discipline.

I therefore respectfully request that the next inspecting officer sent here be instructed to examine rosters and question officers with a view to the equitable adjustment of duty under the regulations. Very respectfully, your obedient s'rvt, signed, R.H. Pratt.[39]

In response to this appalling cheek, Grierson brought Pratt up on half a dozen charges for disobeying orders and behaving disrespectfully toward his commanding officer. In Grierson's opinion, "If I had conducted myself in the disrespectful and contemptuous manner toward my superior officer I should have expected, and justly too, to have been dismissed from the service."

Pratt's court-martial was held on March 4, 1872, at Fort Sill. He was suspended from rank and confined to the grounds of Fort Sill for two months. The episode wasn't a critical one in his career, but it was notable for what it suggested about Pratt's disposition: he struggled to accept orders when convinced he was right, no matter how outranked.

His confinement ended, Pratt was transferred north to the more remote Camp Supply in the midst of the Cheyenne agency, where he chased bootleggers in thirteen-below temperatures wearing buffalo-lined boots and a beaver cap—one raid left thirteen of his twenty men hospitalized with frostbite. To the end of his life, Pratt always claimed bootleggers and white outlaws were more menacing to society than any Kiowa.

But by the close of 1873, Pratt was back in the thick of campaigns against the tribes. Lone Wolf had never ceased to simmer over tribal grievances, and that summer he went wild with grief and rage when his beloved son, Tau-ankia, and nephew Gui-tan were killed after a raid through Texas and Mexico, shot down by the Fourth Cavalry on their way home. When the news of their deaths reached Lone Wolf, he lay down with grief for four days. When he finally rose, he cut off his hair, killed all of his horses, burned his lodges and possessions, and swore to revenge the killings.

In July, Lone Wolf led a war party that cornered a party of Texas Rangers. Ranger David Bailey was the personal conquest of a young warrior named Mamaday-te, who had been Tau-ankia's closest friend. Mamaday-te counted coup and turned Bailey's body over to Lone Wolf. The grieving father furiously chopped the Ranger's head to pieces with an axe and cut out his bowels with a butcher knife. Lone Wolf then mournfully announced that he wished to make a speech: he was appointing Mamaday-te his successor as Kiowa leader, and giving him his own name.

"Thank you, oh thank you for what has been done today," Lone Wolf said. "My poor son has been paid back. His spirit is satisfied. Now, listen! It was Mamaday-te who made the first coup. Because of this, and because he loved my son, I am going to honor him today. I am going to give him my name. Everybody listen! Let the name of Mamaday-te stay here on this battleground. Let the name of Mamaday-te be forgotten. From now on, call him Lone Wolf!"[40]

Lone Wolf I and his war party continued to maraud, and the violence escalated as Comanche and Cheyenne joined in. In August, Kiowa killed five workers at the agency at Anadarko. In September, Cheyenne Dog Soldiers attacked John and Lydia German, murdering the parents and four children and kidnapping four young daughters, to the outrage of the Army.

The Army responded with the Red River War of 1874, less a full-scale conflict than a swift campaign of repression. All the tribes were ordered to come in and be counted at a daily roll call, or else be considered "hostile." For weeks, Pratt rode in endless pursuit of recalcitrants through the Texas Panhandle. On one ride, he was in the saddle for ninety-six continuous miles in icy weather. Pratt wrote his wife on November 7, 1874:

> There seems to be no grounds for a belief that the Indian trouble can last much longer. Buell destroyed nearly all their camp equipage and prisoners in our hands tell us that the Cheyennes

are suffering even now. What must it be in a month more? I feel
sorry for the poor women and children, while I admire the tone
of the men.[41]

Gradually the tribes were forced, starving, cold, and sullen, back to
the agencies. On February 26, 1875, Lone Wolf brought his people in
and surrendered sixty starving warriors with their women and children. Lone Wolf's wars were over.

At Fort Sill, they were put in the stone corral and divested of their
weapons, horses, war shields, lances, and buffalo robes. Their livestock was taken to a prairie and slaughtered, or sold at auction. The
most notorious warriors were put in the guardhouse.

With the war ended, the Army considered how to punish the worst
attackers. It was not an easy question, legally. General Philip Sheridan wanted the raiders tried for war crimes by a military commission.
But President Grant consulted his attorney general and was advised
that "a state of war cannot exist between a nation and its wards."
Criminal proceedings for murder were also impractical; frontier prejudice made a fair trial impossible.

Instead, the government fashioned an extralegal solution. The
combatants would be held indefinitely as prisoners of war, without
trial, at a remote prison site.

Richard Henry Pratt was detailed to make a list of the worst
marauders, and also to identify other agitators who should be deported
from the region. For several weeks, Pratt sorted through evidence and
offenses, and arrived at a list of seventy-two men and one woman
(thirty-three Cheyenne, twenty-seven Kiowa, nine Comanche, two
Arapahoe, and one Caddo). They ranged in age from fifty-nine years old
to just sixteen, and eleven of them were mere teenagers.

Pratt was instructed to escort the prisoners to Fort Leavenworth,
where he was to await further orders while the Army decided where
to incarcerate them. On a raw spring day, he assembled them for
departure. Their families and friends were permitted to come and say
goodbye, and a mass of Indians gathered on the Fort Sill hillside. As
the captives, manacled and in heavy leg irons, were loaded into Army

wagons, their women began to loudly wail. The wailing deepened as the wagons moved out.

Despite Pratt's part in their imprisonment, he didn't relish his role as he rode at the head of the party. He was already wondering how soon he could safely remove their handcuffs. A notion was forming in his mind. Pratt didn't intend to be merely the jailer of these prisoners. He wanted to be their teacher.

3

FORT MARION: FIRST LESSONS

AS THE WAGONS jerked and swayed eastward, some of the prisoners thought about escape and others about death. Escape seemed unlikely, and death seemed preferable. Neither was feasible with their hands manacled. The shackles never came off. At night when they stretched out to sleep on the ground, they were still strung along a length of chain. They bathed in their irons.

They traveled this way for six days, over 165 miles, to a railway depot at Caddo Station, where they transferred to a train bound for Fort Leavenworth, Kansas. The prisoners shuffled onto the rail cars under heavy guard and took their seats with helpless trepidation. Only one of them had ever been on a train before: Lone Wolf, on his trip to Washington in 1863. As the train moved from the station, the Indians stared out of the windows with alarm. The rail cars increased speed and began to sway from side to side. The prisoners slouched down in their seats and pulled their blankets over their heads.

They arrived at Fort Leavenworth nauseated with motion sickness and grimy with train soot. They were placed in the guardhouse, where, at least, they didn't have to endure the hard rocking of the wagons and trains.

They were held at Leavenworth for nine days, growing more and

more despondent, until their jailers took pity on them. The post commander, General Nelson A. Miles, had gotten to know the Cheyenne
leader Gray Beard as well as fight him, and requested leniency on his
behalf. Pratt wrote memos to his superiors pointing out that exe-
crable rations "entirely unfit for issue" had forced the tribes into raiding.[1] But their pleas for clemency were denied, and on May 11, 1875,
Pratt received his new orders: he was to transport the prisoners to a
remote old Spanish fortress in St. Augustine, Florida. They would be
held at Fort Marion until "further notice."

As the prisoners boarded a new train, their fear was palpable. Some
of them were certain Pratt was carrying them east to execute them.
"All the time I think by and by he will kill me," a prisoner named
Bear's Heart remembered.[2] Their fear affected Pratt, who took to
walking up and down the cars attempting to reassure them. At Indianapolis, Pratt's young family joined him, and he took his children
through the cars with him. As he held the hand of his six-year-old
daughter, he paused to speak with Gray Beard. He asked through his
interpreter if Gray Beard had children.

Gray Beard replied that he had only one child, a little girl just about
the same age as Pratt's daughter. Then, his voice quavering with emotion, the Cheyenne asked: "How would you like to have chains on
your legs, as I have? How would you like to be taken a long distance
from your home, your wife, and your little girl, as I am?"

Pratt could not reply. "It was a hard question," he admitted.[3]

As the train neared the Florida state line late one night, a guard
woke Pratt with another breathless report: Gray Beard had leaped
from a window of the speeding train. Pratt jerked at the bell rope, and
as the train braked, he ran through the cars to investigate.

Pratt ordered the conductor to back up, and dispatched a search
party to comb the area. Guards beat through large-leafed palmettos,
their lanterns swaying. When they were unable to find any sign of
Gray Beard, Pratt ordered the train under way again but detailed four
men to stay behind and keep searching.

The train had moved only a few yards when there was a shot and a
call from the soldiers. Gray Beard, believing he was safe, had scurried
from behind a palmetto cluster. As Gray Beard sprinted desperately

down the tracks, the sergeant fired. The bullet caught Gray Beard in the side of the chest. He dropped to the tracks, still barely alive, but bleeding heavily.

Gray Beard was lifted onto a rail car, and Pratt called for his friend Manimic. An interpreter stood by and relayed their conversation to a saddened Pratt. When the Cheyenne murmured his last words, the interpreter translated it: "Ever since the chains went on, and he was taken from home, he wanted to die."[4]

AFTER THREE weeks of travel, the Indians stood at the entrance to Fort Marion, their jail for the foreseeable future. The fortress dated from 1695, and it exuded age, melancholy, and oppression. A moat surrounded massive bulwarks built from blocks of coquina, a local marine rock. The prisoners filed over a drawbridge and through two massive pine doors into a large courtyard, a hundred feet square.

Lining the courtyard on all sides were casemates, rank and damp with green slime, the walls sweating with humidity. Bolted inside these foul and stifling cells, the Indians lay down on the floors, curled up around their chains, and began to sicken.

Within days, there were several deaths. The moist tropical air soured in their lungs, which had never breathed anything but the crisp atmosphere of the plains. They died from malaria, malnutrition, heat ailments, dysentery, and consumption. Some died simply because they wanted to. Lean Bear went on a hunger strike and expired after just a few days.

Pratt believed that one of the worst ailments afflicting the fort was homesickness. The tribesmen longed for their families and begged that they be allowed to join them. Pratt translated a plea from the Kiowa medicine man Mamanti to Washington.

> *You can tell Washington how we have behaved since we left our country and, how we have obeyed you and done everything you told us, we have not been afraid to come down here with you, and wherever Washington wants you to take us we will go, we have thrown our mad away. I am telling you what our hearts all say, only give us our women and children.*[5]

Pratt urged that the request be considered, but President Grant denied it. Mamanti died of dysentery soon after.

Pratt alleviated the prisoners' suffering as best he could. He removed their manacles and relaxed the guard. He escorted them to the roof of the fortress, where there was a broad rampart, called a ter-replein, for daily air and exercise. He organized details to clean the walls of mold and whitewash them.

The close confinement was pointless, Pratt believed; it deepened their depression while doing nothing to reform them. He wished to rehabilitate the prisoners, not just incarcerate them. He wrote to the adjutant general of the Army on July 17, 1875, with a proposition: Why not let him teach the Indian prisoners vocational skills and make them into useful citizens for when they were eventually released? "Constant employment is a necessity and of the greatest importance and benefit," he urged. Pratt even pledged to forfeit his commission if trouble resulted. Pratt's superiors, intrigued, granted him the leeway he requested.[6]

The first thing Pratt did was to liberate the prisoners from their squalid cells. He helped them build a crude shed on the rampart for new sleeping quarters. They outfitted it with bunks made of rough boards and mattresses stuffed with grass. Next, he took them to a secluded beach for bathing, and when they were clean, he replaced their fetid rags and deerskin leggings with clean dark blue Army uni-forms, caps, and boots.

However, when some of the prisoners cut the trousers off at the hip, using the lower part for traditional Indian leggings, this wasn't at all what Pratt had in mind. Pratt mustered the prisoners into a line and displayed a pair of torn trousers. In clipped and firm voice, via the interpreter, he informed them that the clothing they had been issued was the property of the United States Government. It was only loaned to them, so that they might dress in it as the white man did. They would wear the uniform of a U.S. soldier as it should be worn— "Becomingly," he barked.

Pratt instructed the Indians how to press their trousers, shine the buttons, and polish their shoes. To encourage pride in the wearing of their uniforms, Pratt instituted daily inspections. Each morning, every Indian stood at attention at the foot of his bed, which had to be correctly made, with his belongings in order.

Pratt ordered haircuts for the men. The prisoners resisted the loss of their braids, but by now Pratt was determined to transform them, not just reform them. "It seemed best to get them out of the curio class," he remarked.[7]

For exercise, he gave them old guns that wouldn't fire and began to drill them in simple Army maneuvers. He instituted daily formations and parade marches. In essence, over the next few months he turned Fort Marion into a basic training camp. The Indians jogged in formations around the ramparts, as he taught them ever more intricate marching skills.

He put the prisoners to work. The sooner they proved to the government that they would work like white men, the sooner they might be released, Pratt informed them. He hired them out for hard labor: they cleared several acres of palmetto scrub, worked in local orange groves, and packed crates in warehouses. They hauled baggage at the train depot, stacked lumber in a sawmill, and helped drive a well.

One afternoon, he presented the prisoners with local shells, called sea beans. "Make them shine," he said. He contracted with a local souvenir dealer to shine six thousand sea beans at 10 cents apiece, and the prisoners buffed them into such a high sheen that Pratt got a contract for ten thousand more. In just a few months, they earned $3,000, which they sent home to their families or used to buy things to make themselves more comfortable.

The presence of Indians at Fort Marion was sensational news, and as word of Pratt's experiments began to spread, the tourists came to gawk. St. Augustine was a popular and lively winter resort destination, and the fort received streams of important visitors, from local military officers to wealthy sojourners from the East. Pratt proudly drilled his newly martial and clean-cut charges, and showed off their artistry.

The prisoners were avid craftsmen, and they combed the beach for supplies to make trinkets to sell to the local tourists. They whittled bows and arrows, canes, and fans. They painted pictures and hung them about the fort. They asked Pratt to get them supplies from home so they could make moccasins, for which the tourists eagerly paid good money.

The value of propaganda began to dawn on Pratt. He sent a book of one prisoner's paintings to General Sherman, who responded with pleasure at the "very curious, and ingenious" work. Sherman enclosed a sardonic joke, along with a $5 bill for the artist. "He may remember me, if not, Lone Wolf does," Sherman wrote wryly.[8]

Pratt issued day passes so that the prisoners could go into town to buy themselves some personal comforts or to sell their goods at the plaza. St. Augustine residents soon became accustomed to the sight of prisoners in the markets, browsing or hawking goods. One afternoon Pratt treated two of the prisoners, Manimic and Lone Wolf, to a meal at a new oyster restaurant, to see what they would make of it. Lone Wolf was always eager to demonstrate that he had traveled east before and was not afraid of new experiences. He forked an oyster into his mouth and calmly swallowed it. Manimic followed his lead and tossed an oyster into his mouth—and then leaped up and ran out the door. After a moment, he returned, laughing, and signaled that he did not care to try another.

For relief from the summer heat, Pratt took the prisoners camping on Anastasia Island, an isolated bay about five miles from St. Augustine. They set up tents on the cooler eastern side of the atoll, where a hard beach ran for sixteen miles. The Indians exulted in their exposure to the sea, running footraces on the beach and playing games like boys. They learned to fish, sail, and row, and Pratt allowed them to refurbish an old schooner and oars.

The prisoners marveled at the ocean life. One of their favorite pastimes was to fish for sharks, which they called "water buffalo." They captured an enormous sea turtle and kept it as a pet, endlessly entertained by it. They would stand on his back and ride him across the ground, delighted by his slow but sure progress. Eventually, however, they had him as soup.

Pratt's personal relationship with the prisoners grew. Genuine regard seems to have sprung up between him and some of the men, who appreciated his liberality. He used a casemate for an office and left the door open so that any of them could stop in when they had a request. He exhibited interest in their families and encouraged the agency officials back in Indian Territory to forward messages and correspondence. Picture letters flew black and forth that Pratt found both moving and artistically valuable. Manimic received one from his wife that announced three births and three deaths and showed a baby learning to walk, as well as the burial of an elder. Finally, it showed all the faces of the family turned in the direction of Manimic's prison in the East, longing to see him.

Pratt lobbied sincerely for their release. When he was confident they were trained, he replaced their military guards with Indian honor guards instead, and bragged to General Sheridan that they were more disciplined and reliable than some of the regular troops, who got drunk and slept on duty. In January 1876, he wrote to Sheridan:

> *The behavior of the prisoners has been so good that I would recommend their release and return to their people at an early day. There is a difference in guilt, and it might be better that the worst cases be held longer than the less guilty. I am, however, satisfied that all have been cured.*
>
> *I have used them as soldiers and have had no other guard at the Fort for three months. There has not been a single case of breach of discipline and the duty has been performed better and with less anxiety to me than when by the recruits of the 1rst Artillery, for then there were cases of drunkenness and sleeping on post.[9]*

But Pratt could be a punishing gaoler, too. In April 1876, just three months after he wrote to Sheridan requesting their release, he discovered a Kiowa plot to escape. Pratt was trusting, but he was also watchful, and during his morning inspections, he customarily made eye contact with the prisoners to gauge their moods. He began to notice that some of the Kiowa wouldn't meet his eye. When a notorious warrior named White Horse asked to go alone to a sand dune to perform a religious ceremony, Pratt's suspicion turned to certainty, and he ordered his interpreters to press a vulnerable young Kiowa, named Ah-Keah, for information. Ah-Keah turned tearful informant and revealed that Lone Wolf and White Horse planned to lead a mass Kiowa escape at the next full moon. They had made bows and arrows, and had vowed they would not be taken alive.

Pratt locked down the fort, and with a dozen soldiers, he seized the conspirators, along with a Comanche named Wyako, for his surly insubordination. As White Horse was arrested, he told Pratt he expected to be executed. He stood tall, with his arms folded, and said to the interpreter, "Tell the Captain it is all right. I understand and I want him to kill me now."

Pratt replied irritably, "Who said anything about killing anybody?"

Instead, Pratt arrested twenty-four Kiowa, replacing their shackles in front of the rest of the prisoners. He then separated Lone Wolf and White Horse and put them into the dark, evil-smelling casemates.

That night, with the rest of the prisoners watching from their sleeping quarters on the roof, a guard burst into Lone Wolf's cell, blindfolded the chief, and force-marched him around the yard until his knees buckled with exhaustion and fear. The ceremony was repeated with White Horse, but he refused to collapse, and was taken back to his cell still upright.

The night wasn't over. Pratt escorted the fort surgeon, Dr. John H. Janeway, into Lone Wolf's cell, where Janeway drew a large hypodermic needle from his bag and injected the Kiowa with a sedative. In a few minutes, he was unconscious.

Pratt and Janeway proceeded into White Horse's cell. As Janeway prepared the syringe, White Horse stared at the needle, frightened, and began to chatter in his own tongue.

The interpreter said, "Captain he wants to know what you're doing to him."

Pratt replied, "Tell him I know the Indians have strong medicine and do some wonderful things, but the white man has stronger medicine and can do more wonderful things, and I am having the doctor give him a dose of one of our strong medicines."

"Will it make me good?" White Horse asked.

"Tell him I hope so. That is the object."[10]

When both of the Kiowa were fully unconscious, they were carried out of the cells and loaded into a wagon. To the prisoners, watching by the light of the full moon, the Kiowa leaders appeared dead. The wagon carried the limp bodies away.

They were taken to the local military barracks where they awoke in dark solitary confinement, in underground cells. Pratt held them there for four weeks. When he finally brought them back to the fort, he exhibited them to the other prisoners as proof of his ultimate power of life and death over all of them. He then gave the entire Kiowa contingent a tongue-lashing. They couldn't have gone far without getting killed, he informed them, and had they escaped, it would have ended his career.

Pratt added that he could understand how hard it was for the Kiowa to endure the imprisonment and how anxious they were for it to end. But there was no escape except at the hands of the government. Only through good behavior would they be released.

"Every attempt you make to end it your way will react upon you," Pratt said. "There is only one thing safe and best for you to do, and that is to accept patiently all your punishment and await the outcome, and the Government will in its own time bring to pass whatever it thinks best."[11]

The incident was a setback, but Pratt refused to let it discourage him. Pratt informed Sheridan, "They make fine looking soldiers," and made a bold offer calculated to demonstrate his progress. News of the event at Little Big Horn, on June 26, 1876, had reached Fort Marion: Custer and five troops of his Seventh Cavalry had all been slaughtered by an immense force of Sioux and Cheyenne. Pratt's captives were aware of the battle: the Cheyenne among them had received a large pictographic letter from their people back home with an account of the fight.

But the prisoners' loyalties, Pratt asserted, lay with him and not with their tribes. To prove it, Pratt offered to lead a handpicked force of fifty of his captives against any rebellious Cheyenne or Sioux.[12] It was a grand gesture and piece of self-promotion, calculated to reassure his superiors that he was still thoroughly in charge of "his" Indians.

PRATT'S EXPERIMENT with the prisoners might never have amounted to more than military drilling and shell polishing if not for the arrival at Fort Marion of a doughty fifty-seven-year-old school-teacher named Miss Sarah Ann Mather. She had come, she summarily announced to Pratt, to "educate the wild Indians."[13]

The woman had steel-rimmed spectacles covering reading-weary eyes, a mouth as firmly assertive as Pratt's, a gray double bun of hair, a cameo at her ruffled throat, and a cross at her fairly immense brocaded breast. She was broad and dauntless, and as soon as she spoke Pratt realized that his efforts with the prisoners had left something to be desired.

Mather assumed that every person she met was a student, and any room she entered was promptly her classroom. Over the course of her life, she had educated slaves, schoolgirls, poor whites, and any indigents she happened across. In the Indians, Mather saw one more set of students, as well as victims of shameful injustice who caused her to feel that "surely we are guilty as a nation."[14]

Mather was the daughter of a Presbyterian minister, descended from a long line of preachers, and a great-great-great-niece of that unmerciful Puritan, the Reverend Cotton Mather. She was in the first class of women to graduate from Mount Holyoke College, after which she made her way to the spa town of St. Augustine, where she resided for forty years.[15]

She spent many of those years as headmistress of Miss Mather's School for Young Women, a boarding institution for the children of invalids taking the waters of St. Augustine, or well-bred girls from Savannah or Charleston. But she was primarily known as an abolitionist who educated local slave children and helped establish schools, homes, and churches for freedmen by cadging donations of $5 and $10 at a time from her neighbors. Her fellow St. Augustinians were no doubt cowed, and viewed her with a mixture of respect and irritation. Her life was so devoted to her work that little else is discernible about her except that she had a "constant companion, Miss Perit," who is mentioned in her obituary as having preceded her to the grave by a year. At her funeral in 1894, her pallbearers would be four black men.

Miss Mather, with her girth and tightly coiled hair, was one of the few people Pratt ever deferred to. He agreed to set aside three hours each day for schooling. He later confessed that the idea of educating Indians, for which he would receive so much credit, was as much hers as his.[16]

Mather recruited several volunteer schoolteachers from a circle of do-gooder matrons and society ladies of St. Augustine. Mrs. Couper Gibbs and Mrs. King Gibbs were the widows of two brothers who had died in Confederate service. Henry Benjamin Whipple was a prominent Episcopal bishop from Minnesota, known for his missionary work among the Sioux and Ojibwa and for his overbearing reformer's influence in Indian affairs. Anna Laura Pratt and some retired gentlemen from the local school district completed the impromptu faculty.

When the teachers first arrived at the fort, they found the prisoners at work around the yards, talking, singing, or chanting in their own languages. The despised casemates were converted into classrooms, and the first classes were conducted with interpreters and in sign language. But by early 1876, the casemates were decorated with spelling cards, alphabets, and the other bright pieces of paper that bedeck any primary school classroom, and soon the prisoners had a solid command of English.[17]

Classes were held five days a week from 10 A.M. to noon, with another hour in the afternoon. Full-grown Cheyenne and Kiowa bent over their workbooks, learning to write their letters, or sat, upright and attentive, as the widows and matrons led them through their ABCs. From out of the casemates drifted the sound of singsong recitations as they spelled out words or were schooled in phonetics. They learned geography and how to count to one hundred.

An occasional observer of these lessons, from an interested seat in the back of the classrooms, was Harriet Beecher Stowe, the author of *Uncle Tom's Cabin*. Stowe was a winter resident of the area, and she had become a good friend of Sarah Mather's. The author often visited Mather at Fort Marion, and she recorded her impressions of it in a series of articles for eastern publications. The articles are influenced by Pratt's canny propaganda and full of purple rhapsodizing over the Indians' "swart faces." Still, Stowe provided a firsthand glimpse inside the classrooms and at what must have been a fascinating exchange for students and teachers alike.

In the *Christian Union* on April 18, 1877, Stowe observed that when the Indians had arrived from Indian Territory two years earlier, they were "gloomy, scowling, dressed in wild and savage habiliments, painted in weird colors, their hair adorned, they seemed more like grim goblins than human beings. Apprehension was entertained that some day they might break loose from their confinement and carry bloodshed and murder throughout the country."

But after two years, Stowe reported, "We found now no savages. A dark complexioned orderly, with the high cheek bones and black eyes and hair of the Indian race, and dressed in the United States uniform, was pacing to and fro on guard as we and the lady teacher entered." In the classroom, neatly brushed and polished pupils were seated, with books in their hands. They returned the morning greeting of their teacher with smiles. Adorning one wall was a set of spelling cards. "There were among these pupils seated, docile and eager, with books in hand, men who had been the foremost in battle and bloodshed," she remarked. Now, they read in concert and showed satisfaction when they properly pronounced a word.[18]

One afternoon Pratt heard a commotion in Mather's classroom and came to see what the problem was. He found Mather and Stowe doubled over, in fits of laughter, and the class in pandemonium. Mather was trying to teach her pupils to pronounce words ending in *-th*. As an example, she used the word *teeth*. The Indians stared back at her, uncomprehending. Mather, to illustrate, reached into her mouth and removed her dentures. The students erupted—some of the prisoners howled with laughter, and others gasped. When Miss Mather closed her mouth without her dentures, Pratt observed, it made a "remarkable change in her facial presentation," which drove the Indians into further paroxysms.

As the prisoners grasped the rudiments of English, they learned pieces of scripture and to sing hymns. Pratt instituted chapel and prayer meetings. Stowe reported to the *Christian Union* that one Indian service began with the hymn "Just as I Am." Afterward, the Cheyenne Manimic came forward to deliver a lay sermon. He wore a long linen coat, which he had bought with his own money and which he seemed to take great pleasure in wearing.

Manimic said in Cheyenne, "Let us pray."

The prisoners then prayed in their native tongues, asking for release from imprisonment and appealing to the Great Spirit to return them to their families.

"The sound of that prayer was peculiarly mournful," Stowe reported. "It was what the Bible so often speaks of in relation to prayer, a cry unto God. In it we seemed to hear all of the story of the wrongs, the cruelties, the injustice which had followed these children of the forest, driving them to wrong and cruelty in return."

This was the typical Christian reformer's expression of the era. Stowe was part of a growing humanitarian movement that favored educating Indians, just as freedmen were being educated after the Civil War, and she included in her writing on Fort Marion a plea for a policy shift. "Is not here an opening for Christian enterprise?" Stowe asked. "We have tried fighting and killing the Indians, and gained little by it. We have tried feeding them as paupers in their savage state, and the result has been dishonest contractors and invitation and provocation to war. Suppose we try education? . . . Might not the money now constantly spent on armies, forts and frontiers be better invested in educating young men who shall return and teach their people to live like civilized human beings?"[19]

It was a sentiment that came straight from Pratt, and it would lead to the establishment of Carlisle, and last for the life of that institution. That a Christian education might amount to one more form of subtle warfare by the government against tribal life was, for these abolitionists, apparently not a formable thought.

It's impossible to know exactly how each of the prisoners felt about Pratt's first rough attempts to educate them. Some were no doubt force-fed the alphabet and the Bible. For others, the classwork and chapel sessions were probably a welcome distraction from the misery of imprisonment and their longings for home. Added motivation was Pratt's promise of parole for good conduct. But some surely began to learn voluntarily, and to take satisfaction in it when the letters made sense and the sentences became whole. In later years, some of them corresponded regularly with Pratt, and their letters are full of that unique affection students feel for their first teachers.

One of Pratt's favorite students was a young Kiowa named Tsait-Kope-ta. At the end of his imprisonment, he wrote the Captain:

A long time I have not written to you. Now I want to tell you something. I cannot speak good yet. I can read some and understand a good deal, but I cannot talk much. White man's talk is very hard. Long time ago when you first began to teach us, you showed us a card and asked us what that was. It was A.B.C. but I did not know anything about it. I only laughed in my heart But by and by I think yes! He wants to show us the road. . . . You talked a good deal. I could not listen good nor understand. In one year I heard a little, and something I began to know of what you said. Again in one more year I understood a heap. Again in one more year I knew almost all your talk. And now I can write a letter like a white man, and when I open a book I can read a good deal of it. I am surprised and glad. I think, once it was not so—once, all of us Indians knew nothing. Now I am a white man—I think. Now I know that good white men live a good life—no steal, no lie, no hurt anything—no kill, kind to all. By and by I hope I will be the same.

I am very happy now—very glad, some of my friends, old men and young are going home. Capt Pratt may you be glad—I don't know. I think so. Maybe I shall go to school—I shall not forget you—I love you Capt. Pratt. I shall keep you—always I am glad to think of you. You have done so much for me. You have given me everything—clothes, pants, coat . . . all. You have talked to me just the same as to a child and told me what to do and I have done it just the same as one of your little girls would. Capt Pratt you have planted seed just as men do corn, or potatoes or anything, among us young men, and maybe it will be just the same with us as the seed—some will turn out good, and other, good for nothing.

Sometime Capt. Pratt I hope you will write to me. Your friend, Tsait-Kope-ta.[20]

GENERAL WINFIELD Scott Hancock toured Fort Marion in the spring of 1878 and paid the Indians a compliment that must have made Pratt's chest swell. The general was strolling through the fort unannounced when he paused to watch the company of prisoners perform a series of precision exercises.

Pratt noticed Hancock and ordered the Indians to perform an ostentatious hand salute.

Hancock said, "What troops are these, sir?"

Pratt's Fort Marion experiment was becoming influential. Distinguished visitors began to visit the citadel from all over the country. The U.S. commissioner of education came to see firsthand what Pratt was doing, and so did the president of Amherst College. The well-known illustrator J. Wells Champney arrived to draw pictures of the Indians for *Harper's Weekly*. The Smithsonian Institution commissioned Clark Mills, who produced the Andrew Jackson sculpture in the District of Columbia's Lafayette Square, to make plaster casts of the prisoners.

In correspondence with Smithsonian zoologist Spencer F. Baird, Pratt marveled at what the prisoners had accomplished in so short a time. "It is simply just to say that since being here these men have set an example to civilization in good behavior; twenty two of them have learned to read and write, understandingly; while in the matter of labor, at such as could be given, they have not failed or weakened in the slightest degree."[21]

By the time of Hancock's visit, military authorities were at last considering parole. Hancock had come to Fort Marion to gauge the legitimacy of Pratt's reports that some of the prisoners wanted to stay in the East and further their education. As the Indians faced him in a line, he asked, "How many wish to remain and be educated?" Nineteen young men stepped forward, and three more would volunteer later. Hancock decided that they were sincere, and wrote to the general of the Army, Sherman, endorsing the idea as "worthy of consideration."[22]

Pratt was authorized to find places in schools for the prisoners. A physician and his wife from Tarrytown, New York, offered to take three for home schooling, and an Episcopalian school in Paris Hill, New York, pledged to take four more. For the rest, Pratt turned to Miss Mather, who called on her abolitionist contacts. She introduced

Pratt to General Samuel C. Armstrong, the charismatic superintendent of the Hampton Institute, the Virginia school founded by missionaries in 1868 for freed slaves. Initially, Armstrong was not sure that he wanted Indians at his institution, but after some persuading from Pratt, he agreed to take as many of the Fort Marion men as wanted to come. In a short period, Pratt had found places for all twenty-two prisoners who wanted more schooling.

The rest would go home to Indian Territory. In March 1878, the War Department finally ordered their release. Sixty-two prisoners had survived the ordeal of imprisonment. One morning in early April, Pratt and the prisoners walked out of Fort Marion and went to the port of St. Augustine, where a steamer would carry them to Norfolk, Virginia, from where they would proceed to their various destinations. As Pratt said goodbye to the young men who were going to New York, some of them buried their faces in his neck. Their letters afterward reflected just how deeply grateful to him they felt; the young Cheyenne Roman Nose wrote of him, "He is a great good man and his heart is weight."[23]

The residents of St. Augustine had come to know the prisoners well, and a crowd gathered on the waterfront to say farewell. Some of them wept as the prisoners waved from the deck and sang the hymn "In the Sweet Bye and Bye."

The next morning, Pratt said farewell to the Hampton party and escorted the remaining forty prisoners bound for Indian Territory as far as Indianapolis, where he shook their hands, wished them goodbye, and turned them over to a military escort. Lone Wolf and his fellow prisoners reversed the miserable steps they had taken in irons three years earlier. They rode a train to Wichita, Kansas, where an agent loaded them into wagons for the trip back to Fort Sill.

As the wagons wove through the luxuriant spring of Indian Territory, the prisoners' emotions welled up. Some of them leaped from the wagons and raced ahead toward their homes, loping through the soft, knee-deep grass of the plains.[24]

Pratt was due a six-month leave, after which he expected to rejoin his regiment. Instead, the secretary of war appointed him to a one-year term at Hampton assisting in the Indian education program. The assignment made his regimental commander unhappy; Davidson wanted him back in Indian Territory, where a real soldier belonged, not off doing missionary work. "Just now I need the services of every officer belonging to this post and Lt. Pratt will find a large field here for the exercise of his influence for good among the Indians," Davidson wrote. But Pratt persuaded his superiors that he was performing important service.

At Hampton, Pratt worked the same visible transformations that he had in Florida. The students were scrubbed, shorn, and thrown into a curriculum that was part elementary school, part catechism, and part trade school. "I pray every day and hoe onions!" one boy wrote home.[25]

Altering the appearances of the tribal students seemed to count as much as altering their minds. When the Fort Marion prisoner James Bear's Heart finally left Hampton six years later, Hampton instructor Booker T. Washington proudly wrote that "instead of the tomahawk he takes back a chest of carpenters tools . . . His long hair and moccasins he has long since forgotten, and instead of the weak, dirty, ignorant price of humanity that he was, with no correct ideas of this life or the next—his only ambition being to fight the white man—he goes back a strong, decent, Christian man."[26]

But Pratt wasn't satisfied. Hampton, he believed, was just a "steppingstone." He was convinced that Indians should and could be fully absorbed into American society, but stronger measures would be needed. What was required, he decided, was nothing less than the total erasure of their old tribal life and the abolishment of the corrupt reservation system.[27]

The homecoming of the prisoners to their Indian Territory agencies was bittersweet. In the three years they had been absent, their tribes had been weakened, leaderless, and racked by continual hunger. Federal agents forced them to farm corn despite the fact that the soil was not suited to it. General John Pope shook his head at the blank, illogical cruelty of the government toward "these hungry wretches." Pope observed, "These Indians cannot be made self supporting within any calculable time, and the sooner that fact is recognized the sooner will management of them be made to conform to the commonest dictates of humanity."[28]

Not surprisingly, the Fort Marion "cure" had mixed long-term results. Pratt could claim the odd success story, such as a devout young Cheyenne named Making Medicine, who became a missionary, and later the first Oklahoman to be added to the Episcopal Church's calendar of saints. Paul Tsait-Kope-ta wrote gratifyingly to Pratt of his time at the fort, "I felt as if I was born in that place."[29]

Some students stayed in affectionate touch with Miss Mather for years afterward. On one occasion, she received a package from one of her pupils containing a huge buffalo robe and a pair of moccasins. The robe was so frightening that her little dog "screamed like a human being," she reported.[30]

But there were also heartrending letters pleading for help. Quyonah, a Comanche, wrote Pratt from Fort Sill that he wore leggings again because he had nothing else. "When you come to see us I shall have nothing to show you—no corn—no house—nothing at all. A poor country and bad ground. I don't sleep well. I am afraid."[31]

Manimic, the Cheyenne to whom Pratt gave his first taste of oysters, wrote:

> My dear friend Captain Pratt,
>
> A few years ago when I lived with you I used to look around on the white men and saw they had plenty and when I saw it my heart felt glad. Then I came here and looked at the Cheyennes, Arapahoes, Kiowas and saw they were poor. They had been given one thing, the white man's road, and that was all they had—and my heart felt like crying.
>
> . . . The good road you gave me I have not throw away. I wear a white mans clothes but they are getting old and ragged and when I look for money to buy others I have none. I think my good friend Capt. Pratt will either send me some or get some of my friends among the whites to send me some or some money to buy some. When sometimes I feel bad I take your picture and look at it.[32]

Pratt didn't believe he had failed Quyonah or Manimic. Rather, he believed the failure was in the defective, debasing reservation system.

Sending a tribesman back to the reservation, he concluded, was like curing a drunk and then sending him back into the bar.

In the summer of 1879, hunger at the agency was so bad that the Kiowa had to kill and eat their horses. The old Kiowa chieftains were helpless—most of the great warlords were either already dead or would die shortly. The Kiowa Satanta committed suicide in Huntsville Prison, Texas, in October of 1878. The magnificent old braggart was reduced to nostalgic mourning by his imprisonment. He said, "When I roam the prairies I feel free and happy, but when I sit down I grow pale and die." One afternoon he asked a guard if he would ever be released. The guard replied curtly, "No."[33] The next day, Satanta threw himself headfirst from the prison's second-floor balcony to the courtyard below.

Lone Wolf survived little more than a year after his release. His health weakened, he succumbed to malaria in the summer of 1879. He died in his tipi, an unrepentant militant, his passing a relief to local Indian Bureau officials who suspected him of fresh plots. His people carried his body to a secret location on the side of Mount Scott in the Wichita Mountains, where he was buried.

Mamaday-te, to whom he had bequeathed his name, now became Lone Wolf the Younger, a leader of the Kiowa. It would be Lone Wolf II's unenviable job to lead his tribesmen through the coming transitory years, their land and fortunes ever narrowing under the press of Oklahoma land rushes, cattle booms, outlawry, and the righteous blight of allotment.

His nephew and adopted son, Delos K. Lone Wolf, would be a student at Carlisle.

4

CARLISLE

I F Captain R. H. Pratt's requests could sound more like demands and his opinions more like orders, that was strictly the problem of the weaklings who opposed him or stood in his way. Pratt arrived in Washington, D.C., early in 1879 convinced that he had the answer to the "Indian problem." Bureaucracy was a feeble thing in the face of his peremptory certitude.

Pratt was accustomed to commandeering men and materials and building large things with them, and he intended to build a school. After all, he had constructed his own life from scratch, helped raise Fort Sill from the ground up, participated in the assembly of the Tenth Cavalry, and remade the Fort Marion prisoners. He believed he was uniquely qualified to lead men, and even to reshape them. Certainly, he had a charisma that swayed them. Elaine Goodale Eastman, a fellow educator and friend who became his biographer, observed that Pratt felt he could "change the current of a life by just a word."[1]

Pratt stalked the large gray edifices of the federal buildings, banging on office doors and peddling his idea for a grand experiment: What was needed was a large institution devoted to civilizing Indian children and fitting them for citizenship, Pratt urged, not the small, shoehorned trial taking place at Hampton. "The whole fifty thousand children in school is a leverage to settle the Indian question that is worth all the other schemes put together," Pratt preached. Taking Indian pupils straight from tribal camps and putting them into classrooms was a huge proposition, requiring someone with exceptional knowledge in dealing with them—namely, him.[2]

Before long, Pratt gained admittance to the office of the secretary of the interior, Carl Schurz. In Schurz, Pratt found the ideal listener. Schurz was a German refugee who had fought for the Union, rose to the rank of major general, and served as a senator before he was appointed to the cabinet of President Rutherford B. Hayes in 1877. He was the rare functionary who was willing to act, and he was susceptible to the plights of other outsiders.

Pratt and Schurz met in a small side office at the Department of the Interior, and Pratt made a simple declaration that went right to the heart of Schurz's self-worth—and guilt. "You yourself, sir, are one of the very best examples of what we ought to do for the Indians," Pratt said. "You immigrated to America as an individual to escape oppression in your own country. . . . It would have been impossible for you to have accomplished your elevation if, when you came to this country, you had been reservated. . . . The Indians need the chances of participation you have had and they will just as easily become useful citizens."[3]

To make matters easier, Pratt already had a location in mind for a school. Carlisle Barracks, he pointed out, was vacant. Carlisle was a historic old post that dated to the Revolutionary War and had once been the training headquarters for the U.S. Cavalry. But it had been partly destroyed during the Civil War by Confederate cavalryman Fitzhugh Lee, who shelled the town on his way to the Battle of Gettysburg—pockmarks from the cannon shot were still visible in the village—and it had been abandoned and in disrepair ever since. It was ideally placed in the heart of Pennsylvania farm country, perfect for teaching agriculture, and the residents were relatively free from the anti-Indian bigotry that plagued the western states. Why not let him have it?

Schurz was convinced. After a series of hectic meetings and shuttling of paper back and forth with Congress, Pratt had his school. He was authorized to refurbish Carlisle and to enroll an initial class of about two hundred students. Pratt was elated—it was, he said, among the "most eventful days" of his life.

But it came with a catch: a directive from the Departments of War and the Interior. Pratt was ordered to travel to the still-turbulent Dakota Territory, where he was to recruit thirty-six students each from the Oglala Sioux under Red Cloud and the Brule Sioux under Spotted Tail.

Pratt was aghast. Both branches of Sioux were suspicious of whites, and some of their angrier young men had fought at Little Big Horn just three years earlier. They weren't likely to take kindly to the idea of turning their children over to a U.S. soldier. Pratt pleaded—he wanted to draw students from the safer Indian Territory, among tribes "whom I knew, and who knew me."

The order stood. The government specifically wanted him to procure children from Spotted Tail and Red Cloud. Ezra Hayt, the commissioner of Indian affairs, explained the reason.

The children, he said, "would be hostages for the good behavior of their people."[4]

Pratt sat in the driver's seat of a spring wagon, using a black snake whip on a team of mules. Next to him sat Miss Mather, her coiffed head whipsawing with the jolting of the wagon.

The schoolteacher was by now sixty-three years old, and the trip to the Dakota Territory was a test of her pluck. Pratt had urgently telegraphed Mather the news of his school plans. She replied enthusiastically—and insisted on accompanying him, in order to help him "bring in children." Mather yearned to see the West firsthand. "Your trip has been constantly in my mind," she wrote him in response to his telegram, ". . . and the more I think of it, the more I think I should like to go *any where* you go. I know I should be taken good care of and as for the fatigue, I could stand that I know. . . . I hope no old *fogy* will say I can't go."[5]

The pair traveled from Pennsylvania to Yankton by train. From there, they went by riverboat on the Missouri River until they reached Rosebud Landing, the disembarkation point for the Great

Sioux Nation, the sprawling reserve that reached from the northern line of what is now Nebraska into North Dakota, and westward to Montana and Wyoming. A Brule met them with the agency's two-seater spring wagon and a pile of blankets. It was a hundred miles from the river landing to the Spotted Tail agency, through the endless rolling yellow prairie, and the trip was made longer by the jouncing of the wagon, which made Mather so motion-sick that Pratt had to pause frequently to give her some relief.

When they at last arrived at Rosebud, a listless government agent informed them that they'd made the trip for nothing. He'd already brought the matter up with the senior Brule, and they refused to send any children. Pratt testily sized the agent up as incompetent and insisted that a council be called anyway. Like it or not, he would make his case.

Four Brule elders gathered in the council house: Spotted Tail, Two Strike, White Thunder, and Milk. They were a prepossessing group, but the most venerable of them all was Spotted Tail, a legendary chieftain who impressed even Pratt, accustomed to being the largest figure in any room, as a "massive man, with strong and purposeful features." He was a figure of epicurean handsomeness, with large hoop earrings and center-parted hair that flowed luxuriantly over his broad shoulders. He was a storied warrior and a brother-in-law of Crazy Horse, and he owned a scalp shirt bedecked with the hair of a hundred enemy heads.

But Spotted Tail had also earned the respect of the U.S. government for his diplomatic skills and ability to evolve and compromise. Spotted Tail recognized the long odds of battling the federals and had become a conciliator, believing the survival of the Brule depended on it. He was coping with a number of complicated pressures from whites that autumn, as Pratt arrived at the council house. Railroads were seeking right of way, the government was trying to break tribal unity by fomenting factionalism, and the Lakota's already reduced boundaries were being further threatened by politicians who wanted to break up and privatize their land. But resistance was a delicate matter—if they fought the government on any of these issues too strongly, it could invite military intervention.[6]

As Pratt entered the council room, the Brule sat on the ground smoking and talking. The smoking of the pipe was a traditional purification rite for Lakota, who believed the vapors cleansed their minds. Pratt asked the interpreter what they were saying.

"I can't understand them when they talk like that," the interpreter said.

Finally, Spotted Tail gestured that they were ready to listen. Pratt stood and announced that the government had adopted a new policy: it believed Indian youths could become the equals of white youths, and had established a school for the purpose in the East, near Washington. He had come to enroll their children. Their old Indian ways were a liability in the spreading America, Pratt explained.

"They must surely see that being divided into so many languages, and living in small tribal groups away from these opportunities, was a great disadvantage to them," Pratt said. "More and more the white man was occupying the whole country; his railroads and towns and farms would go everywhere and that there was nothing left for them but to become a very part of it all."

When Pratt finished, the Brule spoke among themselves. Then Spotted Tail rose. His speech was brief. "The white people are all thieves and liars," he said. "We are not going to give any children to learn such ways." The white man knew there was gold in the Black Hills and he had made the Indian give up that whole country so the whites could get out the gold, he added. The government had given them a reservation, and when the Indian tried to live there, the surveyors came and made the lines of the reservation far inside of where they should be. "We are not going to give any children to learn such ways," he repeated.

Spotted Tail sat down to a chorus of approval from the other councilors, who said, "Hau, hau." Pratt, undaunted, took a moment to frame a reply. When he spoke next, he looked directly at Spotted Tail.

"Spotted Tail, you are a remarkable man. Your name has gone all over the United States. It has even gone across the great water. You are such an able man that you are the principal chief of these thousands of your people. But Spotted Tail, you cannot read or write. . . . You claim that the government has tricked your people and placed the lines of your reservation a long way inside of where it was agreed that they should be. You put your cross signature on the treaty which fixed the lines of your reservation. . . . You signed that paper, knowing only what the interpreter told you it said. . . .

"Spotted Tail, do you intend to let your children remain in the same condition of ignorance in which you have lived, which will compel them to always meet the white man at a great disadvantage through an interpreter, as you have to do? Cannot you see that it is far, far better for you to have your children educated and trained as our children are so that they can speak the English language, write letters and do the things which bring to the white man such prosperity. . . . As your friend, Spotted Tail, I urge you to send your children with me to this Carlisle School and I will do everything I can to advance them in intelligence and industry in order that they may come back and help you. Spotted Tail, I hear you have a dozen children. Give me four or five, and let me take them back to Carlisle and show you what the right kind of education will do for them."

Pratt turned to the interpreter and asked if the other tribal councilors had children. The reply was that Two Strike had two sons, and White Thunder a girl and boy.

"Two Strike, give me your two boys to take to Carlisle and make useful men out of them," Pratt said. "White Thunder, let me have your boy and girl and take them to Carlisle. I will be a father to them and all the children while they are with me."[7]

His speech concluded, Pratt left the councilors to weigh what he had said. He returned to the agent's porch, where he and Mather sat and waited for a reply.

Pratt sincerely believed that he was offering Spotted Tail the greatest of all privileges: a free American education for his children. But Spotted Tail did not exaggerate the Brule's repulsion at white values. Lakota societies were collectives: land to them was as unparcelable as water, and materialism was a character flaw. Sitting Bull said of whites, "The love of possessions is a disease among them." It was a fundamental cultural difference, and one the Brule parents had to consider.[8]

Still, Spotted Tail and his councilors heard some practical sense in what Pratt said. Perhaps if their children learned the white language, they wouldn't have to rely on untrustworthy government interpreters.

About an hour later, Spotted Tail, Two Strike, Milk, and White Thunder brought their response to Pratt. Spotted Tail walked over to Pratt and extended his hand.

"It is all right," he said. "We are going to give you all the children you want."

Pratt was ecstatic. The Brule pledged to send sixty-six children east with him; four of them were Spotted Tail's own children, plus two grandchildren. But Spotted Tail had a condition—he did not mean to send his progeny off unaccompanied. He asked that his son-in-law, Charles Tackett, a young mixed-blood interpreter and storekeeper, go along with the party to look after the children. Tackett was fluent in Sioux and trusted by the Brule, and would be able to send reports back. Pratt had no choice but to accept, and he did so swiftly. He still had another long wagon trip ahead to see the Oglala, under their leader Red Cloud at the Pine Ridge agency.[9]

In a similar council scene with Red Cloud and assorted Oglala leaders, a weary Pratt met heavier opposition. Red Cloud remained distrustful of white education, and he had no school-age children. But Pratt did not come away empty-handed. One of the prominent Oglala in the council was American Horse. Pratt couldn't help noticing that the former warrior "took a livelier interest" than the others in what he had to say.

American Horse had grown from a warrior into an influential tribal politician. He was also the head of a large personal household, with two wives and at least ten children. He had become a sophisticate, a man who adroitly negotiated his way between the traditional Lakota society he was born into and the new white society encircling him, and he had become fairly affable to the U.S. government. Some of his friendliness, however, was shrewd political calculation, an attempt to win concessions for himself and his people. Above all, American Horse prided himself on his sagacity. It was glaringly apparent to him that his offspring would have to deal with whites, and perhaps even live with them, whether they liked it or not.

Pratt came away with just a small party of sixteen Oglala students—but three of them were from American Horse's household. Bear Don't Scare (Guy) was an elder son of about seventeen. Cut Ears (Robert) was apparently a nephew of about eighteen, although Pratt believed he too was a son. Maggie Stands Looking was a girl of about sixteen or seventeen, who Pratt understood was American's Horse's daughter.[10]

On a late-October afternoon, a huge party of Brule and Oglala gathered at Rosebud Landing to say goodbye to their children. Eighty-two youths, some of them as young as ten, lined up to board the steamship that would take them down the Missouri River. At first, the departure was cause for ceremonial celebration. Fathers on horseback, led by Spotted Tail, showed their pride by shouting aloud, handing out gifts such as calico, and giving away horses. But as the sun began to go down, the reality of the impending separation set in. As names were called for boarding, anguish swept over the embankment. Children clung to adults, sobbing, and had to be pried away. The scene quickly worsened. Parents who couldn't bear the parting tried to snatch their children back from the gangplank.

The boarding area became the scene of a chaotic struggle. White Thunder's family was heartbroken. The Brule leader's son beseeched his father not to make him go. White Thunder had to drag the boy onto the deck and hold him there. Meanwhile, White Thunder's second wife defiantly seized their twelve-year-old daughter and carried her back to shore.

A dispatch from a Rosebud agent, William Pollock, to the *Washington Post* on October 17, 1879, described the event under the headline "Parental Affection Among Indians."

> The hideous wails of the squaws made the night a sorrowful one. But for White Thunder and a few more determined chiefs, the effort to embark would have been a failure. White Thunder, after putting those from his tribe on board, held one, his son by a former wife, by physical force, but his present wife, who has but one child, a daughter, 12 years old, took up the little girl and carried her ashore, telling her husband the child was hers, and that she would rather die than part with her.

At last, Pratt managed to separate the children from their parents and get them aboard. The gangplank was rolled back, and the steamship pulled away from the landing. Dark fell. The ship moved slowly along the river until it disappeared from the view of the adults who wept on the embankment. The piteous crying of the children on deck finally quieted somewhat.

Pratt organized the children for a roll call and discovered that two extra boys had stowed away, bringing the number aboard to eighty-four. The children curled up in their blankets and tried to sleep, but their apprehension for what was ahead, and the thrashing noise of the paddles, kept them awake.

At noon the following day, the children were transferred from the boat to a train. To the uninitiated children, the rail cars looked like "a row of little houses standing on long pieces of iron that stretched as far as the eye could see." They climbed aboard to find the cars sumptuously decorated with soft cushioned seats, which so excited them that they changed places continually before they finally settled down. But as the train rocked and the light posts and telegraph poles flashed past the windows, the children held their blankets in their teeth, certain that the cars were about to tip over.[11]

At Sioux City, news of their party preceded them and drew a huge crush of onlookers to the train station. As the children disembarked for lunch, a cordon of police had to hold back the crowds of whites who pressed in on them from either side. Some in the mob screamed out war whoops and made tomahawk motions with their hands. Others tossed money at the children. When the smaller boys stooped to pick up the coins, the larger boys sharply instructed them not to take it. "Throw it back at them," they said.

Pratt escorted the children to a restaurant, where he arranged them at long tables, but gawkers crowded in the windows, pointing at them and laughing. It was impossible to eat in the pandemonium. Instead, the children shoveled the food into their blankets, and Pratt hustled them back to the rail cars.

As they worked eastward from whistle-stop to whistle-stop, the children grew sore and exhausted from sleeping upright. Some of the older braves told the younger boys that when they arrived in the

East, the place where the sun rises, the white people would dump them over the edge of the earth.

At about midnight on Sunday, October 6, 1879, after four days and nights of travel, the train pulled into Gettysburg Junction, the stop for Carlisle. Despite the hour, hundreds of residents gathered to stare at the disheveled children who climbed wearily down from the train cars. Led by Pratt and Mather, they began a last two-block journey on foot from the station to the campus, shuffling through the dark wrapped in vividly dyed blankets or shawls, clad in soft buckskins and elk-bone breastplates, adorned with softly jingling bracelets and earrings, wearing moccasins covered in intricate beadwork.

They trudged up a long hill to a large gate in a wall. This was the entrance to the barracks, and as they filed through it, the girls were separated from the boys and taken to dormitories on opposite ends of the campus. The buildings glowed with light. But when the exhausted and hungry children got inside, they found only dilapidated, freezing-cold, unfurnished rooms. In the boys' dorm, a cast-iron stove stood in the middle of the room, but it was unlit, with no coal to burn. The light came from a small oil lamp sitting atop it.

Pratt was furious. Before he left, he had requisitioned food, coal, bedding, furniture, and school supplies. Nothing had been received, save for one thing: a small organ. "This article, the least necessary of all the supplies, arrived several days before anything else," Pratt recalled.[12] Teachers and children alike resignedly made camp on the hard wood floors. The boys rolled their leggings into pillows, wrapped themselves in their blankets, and tried to sleep.

The next morning, there was nothing for breakfast but bread and water. Pratt "commenced a lively correspondence" with Washington. He telegraphed for permission to shop for food at the local markets, and by noon he was able to feed the students some meat, bread, and coffee, which made them feel somewhat better. But their homesickness increased; the boys sang mournful songs, and the girls, hearing them from their dormitory at the other end of campus, began crying. It didn't help that there was nothing to do. With no furniture or school supplies for the classrooms, the students were at loose ends. They wandered the campus idly or massed together on the porches of the dormitories, where they shrank from the townspeople who came to gape at them.[13]

But Pratt put them to work. He had the interpreter Tackett pass out large cotton sacks, and explained they would become mattresses. The students took them to a hayloft, where they stuffed them with straw, and then dragged them up the stairs to their dormitory rooms.

Pratt organized work parties to make repairs to the buildings, some of which had holes in the roofs and missing floorboards. A handful of his old Florida students had arrived to help open the school, and they taught the new students how to hammer boards and shingles. Gradually, Carlisle Barracks became a handsome post again. It consisted of sixteen buildings scattered over twenty-seven acres, with two-tiered whitewashed dormitories and an old stone guardhouse on a long rectangular parade ground. After patching the worst of the holes, Pratt's most vital task was to build a seven-foot picket fence around the campus to keep the sightseers out.[14]

Pencils and slates finally arrived, along with secondhand desks and blackboards, and students were ushered into the classrooms. The school's core staff consisted of Alfred Standing, a Quaker who would be Pratt's loyal assistant superintendent for twenty years, a dedicated soldier-volunteer named Lieutenant George Leroy Brown from Cheyenne country, who was on leave to help open the school, and Miss Marianna Burgess, the daughter of a Quaker agent to the Pawnee. In addition, Miss Mather was on hand to help.

After two and a half months, the premiere edition of the school paper, *Eadle Keatah Toh* (Big Morning Star), appeared, with the school motto etched on the masthead: "God Helps Those Who Help Themselves." It contained an account of the first classes.

> Without waiting for the arrival of "white men's clothes" the eighty two Sioux, who were our first recruits, were gathered into the school-room and the difficult work of teaching the language was begun. It would be hard to imagine a more novel sight than that presented by the motley assembly, or to collect a more undisciplined mass of youthful humanity. The faces of nearly all were painted, their arms adorned with bracelets, and their ears,

weighed down by the rings or elk-teeth pendants. Some were wrapped in gaily embroidered blankets; others were happy in the possession of jackets or breastplates heavy with embroidery or elk teeth. All were eager to learn, but it was soon evident that the barber and tailor must take precedence in the work of civilization. The daily sessions were short, and not much was effected until blankets had disappeared. Gradually the frightful vision of bedaubed faces, barbaric ornaments and picturesque costumes ceased to attract the gaping crowd, and now it must be confessed that the school has lost its early charms for the curious. It is fast assuming the characteristics of a well graded, well organized public school.[15]

With basic supplies in place and the Lakota children settled, Pratt departed to meet a second party of students who were en route to Carlisle from his old post in Indian Territory. But before he left, Pratt hired two barbers to visit the campus and give the Lakota a more "civilized" appearance by cutting their braids. This occasioned one of the more traumatic episodes in the history of the school, as Pratt learned afterward from his wife, whom he left in charge.

Tackett got wind of what was about to happen, and warned the boys. Losing their hair was no small matter—their braids were the emblems of their maturity and their manhood. Lakotas cut their hair only as a sign of deep mourning. That evening, the older boys held a council in the dorm, to debate whether they should acquiesce to the haircuts. Robert American Horse took the lead and urged them to resist.

"If I am to learn the ways of the white people, I can do it just as well with my hair on," he said.[16]

But there was no great insurrection on the morning the barbers arrived, just uncertainty and humiliation. The boys sat in their classrooms, drawing on slates quietly, as they were called out of the room one by one. There was never any chance for a group rebellion; a boy would simply disappear and then reappear a short while later, shorn and rubbing his head in confusion. The procession continued through the day, hanks of glossy black hair falling onto the hardwood floor.

As the braids dropped away, some of them wept. Years later, a boy named Plenty Kill, known as Luther Standing Bear, remembered how the tears welled in his eyes. "I do not recall whether the barber noticed my agitation or not, nor did I care. All I was thinking about was that hair he had taken away from me. . . . Now, after having had my hair cut, a new thought came into my head. I felt that I was no more Indian, but would be an imitation of a white man."[17]

By the end of the day, all but one of the boys had been cropped. As this last recusant gazed at the trimmed heads of his classmates, Anna Laura visited the schoolroom and sternly informed him that he would have to deal with the captain when he returned. He still refused.

Late that night, Anna Laura was stirred from sleep by wailing from the parade ground. The boy had cut off his braids with a knife. He was standing in the midst of the green quadrangle crying aloud, and his sorrow spread like contagion. As other students awakened, they joined him in mourning, until the laments echoed all over the barracks and could be heard clearly in town.[18]

THE CARLISLE Indian Industrial School formally opened on November 1, 1879, with an enrollment of 147 students. The youngest of them was just six and the eldest twenty-five, but the majority of them were teenagers. Two-thirds of them were the children of tribal leaders.[19]

But these specificities were irrelevant to Pratt, who did not care who they were; he cared who they became. "When it comes to the Indian I am a Baptist," Pratt said, "because I believe in immersing the Indians in our civilization, and when we get them under, holding them there until they are thoroughly soaked."[20]

Pratt began by issuing new clothes. The boys received suits of gray wool, with vests, caps, work boots, red long johns, suspenders, and socks. The girls got pinafores almost to their ankles, with capes and thick stockings. In one swift change of apparel, the children were reduced to an indistinguishable gray mass with no discernible outward differences.

Initially, the new clothes fascinated the students. The boys examined the pants and puzzled over them—did the button fly go in front or in back? Pockets were ingenious, and their boots made impressive, heavy stomping sounds on the hardwood floors. They stayed up half the night walking around, just to hear the hard trod of their boots.[21]

They received new nightshirts, which enchanted the small boys. The long garments floated around them, a sensation so exhilarating that they snuck out after curfew to race around on the quadrangle. They were forbidden to go on the grass after the dew fell "or we might catch cold and die," Standing Bear remembered, but the boys couldn't resist. They sailed around the lawn with their white shirts trailing in the dark. Suddenly the door to the office opened. The immense shadow of Pratt loomed through the lit doorway, sending them in a mass scurry back to the dormitory. Pratt never mentioned the incident, and was probably amused.[22]

But after the novelty wore off, the clothes were just confining. The red flannel underwear itched unmercifully, the boots made their feet sore, and the pants bit into their crotches. Also, the fabric was cheap. Pratt had contracted the uniforms out to a large respectable American company, but it sent him "the shoddiest of shoddy clothing." The clothes were worn through with holes after just a month. Pratt delivered a bundle to Schurz.

"The boys with their trousers out at the knees and clothing held on by strings certainly cannot feel much of a tendency upward and I know from talking with the teachers that many of them are worn out and discouraged from this one difficulty," Pratt wrote. "I have found the Indians more sensitive to the pride of dress than many civilized people and it seems to me that true economy would favor the adoption of some respectable and durable goods for clothing, especially for the boys."[23] Schurz authorized Pratt to buy decent clothing, and Pratt outfitted the students in surplus military-issue blue uniforms, dark blue jackets, and light blue trousers.

The next step in the students' makeover was to rename them. One morning, they entered a classroom to find teacher Marianna Burgess covering a blackboard with white chalk marks. An interpreter explained that the marks were white people's names. The children stared at the rows of indecipherable squiggles and slashes.

Burgess motioned for a boy in the first row to come to the front of the room, and handed him a pointer. Through an interpreter, she told him to pick any name he wanted. The boy turned hesitantly and stared at the board for a long moment in confusion before he finally touched the pointer to one of the names. Burgess took a piece of white tape and wrote the name on it, and sewed it on the back of the boy's shirt. The chosen name was erased from the board, and the process was repeated.

After the students were renamed, Burgess taught them to scrawl the strange words. She wrote a child's name on his slate and then showed him how to copy the letters.[24] The names ranged from the biblical to those of American presidents; Carlisle's student rolls would be full of Georges, Thomases, and Abrahams.

There were some practical considerations in renaming the pupils. Most of the teachers couldn't pronounce the children's names, or translate them. A classic example was Young Man Afraid of His Horses, which didn't literally mean the young man was afraid of his horses, but rather that he was so brave that the sight of his horses frightened the enemy. Also, anglicizing pupils' names made it easier to keep records.

But the students only knew that a piece of their Indian selves had been taken away, one more profound than their clothes or braids. With their names went entire histories and inheritances. Tribal names were awarded as ceremonial recognitions of feats, attainments, characteristics, mannerisms, quirks, and aspirations. In some cases, they were almost a form of family heraldry. Expunging a child's name essentially meant wiping out his or her personal chronicle.[25]

Some students felt merely disconnected from their new name, but others viewed it explicitly as yet another way of forcibly transforming them into whites. One of Carlisle's later Apache students, "Asa" Daklugie, nephew of Geronimo, resented his white name for the rest of his life as something that was "forced on me as though I'd been an animal."[26]

Still others were simply embarrassed:

Dear Captain Pratt: I am going to tell you something about my name. Captain Pratt, I would like to have a new name because

some of the girls call me Cornbread and some call me Cornrat,
so I do not like that name, so I want you to give me a new name.
Now this is all I want to say. Conrad.[27]

Their braids, clothes, and names were gone. Their language went next. In order to prevent tribal cliques and to discourage speaking in their native dialects, Pratt scattered the tribes as widely as possible in the dormitories and forbade them to speak in their own languages on campus. Each week, he mustered the students in a line and ordered those who had broken the no-Indian-language rule to take one step forward, publicly shaming the confessors.[28]

"Civilization is a habit," Pratt insisted. "Language is nothing but a habit. We aren't born with language, nor are we born with ideas either of civilization or savagery. All these things are forced upon us by our environment after birth."[29]

Nevertheless, the students clung to some vestiges of their old selves. The Lakota especially cleaved together and found ways to communicate via sign language, despite Pratt's rules. During the first few months, Pratt discovered they were actually teaching the Cheyenne and Kiowa how to speak Sioux.

Other instructors who taught at Carlisle over the coming years had sympathy for the homesick, tongue-tied students and refused to report them when they lapsed back into their own dialects. "I just couldn't," said one. "Because you know, it got to be so they'd get, well, remorse. I mean, they'd feel so badly because they couldn't speak their language."[30]

Almost every experience at Carlisle was unfamiliar, uncomfortable, or distressing. The glare of gaslights, the stamp of shoes on hardwood floors, the clatter of silverware, and clanging bells were jarring compared to the hushed natural world in which they'd been raised. Accustomed to soft, circular lodges on plains with vast horizons, they now lived in a hard square world, sleeping in rectangular beds in claustrophobic rooms arranged around a quadrangle.[31]

"We did not think of the great open plains, the beautiful rolling hills, and winding stream with tangled growth, as 'wild,'" wrote Luther Standing Bear later. "Only to the white man was nature a 'wilderness' and only to him was the land 'infested' with 'wild' animals and 'savage' people. To us it was tame. Earth was bountiful and we were surrounded with the blessings of the Great Mystery. Not until the hairy man from the east came and with brutal frenzy heaped injustices upon us and the families we loved was it 'wild' for us. When the very animals of the forest began fleeing from his approach, then it was that for us the 'Wild West' began."[32]

Their sense of artificial rigidity was unrelieved, especially once their daily schedule took shape. They rose at 6 A.M. for chores and military exercises. Pratt drilled them as he would a new company: they learned to march and to stand at attention during inspection. He examined them from head to toe for properly combed hair, clothes brushed free of lint, and shoes shined. He lifted their mattresses to make sure the floor was clean underneath, and opened their trunks.

Then came breakfast. Meal times were no solace. Students were marched into a dining room where they sat on benches at long tables and fumbled with the strange forks, spoons, knives, and glasses. The Carlisle diet was based on the Army schedule of rations and seemed like tasteless slop compared to the roasted game they had grown up on. The first mouthful of bland oatmeal was revolting, the first sip of unsweetened tea like drinking a glass of stirred dirt. There was a tiresome sameness to the servings, too. Breakfast was invariably oatmeal, milk, bread, syrup, and coffee or cocoa. At noon, they had a thin beef stew called "gravy" or a hash with dumplings or potatoes, perhaps a prune pudding, and tea. For supper there was soup or beans with cornbread, and fruit if it was available.[33]

Mornings were devoted to academics—mostly English at first— and afternoons were for trade and shop classes in wagon building, cobbling, blacksmithing, tin- and coppersmithing, carpentry, painting, tailoring, and harness making. The girls were taught sewing, cooking, canning, ironing, child care, cleaning, and later stenography, bookkeeping, and typing.

These were exercises in bewilderment. The most basic elements of a Victorian-era school were unfamiliar to the pupils: folding hands, sitting in chairs, climbing stairs, and walking in line. But there were moments of electrifying discovery, too. A professor from Dickinson

College, Charles Himes, delivered a science lecture to forty students, using props with a magician's flair. He ignited a pile of gunpowder with a small drop of liquid, to delighted shrieks. He displayed a model house—and then exploded it into a pile of sticks with a bolt of electricity, startling the boys and causing the girls to run from the room.

Next, Himes passed a jolt of electricity from Roman Nose's nose to High Forehead's knuckle, convulsing them with laughter. He invited them to test the strength of the voltage, and a dozen students, including Spotted Tail's daughter Red Road and American Horse's Maggie Stands Looking, joined hands while Himes zapped them. As the current jerked them, the students held on until they couldn't stand it anymore.[34]

Sometimes the teachers were as perplexed as the pupils. One morning the students were called into a classroom where a tiny white woman stood in front of a long table piled high with packages wrapped in paper and string. Their teacher opened the packages and pulled out an assortment of gleaming bugles, trumpets, cornets, trombones, and French horns, which she handed around to the class. She then opened a black leather case from which she pulled her own horn. She put it to her mouth and blew into it, trumpeting a long, beautiful note. Then she motioned to the students that they should imitate her and blow into their horns.

The room exploded in a sputtering, discordant cacophony. Some of the boys tried to blow into the horns from the large end. The teacher began chattering at them and pantomiming instructions. The class stared back at her, unable to understand a word. She demonstrated how to wet the end of their mouthpiece, but this further confused matters. The boys thought she wanted them to spit on the horns. They covered the shiny brass instruments in saliva. The teacher burst into helpless tears.[35]

Still, after just a few weeks of struggle, the pupils began to learn. They mastered the basics of the English language, willfully forcing the strange consonants, articulations, and tenses from their mouths. "Good morning," a teacher would say as she entered the classroom. The students would respond with a rote, thickly accented "Good monnick."[36]

Presiding over it all was Pratt, who punctuated the beginning and end of every day with his commands and lectures. On Monday and Tuesday nights, they had study hall. On Wednesday and Thursday nights, they gathered in the chapel for hymns, prayers, and religious instructions. On Friday nights, they received a weekly health lecture.

On Sundays, they went to church, marching into town in columns of fours. There was nothing voluntary about the religious instruction—attendance at services was mandatory. In the debut issue of the school paper, *Eadle Keatah Toh*, Pratt pronounced the mission of Carlisle: "Instead of educating soldiers to go to the western plains to destroy with powder and ball, it is proposed to now to train at this institution a corps of practical, educated, and Christian teachers, who will by precept and practice induce their tribes on the plains to adopt the peaceful pursuits of Christian people."

One evening a week, Pratt delivered an address to a school-wide assembly. "You've got to stick to it," Pratt would boom. "S-t-i-c-k-t-o-i-t!"[37]

AFTER JUST a few months, the Carlisle students were the picture of order and obedience—literally. Pratt cannily hired a local photographer, J. N. Choate, to document the alteration in the students' appearances. Choate had photographed them on arrival, in feather-bedecked hair and buckskins, blankets falling around them, pendants in their ears and elk-bone breastplates on their chests. Just a few weeks later, Choate photographed them again, trimmed and buttoned up in their uniforms. Pratt sent a packet of the photos to Schurz. "Astonishing," Schurz pronounced.

Pratt also sent a packet for the president, Rutherford B. Hayes. "I hope your interest in this feature of your administration will increase as it ought," Pratt lectured Hayes.[38]

Pratt had an urgent reason to curry favor in Washington: his superior officers deeply resented his absence from the ranks and threatened to recall him. General Sherman declared that teaching was "old woman's work," and six months after Carlisle opened, he wrote Pratt a scathing letter pressuring him to return to his regular duty in Indian Territory. "Officers who leave their lawful stations for this kind of work are fast sapping the foundations of our profession," Sherman scrawled. He all but accused Pratt of shirking while the men in the Tenth Cavalry "are today fighting the enemies of Civilization."[39] To add injury to insult, Sherman refused to let Lieutenant Brown, whom Pratt had hoped to keep permanently, remain on the Carlisle staff.

Pratt, livid, went over Sherman's head and wrote a dramatic letter straight to President Hayes. West Point had an entire staff of sixty instructors, he pointed out, while he was denied a single volunteer soldier. "I am at this time 'fighting' a greater number of the 'enemies of civilization' than the whole of my regiment put together and I know further that I am fighting them with a thousand times more hope of success," Pratt wrote. "Here a Lieutenant struggles to evolve order out of a chaos of fourteen different Indian languages! Civilization out of savagery! Cleanliness out of filth!"[40]

Pratt's powerful photographs showing his quick results helped persuade Washington that he was doing vital work. Brown went back to his regular duty, but Pratt remained firmly in place as Carlisle superintendent, and would fend off repeated attempts to pull him back to active duty over the next twenty-five years.

But the pictures didn't tell the whole story at Carlisle, as Pratt well knew. The transition of the students was not as swift or easy as he made it look. Those Carlisle students who seemed so outwardly neat and placid boiled with resentments. What Pratt didn't tell his superiors was there were clear signs of emotional stress in even the most eager-to-please pupils: tantrums, sullen work stoppages, and quarrels.

Clarence Three Stars was the son of an influential Lakota and grandson of a man named High Forehead, who had played a key role in a famed early victory over U.S. troops known as the Grattan Massacre. Clarence was ordinarily a keen student, but for some unknown reason he began behaving disruptively in the math classroom one day. Pratt was summoned, and arrived with an interpreter. Insubordination came with a price; Pratt was a swift and hard disciplinarian, and he employed one of his favorite old-fashioned tactics on Three Stars. He "braced" the boy, calling him to attention.

"Stand up!" he barked.

Three Stars stood.

"Hold up your head! Put your hands down by your side! Palms front! Heels together! Push your shoulders back!"

As Pratt issued his commands, he too reared up in his full, imposing military bearing. Then Pratt said, "What is the matter?"

Three Stars began stuttering in Lakota, and in his upset and nervousness, his voice quivered. Robert American Horse said something in Sioux, which made the others snicker. The interpreter translated.

"If you are so brave what makes your voice shake so?"

Three Stars was humiliated. But Pratt was satisfied—public embarrassment was one of his oft-used correctives. He had impressed his authority on Three Stars. With the boy still standing erect at full attention, Pratt said to the teacher, "He seems to obey promptly. I guess things will go all right now."[41]

Another sudden outburst came from American Horse's young relation, Maggie Stands Looking. One morning a Carlisle matron, Miss Mary Hyde, corrected the girl in the performance of some menial domestic chore. The girl stared levelly back at the matron and then deliberately reached out and slapped her across the face. Hyde said, "Why Maggie!" Maggie then burst into tears and, according to Pratt, "cried bitterly." The matron wound up comforting the girl, who was otherwise such a dutiful student that Pratt eventually sent her back to Pine Ridge to recruit other Lakota.[42]

Pratt relied on traditional forms of military discipline: student court-martials, stints in the old Hessian guardhouse, and punishing work details. And though he publicly denied it, he also approved of corporal punishment, and used it.[43] Privately he acknowledged keeping a "raw hide" for the purpose of whipping the most defiant pupils; an old black snake whip was stashed behind the bookshelf in his office, and when a pupil was unruly, he would reach behind the shelf and pull it out.[44] But Pratt preferred to solve problems before they reached that point, and his sheer size and innate authority were usually good enough to do the job.

Pratt was strict, but he was also encouraging, and he was not insensible to the troubles and inner lives of his pupils. A typical form of student resistance was to lapse into silent, sullen passivity. Pratt understood this was a form of pride, and dealt with it patiently. One afternoon a Lakota named Amos Lone Hill balked when he was assigned to dig a trench for a sewer pipe. Lone Hill simply stood by the hole, "stubbornly inactive," Pratt recalled. The superintendent didn't overreact. Suspecting that the boy felt the work was beneath his dignity, Pratt grabbed a shovel himself, jumped into the trench, and began to dig, tossing up huge mounds of dirt.

"Amos, go to work," he said mildly.

After a while the young man clambered down into the ditch, and the two men shoveled side by side.[45]

Still, Pratt's immersion methods were deeply stressful to students—and they took an obvious toll on the students' health. Illness was a constant at Carlisle: With one smothered cough an epidemic could sweep through the common rooms. A single sick child passing a pitcher of water at supper might put half the student body in the infirmary. On one occasion, Pratt reported in a letter to a benefactor, "We are passing through a thorough siege of the mumps. Over 60 are sick today."[46]

The infirmary was filled with victims of tuberculosis, pneumonia, influenza, and trachoma (a potentially blinding eye infection). In the first year, six boys died. By 1881, the number had risen to sixteen, and eight more were sent home with failing health.[47] The *Eadle Keatah Toh* regularly reported student deaths:

> One of the Cheyenne pupils, Abraham Lincoln, died on the 16th inst. His disease was Plenro Pneumonia followed by Cerebro Spinal Meningitis. The funeral services were held at the chapel conducted by the Rev. Dr. Wing, of Carlisle. [January 1880]

> Died, on the 10th inst., after an illness of fifteen days, John Renville, son of Gabriel Renville, chief of the Sisseton Sioux. John was full of life and health when the boys marched out of the camp in Perry Co. The day was hot and at a spring on the way he drank heartily, from that drink began his illness. He returned to the barracks with a fever and hemorrhages from the nose. At the last these defied all skill and he died. [August 1880]

Demoralization, homesickness, climate change, unappetizing diet, fatigue, and the constant emotional distress of dealing with the untried and unknown all combined to undermine their physical health. "That was one of the hard things about our education—we had to get used to so many things we had never known before that it worked on our nerves to such an extent that it told on our bodies," Standing Bear remembered.[48]

But Carlisle was harder on one student than any other: White Thunder's son. The boy who cried and fought when his father forced him onto the boat at Rosebud Landing continued his fight at Carlisle. He neglected his schoolwork, except for drawing, and was stubbornly uncommunicative with teachers. There was a school dictate that students must write a letter home every month in English, but Ernest refused. When he did write to his father, it was to complain bitterly.[49]

Pratt's kindness failed him in dealing with the boy. Instead, he singled him out for special public chastisement in the school paper. "The son of White Thunder has been exceptionally idle, and sometimes disobedient," the April 1880 edition of *Eadle Keatah Toh* reported. When Ernest was encouraged by his teachers to write a letter, the boy sullenly replied, "I have no friends to write to; I had an aunt once, but the bears eat her up."

To add to Ernest's humiliation, Pratt published a supposed rebuke from his father in the same edition of the paper. Pratt had written to White Thunder about the boy's behavior, and Pratt claimed the father's reply, presumably written with the help of an agency interpreter, was as follows:

> *My son: I want to tell you one thing. You did not listen to the school teacher, and for that reason you were scolded. . . . At this agency there are over 7000 people and there are four chiefs. The chiefs sent their children to school and others followed their lead.*
>
> *I want Capt. Pratt to take good care of the children of the chiefs. Your letter did not please me and my people. When the children went to school, many of the people found fault with us for letting them go; and now if what your letter says is true they*

will find still more fault. Capt said he would take care of the children the same as if they were his own. . . . I want you to attend to your books and let play alone.

If you can write a word in English I want to see it and I will be glad. You wrote to me that you were all soldiers and had uniforms. I send you $20 for you to get a large picture in your uniform so that I can see it. I am ashamed to hear every day from others in the school that you act bad and do not try to learn. I send you there to be like a white man and I want you to do what the teacher tells you.

I hope Capt. Pratt will not lose patience with you and give you up, for when I come in the Spring I shall talk to you. You had your own way too much when you were here. I want Capt. Pratt to know I shall talk to you in the Spring and if you don't mind then I shall fix you so you will. I hope you will listen to your teachers for it makes me feel bad when I hear you do not.

Remember the words I told you; I said if it takes five or ten years if you did not learn anything you should not come back here. Your grandfather and mother would be glad to hear from you if you can write a word in English. When you get this letter take it to Capt. Pratt and have him read it and I hope he will write me. Your father White Thunder.

In June 1880, White Thunder came to Carlisle to see his son. He arrived for a grand occasion: the completion of Carlisle's first term. Several influential Lakota had petitioned the government for permission to make the trip, among them American Horse, Red Cloud, and Spotted Tail. All were anxious to see the school and how their children were faring.

It was not a happy visit.

THE LAKOTA scarcely recognized their children. Reports had reached the agencies that their offspring were being made into copies of whites. Tackett wrote to Spotted Tail that all of the children had been given Christian names, and that thirty-four of them had been baptized Episcopalian. But they were still hardly prepared for the sight of the clipped and grim-faced students in their counterfeit Army clothes.[50]

Pratt intended for the celebration of Carlisle's first term to be a political showcase for the school. He invited several dignitaries to attend an elaborate program of events and performances by students. The guest list included the Episcopal bishop of the Dakota Territory, William Hobart Hare. President Hayes and the First Lady were also invited, but, fortunately for Pratt as it turned out, could not come. In addition, Carlisle hosted thirty-one Lakota chiefs, as well as Kiowa, Comanche, Apache, and Wichita representatives from Indian Territory.

Somehow, Pratt seems to have deluded himself that the Indian parents would be as cheerfully astonished by the changes in the students as Washington politicians were. As Pratt greeted the Lakota on campus, he asked them to pose for photographs with their children. The Lakota politely acquiesced. Spotted Tail sat, his braids swathed in fur, eagle feather in his hair, elk-bone breastplate, and blanket falling to his porcupine-quill moccasins, surrounded by his four boys with collars buttoned tightly to their necks under vests and coats.

But after the photo session, Spotted Tail spoke privately with his sons and some of the other children from the agencies. The students poured out their miseries: they were uncomfortable with the stiff clothing and rigid discipline, and offended by the menial work they were forced to do. Worst of all were their descriptions of the guardhouse and corporal punishments. This the Lakota found intolerable—they never struck their children.

In a general welcome assembly, Spotted Tail rose to speak. Through an interpreter, he vented his wrath, in a rising voice cataloging complaints against the school. Pratt had made the school "a soldier place," he angrily charged. He had turned their sons into common laborers, teaching them bricklaying when they had been sent to the school to learn English from books. His son, Stays at Home, who should have been training as a leader of men, worked in a harness shop. Also, his youngest son had been thrown into the guardhouse for a week.

For Pratt, it was an extremely public embarrassment in front of an assembly packed with benefactors. As Spotted Tail finished, the superintendent rose to counter the Brule leader's charges. Military drilling was essential to good health, he argued. As for the uniforms, they were the best clothing available for the price. He had put the youngest Spotted Tail in the guardhouse, it was true, but that was because the boy had stabbed a schoolmate in the leg with a jackknife during a quarrel. The sentence was not harsh under American law.

But as the assembly ended, Spotted Tail wasn't mollified. The superintendent realized he could have a disaster on his hands if he didn't find a way to satisfy the Brule. Pratt had arranged a carefully stage-managed schedule of assemblies, tours, luncheons, and declamations to show off his students' accomplishments, and he could only hope their opinion of the place would change.

He asked the Dickinson science professor, Himes, to give one of his magical lectures to the chiefs, and impressed on Himes the need to make it a success. It was crucial that the visitors take back a good report, or at least not discourage others from sending their children to Carlisle, he told Himes. "It was desirable, not simply to remove distrust, but to impress upon these leading men of their tribes, in every way the superiority of the White Man's Way," Himes recalled Pratt saying.

Himes delivered one of his engaging presentations to an audience that included Spotted Tail, American Horse, Red Cloud, Young Man Afraid of His Horses, White Thunder, Two Strike, Milk, and others. The thoughtful demeanor of the Indian leaders, who paid attention with more than idle curiosity, struck Himes. "They were in their way practical, shrewd observers, alert to everything," he remembered.

He showed them the workings of a compass, advising them, "The surveyor uses this in running the lines of your lands." He explained magnetism, borrowing a knife from one of them, magnetizing it, and using it to pick up iron fillings. When he returned the knife, his audience looked it over, rubbed it, smelled it, and tasted it with their tongues.

"The White Man has no secrets," Himes said. "Whatever he knows your boys and girls will be taught."

The chiefs found the presentation so engrossing that after it was over, some of them came to the front of the room to meet Himes and examine his apparatus. "Howdy," they said, and offered him their hands.[51]

But it was a rare exchange of pleasantries in an otherwise tense occasion. The tribal leaders were scheduled to break up their Carlisle visit with a trip to Washington to discuss pressing issues such as the railroads' right of way. Pratt was relieved to see them go—the pause gave him an opportunity to think about what to do next.

The Lakota traveled via horse-drawn railway cars to the capital, where they were put up at the Tremont House hotel and escorted to A. Saks and Company, where they were outfitted in complimentary suits. The suits, which normally would have cost $23.50 each, included hats, a box of reusable collars, socks, shoes, underwear, and neckties. They toured the still-rough, muddy city, and gazed at the unfinished Washington Monument, a stunted pillar of stone that wouldn't reach its full height for four more years, until it was finally completed in 1884.

This was all part of a familiar routine; Indian delegations had been visiting the capital regularly since the 1840s, and Washingtonians were accustomed to seeing the tribal parties lounging in hotel lobbies smoking, taking in the sights, or shopping. They were entertained at state dinners, awarded large and impressive-seeming "peace medals" with the president's likeness, and given gifts of clothing. But while the tribes thought they were there to negotiate, federal authorities saw the visits less as diplomatic missions than as chances to demonstrate the reach of American civilization, and thus the futility of resisting Washington's will.[52]

While they were gone, Pratt maneuvered, telegraphing Washington to ask that their return visit to Carlisle be canceled. Nevertheless, on June 21, the Lakota came back by train to Harrisburg, Pennsylvania. Pratt threw them a lavish dinner, hoping to improve their mood.

Spotted Tail sported a linen duster, a derby, and a cane, which he had received as gifts in Washington. But despite his new garb, he was no happier about the treatment of his children than he had been before. He demanded another council, and with the entire school gathered in the chapel, he announced that he was taking the Rosebud children home.

Other chiefs rose and spoke in support of Spotted Tail. American Horse, Red Cloud, Red Dog, and Two Strike each made angry speeches protesting the methods of Carlisle. "All of them," Pratt said, "were offensive and prejudicial to the discipline of the school."[53]

But Pratt had Washington on his side, and he used it. He waved a telegram from Schurz, stating that they were forbidden to withdraw any students. The Lakota had pledged their children for a term of three years, and officialdom would be deeply displeased if they removed any children before then, Pratt sternly advised.

"The children came here for three years and must remain until the period expires," he insisted. "You have a right to speak your wishes only about your own children . . . besides they have not learned enough to be useful to you."

In the face of these arguments, the parents wilted, even American Horse. Only Spotted Tail was adamant: others could do as they wished, but the Rosebud children were going home.

Pratt hurriedly telegraphed Schurz once more. The secretary replied that Spotted Tail was not entitled to any children but his very own, and he would have to foot the bill for their train fare home. Spotted Tail responded that in that case he would pay for it himself.[54]

Spotted Tail collected his four sons and two grandchildren, and the party departed for the train station. Spotted Tail didn't doubt Pratt's word that the government would be displeased, and as a precaution, he surrounded the children with a tribal guard.

At the station, Spotted Tail quickly hustled his family onto the rail cars, and a harrowing scene ensued as the other Lakota fathers bid their own children goodbye. Weeping pupils had to be pulled from the train by Carlisle staff. In the emotion and confusion, three children tried to stow away. As a small girl was dragged, screeching, from the rail car, Spotted Tail clasped another little girl to him and refused to let her go, claiming her as a relative.

The third stowaway was White Thunder's son, Ernest. The boy made it as far as Harrisburg before he was discovered and forced to return to campus by his father. He would never recover from a bitter sense of rejection.[55]

The parents who had left their children behind understood it was a risky proposition to defy the government's Indian policy, as Spotted Tail's fate would prove—the incident ruined the Brule leader. Even before he arrived back at Rosebud, wires from Washington informed the local agent that he was in deep disfavor with the White Father.

This fatally weakened him politically within his tribe, and his reservation enemies promptly began plotting against him.

Little more than a year later, on August 5, 1881, Spotted Tail was assassinated by a minor factional rival named Crow Dog, who shot him off his horse as he rode home from a meeting at the agency office. The aging Brule tumbled heavily into the dusty road, but he managed to get to his feet and pull his pistol before he collapsed again, dead.[56] A *New York Herald* obituary paid tribute to a man who was an irreplaceable loss to his people. "He was never double faced," the *Herald* wrote. "His public and private councils were the same. He met the white man with candor and courtesy, displaying a depth and breadth of intellect that are seldom looked for in a savage chieftain. His bearing was truly majestic, as his person was noble and handsome."[57]

THE STUDENTS left behind at Carlisle were torn between longings for home and a genuinely developing loyalty to Pratt and to the school. The constant drumbeat of Pratt's voice and the missionary-tinged schooling from their teachers slowly but surely wore away at them. Their letters home expressed competing allegiances: "My dear Uncle, I am not afraid to try learning, working and reading too, all the time. White men is very good and Dakota way is not good I guess."[58]

In July 1880, a boy named Joshua Given, the nineteen-year-old son of Satank, the old Kiowa leader who had been shot trying to escape at Fort Sill, delivered a speech before the Cumberland Valley Sunday School Convention. It was a testament to the swift effectiveness of his Carlisle indoctrination.

> *My friends I speak to you a few words. The Indians are not much civilized. We live in houses made of the skins of buffaloes. The Indian women have very hard work making moccasins for the men, and work all the days long. The Indian men do nothing, just we think about fighting and they don't know anything about God. Now they had children to send to school. I say the Indian children do much better because we have something to do now. . . . Capt Pratt is a very good friend to the Indians, and he teaches us a good many things and we love him too.*[59]

On October 6, 1880, Pratt held a general assembly to mark the one-year anniversary of Carlisle. He recalled the arrival of the first bedraggled, weary, frightened pupils at Carlisle, and then he posed a simple question to the student body. "Should the work be carried forward?" he asked. According to Pratt, every hand in the room went up.

But one hand went more slowly and grudgingly than all the others. Ernest White Thunder was more melancholy and brooding than ever. His father's departure must have cut him deeply, because the boy lapsed into despondency, which turned into a serious illness. One October morning shortly after Pratt's assembly, he refused to go to class, complaining he was ill with a sore throat. He was carried to the infirmary.

There he went on a hunger strike. On December 6, Pratt wrote worriedly to Washington, and the tone of his letter made clear his enormous frustration with the boy. "White Thunder's son is very sick and I doubt if he recovers. I consider that it is entirely his own fault as I explained to you. He is still very obstinate [and] seems to rather want to die."[60]

What keen emotional suffering caused a fifteen-year-old boy to try to starve himself to death can only be conjectured at, but what's clear is that Ernest White Thunder fought like hell against the Carlisle method. He fought everything. He fought to get out of bed—Pratt had to hide his clothes to keep him in the hospital. He fought against food or medicine, until Pratt physically held him down and poured it into him. No sooner would he get a draught in Ernest's mouth than the boy would spit it out. Pratt had met his match.

At the bitter end, Ernest seems to have decided he wanted to live, because he began to eat. His closest friend, Robert American Horse, helped to feed him and coaxed him to take his medicine "as if he was his own brother," Pratt remarked. But by then, it was too late. Robert was at his bedside when he passed away at daybreak on December 14, 1880.

"It is with a sad heart that I write to you this morning," Pratt wrote to White Thunder. The boy died "quietly without suffering like a man," Pratt informed him. But Pratt knew what small consolation that must have been. "I know how a father loves his boy," he wrote.

"It was because you loved him so much that you gave him to me to come far away to this school."

The entire school was abject with grief. That same night, Carlisle had lost another child from Rosebud, Maud Swift Bear, to pneumonia. Apparently, the sobbing in the girls' dormitory lasted all night long. The following day, Carlisle held a double funeral. Six Lakota boys, including the sons of American Horse, carried Ernest's coffin.

Pratt wrote White Thunder with the details of the ceremony and tried to console him by suggesting that his son had died in a heroic cause, much as young men sometimes died on a dangerous buffalo hunt. It was not such far-fetched sentiment: by now the Lakota parents surely felt that their children's attendance at Carlisle was perilous and a supreme sacrifice.[61]

White Thunder's immediate feelings are not recorded. But he was upset at the news that his son had been buried in a white man's funeral, and petitioned Washington for the return of the body. He was refused. To Pratt's immense relief, however, White Thunder wrote him a kindly letter, in which he refrained from blame. He only cautioned Pratt to tend to the children they had surrendered to him. "You, my friend, are a good man," White Thunder wrote. "For that reason you now have with you children of three of the chiefs. Therefore, my friend, take good care of those children. They belong to us who are chiefs. I am White Thunder who say this." Two years later, a second White Thunder, Clarence, would arrive at Carlisle.[62]

Despite the ordeal of the White Thunder family, Pratt had no qualms about his undertaking. Pratt's critics increasingly questioned why Indian children had to be taken from their parents and spirited across the country to be educated. But any suggestion that the children should not be removed from their homes, or that their tribal families were worth preserving, Pratt viewed as pure sentiment. After all, his own childhood had been shattered and he had been forced to go to work as a boy, and look what it had done for him. "The devastating effect of his program upon clan and tribe seems not to have seriously disturbed him," according to his biographer and fellow teacher Elaine Goodale Eastman.[63]

In March 1881, Pratt informed Senator Henry L. Dawes that the

Carlisle student body had grown to 286 children from twenty-three tribes. The photographer J. N. Choate continued to chronicle the conversions of the students: A panoramic photo from the early period shows pupils lined up like toy soldiers in the quadrangle, their clothes stiff and their faces stony. Pratt wrote to Dawes:

> I suppose the end to be gained, however far away it may be, is the complete civilization of the Indian and his absorption into our national life, with all the rights and privileges guaranteed to every other individual, the Indian to lose his identity as such, to give up his tribal relations and to be made to feel that he is an American citizen. . . . The sooner all tribal relations are broken up, the sooner the Indian loses all his Indian ways, even his language, the better it will be for him and for the government and the greater will be the economy to both.[64]

It's easy, in reviewing the events of the first year at Carlisle, to write Pratt off as his students' oppressor. But the truth is more complicated than that. Beneath his bullying lay a fundamental belief in his pupils. A Carlisle teacher, Katherine Bowersox, said of him, "He saw great possibilities in each boy and girl and forgot absolutely that they were Indians."[65]

Pratt had the Victorian American male's full confidence of the era in the ability to make oneself out of nothing, to literally mold one's own body and destiny. He believed his students had the very same ability. In his more temperate moments, he could be quite articulate about that. The Indian, he said, "is born a blank, like the rest of us."

It was that belief, coupled with his self-righteousness, that allowed Pratt to be cruel. He had the same quality ascribed to his younger contemporary Theodore Roosevelt: a "righteous ruthlessness."[66] He was absolutely certain of what was best, and he quashed any misgivings he may have felt when he read letters such as the one from White Thunder. He never once doubted that he was doing the right thing by taking his students from their homes and all they had known—he did it to plunge them into his boundless America.

Pratt's favorite lounging spot on campus was the bandstand, a quaint Victorian gazebo in the center of the lawn. From it, Pratt viewed the entire Carlisle grounds, from the two-tiered balustrades of the whitewashed dormitories to his own white-columned residence. At the close of Carlisle's first year, Pratt could prop his feet on its railing and survey with pride a campus alive with students, studying, working, and playing.

"What is home?" Pratt demanded. "Is it your father's home? Or your grandfather's? Or is it the home you create for yourself to fit your own powers and aspirations?"[67]

5

THE LAST FIGHT AND FIRST GAMES

MERICAN HORSE'S HOME was part camp and part farmstead at the foot of some honey-colored bluffs, where a creek named Medicine Root twisted through a verdant bottomland, glinting like a lost necklace. Amid a circle of faded, smoke-smudged tipis rose a new house: it was a tall plank structure with a peaked escarpment of a roof, furnished with a wood-burning stove, some trunks and chairs, and a frame bed. White canvas covered the walls, hung with mementos, including a large portrait of American Horse himself.[1]

By 1889 American Horse had become firmly "progressive," a tribal politician who recognized that military victories against the United States had been satisfying but ultimately futile. In the bloodstained grass, the warrior had understood that some accommodation would have to be reached with whites to avoid total destruction. The question was how much. The new house he dwelled in was government-built, an encouragement to take the white man's road. Gradually, he did—sort of.

As American Horse's family milled between camp and house, they passed between the old Lakota world and the new one, ruled by the missionaries and federal agents of the Pine Ridge reservation. Robert American Horse returned to Pine Ridge in 1887 after eight years at

Carlisle, so thoroughly Christianized that he became a catechist under the local Episcopal bishop, William Hobart Hare. But when he preached sermons on Sunday, he did so in Lakota—to Pratt's disappointment.[2]

The elder American Horse was of two minds about Carlisle. He was eager for at least some of his children to be white-educated, yet he was wary of Pratt's methods. He kept his eldest son, Tom, home to fill a more traditional Lakota role, suggesting the extent to which he was conflicted. He had received a nasty shock at finding his children shorn and in military uniform on his first visit to the school. But subsequently, he had come to appreciate that they were well fed and cared for there. Still, he didn't like sending his children so far away, believing the climate change was bad for their health, and he was continually anxious about their welfare. Over a decade, he would make no fewer than a dozen trips to Carlisle to check on his children, as he struggled with the question of how to prepare them for what was to come without totally destroying their Lakotaness.[3]

One day in 1889, the question posed itself in the shape of his younger son, Ben. The boy made an announcement: he wanted to go to Carlisle, he said. Two of his sisters were to be sent off to the school, and they needed somebody to look after them. Ben wanted to go with them.

American Horse flatly refused—he had sent enough sons to Carlisle for the time being. The boy in front of him stood just five feet tall and weighed little more than 103 pounds, and wasn't ready for the trip. But Ben would not let the matter drop. "Why can't I go?" he demanded.

American Horse replied that Lakota men were needed to protect their homes. "If something happens, I need you here," he said. "We need warriors."

But Ben packed his belongings anyway. If his father didn't let him go, he would get there on his own, he said. It wasn't an idle threat. Over the next few days, Ben twice ran away, and his father had to find him and bring him home. Finally, American Horse relented. He was due in Washington on diplomatic business, and he decided to take the boy with him and send him on to school.[4]

American Horse and his son rode to Omaha, where they boarded a train for Washington. From there, Ben continued on alone to Pennsylvania. He sat in the rail car unaccompanied, unable to speak a word of English. As the train chugged through the countryside, Ben took note of the changing landscape. At the periodic whistle-stops, he carefully marked the ground. He intended to find his way back again in case he didn't like the school.

A conductor gruffly looked after Ben, and by listening closely to him, Ben learned to say three things in English. "Sun" told him what direction they were heading. "Eat" meant he would be fed. "Come on" told him to get back on the train.

Ben pulled into Carlisle junction on December 16, 1889. "A little son of the Sioux Chief American Horse has arrived," the school paper reported.[5] Like the Lakota students before him, Ben walked through stone gates into a world that was dissonant and strange. But Carlisle was a larger, more comfortable, and prosperous place than it had been a decade earlier. The institution had grown and matured. More than fifty teachers and four hundred pupils wandered the sprawling campus, including forty-four young Apache from Geronimo's recently defeated band.[6] The students wore dashing blue uniforms with yellow-lined capes turned back at the shoulder and red braid at the sleeves of the student officers.

Freshly painted cream-colored buildings lined an immaculately landscaped quadrangle. Behind the dorms were new workshops and stables, and on the outskirts of campus students worked in rows on three hundred neatly farmed acres that reached into the distance. Pratt had built Carlisle with furious energy over ten years, raising money from private benefactors for capital improvements. Ben's residence was a brand-new, three-story dormitory, with eighty-six rooms and a large common assembly room. Newly installed electric lights and central steam heat had recently replaced the old oil lamps and coal stoves.

As Ben settled in, he began to take pride in the marching and drilling of the students in their handsome uniforms, which appealed to his soldierly Lakota sensibility. So did the school's brass band, which in just a few short years had become one of the most renowned in the country, playing national parades and festivals, delivering airs from the classical to the martial with spirited, high-stepping delivery under their Oneida conductor, Dennison Wheelock.[7]

In class, newly shorn, Ben stared at a blackboard covered with indecipherable chalk marks, and learned to write his new name. Carlisle's curriculum had evolved: the school offered grades one through ten as well as manual training, a teaching program, and college preparatory classes from nearby Conway Hall, a local prep school. But most of the students still arrived with little or no previous education—in 1886 just six pupils came in above third grade. Ben spent the first half of each day in classrooms as teachers conducted rhythmic choruses of vocabulary, painstaking chants in single syllables.

"Boy."

"Box."

"Cat."

Gradually, Ben and his fellow students learned to string a few words together: "The cow is white."

The second half of each day was spent in shop classes. Ben was assigned to the bakery, where he rolled heavy barrels of flour and learned to mix ingredients and bake the airy loaves that supplied the entire school at mealtimes.

One afternoon, Ben noticed a line of students in front of a bulletin board, writing their names on a sign-up sheet. Ben put himself in line with the rest of them and pretended he knew how to read when it was his turn to scan the notice on the board. He added his name to the other signatures.

Ben didn't realize it, but he had signed up for Carlisle's "outing" program. This was the most distinctive feature of a Carlisle education, and it was wholly Pratt-conceived: students were sent out to work and board with local families, usually on farms, in the name of total cultural immersion.[8] The outing program was meant to introduce students to American society and teach them to be wage earners. But it could be a less than educational experience. While some patrons were genuinely interested in helping Indian children, some were just looking for cheap labor. Ben was lucky: he was sent to a kind Quaker family with two daughters, and between heavy farm chores they taught him to read.

Life on the Carlisle campus was not all drill, prayer, and drudgery, Ben discovered. Pratt insisted on discipline, but he also encouraged the age-old impulse of children to play. He believed in strenuous activity of any kind, and the lawns teemed with games and exercises, native contests, white pastimes, romps, and footraces. A creek named Letort Spring ran by the campus, and students built a dock and a rope swing for summer swimming. They put a plank over a wagon wheel and used it for floating; and, most ingeniously, they ran a cable and a small platform through the woods, so they could ride through the trees. When there were blizzards, Pratt sent the boys out to shovel the town trolley tracks, and they would use the shovels as sleds, riding them, sometimes standing up, down the banks.[9]

Pratt even tolerated pranks, as long as they were enterprising. One evening, a matron named Ella Patterson heard a racket coming from the small boys' dormitory. She opened the door to find a dozen boys whooping with excitement, surrounding a ringleader, who held a piece of string in his hand. The string tailed along the floor and disappeared under a bed. Patterson demanded the string, and the boy handed it over. As she jerked it away, three rats came racing out from the bed, harnessed as a team. The horrified matron leaped onto a chair while the boys pelted out of the room, howling with laughter.

Shortly afterward, Patterson heard scrabbling noises at her chimney hole. Here came the rats, dangling by the string, down the flue.

When the matron reported the episode to Pratt, however, he reacted delightedly. "Splendid industry!" he bawled. "Push it, Miss P. Push it! I will give a reward of five cents for every rat scalp presented at the office which shows up with two ears."[10]

Like most school headmasters in the late nineteenth century, Pratt was a subscriber to "muscular Christianity," the notion that a strong body led to a strong mind and a strong soul. It was an attitude borrowed from the British public schools and exemplified by the Anglican author Thomas Hughes, who celebrated the playing fields of Rugby in his novel *Tom Brown's School Days*. Pratt, in step with the times, made a gymnasium one of his first major projects at Carlisle, converting an old stable for the purpose. "We need a gymnasium so we may build up physically at the same time we build up the brain," he trumpeted. "Strong minds and weak bodies will not do."[11] When the gym was completed and the hardwood floor was laid, Pratt hosted a school roller-skating party on it. Roller-skating had originated among the wealthy families of Newport, Rhode Island, but it had rapidly caught on around the country, as did any new pastime involving wheels.[12]

Bicycles came into vogue, and Pratt urged the children to start a cycling club. He frequently took students on traipses in the woods surrounding Carlisle so they could fish, camp, and shoot bows and arrows. In the coming years, he also encouraged cakewalks, dance socials, and debate societies. He booked lively entertainments for campus performances, including Italian magicians, and brought the Barnum circus to town.[13]

But there was one game that captivated Ben American Horse and the rest of the Carlisle students above all others: football. In the fall of 1882, the first students had leveled and graded a playing field and begun to learn the basics of the game from the school's disciplinarian, W. G. Thompson, a Victorian gentleman with a drooping mustache and a manner of prim rectitude who was in charge of physical activities. Student Harry Shirley, a Caddo, wrote home to his father:

My Dear Father:—I thought I would write you a few lines and I like the place very much and there was one Negro boy got killed on the railroad and we have a very nice farm and cold water to drink and would send my Bow and arrows and how is my little pony getting along I would like to know how are you getting and would please send me some money and we have a great many boy and is great many girls and the boys have a small house I wish they play the band and I have a bed to myself. And I am coming home in two years from now if Capt. Pratt will let me and how are you getting along with the big house and will you tell me in your letter when you write and we got at Carlisle on Thursday and when we got here I did not like the place but since I have being here two or three days I have got used to the place and I like it very well but when we got I felt very home sick and be sure and send my bow and some spike arrows.

And we go to church every Sunday. And I have a blue suit to where and there was one Shyenne boy shot himself with a pistol and . . . the boys have a nice green lawn in which play Kicking a football and how are you getting along with your stock.[14]

By the fall of 1887, football was so popular on campus that the boys took up a collection from among the student body to buy a new ball. By 1890, intramural games were a regular part of the school day, with competitions between the shop classes. Ben's bakers played against the blacksmiths, tailors, and so on, for the school championship. They practiced in the evenings, between supper and the call to study hall.[15]

Other sports were just mild amusements, diversions, compared to the staggering physical punishments and rewards doled out in a game of football, Ben found. Only football offered the satisfaction of physically forcing another human to give way. Ben locked his arms together with the other boys and charged, feet threshing in the grass until sod flew. They plunged forward and dove at each other's legs while a ball carrier struggled to break the muddy impasse. Eventually, the shoving action on the field would end in a large pile of limbs. Boys unpeeled themselves, rising gingerly, and felt their arms and legs to make sure nothing was broken. Afterward, they limped around campus with sore muscles and livid purple welts, gratifyingly tired and proud of their scars.

But Pratt, from his favorite viewing spot on the bandstand, had serious qualms about the new game as he watched it take hold of his campus. "I was not especially pleased to encourage it," he recalled.[16]

W HEN IT came to football, the trouble with muscular Christianity was that American boys showed a tendency to shuck the Christianity part and indulge in sheer muscularity.

The game began as an Ivy League undergraduate riot, an annual rite of mock warfare between privileged sons. At Harvard, the free-for-all between freshmen and sophomores was dubbed "Bloody Monday." At Yale, the yearly "rush" on the college green was such a chaotic melee that on one occasion the overly enthused undergrads took on local firefighters, too.

November 6, 1869, is officially identified as the date of the first formal intercollegiate game, between Princeton and Rutgers, but it was just an unruly brawl between men who removed their velvet-collared coats to play "kill the ballcarrier." Students rode in buckboard wagons or a train hauled by a huffing engine to an open field, where "grim faced players were silently stripping" as their supporters gave them urgent advice. The high point of the game came when J. Edward Michael of Princeton and George Large of Rutgers hurtled into a split rail fence. Sitting atop the rails were supporters from both sides. The fence collapsed, and spectators were dumped in the grass like a heap of garments.

The game grew haphazardly. Fields were irregular patches of ground; there was no set number of players, and no such thing as a regulation-sized ball. On November 15, 1873, Princeton and Yale played the first of their "classics." Early in the game, there was a loud pop during a massive pileup in front of the Yale goal—the ball had exploded.[17]

A starchy young elitist brought some order to the mayhem. One night during a Yale rush in New Haven, a bullying upperclassman named Louis Hull piled into the melee and tackled all the freshmen he could lay his hands on. He peered through the dark looking for more candidates, and spied a slim figure on the fringe of the crowd that seemed a likely victim.[18]

"Come to it, freshman," he said.

A moment later, he found himself pinned on his back in the grass. "What is your name, freshman?" Hull asked, chastened.

"Walter Camp."

Walter Chauncey Camp was the son of a New Haven school principal, descended from a family that traced itself to the first post-Pilgrim generation. He was a priggish, fleshy-cheeked boy who covered his baby face with muttonchop whiskers and a luxurious mustache. His center-parted hair curled on either side of his forehead like virtuous wings, and he favored stiff white collars with an ascot knot under his tweed jacket, pinned by a Skull and Bones insignia. One kindly biographer describes him as "gently autocratic" even as an undergrad.[19]

In the fall of 1876, while the country still reeled from the events at Little Big Horn, Yale, Harvard, Princeton, and Columbia formed the

Intercollegiate Football Association. Camp would sit on every rules committee from 1878 to his death in 1925, and his personal interventions would set the game apart from rugby. Between 1880 and 1881 he proposed the structure that the modern audience would recognize: he set the number of players at eleven, introduced the pause in the action known as the line of scrimmage, and established a system of three tries, or "downs," in which to gain yardage or face forfeiture of the ball.

Just as important, Camp brought a philosophic rationale to the game. To Camp, football was an exercise in social Darwinism and military science. The best teams were a product of good breeding, and vice versa. "As the 'dandy' gentleman regiments in the war outmarched, outfought and outplucked the bloody 'rebs,'" he wrote, "so gentlemen teams and gentleman players will always hold the football field. Brutes haven't the pluck."[20]

But Camp's rules and justifications were like his facial hair: a handsome veneer on what was fundamentally a lawless indulgence. From the beginning, the American game differed from its British public school antecedent, rugby, in three major ways: its creativity, its violence, and its total lack of principle. The English played according to an honor code. But in American football, competitors viewed every regulation as something to be cagily outwitted. Invention was rampant, and so were slugging and cheating. They led to that distinctly American necessity: the referee.[21]

No tactic was out of bounds. Linemen picked up handfuls of dirt and flung it in the eyes of their opponents. Punches to the face and kicks in the shin were the norm, as was biting. A typical tactic was to identify a star player on the opposing team and cripple him. Strategy consisted of crude "mass" plays, machine-like formations that mowed down opponents as if flattening hay. The center of the action was nicknamed "the pile" by its participants, who sometimes emerged from it with cracked ribs or broken collarbones and were expected to play through them.

The painter Frederic Remington was a rusher on the 1879 Yale squad, and his sense of bloody color was evident when he earned renown for a stunt before the almightily important game against

Princeton. He took his jersey to a local slaughterhouse and dipped it in blood, to make it look "more businesslike."[22]

After the 1886 game against Harvard, Amos Alonzo Stagg of Yale recalled that his teammates looked like they had been beaten with clubs. One of them, George Woodruff, had a badly broken nose, another needed eight stitches over his eye, and still another had both eyes closed by swelling, and two fat lips.[23]

When baseball hero Mike Kelly, the famous Boston catcher, was asked whether he would like to play football, he replied, "Not me! Say, when I want to get knocked out, I'll go up against Corbett or John L. They'll do it quick and easy."[24]

At Cornell, a behemoth guard named Glenn S. Warner worked his way through school from 1892 to 1894 by waiting tables and painting amateurish watercolors, but he was often so sore he couldn't lift a tray or even a paintbrush. He recalled that players "free lunched" on each other's legs at the bottom of a pile. "Such a game, obviously put a premium on beef, and 'human mountains' were sought and valued by every coach. I can remember lines that looked like a herd of hairy mammoths," Warner remembered.[25]

No team was more punishing than Yale. A football man at Yale was a specimen of hulking institutional manliness. He was thick-haunched, stern-faced, and stiff-whiskered, and he threatened to break the wobbly-legged furniture of the Victorian period simply by sitting in it. At the training table, he grubbed on massive slabs of carved meat, called "chops," which he chased with whole milk and puddings.

Yale's captain and quarterback in 1887 was Harry Beecher, nephew of Harriet Beecher Stowe and grandson of the grandiloquent old abolitionist preacher Lyman Beecher. The old man was said to be such an ardent football fan that he paid his grandson $25 every time he scored. The Yalies enthusiastically set up goal opportunities for Harry, and then swilled the champagne he treated them to when they won.

The 1887 season must have been booze-soaked, because Yale won nine games as Beecher scored nineteen touchdowns and kicked thirty-three goals. But even without champagne, it was a rowdy team. Teammate Stagg, the future University of Chicago football coaching legend, paid his way though Yale by waiting on tables in the student dining club, and he recalled seeing "everything on the table, wet or dry, hot or cold, hurled by the diners at one another out of sheer good feeling"—including applesauce and large balls of butter, which would stick squarely to the foreheads of victims. Beecher usually started the fight and then ducked under the table.[26]

As scandals and brouhahas became chronic, colleges and universities began to wrestle with the issue that tortures them to the present day: professionalism. Faculty members across the country debated the moral content of the new game. As early as 1883, a Harvard committee on athletics complained that instead of "a manly spirit of fair play," football encouraged "a spirit of sharpers and of roughs." In 1889, one of Harvard's players was said to have been a brakeman for the Boston and Maine line. Charles W. Eliot, the president of Harvard for forty years, toyed with banning the sport altogether, arguing that it reduced athletes to "powerful animals" and campuses to centers of "mere physical sport and not of intellectual training." Football, he declared, was "more brutal than prize fighting, cock fighting or bull fighting."[27]

But for every critic there was an enthusiast. No criticism, scandal, or snobbery could slow the popular spread of the game. At first, spectators would simply pull up to the fields in their surreys, traps, and buggies, but by 1880, the Yale-Princeton game drew five thousand fans. Just ten years later, forty thousand people packed Manhattan Field at the Polo Grounds in New York to see the two teams play on Thanksgiving Day. Thousands more hung over the rails of a nearby viaduct or climbed the adjacent Coogan's Bluff, nicknamed Deadhead Hill, to look down into the field for free.

The Yale-Princeton game was so hugely popular that church services were held an hour earlier so New Yorkers could get to the game. Journalist Richard Harding Davis vividly rendered the siege-like state of the city for *Harper's Weekly*. Fifth Avenue mansions were draped in school colors, depending on the allegiance of the household: blue banners with a white *Y* fluttered from the Vanderbilt and Whitney mansions, orange flags with a black *P* from the manses of the Sloanes, Alexanders, and Scribners.

Collegians swarmed over the city, packing Broadway and striding cockily down the boulevard in their fluttering Newmarket greatcoats and curl-brimmed hats, silk kerchiefs wound around their throats, twirling canes wrapped in school-color ribbons. In taverns, restaurants, and wagering parlors, $50,000 might exchange hands amid "the rifle like cheer of Yale and the hissing sky rocket yell of Princeton."

Every vehicle that could hold a passenger was commandeered for the ride to the Polo Grounds, twenty men at a time balanced perilously atop omnibuses from Washington Square to Harlem. The buses were "draped from top to hub with festooned colors," and they were stocked with bourbon, champagne, sandwiches, whole cold salmon, and roasted chickens.

At the game, the scoring team did handstands in the muddy end zone, "their chins in the hands and their elbows in the mud, and the rest of their bodies in the air, kicking and dancing with ecstasy."

Afterward, roaring undergraduates packed into Koster and Bial's Music Hall on Twenty-third Street so densely that a man who wanted to leave had to be passed out over the heads of the crowd until hc was thrown, hatless and scarfless, into the lobby. The music hall was threadbare and dimly lit, and the ceiling was so low that the cigar smoke seemed to roll in waves around the horseshoe balcony.

Men rode on each other's shoulders, stepped across tabletops, hung over the balcony railings, and dropped to the floor. They walked "unsteadily on to the heads of the crowd without exciting any ill humor on the part of the gentlemen so trampled upon. They yelled the entire time . . . and at moments of greatest enthusiasm clambered upon the stage, and were pitched off into the arms of their companions and on to the heads of the frightened orchestra by the irate German managers."

The orchestra and the vaudeville performers were unheard in the drunken din. The leader waved his baton and the lips of the singers and comedians moved noiselessly, while the college boys roared the dance hall refrains:

> They're af-ter me
> They're af-ter me
> For I'm the individual they require![28]

What was it about the game that fascinated boys from Yale to Carlisle? One answer is that football took hold of the American imagination at the same historical moment that the West was won. Scholar Frederick Jackson Turner would identify 1890 as the year in which America became fully colonized—if a frontier was defined as "the existence of an area of free land," he argued, then it had vanished, replaced by settlements. Technology was fast outstripping the human body, and men no longer relied for their livelihoods on their ability to conquer the land. In the streets, mechanized vehicles vied with horse-drawn ones—sometimes with catastrophic results, as horses stampeded and trains ran off rails. Electrical and gas-powered apparatus gave off great bursts of light that illuminated fast-growing cities.[29]

But with urbanity came anxiety. When electricity was installed in the White House in 1889, President Benjamin Harrison and his wife were so afraid of the light switches that they refused to touch them. They left the lights burning all night, until an orderly arrived in the morning to douse them.[30]

America experienced a collective fear that mechanization could result in male atrophy and even effeminacy. Increasingly, Gilded Age young men turned to sport as an antidote for pervasive cultural weakening. If football was a game of excesses, its enthusiasts considered it well worth it. Violence and moral edginess were its chief attractions, because they toughened the sons of the rich and prepared them to wield authority. Henry Cabot Lodge remarked at a Harvard commencement dinner: "The time given to athletic contests and the injuries incurred on the playing field are the price which the English speaking race has paid for being world conquerors."[31]

The game at once reaffirmed the exclusivity of a close Ivy League circle while demonstrating that upper-class refinement didn't mean a loss of physical virility. Between 1875 and 1899, Yale wouldn't lose to a team that wasn't Princeton or Harvard. Similarly, between 1901 and 1921, the White House wouldn't be occupied by anyone who hadn't gone to one of the Big Three.

It was the perfect contest for young men of a newly industrialized society. Camp rationalized that it was less a game than a "science" requiring intelligence, execution, strategy, timing, and collaboration, as well as strength. The football player was uniquely positioned to straddle the old and new worlds: he employed his body and yet he was able to intellectually grasp and employ new mechanics, methods, and industries. The game was therefore the ultimate teaching tool for a new kind of robust managerial executive. As historian David Wallace Adams puts it, football was "an ideal forum for creating the new American man—half Boone, half Rockefeller."[32]

But by the fall of 1890, Pratt was still not persuaded that the game belonged on the Carlisle campus. He could not overcome his distaste for the crude violence of it. That autumn, injuries to two of his students made up his mind on the subject.

Impromptu rivalries had sprung up between the Indian students and locals. Town boys would break up the boredom of an afternoon by storming the Carlisle fence line. "Let's go fight the Indians," one of them would say, and they would pick up rocks from the freight tracks behind the school and chuck them over the fence. The Indian boys would throw rocks back, and a pitched battle would ensue until Pratt or the railroad police broke it up.[33]

Carlisle's football boys began to scrimmage with students from Dickinson College, a gracious, gray-stone, Revolutionary War–era institution that sat just on the other side of town. Dickinson was a natural opponent, and the relationship quickly grew heated. One October afternoon there was a vicious pileup on the field, and at the bottom of it, a Pawnee boy named Stacy Matlock lay trampled and clutching a badly broken leg. As Matlock writhed in the grass, the Carlisle players gathered around him and added to his cries with their own wails of grief.[34]

Matlock was put in a carriage and brought back to campus. Pratt helped carry the boy to an operating table and assisted in setting the bone, which was broken in two different places below the knee. Pratt was shaken—it was the second instance of a broken bone just that week. Another boy, named Paul Shattuck, had had his collarbone broken in a "fiendish" intramural game on the Carlisle field, according to the school paper.

The injuries appalled Pratt. His mission at Carlisle was to pacify and civilize his students, not make them more combative. He banned any more games beyond school walls. "This ends outside football for us," he announced.[35]

But Pratt may have had another reason for banning the sport as well. There was enough conflict at Carlisle in 1890 and 1891 without football. The student body was caught squarely in the middle of a very real and agonizing conflict, the Ghost Dance War.

ON THE afternoon of December 16, 1890, a fistfight broke out in the school reading room. The cause was the death of Sitting Bull: the Hunkpapa Sioux chief had been shot to death in the midst of the Ghost Dance passions by Indian police. "Sitting Bull is dead, and nobody weeps," the school paper announced. A Crow student made the mistake of openly celebrating the news in front of a nephew of Sitting Bull's. The nephew lunged, and the two boys thrashed around the room in a brawl until Pratt arrived to separate them.[36]

Though it took place far to the west, the Ghost Dance movement intimately involved Carlisle students and their families—and divided them. It began as the messianic vision of a Nevada Paiute named Wovoka, who preached of a trance-inducing dance and impending apocalypse. According to Wovoka, the world would be wiped clean, the dead would come back to life, and the buffalo would be plentiful on the plains again. News of Wovoka's word spread through the American West, carried to other tribes by emissaries who trekked to see him. A significant number of his apostles were former Carlisle students. Four ex-pupils, Grant Left Hand, Paul Boynton, Arnold Woolworth, and Caspar Edson, served as interpreters of the dance to the Arapahoe and Cheyenne.[37]

The Ghost Dance religion took on a unique potency when it reached the Lakota reservations, where a mix of unfortunate personalities and fulminating circumstances resulted in a catastrophe. Ghost Dance disciples Short Bull and Kicking Bear emphasized the revenge implicit in Wovoka's apocalyptic tidings: the dead would revive, the buffalo would teem again, and whites would be wiped off the earth. The Lakota would be made impervious to bullets by "ghost shirts" painted with certain symbols, and triumph.

By fall of 1890, thousands of Sioux were dancing, and whites were nervous. The witless Pine Ridge agent D. F. Royer, an inexperienced political appointee and a man so easily affrighted that the Oglala nicknamed him "Young Man Afraid of His Indians," tried to order a halt to the dancing but was met with furious defiance. "White men dance when they please and so will we Indians," a Sioux said. Royer called for federal troops.

For American Horse and his family, the tensions were particularly excruciating. He was a nondancer and a firm progressive, an unpopular stance in the face of rising militancy. When his elder son, Tom, witnessed a Ghost Dance ceremony and pronounced it fantastic nonsense, he was accused of siding with whites.[38]

American Horse was, as ever, still deeply immersed in the worldly affairs of the tribe. He always seemed to be at the forefront of events that affected the Oglala Sioux. He toured the country with the new theatrical sensation, Buffalo Bill's Wild West Show, in 1886–1887, from St. Louis to Staten Island to Europe. When he came home, he took an unhappy lead role in the fractious discussions with the Crook Commission of 1888–1889, which strong-armed the Sioux into selling a substantial portion of land.

Along with just a handful of other progressives, American Horse decided in favor of the 1889 treaty. He wanted "the satisfaction of knowing that I can leave a piece of land to my children, that they will not have to say that for my foolishness I deprived them of lands that they might have had, had I accepted the reasonable terms the government has offered."[39]

But the land concessions left many other Sioux embittered, and anger turned to rage when, in the wake of the treaty, Congress suddenly halved their food rations. This was a disastrous betrayal of progressive leaders such as American Horse, who had assured his people that the land sale would be beneficial, not harmful. American Horse protested vehemently to Crook that it was "like cutting our heads off."[40]

One day in early November, Royer issued the scant monthly allotment: just ninety-three lean steers were supposed to feed thousands of hungry Oglala who crowded around the agency dispensary. The animals were quickly slaughtered, and when nothing was left, the crowd became an angry, pushing, surging mob. Royer ordered the Indian police to arrest a defiant ghost dancer named Little. This only incensed the crowd. Young men drew their knives, pointed their rifles at the police, and began screaming for blood.

But American Horse pushed his way in between the armed men.

"Stop! Think!" he shouted. "What are you planning to do? Kill these men of your own race? Then what? Kill all these helpless white men, women, and children. And then what? What will these brave words and brave deeds lead to in the end? How long could you hold out? Your country is surrounded by railroads. Thousands of white soldiers could be here within days. What ammunition have you? What provisions have you? What will become of your families? This is child's madness! Think my brothers, think! Let no Sioux shed the blood of a brother Sioux!"

Jack Red Cloud, son of Red Cloud, pointed a revolver in American Horse's face. "This is the one who betrayed us!" he yelled. "Here is the man who sold us out! Here is the one who brought on this trouble by selling our land to the whites!"

American Horse stared into the barrel of the gun contemptuously. Summoning his full dignity, he turned his back on the gun and without another word walked slowly up the steps into the council house.

Witnesses to the incident, such as physician Charles Eastman and his fiancée, the schoolteacher Elaine Goodale, believed American Horse's words quelled a bloody disaster. But it was just temporary.[41]

In the midst of these difficulties, American Horse worried about the children he had packed off to Carlisle, especially Ben. As tensions ratcheted, so did anti-Indian feeling across the country, thanks to newspapers that hysterically predicted "outbreaks." American Horse was unhappy to hear that his son was in the outing program, living among whites doing farm chores. He wrote anxiously to Pratt, concerned that Ben was out of his immediate care.

On November 11, 1890, Pratt responded with one of his meant-to-be-bracing lectures.

Dear Friend, I am sure that I am doing for your boy that which is the very best thing for him to do just now, and if the Indians were wise they would send their youth here and there through-

out the United States, everywhere, in order to meet with the
people and get acquainted with them, learn their language and
how the white people do. . . .

You entrusted your boy to me and I look after him as I would
my own son. I did just this way with my own son and it made
a man of him . . . so I hope you will trust me in this matter and
not listen to those who would make you discontented, nor even
to the complaints of your boy. He needs to be made a strong
English speaking manly man, not afraid to go among the whites
and to meet them in any way, and he cannot learn these things
in any school, not even in Carlisle. I am glad to know you are
interested, and I am glad to receive your criticism. I like to
know what parents feel and think about their children. In this
case you must trust to my judgment. Faithfully, your friend,
RH Pratt.[42]

As it happened, Ben was safer at Carlisle than at Pine Ridge.
Increasing numbers of Lakota were dancing, fainting, and having
visions of imminent Lakota resurrection. On November 15, Royer
telegraphed Washington, "Indians are dancing in the snow & are wild
& crazy." He begged again for troops.[43]

General Nelson A. Miles wrote to Washington on November 28:
"There never has been a time when the Indians were as well armed
and equipped for war as present." He warned that the "most serious
and general uprising" could be brewing. By the first week of December, the Army had mustered between six thousand and seven thousand soldiers, the largest concentration of troops since the Civil War,
to suppress four thousand to five thousand Ghost Dancers, most of
them women and children. The intent was for the display of force to
intimidate the dancers into surrendering.[44]

Instead, the arrival of the military started a human stampede;
Sioux dancers and nondancers, fearing reprisals, took flight into the
rough country known as the Badlands, where they hunkered down in
a refuge called the Stronghold. It was a table of land amid a bleak
landscape of carved gorges and sheer bluffs. During the dash to the
Badlands, homes were destroyed and herds of livestock killed. Amer-

ican Horse lost everything. His furniture was smashed, fabric was torn from his walls, and his portrait was pumped full of bullets. His stock was either stolen or slaughtered. The family was left with their tipis and the clothes they were wearing.[45]

For the next month, Pine Ridge was in a state of siege, as dust clouds rose from the frenzied dances all day and night. In mid-December, Sitting Bull was killed after threatening to attend a dance. So-called friendlies were ordered to come to the agencies or be labeled hostiles. Pine Ridge was covered by rows of military A tents. When a group of young warriors threatened to kill American Horse while he slept, he moved into the dispensary with Charles Eastman. From there, he and a handful of fellow peacemakers worked to defuse the situation, serving as go-betweens to the Badlands.

At Carlisle, Pratt kept his pupils updated on the crisis via the school paper, with the usual drumbeat of lecturing mixed in.

> What a shame and an outrage it is! What is the real reason for it all? Ignorance on the part of the Indians and nothing else. Our boys and girls who have learned to read and reason, know better than to be led into trouble in that fashion. Thousands, perhaps, of your people will suffer and many be killed before they get their eyes open. Be content that you are where you can get the education that will save you from such a fearful mistake in the future.[46]

Pratt was loath to admit that at least a dozen former Carlisle students were dedicated dancers, probably more. There were sixty-three ex-pupils living at the Pine Ridge agency during the siege, including Luther Standing Bear, who had become a teacher; Clarence Three Stars, the boy Pratt had braced in class, who worked as a clerk; and Pratt's old ditchdigging friend, Amos Lone Hill, an agency carpenter. Most of the students were nondancers, but even they felt conflicted loyalties at times over the coming weeks.[47]

By the end of December, in part thanks to the efforts of tribal diplomats such as American Horse, the crisis seemed averted. Most of the bands trickled peaceably back to the agencies. Then, on December 29, the Seventh Cavalry confronted and disarmed Big Foot's band of

Miniconjous as they camped on Wounded Knee Creek, twenty miles east of the agency. Amid flaring tempers, a shot was fired. The troops, eleven of whose officers had served with Custer, unleashed their Hotchkiss guns, and for the next few hours they relentlessly stalked and massacred at least 250 people, maybe more, mostly women and children.

At the Pine Ridge agency school, the doors had been bolted to keep the children safe. Charles American Horse, one of the children shut inside, for the rest of his life remembered hearing the distant sound of the Hotchkiss guns.[48]

As wounded survivors began streaming into Pine Ridge, panic ensued. Terrified Lakota fled back toward the Stronghold, including all of those who previously had been talked back into the agency. It would take weeks of diplomacy to bring them out again. A blizzard struck. When it broke on New Year's Day, a relief party of Lakota and whites from Pine Ridge trekked through the snow to the battlefield, American Horse among them. He followed the bloody tracks to find bodies frozen into contorted shapes.

When the news reached Carlisle, the stricken students immediately took up a collection to help the wounded. Pratt wrote to Elaine Goodale on January 15, 1891, with an enclosed check for $64 that represented the life savings of seventeen male Lakota students, including Clarence White Thunder, who donated the money they had earned in their outings. "Some had given all they had and others nearly all," Pratt remarked. A week later, Pratt forwarded another check, this one for $40. He added, "Should your emergencies become great I will bring the case before the whole school."[49]

Pratt was sickened by the affair, which he viewed as instigated by whites. He wrote an acquaintance, "The great Indian war seems to be drawing to a close. There has been a good deal of slander and slaughter, the full purposes of which we may never know."[50]

At the end of January, American Horse and nearly forty other Lakota leaders went to Washington to demand reparations and relief. They met with the commissioner of Indian affairs, Thomas Morgan, and interior secretary John Noble. The conference was "intensely melancholy," according to *Harper's Weekly*. In an office crammed to capacity with rows of Washington bureaucrats who had brought their wives and daughters to gawk at the sight of real Indians, the delegates sat in their ill-fitting Saks suits and disposable collars, held their hats in their hands, and sweated from the steam radiator. As they testified to conditions on the reservation, Secretary Noble listened to their complaints with an expression that veered from "amusement to concern."[51]

The Lakota elders were dispirited. But American Horse summoned his eloquence and delivered a deeply felt speech. He had come to Washington, he announced, "with very great blame on my heart" for the government. He then gave a riveting account of what he saw as he followed the blood at Wounded Knee. "There was a woman with an infant in her arms who was killed as she almost touched the flag of truce, and the women and children of course were strewn all along the circular village until they were dispatched. Right near the flag of truce a mother was shot down with her infant; the child not knowing that its mother was dead was still nursing, and that especially was a very sad sight. . . . Of course we all feel very sad about this affair. I stood very loyal to the government all through the troublesome days, and believing so much in the government and being so loyal to it my disappointment was very strong."[52]

The visit accomplished the most important thing: full rations were restored. The trip also gave American Horse a chance to detour to Carlisle and see his children. Pratt brought Ben in from his farm outing so that he could be with his father. After a greeting in the chapel, American Horse ate in the dining room with his children. He apparently returned home satisfied that his children were well cared for. It didn't prevent him, however, from suggesting to Washington that Carlisle be moved out west, so pupils didn't have to be taken so far from their homes.[53]

Pratt didn't dare pry too deeply into the real feelings of his students or their parents after Wounded Knee. He had staked his credibility on Carlisle's ability to turn out pacified citizens, and he insisted that was exactly what the vast majority of his pupils were. He published a precise tally in the school newsletter, the *Indian Helper*, to demonstrate how few of his sixty-three Pine Ridge pupils were "hostiles."[54]

Working at various employments and doing well	22
Working as scouts or police	12
Doing nothing in particular	4
Dead	6
No information	1
In penitentiary, on doubtful charge	1
Hostiles, including Julia Walking Crane, little Robert Cow Kill, and Mack Kutepi, a steady worker before and since	6
Gone to other agencies	11
Total	63

There were some things Pratt simply didn't want to know. Above all, he wanted to know nothing about a former Carlisle student named Plenty Horses, a Rosebud Brule. On January 7, in the livid and grief-stricken aftermath of Wounded Knee, the ex-pupil shot to death a popular young officer, Lieutenant Ned Casey.

Plenty Horses had spent five years at Carlisle, from 1883 to 1888, where he was regarded as a quiet and average student. But when he returned to the bleak, hunger-plagued Rosebudland, he was accepted as neither white nor Indian. Instead, he inhabited a confused nether-world. It was a common grievance among returned students, who no longer knew where they fit in. There were no jobs, nothing to do. They were trained to eat with a knife and fork at a table, while their fathers and mothers sat on the floor to eat. Some old friends were glad to see them, while others refused to shake their hands. They were self-conscious speaking English but ashamed to speak their own language.

"I was lonely," Plenty Horses told the grand jury at Deadwood that indicted him. "I shot the lieutenant so I might make a place for myself among my people. Now I am one of them. I shall be hung and the Indians will bury me as a warrior. They will be proud of me. I am satisfied."[55]

Before Wounded Knee, Plenty Horses was merely distressed. After Wounded Knee, he fled to the Stronghold and joined the militant dancers. "Of course I was in a bad frame of mind," he said. "Our home was destroyed, our family separated, and all hope of good times was gone. There was nothing to live for."[56]

On the morning of January 7, Plenty Horses was on guard with several other Lakota when he met Casey, a promising field officer and commander of an elite troop of Cheyenne scouts, who was approaching their encampment to talk. Casey was well liked by Indians and whites equally, and a figure of some glamour. He was a friend of the Yale-educated artist Remington, who rode with his unit and painted him, lanky on horseback in his sky blue trousers and dark blue tunic, a blond cascade of a mustache under his slouch hat.

Casey was warned that the young men were in a killing mood, and to leave. But he was slow to turn his horse. As he sat in his saddle, conversing, Plenty Horses raised a Winchester from under his blanket, put it to his shoulder, and fired one shot into the back of Casey's head.

In April 1891, Plenty Horses was tried for murder in Sioux Falls. On the eve of his trial, he granted an interview to a reporter from the *New York World* in his jail cell. He insisted on speaking through an interpreter, for fear of misspeaking, but frequently lapsed into English.

"We were at war, and the Indian style of fighting to the bitter end is just as fair as the white man's," he said. "Besides, we were only fighting for our rights."

The next morning, several Lakota leaders arrived to attend the trial. On the edge of town, they were overjoyed to find a small herd of seventeen tatty, aging buffalo held in a pen. The Lakota began to dance "like a lot of boys," the *New York World* reported. Two of them even climbed into the pen and tried to hug the beasts, "and generally made so free with the animals that the latter looked around as though dazed at the proceedings."[57]

The trial revolved around the central issue of whether Plenty Horses committed an act of war or murder. But if he committed murder, then what was the massacre by the Seventh Cavalry at Wounded Knee? A first trial ended in a hung jury. A second trial opened on May 23, and among those who testified was American Horse, who described the state of siege at the agency. But the highlight of the trial, and the thing that ended it, was the testimony of an officer,

Frank Baldwin, sent by General Nelson A. Miles to testify that a state of war existed. When Miles was asked his own opinion on the matter, he had replied, "My boy, it was a war. You do not suppose that I am going to reduce my campaign to a dress parade affair?" The judge announced that there was no need for the trial to proceed, and Plenty Horses was acquitted, to roars of approval from the courtroom, packed with his family and friends.

Outside the courtroom, American Horse shook hands with Plenty Horses and told him, "I am glad you are free. You killed Casey, that was bad. He was a brave man, and a good one. He did much for the Indian, but the whites cruelly starved us into such a condition that the young men are crazy and you did not know what you did."

American Horse then said to a reporter, "It was good. Enemies may kill in war."[58]

The next morning, a party of twenty Lakota went to the rail station to board a train for home. The trial effectively concluded major armed conflict between Lakota and whites. From then on, there would be no more wars, only skirmishes. American Horse seemed to recognize that it was the end of something, because he paused in the station and turned to deliver a speech to a large crowd that had gathered. He called to an interpreter to translate his words.

It was a speech of deep recrimination, a lament about lies and starvation. The government mistreated them, traders cheated them, and soldiers shot them down. "That's what the white people do for us," he said.

"What must the Indian do?" American Horse asked. "Die, starve or fight? We ask not much. Give us a chance to learn your ways and do not charge us three prices for what the white man gets for one. The spot of snow is melting. Soon the Indian will be no more. Give us a chance, keep your treaty."[59]

ONE DAY a few months afterward, forty or so of Carlisle's best athletes trooped into Pratt's office. They had come to plead for the reinstatement of football.

Pratt was willing to consider football in a new light. Altering popular perceptions of Indians was much on his mind. He had done his best to counter the bad publicity of the past couple of years by por-traying his students as enlightened Christians, lacking any outward or inward Indianness. But stereotypes of "wild Indians" were hard to fight. Citizenship would be hard to achieve as long as the populace viewed them as lazy, savage, or, as one murderous white rancher at Pine Ridge labeled them, "damned government pets."[60]

Pratt simply didn't believe someone could be a citizen and an Indian, too. He was still convinced the best chance his students had was to leave the reservations, which he considered the "ruin and wreck of manhood," and be colorlessly absorbed into "our American family." He often quoted a like-minded man, Senator George F. Edmunds of Ver-mont, chair of the Judiciary Committee. When asked what the tribes needed to do to attain citizenship, Edmunds replied, "Quit being an Indian, pay taxes, and be ready to fight for the government."[61]

Quit being an Indian—there it was in a nutshell. As if Wounded Knee wasn't enough evidence that "being an Indian" was a dead end, there was the letter Pratt received from Stacy Matlock, the boy who had broken his leg playing football. Against Pratt's stern advice, Mat-lock had returned to his Pawnee agency in Indian Territory. He was unable to find work. The best the local agent would offer him was a job as a stable hand. Next, his fiancée broke off with him. Pratt received a desperate letter on September 29, 1892. "I am getting scared," Matlock wrote.[62]

Pratt was sorry but not surprised. Sometime later, another report on Matlock was even more disquieting. The former YMCA boy had apparently reverted to his former self, according to notes Pratt kept on returned students.

"Not doing well," a notation read. "Has long hair."[63]

Pratt tried desperately hard to show that his students had quit being Indians—they didn't have a trace or token of separateness, no braids or blankets. He marched his clean-cut students under a banner that said, "Into Civilization and Citizenship." He entered them in cultural fairs, where they displayed their peaceable agrarian and trade skills. He paraded them in the 1892 World's Columbian Exposition, quick-step-ping in neat squadrons with agricultural tools on their shoulders, like guns. They carried carpentry tools, shears, mallets, and rakes.

Pratt proudly marched Ben American Horse and the other students over the Brooklyn Bridge and for seven miles before the New York crowds, their blue uniforms crisp under flying flags. When the students tired, Pratt rallied them by pointing to some nearby soldiers and saying, "Boys, I don't remember that I was ever more tired in my life than I am now. My feet are sore and I admit it is very difficult to keep my legs going, but I am not going to let a single one of those regulars see that I am a bit tired."[64]

He was gratified by the next day's edition of the *New York World.* "They march better than the National Guard," the paper announced.[65]

But the public hardly cared about expositions or cultural fairs. They preferred Buffalo Bill's Wild West Show. Pratt despised Cody's spectacles, which he believed perpetrated "evil impressions."

"Buffalo Bill travels all over the land parading what he intends the people to believe to be the particular qualities of the Indian," Pratt said. "No man ever put a greater lie before the public than Buffalo Bill."[66]

But the football field was a stage too, Pratt realized—a stage on which Carlisle could exhibit a different kind of "show Indian" to the public, one who was every bit as intelligent and civilized as the elite college boys.

As the athletes stood in front of his desk and made their case, Pratt didn't need much persuading. Every other school in the country was playing the game, from the newest universities in the West to the primly honor-bound service academies. On November 29, 1890, in the midst of the Ghost Dance affair, the first Army-Navy game was played.[67] As for injuries, students could just as easily hurt themselves doing farm work, Pratt realized. The boys gave "practically all the arguments in favor of our contending in outside football that it seemed possible to bring, and ended by requesting the removal of the embargo," he remembered.

The boys knew that a display of public oratory and sound grammar would please Pratt. They had chosen the school's debate star as their spokesperson, and he invoked a famed speech by the great Chief Logan, a pre–Revolutionary War leader of the Shawnee. The speech, known as Logan's Lament, was recounted in Thomas Jefferson's *Notes on the State of Virginia,* and they had learned it in class.

"'I appeal to any white man to say, if ever he entered Logan's cabin hungry, and he gave him not meat; if ever he came cold and naked, and he clothed him not,'" the boy quoted. "'. . . For my country, I rejoice at the beams of peace. But do not harbour a thought that mine is the joy of fear. Logan never felt fear. He will not turn on his heel to save his life.'"

As the orator carried on, Pratt was thoroughly disarmed, and struggled not to laugh. By the time the speech was finished, Pratt was won over.

"Boys, I begin to realize that I must surrender and give you the opportunity you so earnestly desire," he said. But Pratt had two conditions, and now it was his turn to deliver a speech.

"First, that you will never, under any circumstances, slug," he said. "That you will play fair straight through, and if the other fellows slug you will in no case return it. Can't you see that if you slug, people who are looking on will say, 'There, that's the Indian of it. Just see them. They are savages and you can't get it out of them.' Our white fellows may do a lot of slugging and it causes little or no remark, but you have to make a record for your race. If the other fellows slug and you do not return it, very soon you will be the most famous football team in the country. If you can set an example of that kind for the white race, you will do a work in the highest interests of your people."

Pratt paused and looked at the athletes for an answer. The boys agreed. "All right Captain," they said.

"My other condition is this. That, in the course of two, three, or four years . . . you will whip the biggest football team in the country."

They stood silent for a moment. The debater said, "Well, Captain, we will try."

"I don't want you to promise to try. I want you to say that you will do it. The man who only thinks of trying to do a thing admits to himself that he may fail, while the sure winner is the man who will not admit failure. You must get your determination up to that point."

They thought that over for a moment, and then the orator replied. "Yes sir," he said. "We will agree to that."[68]

Sometime afterward, the Carlisle boys gathered on a muddy, unlined field for their lesson in intercollegiate football. Standing before them was the dapper Mr. Vance McCormick, lately of Yale. Pratt could not have found a more illustrious or aristocratic coach for his team.

McCormick was just out of school and fresh from his triumph captaining Yale to an unbeaten championship season. A native of nearby Harrisburg, he had returned home after graduating with the class of '93 to begin a career managing the family interests in coal mining and railroads. He would soon turn to politics, however, and go on to win renown as a campaign manager and advisor to another football man, Woodrow Wilson.

But that autumn, McCormick was still just a young man with noblesse oblige. An old teacher of his, Miss Anna Luckenbaugh, was on the faculty at Carlisle, and she wrote McCormick with a request: the Indian boys had become captivated by football and formed "an enthusiastic squad of players." But they had no coach. Would he consider coming up to Carlisle to help them?

As the boys watched, McCormick hurled the fat oval-shaped ball downfield. He waved his arms, demonstrating to the Carlisle players that he wanted them to chase the ball and "fall on it." The boys followed halfheartedly, not quite certain of his meaning.

Pratt stood off to the side, observing, curious to see how the young Yalie would deal with the Indian students, some of whom still barely grasped English. But McCormick was an animated teacher. Without removing a single article of his natty clothing, not even his hat, McCormick sprinted downfield after the ball and dove headfirst on the moist, rain-softened ground. He jumped back up, splattered in mud but satisfied that he had properly demonstrated how to play football, Yale style.

"His hat and clothing were some admonition against too sudden enthusiasm," Pratt remembered. But McCormick took no notice of his ruined clothes as he strode back and forth across the field positioning players and pointing out what he wanted them to do.[69]

The Carlisle students were surely in awe of McCormick—anyone who followed football knew that he was one of the most lionized heroes in the game that year, the embodiment of everything praiseworthy about Yale. He was superbly built, with shoulders that strained his suit jacket, and a jutting, battered-looking chin only enhanced his handsomeness, topped by his glossy side-combed hair. He had led the Eli eleven to their unbeaten season in '92 with an inspired stand against the hated Harvard.

Yale was 11-0 and Harvard was 10-0 when the two teams met, and the collision between them was so heated that Yale football alum Pudge Heffelfinger leaped the fence and tried to run onto the field, fighting off three cops before he was wrestled down and tossed back into the bleachers.

Harvard nearly won the game with a startling and dangerous new formation, a flying wedge. Two groups of players lined up behind the quarterback and started running, converging in a high-speed V that plowed like a spear into the surprised Yale team. The first time Harvard tried the play, it gained thirty-five yards before McCormick stopped it. McCormick then steadied his team by stalking up and down the Yale line, shouting encouragement and instructions. "Boys this is something new, but play the game as you have been *taught* it," he called. Yale stiffened and held, and the Elis went on to win 6-0, finishing a perfect season.[70]

To someone of McCormick's stature, the Carlisle pupils in their baggy, ill-fitting, mismatched canvas garments must have looked hopelessly raw. He had to teach them the most basic elements of the game, even the scoring—which, granted, was confusing. (A kicked field goal counted for five points, a touchdown for four points, a goal after a touchdown for two points, and a safety for one point.) But after just a few instructions, the mud-caked McCormick found himself excited by the Carlisle athletes, who were "willing, intelligent and receptive."[71]

Jonas Metoxen, a twenty-year-old Oneida from Sagola, Wisconsin, showed the strength and speed to be a brilliant running back. Frank Hudson was a slight, sixteen-year-old Laguna Pueblo who no sooner picked up a football than he seemed to know how to kick it. Bemus Pierce and his brother Hawley, tall Seneca farm boys from upstate New York, were made linemen.

Delos Lone Wolf was twenty-two, round in the face but strongly built like the other Lone Wolfs of the Kiowa, barrel-chested at five foot nine and 180 pounds, and he had the same independent-minded streak, too. Ben American Horse was still slight and fine-featured, with a shock of hair falling over his eyes, but he also had his father's toughness, as well as speed and leaping ability. Farm work had filled him out, and he had grown a foot taller since he arrived.

They didn't have proper equipment, and their field was a piece of converted farm acreage, but they had promise. The popular term for a good football player in the industrially obsessed 1890s was "material." The Carlisle players struck McCormick as "excellent material." Soon, McCormick found himself returning to Carlisle regularly. "I was very much impressed with the material and became so much interested that I made several visits a week as a volunteer coach," he remembered.[72]

The more McCormick was around, the more he realized that the Indians were determined to compete on the national stage. "I remember distinctly that Captain Pratt . . . was very much interested in the development of the team as he recognized its value in bringing the school to the attention of the public."[73]

They didn't just want to play football, McCormick discovered. They wanted to play Yale.

It was a heady ambition, maybe even a foolish one. No team of the era was more dominant than Yale, which was in the midst of a four-year streak in which it would lose just one game. Its record between 1883 and 1910 would be a staggering 285 victories to just 12 losses, with 14 ties. Moreover, football had only grown more bruising since Pratt had banned the game three years earlier, and no team was more injurious to an opponent than Yale. The 1894 varsity, in particular, had a reputation for viciousness, thanks to senior leader Frank Hinkey.

Hinkey, a player of just 143 pounds with a wan, brooding appearance, had a mean disposition. He once said of another player, "Why is he leaving the field? He can stand, can't he?" He so rejoiced in dealing out broken bones and abrasions that a writer for the *New York Post* editorialized, "No father or mother worthy of the name would permit a son to associate with the sort of Yale brutes on Hinkey's football team."[74]

Hinkey's influence had turned the Harvard-Yale game of 1894 into a bloodbath. Seven of the twenty-two participants were carried off the field, and two more were ejected for fighting. Yale won 12-6 in what was dubbed "The Springfield Massacre," but the score was merely a detail. Harvard's Charlie Brewer played part of the game on a broken leg. Yale's Frank Butterworth was almost blinded by a finger intentionally jabbed in his eye. As for Hinkey, he piled into Crimson halfback Edgar Wrightington after the latter signaled a fair catch, and broke his collarbone. A Harvard lineman responded by landing a right to Hinkey's face.

"My friend if you hit me another blow like that, you will break your hand," Hinkey said in a sinister tone.

While the officials were talking, Yale's Fred Murphy punched Harvard tackle Bob Hallowell and crushed his nose. Two plays later, the Crimson hit Murphy so hard that from then on, when he turned his head at a certain angle, he passed out. After the game, the student bodies engaged in at least half a dozen brawls, and the Crimson fans had to fight their way from the field at Hampden Park to the railroad station.[75]

This was the team Carlisle aspired to play.

But the Indians were not ready for Yale yet. Instead, they spent a season practicing against lesser opponents. In the fall of '94, while Yale was bloodying other teams, Carlisle introduced itself to collegiate football with a modest schedule against second-tier opponents: Navy, Lehigh, Dickinson, Bucknell, and some club and YMCA teams.

That November, Pratt and his wife made a depressing visit to Indian Territory. He had not been to Fort Sill since leaving twenty years earlier, escorting the manacled prisoners. "About one half of the old fellows are still alive," he wrote sadly to a friend. "Things are down at the heel among the Indians. I used to admire the clean manly character of the Comanches and Cheyenne particularly, but the mighty are fallen. They are killed with disease and are fading away rapidly . . . and such a sore-eyed, scrofulous, syphilitic lot I have never before seen."[76]

In his football team, Pratt hoped to rebuild Indian manhood. The Carlisle Indians had no stadium of their own and played all of their games on the road, against opponents who were invariably larger, more experienced, and backed by home crowds. But they fought their way toward respectability in a succession of losses: to Navy 8-0, to Bucknell 6-0, and to Lehigh 22-12.

Newspapers began to take note of them at first, for no other reason than it was a novelty to see Indians play the game. Soon, however, they won plaudits by giving a good account of themselves. Jonas Metoxen quickly earned a reputation as such a tough runner that the papers dubbed him "Met the Oxen"—trying to take him down was like trying to take down an ox.

But Carlisle learned some hard lessons before the season was over, too. On November 24, the Indians traveled to Washington, D.C., for a game against the Columbia Athletic Club at National Park. It was an important contest, a chance to make a point in the nation's capital, in front of a correspondent from the *Washington Post*.

Instead, the Indians suffered their worst defeat of the season. CAC, a team of former varsity players, significantly outweighed the Indians, and they added to the punishment with their bare fists. The Indians took such a physical beating that the reporter from the *Washington Post* remarked it looked like a boxing match "without the regulation five ounce gloves." The headline read, "Lo, the Poor Indians."[77] Four Carlisle players were carried from the field, Ben American Horse one of them.

Ben was a starter at the end position, where he earned the nickname "Flying Man" from his teammates for his ability to gain chunks of ground by leaping through the air. The Indians would send the heaviest players up front, including Lone Wolf, to plow into the opposing line. Ben would take a running start and vault over the line.

But in the first quarter, as Ben sailed through the air, he was met by a blow flush in the face. He dropped to the turf, blood spurting from his badly broken nose, so displaced it had to be reset. Ben screamed as the doctor mashed it back into shape—the pain was so bad that when he broke his nose a second time a few months later, hit by a bat during a baseball game, he refused to have it fixed. For the rest of his life it had a flattened, concave shape.

Despite the beating, Carlisle earned grudging respect from the *Post* correspondent, who was apparently surprised to learn that Indians weren't always lazy. While they still had much to learn, he noted, they showed outstanding speed and potential. It was exactly the sort of thing Pratt had hoped for.

"It is an unusual thing to see an Indian bestir himself sufficiently to take part in any sort of amusement which is liable to disturb his peaceful serenity," the *Post* reporter wrote, "but in the Carlisle Indian School they have a set of young bucks who have taken up the American game of football. . . . They are a most energetic set of youngsters, with no idea whatever of interference, a fair idea of the principles of the Rugby game, and the speed, when once under way, of a jackrabbit making for his hole. The hero of the day yesterday was Met Oxen, a tall and robust youth with a chrysanthemum head of hair and a surprising amount of endurance. . . . The red men had a hard row to hoe with the locals and four of them fell down so hard they had to retire."

They lost the game, 18-0. But Carlisle's mere presence on a field in Washington was a victory of a sort. Huddled together in a corner of the park were some unanticipated guests: several elderly Indians. They were a delegation of Assiniboine and Gros Ventre from Belknap, Montana, who were in town on a diplomatic mission to meet with the Great Father, Grover Cleveland.

"A dozen or more old rounders," as the *Post* described them, "watched the cruel white men handle their sons and friends." They shivered in the grandstands as the autumn afternoon grew cool and Carlisle went down to defeat. But they stayed to the end.

B EN AMERICAN Horse's football career at Carlisle was brief, lasting from 1894 to 1895. In the summer of '95, after more than five years at the school, he returned home to Pine Ridge. But he always took satisfaction in the fact that he helped launch the school into national prominence, and to the end of his life he was proud to say that he had played on the first, pioneering football team at Carlisle.

Like other Carlisle students before him, Ben came home to find that his family barely recognized him. He was altered—literally. His broken, flattened nose had changed his face, toughening it. He had a misshapen finger on his right hand, which had been crushed between two barrels of flour while he was working in the school bakery.

The family he returned to was altered, too, and in some ways divided. His sisters had gone to Carlisle in braids but came home in corsets, converts to Catholicism. Ben barely knew some of his younger siblings. Alice American Horse, for instance, was just seven when she went to Carlisle, and she would not return home until she was seventeen. She was away for so long that she lost her command of Lakota and could barely communicate with her own father and brothers. When her youngest brother, Charles, spoke Lakota at home, the thoroughly anglicized Alice disapproved. "If you don't speak English, I'm going to slap you," she said.[78]

American Horse nevertheless continued to send children to Carlisle. He had reached a state of resignation and peace with the school. Pratt, in his turn, had come to admire American Horse as a great leader, and their communications over the years reflected a growing mutual if wary regard. In March 1892, when American Horse visited his children at Carlisle, Pratt urged him to deliver an address to the entire student body through an interpreter.

"Look at me!" American Horse said. "I have long hair. My skin is red. I cannot speak English, nor do I understand it. As I look back to the time when I was a boy, I wish that the Government had given me such a chance as this, so that I might have learned something too. When the Captain and others come out for pupils, we look forward to your future and let them have the children. . . . I take children myself, and get them to go to school without being asked to do so, because I see the great benefit it is to you.

"When you go out among the whites you will not find everybody so kind and good as your Superintendent, and it makes me feel sorry for you when I think of what you will have to meet when you go out in the world. So I urge you to learn all you can, and take courage."[79]

But Ben's education was of little immediate use at Pine Ridge, where employment was hard to find. He was in a strange half-state, he found, his skills of small use on a reservation that was still undeveloped. The Lakota elders laughed when another Carlisle student brought home light fixtures to the reservation—which didn't yet have electricity.[80]

Instead, Ben went to work as a ranch hand and helped farm the family allotments. To make ends meet, he worked as boss of a road crew—for $2.50 a day. He helped install the first phone lines in Pine Ridge.

Irony of ironies, the best-paying job Ben found was as an interpreter for his father's old acquaintance, Buffalo Bill Cody. Each spring and summer Ben toured with the act, to Pratt's great frustration. What few qualms Ben had about working as a "show Indian" were overcome by the affection he developed for Cody, who paid handsomely, respected his Indian employees, and even took the trouble to learn some Sioux. Ben's job was to help communicate what Cody wanted from the Indians in the show, and occasionally fill in when someone got sick, mounting a white horse to ride in the parade. The job took him all over the country and on two tours of Europe. He would be among the old Lakota friends Cody requested at his bedside just before he died.[81]

When Carlisle sent out surveys to former students, in the interest of finding out how they were using their education, Ben replied faithfully. Among the questions asked were what their occupations were, what sort of homes they were living in, and whether they had money or property. In 1910, Ben responded in broken English, using *had* for *have*, but he still displayed the sloping, elegant script taught him by Carlisle's lady schoolteachers.

He was living in the township of Kyle, South Dakota, at Pine Ridge, on his family property. "Had a good house for three rooms, and Barn too," he reported. He didn't have much money, but he did have thirty-eight head of cattle, seventeen horses, two farm wagons, a carriage, a spring wagon, and two plows. He was doing fine, but he was nostalgic for his school days, when life was a reassuring routine of drill, study, and play.

"I had lots time thanks for Carlisle School had done me some goods," he wrote. "I never forget Carlisle School yet. Lots time I wish I would be at school now. I am getting along O.K."[82]

Eventually, when there were no more Wild West Shows, Ben enlisted in the Indian police at Pine Ridge. He spent his days patrolling the reservation on horseback as a peace officer, growing into an increasingly respected tribal elder, and eventually the last appointed head of the Oglala after old American Horse finally died in 1908. His job, his father told him, was to "guard the boundaries" of his people.

Ben became a bridge. He was a repository of old lore, one of the few people who could recall the rituals of a Sun Dance. He tried to show the way forward, as his father always had, but he also looked backward. When important news came over the radio, crowds would gather at Ben's house while he translated and tried to make sense of current affairs for them.

Sometimes in the evening, he read the Bible aloud. But other nights, he lit a burning ember in a traditional sacred pipe. He would breathe in the smoke and murmur, praying in Lakota.

6

CHEATS AND SWINDLES

IN THE AUTUMN of 1895, newly metropolitan Americans needed entertainment. Bored and pent-up city populaces congregated for anything that promised to be a show, from ball games to society weddings. Mass spectacles were born. With large entertainments came little things, on the cheap: it was the year Cracker Jack and the Tootsie Roll were first made.

On Thanksgiving Day, the Carlisle football team debuted on the largest sports stage in the country, New York City, in a game against the YMCA at the Polo Grounds. To Delos Lone Wolf and his team-mates, the metropolis itself seemed to be a large, overlit playhouse, incandescent with Thomas Edison's bulbs. From the doorways of music halls came the jingle and chime of commercial entertainments, *Sweet Rosie O'Grady,* and *Hot Time in the Old Town.*

The town writhed with human and automated movement. An impromptu football game broke out on the floor of the New York Stock Exchange, brokers chasing a ball through the air in their frock coats and neckties. In saloons and pool halls, telegraph receivers spat out the latest sports scores for customers. Newspapers cranked out twenty thousand sheets an hour with revolving cylinder presses, and the first major sports section appeared in William Randolph Hearst's

New York Journal. At *Harper's Weekly*, sportswriter Caspar Whitney, a thin-necked, pince-nez-wearing snob, dubbed the new sport-crazed masses "the great unwashed."[1]

The Indians attracted the attention of this game-hungry public, and the penny press that fed it, despite the fact that they arrived in the midst of a particularly busy November, judging by the headlines. Henry Irving and Ellen Terry starred in *Macbeth*. A group of young women were arrested for wearing bloomers that fit too close. Miss Evelyn Pook, heiress of a storied old shipbuilding family, eloped with a popular singer named Henry Brandon, for which her brother had her arrested, claiming she was insane. Throngs gathered daily at the corner of Seventy-second Street and Madison Avenue to watch the comings and goings from the baronial Vanderbilt mansion, where the socially ambitious Alva Vanderbilt browbeat her unwilling daughter, Consuelo, into marrying the Duke of Marlborough. The prenuptial parties were so numerous that the Duke needed an entire day of bed rest before the wedding. The bride wept behind her veil.[2]

The Indians stared curiously at the magnificent dwellings as they rode through town in a horse-drawn carriage, called a tally-ho, en route to the Polo Grounds. It took an hour and a half to make their way to the stadium at 155th Street and Eighth Avenue.

Finally, the Indians arrived at the Polo Grounds. A sparse paying crowd of about fifteen hundred sat in the steep, enormous double-deck bleachers that ringed Manhattan Field, but about four thousand more were seated for free on Deadhead Hill or hung over the railing of the nearby elevated train viaducts. The spectators greeted the Indians boisterously with screeched war whoops as they took the field.

Football was only part of the attraction for these rowdies—they had come to see Indians. Apparently, they half expected the Carlisle team to put on a Wild West Show. The name Lone Wolf, well known from bloodcurdling western dispatches, especially excited the viewers. "Everybody wanted Lone Wolf pointed out to them," the *New York World* reported. "Lone Wolf was the man of the hour with the crowd."[3]

But as the Indians warmed up, the onlookers murmured with something like disappointment. Apart from their darker complexions, the Carlisle players were indistinguishable from any other collegians. Delos Lone Wolf turned out to be a stout young man with cropped, center-parted hair that flopped on either side of his forehead over his eyebrows.

In the bleachers, a female fan felt distinctly shortchanged. She imagined that she had come to see vermilion-painted savages wielding tomahawks. Instead, she found a collection of Seneca, Oneida, Chippewa, Kiowa, Pueblo, and Winnebago players, neatly attired in denim and canvas uniforms, chewing gum.

"Oh, dear me," she said. "Are those the Indians? Why, they don't look any different from our boys."

"That crowd couldn't do a thing to you if they had you out west on a prairie," one of the YMCA substitutes said, according to the *World*.

But they could. The Indians had plenty of fight in them, despite their nondescript appearance. Though still relative novices, they had a hard-earned record of 3-4, and they were toughened by some difficult losses and the continual cheap shots of their opponents. They had been punched bloody in a 34-0 loss to the Naval Academy, while the referee, a Midshipman, looked the other way. They lost 39-0 to the University of Pennsylvania, a game in which their only measure of satisfaction came when they threw a Penn player named A. E. Bull to the turf.

"Look," one of the Carlisle players said. "Sitting Bull."[4]

When they finally won a couple of games, a cartoon appeared in the student paper. It showed two scenes. In the first, a settler shoots an Indian dead. In the second, a Carlisle football player stands with his cleats on top of a prone opponent. A black ink headline reads: "Revenge!" The caption says, "A hundred years have passed and the Indian comes out on top."[5]

The YMCA team was no match for such combativeness. The Indians won 16-4, scoring a trio of touchdowns, two by Bemus Pierce before he retired with a wrenched knee. The score would have been even more lopsided, the Indians knew, if the referee hadn't baldly cheated them.

Three times the Indians drove the ball to within a few yards of the YMCA goal only to lose the ball to decisions by the palpably prejudiced official. The injustice was so obvious that the sentiments of the crowd actually shifted to the Indians' favor. The spectators began to hoot and boo at the officials.

"Those Indians will go away with a pretty poor idea of Christianity if that robbery keeps up," one fan said on the sideline. "Talk about your hold up!"

The Indians, however, accepted each decision without protest, true to their promise to Pratt. They simply stood along the line impassively, hands on hips. "The players chewed gum and said nothing," the *World* correspondent observed. He added, "An Indian chewing gum upsets tradition."

For the Indians, the satisfaction of finishing the season with a break-even 4-4 record took the sting out of the wrongs committed against them by the referee. It was an important first step. They had won before a large New York audience, and just as importantly, their performance had contradicted a number of distorted perceptions of Indians.

That evening, the Carlisle players attended a banquet at the YMCA, at which they made it clear they had come to New York to do more than play football. They were there to exhibit their other qualities as well. Delos Lone Wolf rose to give a toast—one of impeccable diction.

"I play football because I like it; because it has taught me to control myself as I never could before," he said. "It has strengthened me physically and so helped me in my work for God. We do not put off our Christianity when we go to the football field. We play not only for the good benefits of the game to us as individuals, but for the advancement and glory of our school."

Next, his teammate William Leighton rose. "You notice," Leighton said, "we like what you like, we eat what you eat, and we eat just as you eat."[6]

The following morning the Carlisle players went sightseeing— they walked over the Brooklyn Bridge, visited a firehouse, and examined the pneumatic tubes at Western Union. Then they boarded a train and returned to campus, where they were met by a celebrating student body and a delighted Pratt. The Indians had earned glowing coverage from the newspapers not just for their ability but also for their sportsmanship. The December edition of the school's monthly newsletter, the *Red Man*, published a wrapup of the 1895 season: "But we are especially proud of the fact that our boys played a clean, gentlemanly game throughout, and showed themselves men of grit, endurance, self control and brains under the trying conditions of a foot ball game. . . . 'A fair field and no favor' is all (the Indian) asks, and he will render a good account of himself, whether in business, music, art, education or athletics."

INDIAN TERRITORY was becoming nearly as crowded, and crooked, as New York. A variety of men and scourges had streamed into the territory during the land rushes of 1889 and 1891: homesteaders, peyote men, flimflammers, cattle rustlers, easy creditors, and peddlers who sold celery juice as a cure-all. The one thing you couldn't find was a man who didn't wear a gun belt.

In the summer of 1892, Delos Lone Wolf's uncle, Lone Wolf II (Mamaday-te), made an appeal on behalf of the Kiowa, who were increasingly overrun by the opportunists flooding the territory.

"When the Great Spirit created the world He divided it into two great seasons—the warm and the cold," Lone Wolf II said. "The warm season brings life and light; the grass springs up, the birds sing, there is growth and development to fruit, and joy, and gladness. The cold season brings death and desolation; the grass dies, the trees are bare, the fruits are gone, the animals become weak and poor, the water turns hard; there is no joy, no growth, no gladness. You Christian white people are like the summer. . . . We poor, wild Indians are like the winter. We have no growth, no knowledge, no joy, no gladness. Will you share your summer with us?"[7]

The answer was plain no. The U.S. government didn't believe in sharing. It believed in private ownership—and that meant allotment. The hoary-bearded Senator Henry L. Dawes of Massachusetts was determined that tribes till their own plots. As one Indian Commission put it, the Indian "must be imbued with the exalting egotism of American civilization so that he will say 'I' instead of 'We' and 'This is mine' instead of 'This is ours.'"[8]

But in fact, the practical result of the General Allotment (Dawes) Act of 1887 was to strip Indians of their property. Government agents used it to force sales of tribal land and open it to homesteaders. In Indian Territory alone, fifteen million acres were pried from the reservations and sold to settlers in the name of allotment, with catastrophic results for the tribes. In 1880, just seven thousand whites lived in the region. By the turn of the century, more than one million would occupy it.

As the Sooners and settlers charged across the territory driving homestead stakes, tribesmen struggled to learn how to farm the small parcels they had been reduced to. Indians, in nothing but leggings, pushed plows and fought with stubborn livestock. When a land commissioner tried to argue a Shoshone chief named Washakie into farming his 160-acre plot, Washakie shouted back in frustration, "God damn a potato!"[9]

Lone Wolf II recognized allotment for what it was, one more land seizure, and resisted it. Local agents labeled him an "implacable." He refused to farm or be Christianized, and he rejected corn doled out by the government because it was what whites fed cattle with. He jeered Indians who tilled soil, and called those who lined up to accept federal rations "sugar eaters."[10]

In the fall of 1892 a land commission came to Fort Sill to force allotment on the Kiowa, Comanche, and Plains Apache. The commission, named for chairman David Jerome, tried to persuade the Kiowa to sell most of their three-million-acre reserve to the government. Lone Wolf II opposed them, declaring that allotment would be "the downfall" of his tribe. Talks became fractious, and then openly dishonest, as the commission used fraud and coercion to procure signatures on an agreement. Negotiations deteriorated into shouts, and Lone Wolf II insisted that his name be stricken from any accord. Chairman Jerome simply informed the tribes, "Congress has full control of you, it can do as it is a mind to with you," and the panel returned to Washington claiming it had a deal. The legally dubious "agreement" left the Kiowas with just half a million acres.[11]

But Lone Wolf II followed the land commissioners back to Washington, charging swindle. Congress hesitated to confirm the so-called Jerome Agreement, in part thanks to the vehement efforts of the Kiowa elder, who, aided by other Kiowa, Comanche, and Apache activists, launched a legal battle to prevent the opening of the reservation. Their efforts would forestall allotment for eight full years. On his repeated trips to Washington, Lone Wolf II leaned heavily on his educated nephew and adopted son as his interpreter.

Delos had arrived at Carlisle in the midst of the political storm of 1892, just as his uncle began fighting the Jerome Agreement. He was a young man who looked as if he had been bred for leadership his whole life, which he was. Born in 1870, to Lone Wolf II's elder brother Black Turtle, he had lost his father in childhood and been adopted and reared by his uncle. He must have watched closely as Lone Wolf II helped steer the Kiowa through the difficult transition years from nomadic to reservation life.

Lone Wolf II was not insensible to the changes taking place around him, and by the 1890s, he recognized the inevitable: the question was no longer resistance, but how to avoid total eclipse. He adopted some aspects of the "white man's road": he became a rancher and joined the Baptist Church at Elk Creek. And he became a staunch advocate of education for Kiowa children, recognizing that it would be vital. He sent his nephew to the government boarding school in Anadarko, and to the Chilocco Indian School. By the time Delos entered Carlisle, at the age of twenty-two, he already projected authority and was clearly being groomed to accept his future responsibilities.[12]

A team photograph shows a young man with crossed arms, cocked head, and the countenance of a lord. His chin was short and outthrust, his mouth was full, and lustrous center-parted hair flopped over alertly searching eyes. He was so generally splendid-looking that, in November 1892, artist H. K. Bush-Brown borrowed him as a model for a sculpture called "The Buffalo Hunt."

Delos immediately became one of Carlisle's star pupils and athletes. He joined the school's debate society, called the Standards, and the YMCA, and helped to launch the football team. No activity or game could have been trivial to a young man whose education was punctuated by his frequent trips to Washington for diplomatic conferences.

At the end of the 1895 season, Delos literally went from being cheated on the football field to discussions about the Jerome commission, which cheated the Kiowa out of their land. On January 30, 1896,

Lone Wolf II stopped in Carlisle, en route to Washington, to pick up his nephew for yet another trip to the capital. That evening, Lone Wolf II addressed a reception of Carlisle students. With Delos by his side translating, the elder man began to speak in Kiowa.

At the sound of the strange old tongue, the students tittered. But they quieted as Delos translated Lone Wolf II's grim explanation of the reason for his trip to Washington.

"The first thought I wish to present to you is in a line concerning our business," the old warrior said. "We are on our way to Washington to adjust some matters concerning our people. Commissioners were appointed to treat with us. You no doubt have read of the proceedings. . . . The Commissioners saw that the old chiefs were weak and they made things go their own way. We found that we will receive rations only two years, and not half of our people are farmers and are not able yet to take care of themselves. The time is too short. I am doing what I can in my feeble efforts to help my people. . . . I have said time and again, we men are as children. Our children who have learned the English language are stronger than we are."[13]

It would be up to Delos to demonstrate that strength. And the first place he would show it was on the football field.

As the 1896 football season began, Carlisle adopted school colors for the first time: the Indians would wear old gold and red. Not just any red either, but a splash of bold primary color, the most vivid red imaginable. Carlisle red wasn't claret, ruby, blush, crimson, or any other subtle derivation or blend. It was the kind of red that came from a bucket of paint or an artery.

The prideful new colors appeared on pennants and sweaters just in time for a season that represented the height of aspiration. In only their third season, the Indians were about to undertake the most difficult schedule anyone had yet played in college football. They would meet Princeton, Yale, Harvard, and the defending national champion, Pennsylvania, all in the space between October 14 and November 7. No school had ever played the Big Four in the same year, much less in a row. Even the Ivy swells regarded such a schedule as too difficult, if not downright physically dangerous. For Carlisle, it was an act of potential self-slaughter. But then, the Indians had more to prove than other teams.

To make matters more difficult, the Indians were taking on the challenge with only limited help from Vance McCormick. The young industrialist couldn't devote any "steady" time to the Indians due to his business concerns. Instead, he proposed that another former Yale star take his place: William O. Hickok. "Hickey," as he was known, was from a wealthy Harrisburg manufacturing family and had been a two-time all-American at Yale, where he played guard, and also won a national championship in the shot put. He was thickset and stolid, with masses of blond hair that fell on either side of his head like petals. The Indians would bitterly regret his presence on the sideline, preferring McCormick.

The fourteen Carlisle players who traveled to Princeton on October 14, 1896, were badly outnumbered and undersized. Almost to a man, they were considerably lighter than their Ivy opponents. Left end Jacob Jamison, a gangly, open-faced twenty-one-year-old Seneca farm boy, weighed just 152 pounds. Quarterback Frank Cayou, an Omaha from Decatur, Nebraska, weighed just 150. Cayou was something of a marquee idol at the school, with a handsome angular face, pouting mouth, and waves of side-combed hair. His melodious singing voice would eventually land him onstage in New York in a vaudeville revue. But he was a fleet, skittering runner.

The closest thing the Indians had to conventional power was provided by their staunch 180-pound center, Delos Lone Wolf. Delos had graduated in the spring of 1896 but stayed on as assistant disciplinarian in the boys' dorm while he took classes at nearby Metzger College. He plowed the way for running back Jonas Metoxen, lantern-jawed and thick-legged at five foot nine and 170 pounds. Lined up next to Delos at right guard was the Indians' stalwart captain, Bemus Pierce, at six foot one, and 200 pounds. Pierce was a serious-minded twenty-three-year-old Iroquois from upstate New York with a long, solemn face projecting authority. He was the oldest of farmer Jacob and Jane Pierce's six children, and his younger brother Hawley was also on the Carlisle team.[14]

From the opening kickoff, the Indians met the Tigers blow for blow and appalled the Princeton crowd by taking a 6-0 lead at the half. Three minutes into the game, the Indians had forced a fumble, and Metoxen returned it for a touchdown in a wild romp. Princeton's Billy Bannard, humiliated, lodged a protest. He claimed he had yelled "Down!" which should have ended the play. The referees let the score stand—but it was the last decent call the Indians would get.

After a halftime harangue from their coaches, the Princeton eleven retook the field scowling. Shoulders met shoulders and knees met hips; players ground their shoes into whatever limb was underfoot. Princeton tied the score four minutes into the second half—and then the referees began to call fouls on the Indians.

Time after time, a whistle blew and the Indians were penalized. Late in the game, when the whistle blew with yet another call against the Indians, their captain finally had enough. Bemus Pierce called time and stalked over to the referee. Spectators waited for an outburst or complaint. Instead, Pierce spoke one polite sentence.

"You must remember that you are umpiring for both sides," he said.

The physical play and the whistles of the referees wore the Indians out, and their line turned to sand. They lost 22-6. To the *Philadelphia Press* correspondent, the outcome was a case of ancestral superiority asserting itself. "The race with a civilization and a history won the day. It was a clear victory of mind over physical force."

In fact, Carlisle had given Princeton one of the stiffest tests it would face all season. The Tigers would go on to a 10-0-1 record and be declared national champions. Only one other team would score on them all season: Yale.

The Carlisle boys had just a few days to regroup, put balm on their injuries, and practice for their next game, against Yale. It would be their most important, visible game yet, against the traditional power-house. Heightening the tension was the fact that they would be playing on famous old Manhattan Field at the Polo Grounds, and this time the audience promised to be far larger than the curiosity-seeking throng that had come to see them play the YMCA a year earlier.

"While we hope to win the game there is of course a good deal of doubt," Pratt wrote to a friend, "but our boys are putting up a strong game, and I am glad to know, so far are gentlemanly about it."[15]

On October 24, the steep, peaked-roof grandstands were packed with eight thousand spectators, making the field seem like a green carpet at the bottom of a crater. Countless more covered the slope of Deadhead Hill and lined the railings of the viaducts. The open side of the field was lined with buggies and carriages.

Seated in a prime box in the covered grandstand was Pratt, along with his youngest daughter, Nana. Pratt was a growing football fan, despite the fact that he still confused an inning with a half. He had come to the game as the invited guest of a wealthy New York bene-factor, Russell Sage, a railroad magnate, philanthropist, and onetime congressman, and his wife, heiress to an old Yankee seafaring family. The Sages were such Carlisle enthusiasts that before the game, they delivered gold chrysanthemums and red roses to the team hotel, the Ashland House on Fourth Avenue at Twenty-fourth Street. Mrs. Sage wore a corsage of the same flaming flowers, as did young Nana. Also sharing their box was the president of Hamilton College, Dr. W. M. Stryker.

Correspondents for all of the major New York papers, warring for circulation, were on hand: Joseph Pulitzer's *World*, Horace Greeley's *Tribune*, Hearst's *Journal*, James Gordon Bennett's *Herald*, Charles A. Dana's *Sun*. They anticipated a sensational story: Indians against the cream of civilized society. In the highest-circulation paper of them all, the *World*, the game dueled for space with Ada Parker, a cigarette-smoking four-year-old—"Loves a Pipe or a Cigar Better than Her Dolly"—and the amazing A. J. Salisbury, who claimed his eyes had X-ray powers and could "pierce clothes and flesh."[16]

"On one side were the undergraduates of an old and great univer-sity," wrote the *World* correspondent. "They represent, physically, the perfection of modern athletics and intellectually the culture and refinement of the best modern American life. On the other side was the aborigine, the real son of the forest and plain, the redskin of his-tory, of story, of war, developed, or veneered, as the case may be, by education."

As the Indians took the field, their flaming red sweaters made their hair seem more intensely black. The blue of Yale's sweaters seemed almost dull by comparison. In the stands, the small party of Carlisle fans gave the school's cheer: "Hello! Hello! Hellee! Hellee! Who are we? *Carlisle!*"

As the Indians warmed up, the roisterers on the viaducts clapped their hands over their mouths and uttered imitation war whoops. From the box seats came a more courteous but almost disinterested applause, as the crowd settled down for what surely would be an over-whelming Yale victory. Dr. John Hartwell, the referee, strolled over to the Carlisle coach, Hickok.[17]

"Say Hickey, it's 3 o'clock. Get your men out on the field."

Hickock turned to his players, who were so nervous they were all but silent.

"Come on fellows, get out there."

As the Indians lined up for the kickoff, Hickok also took the field, to serve as a game official. There was not yet a formal officiating system in college football, and referees were drawn from a small pool of representatives from various schools. Often the coach of one team also held a whistle in his hand. In this case, Hartwell and Hickok, both former Yalies, would officiate Yale's game, which wouldn't strike anyone as outrageous—until later.

As Pierce kicked off for Carlisle, the crowd gave another languid cheer. The ball fluttered down into the hands of Yale's Paul Mills, who started back with it. Lone Wolf met him and instantly dropped him.

As the two teams lined up, the Yale men seemed like tall stalks compared to the smaller Indians. But when the ball was snapped the Indians surged forward—it looked as though they had picked up the entire Yale team and thrown it backward.

Three minutes into the game, in the midst of a pileup, Yale's Leonard Van Every fumbled. A hole opened between blue jerseys. A single red-clad figure burst through the space. It was Frank Cayou, running freely with the ball. A cadre of Indians surrounded him and began bowling over Yale pursuers.

A last figure in blue dove at Cayou's hip, but he shook him off. After a sixty-yard run, Cayou scurried across the Yale goal line, and planted the ball on the ground for a touchdown.

The crowd came alive. "The 'bleachers,' the 'bridges' and 'dead-headers' were drunk with excitement," the *World* reported. "People in the covered grandstand even awoke to fine enthusiasm." On the sidelines, while the Indians leaped around in a frenzy of celebration, the Yale players stood stock-still. In seven previous games, they had held their opponents scoreless. Once again, the Indians had shocked an Ivy superior.

The score awoke the Yale men, who went bruisingly to work and scored twice before halftime, for a 12-6 margin. But they couldn't increase the lead, hamstrung by the speed of the Indian defenders. Half a dozen times a Yale runner threatened to break away only to be met or yanked down by an Indian tackler, usually Pierce or Lone Wolf.

With just a few minutes remaining, play was an impasse of heaving, shoving men. Yale captain Fred Murphy swung at Carlisle's Pierce. In response, the Indian "only smiled a trifle grimly," the World reported.

Carlisle's halfback Isaac Seneca charged the center of the line—and ran straight into a pileup. But in the stalemate, Seneca slipped the ball to Jamison, who wiggled free of the pack. Jamison found an open field around the left end. Instantly, three blockers appeared at his side.

Jamison raced toward the opposite goal, with the entire Yale team chasing him. He dodged a last blue jersey and hurled himself across the goal line. Joyously, he planted the ball on the ground for the touchdown. The Indians prepared to kick the extra point—the point that would give them a tie with mighty Yale.

A whistle sounded.

The Carlisle players stared in disbelief. It was Hickok.

He was calling the play back.

A burst of catcalls and boos came from the crowd. Players from both sides congregated around Hickok for an explanation. Hickok explained that he believed Metoxen had gone down before he gave the ball to Jamison. He declared the play dead.

The Carlisle players erupted in furious protests—none of them had heard a whistle during Jamison's run, and neither had their team disciplinarian, W. G. Thompson, standing on the sideline. Jamison had scored fairly. "For about a minute everyone thought the Redmen would whip out their tomahawks and simply scalp the sons of Eli in their tracks," the Journal reported. As the catcalls grew louder, a

Carlisle faculty member on the sideline threatened to pull the team off the field if Jamison's touchdown didn't stand.

Hickok consulted with the referee, Hartwell, and then jogged over to the Yale captain, Murphy.

"Look here Murphy if we don't allow that TD the Indians will quit," Hickok said.

"Let 'em," answered Yale's captain. "I heard the whistle and the touchdown don't go."

"Say Hick," said Hartwell, "when you make a decision stick to it."

"I know it," answered Hickok testily.

Hickok ran back to the spot of the original play and stamped his foot in the sod.

"The ball down right here," he said.

With that, the stadium exploded in jeers and hisses. The uproar continued for five minutes, unabated. In the covered grandstand, Pratt was beside himself, and so were his hosts, the Sages. Angriest of all was Dr. Stryker, who kept shouting with all his force, "Carlisle! Carlisle!"

As Pratt watched the ugly scene, he realized his players were about to walk off the field. Pratt bolted from the box and ran across the field to the Carlisle sideline, where he gathered the players around him.

"You must fight the battle out," Pratt insisted. "If you leave you will be called quitters and probably lose us future opportunities. Listen, can't you hear that the crowd is with you? Now go back, and play the game out and don't quit for any reason whatever."

Jamison was still indignant.

"Captain that was as fair a touchdown as was ever made," he said, "and it belongs to us."

"Jakey, it is ours," Pratt said. "The umpire's decision will not take it from us. Go back and do your best, and wait for tomorrow morning's papers, and you will find that you are a bigger man because the touchdown was denied you than would be if it had been allowed. Now go and help the boys keep Carlisle at the top."

"All right Captain," Jamison said.[18]

The Indians returned to the field and played on determinedly—but uselessly. "You could see them standing calm, perfectly motionless, and at the word springing forward with tremendous intensity and fighting with everything in them," the *Journal* reported. But after just a few more minutes, another whistle sounded. Time had run out. The game was over, and they had lost.

As the Indians left the field, a huge ovation swept through the crowd. Spectators from the grandstands emptied onto the field and began to lift the Indian players off their feet. The crowd carried them out of the stadium and all the way to the train station. Back at the Ashland House hotel, a moved Mrs. Sage took off her corsage and pinned it on Cayou for his touchdown. Nana Pratt stripped hers off and presented it to the downhearted hero, Jamison.

The following day, as Pratt predicted, the newspapers were full of outrage at how the Indians had been treated by Hickok and Hartwell. The *New York Sun* commented acidly that the botched call was "characteristic . . . of nearly all the crimes committed against the Indians by the whites, for it was accomplished by the man of all men who should have looked out for their interests and their rights." Hickok was no different from a crooked Indian agent back home. "Just as many an agent has proved false to his trust so this referee was to his."[19]

The *World* called it "as fair a play as could have been." Even Harry Beecher, the former Yale star, seemed unsure of how to feel in a sidebar he wrote for the *World*. Of the disputed call, Beecher said, "This decision was at least questionable to an outsider." In conclusion, he wrote, "The Indians deserve the credit of a practical victory."

Since it was a Sunday morning, Pratt took the team to church, no doubt in part to try to cure their bitterness. They attended the Plymouth Congregational service in Brooklyn, where preacher Lyman Abbott had succeeded Henry Ward Beecher as pastor. Abbott waggled his long white beard as he singled out the Carlisle boys. Their performance on the field, he said, proved they were capable of rising above "degradation and ignorance."

Painful as the Yale loss was, it thrust Carlisle into the national spotlight. As the controversy raged on, magazine and newspaper writers streamed to Carlisle to see what the Indian school was about, and to interview the players. A New York baseball club wrote to offer Jamison the royal sum of $150 to play baseball for a season. Pratt declined on his behalf. "Jacob is just now getting his education . . . the 150 a month would be so much more than is necessary for him that he would undoubtedly be led into loose ideas, and when his baseball days are over would be practically spoiled for the hard tussle with life that he must eventually make."[20]

Mail streamed in from well-wishers. Walter Camp wrote Pratt a note of apologetic kindness and enclosed a copy of his work *Football Facts and Figures*. Pratt engaged in a lively correspondence with the *New York Sun*'s ace reporter J. R. Spears, who was full of praise for the play of Cayou, Jamison, and Lone Wolf. As for Hickok, Sears opined, he should be fired. Pratt tended to agree.

The players could barely bring themselves to take the field again with Hickok as their coach. Pratt replied to Spears, "I may say in justification of your views that our boys have practically lost faith in Mr. Hickok as a friend to their cause and their practice is lifeless compared with what it was before our trip."

But the Indians took heart from the kind treatment they had received in the press. "The boys say so long as the public will referee their game so fairly as they have, they will fight the campaign out to the finish, whatever may be the partisan conclusions of referees and umpires acting on the field," Pratt added.[21]

Gradually, the spirits of the players lifted. McCormick came to visit, and on the twenty-ninth, Pratt was able to tell Spears that "in practice last night there was better playing than we have witnessed before, even better, we thought, than that on Manhattan Field." Nevertheless, they continued to insist they had been robbed.

"Our boys one and all, as well as Mr. Thompson, who was on the sideline, disclaim having heard Hickok's whistle," Pratt said.

The Indians remained a favorite cause of the New York papers through November—which was saying something, given that the country was in the grip of a heated presidential campaign between William McKinley and William Jennings Bryan, and on the lighter side the penny press was obsessed by the dance hall antics of Lona Barrison, star of Koster and Bial's, aboard her trick horse Maestro, whom she threatened to enter in the upper-crust New York Horse

Show. "Society is now wondering if she will appear in the Light and Airy Costume she wears at the music hall," the *World* reported.[22]

Buoyed by popular support, the Indians played Harvard to another near standstill before losing, 4-0. Then, in their final game of the four-week stretch, the overtaxed and exhausted team lost to defending national champion Penn, 21-0.

They had dropped all four games. But it was an unprecedented streak in terms of guts, and audiences seemed to feel as if the Indians had won something. Every game had been played on the road, in front of hostile observers, with nothing close to the manpower of their opponents. They never substituted against Harvard, and only once with Yale and Princeton, respectively. They had been fouled, without complaint. Frankly, they had given football players a good name, and the sons of gentlemen a lesson in comportment.

The opinion maker Caspar Whitney paid them the ultimate compliment when he devoted a significant portion of his *Harper's Weekly* column to them. He singled out Delos Lone Wolf and Bemus Pierce, who had made "the center impregnable." As for Carlisle as a whole, "Too much praise cannot be given this Indian team for its showing this year; for the quality of its football after but three years of the game at Carlisle, and above all for its sportsmanly conduct and clean play," Whitney wrote. "They were much harassed at Princeton by questionable umpiring; an unjust referee's decision lost them the Yale game—and yet they played ball on both occasions. I regard the conduct of these Indians to have had a more wholesome influence on the game than any occurrence of recent years. All honor to them!"[23]

Carlisle also attracted notice from the political press, which treated the performance as a wholesale ratification of Indian education. *Harper's Weekly* announced in a separate editorial: "When one sees the headline 'What Education Does for the Indian' standing as the headline of a newspaper editorial, it seems hardly necessary to read what follows. We all know what education has done for the Indians of the Carlisle School. It has enabled them to turn out a football team that played what apparently ought to have been a tie with Yale, and kept Harvard down to four points. Incidentally, it has done much more, but that particular achievement is unquestionably the most impressive at the present moment, and not altogether on frivolous grounds, either."[24]

But not everyone was delighted by Carlisle's football success. One influential Carlisle patron wrote to Pratt to protest the school's sudden emphasis on a sport with such an unsavory reputation. The game was too violent and distracted the public from the real work Carlisle was trying to accomplish, according to Abram Vail of Quakertown, New Jersey. Pratt appreciated Vail's objections, but he was overwhelmed by the public praise the Indians had received. After years of trying to show the school off in expositions, parades, and cultural fairs, Pratt wasn't going to quibble because Carlisle had finally won notice in a football game.

Nothing else the school had accomplished "in the whole seventeen years of our history, attracted the attention and comment that this Fall's football campaign has!" Pratt replied. He had become an unabashed cheerleader.

> There is another feature in it, personal to myself. I have considerable elation and reward in seeing my boys shake up and even overcome trained college athletes with all their centuries of development and intelligence backing them. . . .
>
> I am keeping my hand on the throttle, and watching carefully the ongoing of this train. So long as I believe as I do now that it is doing good to the cause and will probably lead to deeper public thought as to what is best and right for the Indians I shall accelerate it. If I discover that the contrary is likely to result I will stop it. In the meantime I think we had better have work a plenty, study a plenty, civilized experience a plenty, and play a plenty.[25]

THE CARLISLE Indians were a hot ticket. Their performance against the Ivy schools had made them the most sought-after team in the country—and they followed it up with three straight victories over lesser opponents. According to *Outing* magazine, "They have just finished a four weeks campaign that no other team we have ever seen would think of undertaking . . . they are the most popular team with the spectators now playing the game."[26]

With their popularity came new opportunities. Although the football season was ending, the Chicago Press Club made Carlisle a handsome financial offer to play one more game: a matchup with the strongest team in the west, the University of Wisconsin. The game would be played under unprecedented circumstances: the first ever under electric lights. It would be held at night, in the Chicago Coliseum.

Pratt weighed whether to accept. He had a lot to think about. The proposal earned sharp criticism from the fussy eastern press, which considered it unsportsmanlike to play purely for money. The dread sin of professionalism and the murky issue of college "eligibility" were particularly sensitive topics in the 1896 season. The sentiment of the era was expressed by the *New York Times* in an editorial: "A young gentleman engaged in getting an education ought not to exhibit himself for money and he and his fellows ought not to raise a mere sport to the dignity of an occupation."[27]

It was obvious that some Ivy stars were nothing more than hired hands with only the most vague connection to their schools. Five of the eleven men named to Walter Camp's all-American team that season were twenty-four or older. Harvard had feuded with Princeton over the legitimacy of two of the Tigers' key players, who had already played football at smaller colleges.[28]

But in addition to the public relations value of such a game for Carlisle, there were the gate receipts to consider. College football, Pratt discovered, had become a moneymaking enterprise. By 1890, a ticket to the Yale-Princeton game cost $15, and by 1896 a big game yielded a box office take of $15,000 or $20,000. It was customary for schools to negotiate financial splits from proceeds, and the prospect of such income was tantalizing to Pratt, for whom finances were a constant, ulcerous worry.

Carlisle was chronically underfunded. Pratt had to badger Congress for basic appropriations for the school, and the Capitol was filled with men who believed federal funds were wasted on Indian education, as well as western politicians who resented that appropriations were sent to the East instead of to their states. Pratt's correspondence in the fall of 1896 shows that he had 820 pupils on the rolls, about 250 more than appropriations called for. He was also trying to raise funds to build a new laundry and a second story for the trade building. He constantly sought to supplement Carlisle's income with private charitable donations. Among the things Washington refused to pay for was an athletics program. The Chicago game would give Carlisle a tidy profit and allow it to buy decent athletic equipment.

Pratt decided to let Carlisle participate. The benefits, and profits, would far outweigh the cost to the school's reputation. "We need greatly an athletic field and better equipments, which must come from outside sources," Pratt wrote to editor C. E. Patterson of the *Illustrated American*, defending his decision. "I therefore concluded to let the boys play one more game and that they do Saturday in the Coliseum in Chicago, from which, if all present indications are realized, we shall have means to work with. I am aware that playing for money is scarcely sportsmanlike, but it has been a long and heavy pull upon me all the years to keep up the athletic spirit. Our gymnasium, its equipment and almost everything the boys have had to work with, I have had to supply from charity resources."[29]

The shoestring budget of the football team made the trip to Chicago uncomfortable. Accompanied by the marching band, they traveled via the Pittsburgh-Niagara Express and then transferred to a sleeper for Chicago, aboard which forty-four students crammed into just thirty-two berths. It was all Pratt could afford. The return trip would be even worse, with just twenty-eight berths for the party. Pratt had actually splurged on the outbound trip, so the players could sleep somewhat decently.

One of the ways in which Pratt justified the trip was to tell himself that it would be good for Carlisle to play before a western audience, one that had formed its opinions of Indians largely from sensational news reports of uprisings. When the Carlisle team arrived in Chicago early in the morning before the game and checked into the Palmer House hotel, a *Chicago Tribune* correspondent was waiting in the lobby to report his impressions of them, and accompanied them on a round of sightseeing.

After a team breakfast, the players visited the Chicago Board of

A careworn Richard Henry Pratt in the uniform of a U.S. cavalryman, shortly before his retirement in 1904.

The splendidly clad Sioux leader American Horse sat for a studio photograph during an early visit to the Indian Training School at Carlisle Barracks.

The lean young Captain Pratt and some of the Indian prisoners at Fort Marion, St. Augustine, circa 1875, wearing military-issue uniforms. Note the bars on the casemate in the background.

The first Sioux students and their chaperones, shortly after arrival at Carlisle Barracks in October 1879. Pratt stands at left in civilian dress.

A dozen new Navajo students, some still wearing native dress, gathered in front of the Carlisle bandstand on the parade ground. Pratt is seated behind them in his favorite spot.

Yale football captain Vance McCormick in his glory in 1893. He was Carlisle's first real coach and led them to their earliest successes.

Carlisle's 1894 football pioneers. Delos Lone Wolf is seated in the middle row, second from left. To his right is Ben American Horse. Team captain Bemus Pierce stands in the top row, second from right, with arms folded.

A studio portrait of the young Kiowa Delos K. Lone Wolf, center-rush on the football team, debate star, YMCA leader, and future litigant who would fight allotment all the way to the U.S. Supreme Court.

The heroes of the notorious hidden-ball trick in 1903. Charlie Dillon stands in the top row second from left. To his right is Antonio "The Wolf" Lubo. Albert Exendine, who held Dillon's jersey, is in the middle row, second from left.

The dapper young innovator, Glenn S. "Pop" Warner.

Albert Exendine, star end and captain of the 1906 team, who helped demonstrate the possibilities of the forward pass to the rest of the collegiate world.

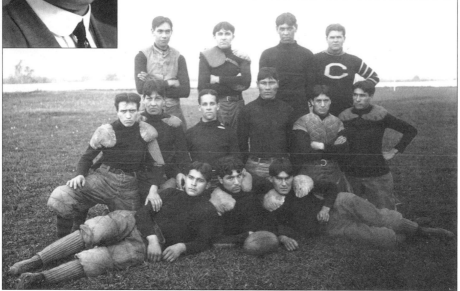

Pop Warner poses with his first Carlisle squad in 1899. Famed drop kicker Frank Hudson kneels in the middle row, second from left. Future all-American Jimmie Johnson appears noticeably smaller than his teammates in the middle row, third from left.

Pop Warner, trainer Wallace Denny, and Exendine (in football uniform) stand on the Carlisle athletic field, which was graded and seeded by the players themselves.

The Carlisle student body, in uniform and formation on the parade ground. Behind them are the dormitories.

American Horse, a man of two worlds, with his children and other young relatives at Carlisle in 1889.

The six Indian leaders who rode at the head of Theodore Roosevelt's 1905 inaugural parade. From left to right: Little Plume, Buckskin Charlie, Geronimo, Quanah Parker, Hollow Horn Bear, and American Horse.

Jim Thorpe works out against one of Warner's many homemade inventions, a rudimentary blocking sled.

Carlisle's quick, low-charging line in one of Warner's myriad trick formations. Warner wears a winter cap in the background.

Quarterback Gus Welch carries the ball in practice. The tackler is Thorpe.

The Carlisle team of 1912. Top row: Charles Williams, Gus Welch, Jim Thorpe, coach Pop Warner, Robert Hill, and William Garlow. Middle row: Pete Calac, Joe Bergie, Joel Wheelock, Stancil "Possum" Powell, Joe Guyon, and Elmer Busch. Bottom row: George Vetterneck, Roy Large, and Alex Arcasa.

Thorpe takes a pitch. From the Carlisle single wing, anything might happen: run, pass, or kick.

The world's greatest athlete in his prime, 1912.

Welch and Thorpe, grinning best friends and roommates, with their companions in the Carlisle backfield of 1912, Alex Arcasa and Possum Powell.

Captain Gus Welch of the Allied Expeditionary Force, who would win commendation while fighting in France despite a near-fatal head injury.

Carlisle's greatest team on the practice field. From 1911 to 1913, the Indians would win thirty-eight games and lose just three.

Trade, where they filed into a private gallery. They stared, dumb-founded, down onto a floor where commodities traders frantically screamed bids at each other. In the wheat pit, the hoarse exclama-tions and the leaping gesticulations of the traders drew a wry com-ment from Delos Lone Wolf. "Savages," he said.[30]

Next, the Indians went to the stock exchange, where they were raucously greeted by a football flying through the air. Lineman Mar-tin Wheelock caught it and tossed it back, which incited the brokers into a punting contest.

A nervy broker named J. Townsend approached the Indians. Town-send was a boxer from the Chicago Athletic Association who appar-ently wanted to try his strength. He suddenly lunged at Bemus Pierce and tried to tackle him. "In an affectionate way he embraced the big fellow below the knees," the *Tribune* reported. Pierce calmly shook the broker from his pants cuff, and "in a moment [Townsend] was on his back. It was only a simple movement of the leg that put him there, but he did not again seek to test the red men's physical power."

Somehow, the Indians maintained their sense of humor. They exhibited "pleasant smiles" as they got ready to leave, and paused to serenade the brokers with a song: "America." Moreover, they delivered the anthem "with a right heart will," according to the cor-respondent.

With some relief, the players returned to the hotel. They spent the rest of their time in Chicago dining, strolling around town, or reading newspapers in easy chairs in the corridors.

On the night of December 19, a crowd of fifteen thousand gathered at the Coliseum to see Carlisle play Wisconsin. The game was a major attraction in a town that loved its entertainments; the Chicago Opera House, the Haymarket, and the Olympic featured continuous vaude-ville all day and all night, with performances beginning at ten-thirty in the morning. Promoters advertised the Carlisle-Wisconsin game in the theatrical section of the papers as a high drama: a spectacle to be played out under electric light, a collision between the East and the West. And of course it featured Indians. "Kiowa, Omaha, Oneida, Pueblo, Seneca, Chippewa, Nez-Perce, Tuscarora, Stockbridge," read a *Tribune* advertisement in thick black letters.

Back at Carlisle, Pratt was uncharacteristically nervous. On the morning of the game, he sent a telegram to Bemus Pierce. "Tell the boys one and all to play the strongest, cleanest game they can from start to finish, and then the score will take care of itself," he wrote.

But Pratt was worried that Carlisle could be cheated again. He had heard reports that the Wisconsin coach was known to behave illegally on the sidelines. "I have given the subject of football more thought this year than in all the previous years, and am becoming convinced that good honest, fair, straight football is almost an impossibility," he wrote to an acquaintance.[31]

After Pratt telegraphed Pierce, he sent another telegram, this one to the team chaperone, W. G. Thompson, warning him to beware of cheating. "Am anxious to know your officials and that Coach King and all coaching has been driven from the field and side lines."[32] Pratt was right to be concerned. The Wisconsin team would be led by a recent addition to the team—a ringer named Pat O'Dea, the champion dropkicker of Australia.[33]

But there was nothing Pratt could do about it except wait. That night, a group of faculty and students gathered in Pratt's office, "all excitement and anxiety," as they awaited periodic game bulletins that came in by telephone. It was a night of long silences punctuated by a shrieking phone and three dramatic lead changes. Pratt would pick up the receiver, and as he reported the latest score, either cheers or groans would fill the room.[34]

Inside the Chicago Coliseum, Carlisle took the field at 8:15 P.M. Rows of arc lights gave off a sodium glare, and a heat so intense it was as though the game was on a warm, sunny October afternoon. The arena echoed and hummed with the excitement, as cigar smoke swirled upward.

As the game got under way, an odd event reminded spectators and players alike of what an unusual setting it was. A punt caromed high into the air—and into the arched iron grids that supported the Coliseum ceiling. The ball bounced into the struts and then rolled lazily along a slanting iron girder, until it came to rest against an upright beam, stuck.

Players and officials stared up at the motionless ball. Laughter rippled around the stadium. The collective gaze of fifteen thousand shifted to the figure of a small boy scurrying up one of the uppermost bleachers. The boy climbed from the gallery into the rafters, scaled the girders, and worked his way to the ball. He plucked it from its wedged place and dropped it to the ground, to applause.

The game resumed. There was no score for the first half hour. But then a flurry of lead changes kept Pratt jumping to the phone in his office. Carlisle led, 6-0, until Wisconsin scored twice in succession to overtake the Indians 8-6 early in the second half.

The Indians' runners began to assert themselves. They stepped out of the grasp of tacklers, dodged, and quick-jumped and scrambled past the chalk marks. The Wisconsin men grew winded and began to double over, trying to catch their breath. Holes began to open up left, right, and center.

At eleven-thirty, the phone rang in Pratt's office. The report was that Carlisle led 12-8 and that the game would be over in ten minutes. Pratt hung up, and the group in his office settled down to wait for the hoped-for final result. The ten minutes stretched out into an hour. It was after midnight when the phone finally rang again, this time with W. G. Thompson on the other end: Carlisle had won, 18-8.

The Carlisle players were weary but jubilant; the victory completed their first winning record at 6-4. As they rode the Illinois Central train back to their hotel after the game, they preened in "the center of an admiring group of young women, anxious to gaze at the descendants of the natives, who had beaten the sons of their fathers conquerors at their own game," according to the *Tribune* reporter who made the trip with them. Back at the Palmer House, the men luxuriantly lit cigars and enjoyed a smoke. They were out of training, they announced.

At Carlisle, Pratt was exultant. The game had "changed the opinions of many of the westerners in regard to the Indians," he believed.[35] The grateful and perhaps guilty superintendent rewarded the exhausted players with a fortnight's leave of absence so they could visit their families for Christmas and rest. Pratt spent his own holiday season marveling at a campus demonstration of Thomas Edison's latest invention, the moving picture Projectoscope, and defending his decision to allow Carlisle to play a game for money.

He was rewarded with a commentary in *Harper's Weekly* from Caspar Whitney, who explained Carlisle's financial condition and the sorry state of their weed-strewn field. Whitney exempted Carlisle from criticism for the sin of "touring" because circumstances revealed the object of the game to be "entirely worthy and healthful."[36]

In the New Year, Pratt turned his attention back to Carlisle's fight for funding. He found that the Indians' stunning success in football had not gone unnoticed in Washington. On January 27, the House of Representatives considered the latest Indian appropriations bill. One of Pratt's political opponents, Arizona congressman Nathan Oakes Murphy, rose and delivered a diatribe against Carlisle, claiming that funds for it were wasted and that its students invariably reverted to tribalism. Murphy questioned the "good results of the present Indian educational system" and declared heatedly, "Every Apache who was educated in the East and who returned to his reservation, is wearing breechclout today."

But Congressman Charles Henry Grosvenor of Ohio rose to defend Carlisle's honor.

"Have not the Indians developed great powers in football?" he asked with good humor.

"I believe they have," another congressman answered.

"And is not football considered in our modern colleges the highest level of culture and civilization?"

The chamber erupted in laughter.[37]

Delos Lone Wolf delivered an oratory at Carlisle's 1896 commencement ceremony. It was entitled "Our Development: A Necessity." But the only development taking place in Indian Territory was the spread of allotment and a steady increase in lawlessness. While Delos was still at Carlisle, Lone Wolf II's home was broken into and ransacked by thieves.[38]

The young man finally returned to Indian Territory at the end of 1896, no doubt with the belief that he could change things. He was the personification of all of Pratt's hopes and theories, the seemingly perfect new young Indian leader, schooled and Christianized. "Delos can make things move his way if he will," Pratt said of him.[39]

At first, things went smoothly for Delos. He determinedly found work on his very first day back on the reservation, as a carpenter. He hired himself out with a hammer and a saw for $2.50 a day. The agent at Anadarko was impressed by his work ethic and offered him a position as clerk and interpreter.

In the summer of 1896, during a camp meeting in the hills near Fort Sill, Delos married fellow Carlisle student Ida Wasee. He and his wife moved to the Kiowa and Comanche agency at Anadarko, where he steadily rose to the position of agency farmer, a coveted job with a good income. He and Ida started a family, which would grow to six children.[40]

In 1898, Delos moved his family to what is now Carnegie, Oklahoma, an area of steep, grassy hills, where he and his wife took up adjoining allotments. Pratt wrote to Delos in October of that year. "I am glad to know you are getting on so well. I trust you will stand your ground clear through to the end. No man accomplishes much in this world, who does not stem the current. To float with the stream is easy, and weak human nature is so prone to do that. Those who would resist not only have to pull themselves forward, but often have to drag those who would otherwise float."[41]

Delos took Pratt's words to heart—but he employed them in a way Pratt could never have anticipated. On June 6, 1900, the Kiowa's long efforts against the despised Jerome Agreement failed. With an act of Congress, the United States seized 2.9 million acres of the Kiowa, Comanche, and Plains Apache reservation, paying just 93 cents an acre for land valued at $2.

The government held a lottery for the new land. Ten thousand people camped near Fort Sill. In just two weeks, there were 165,000 registrations for parcels.[42]

Delos and Lone Wolf II once more traveled to Washington to fight against opening the reservation. This incensed the local Kiowa agent, Lieutenant Colonel James Randlett. He berated Delos for traveling without his authorization, labeled him a troublemaker, and fired him from his job as agency farmer and interpreter.[43]

But Delos was not done—not by a long shot. The Kiowa now pursued justice the way he had been taught at Carlisle: he put his faith in the American system.

He sued. The Lone Wolfs filed suit to block execution of the Jerome Agreement, asking for a restraining order against the secretary of the interior, Ethan Allen Hitchcock, to prevent him from opening the reservation to white settlement. They argued through their attorneys—William M. Springer, a former federal judge and Congressman, and Hampton L. Carson, founder of the Indian Rights Association—that the 1892 agreement violated the Medicine Lodge Treaty of 1867, which stated that a deal had to be ratified by three-fourths of the adult males. They charged that signatures had been obtained by fraud, forgery, and bribery, and that the proposed payment for the land was inequitable.

Carlisle had unwittingly created a new brand of Indian activist, personified by Delos. He was not the only one. Another Carlisle-educated student, a Comanche named William Tivis, also joined the effort to halt the opening of the reservation. All across the country, in fact, Carlisle men and women, groomed to lead, schooled in debate, and with command of English and American history and values, went back to their homes to use their education against local authorities. In Wisconsin, a Carlisle grad named Neopit Oshkosh fought the federal government for control of his tribe's timber reserves. In Yuma, Arizona, Patrick Miguel, another Carlisle alum, helped organize tribal elections and confronted the local agent when he struck an Indian, warning him "not to touch the Indians again" or he would report him to the government.[44]

But *Lone Wolf v. Hitchcock* was, in the end, a crushing defeat. On January 5, 1903, the Supreme Court ruled against the Lone Wolfs. Justice Edward Douglas White announced the opinion: Congress could abrogate an Indian treaty at will. In effect, the government could seize Indian land without consent.

The decision, regarded in legal quarters as "one of the blackest days in the history of the American Indian," meant the all but total dissolution of reserved lands. It also stripped the tribes of any meaningful legal and political rights. By 1925, Indians would lose 90 percent of their territory.[45]

Delos, as it turned out, could not "move things his way if he has a will." The beaten young farmer retreated to Carnegie, where he tried to cadge a decent living from his crops on his allotted acres. Somehow he maintained his confidence, however. In February 1903, he was invited by Pratt to revisit Carlisle and to speak at commencement. He accepted. The Delos who returned to Carlisle was somewhat older and stouter, but not subdued. He participated in a ceremony that featured a number of other former football players, including Stacy Matlock, who had become a schoolteacher in Utah. When it was Delos' turn to step to the podium, he delivered a speech of determined hopefulness.

"I feel that I am still a student in the big school of the world," he said. "I have struck out by myself, and am doing what Carlisle taught me. I am not dependent on the government, but upon what knowledge Carlisle has given, and am thankful for what little I know."[46]

7

NOT A PARLOR GAME

THE CARLISLE PRACTICE field was a stubborn piece of hardpan that could chip the blade off a shovel. It was an uneven, rock-strewn acre, furrowed with the Indians' own sweat. The players dug the field themselves, measured it, graded it, and sodded it. It was an ordeal each summer to sow grass seed into that patch of sun-baked clay and dirt.

Bemus Pierce needed a team of six horses just to plow it. While three men guided the horses, Pierce rode on the beam of the plow, straining as he drove it nose down into the earth. Even then, the field resisted and the plow nearly bucked him off. A passage in the school paper described Pierce "plunging and leaping and almost falling over the great clods of clay turned over by the plow, [but he] stuck to it with all the fierceness manifested in a football match, and is hardening his muscles by such work ready for the coming games in the fall."[1]

The Indians practiced with the same perseverance. Quarterback Frank Hudson spent hour after hour working on his dropkick. Hudson was a twenty-year-old Laguna-Pueblo from Paguate, New Mexico, a village about forty-five miles west of Albuquerque, reachable by a wagon road that would become Highway 66. He had practically been raised at Carlisle, arriving on campus in 1886 at the age of just ten. A decade later, he still looked like a little boy, with an elfin face under short, curling bangs, and he stood just five foot five. Team captain Pierce called him "the smallest man I have ever seen on a gridiron." But with dedicated practice, Hudson had become the best dropkicker in the nation, mastering a technique of impeccable athletic timing: he dropped the balloon-sized ball to the ground, let it bounce once like a basketball, and then caught it with his toe and sent it straight toward the uprights. In football lingo, Hudson could boom the ball.

In winter, Hudson moved indoors to the gymnasium, where he used a set of parallel bars as a target. He would stand two-thirds of the way back in the gym and kick the ball over the bars—with either foot. Next, he hung out a three-foot gymnastics ring and practiced until he could kick the ball through the ring five times in succession. His became such a forceful, accurate kicker he could boot the ball through the goalposts from the fifty-yard line.[2]

The Indians fashioned a sort of trophy room in the vestibule of the gym to commemorate their feats. They hung rows of colorful footballs, painted in team colors, with the final scores of their victories written on the sides. They posted the college flag of each defeated team on the wall above it. But there was one missing item. Underneath the Yale banner sat a football without a score. It represented the 1896 Yale game, and the touchdown they were denied.[3]

There was something else the Indians felt they were denied: proper credit. The press had an irritating habit of attributing their victories to the Yale men who coached them—in the 1897 season another former Eli, William T. Bull, replaced the unloved Hickok. Carlisle went 6-4, but when the Indians won a game, it was never their own doing. Their losses, on the other hand, were always the inevitable evidence of their Indian character flaws. "Indians Lacked Science," a typical headline read after they lost to Brown by just 18-14.[4]

When Walter Camp reviewed Carlisle's season for *Harper's Weekly* it was William Bull he applauded rather than Carlisle. Hudson's spectacular kicking, Camp observed, was a reflection of "Bull's own playing days at Yale." Camp assumed an Indian couldn't possibly have become so proficient on his own, and what's more, he implied that the Carlisle players were hampered by their native emotions. The Indian was "much more mercurial in football than his brother the pale face," Camp remarked. "His depression when losing ground is extreme, and his elation correspondingly high when his team gains some especial advantage."[5]

Nobody seemed willing to give them their due, not even their own Carlisle teachers. At the end of 1897, the team celebrated their winning season with a banquet in the campus YMCA hall. Grand speeches followed a sumptuous meal of oysters, sliced turkey, and ice cream and cake, served on football-shaped placemats.

But in the midst of a toast, assistant superintendent Alfred Standing reminded the team that "they still need a white man to coach and to manage their finances."

Even Pratt managed to insult his own students. To him, the Indians' accomplishments on the field were mainly a demonstration that the Indians were not always slothful. "During the past eighteen years we have been demonstrating that the Indian is not lazy, that he is industrious, and proved it beyond all peradventure," he said. "We have talked about it, and published it everywhere, but it had little effect. Nothing has helped us into public notice so much as football."[6]

But when Dennison Wheelock, the leader of the Carlisle marching band, rose to speak, he made it clear that the Indians' exploits were far more than a demonstration of their industry. Football, as he saw it, was nothing less than another form of resistance.

"Long ago, it was said that the Indian could not understand civilization," Wheelock said. "It is repeated even at the present time. I deny it. I assert that what the Indian could not understand was the greed, the grasping selfishness of the white man in this country, and when the Indian learned that his habitation and the hills he so dearly loved were being invaded, he justly cried, 'there will be eternal war between me and thee.' And when he resisted, who will say that he did not do right? Who will say that he would not have done the same? He resisted with a thousand warriors but he had to retreat westward like a hunted fox. . . . Today the Indian is beyond the Mississippi. The only way I see how he may reoccupy the lands that once were his, is through football, and as football takes brains, takes energy, proves whether a civilization can be understood by the Indian or not, we are willing to perpetuate it."

When it was Bemus Pierce's turn to speak, it was clear he too did not take kindly to the patronization by his teachers. The tall team captain was such a notable campus leader that some of the town residents who followed Carlisle's football team joked that "he runs things out there." Pierce was ordinarily a laconic sort, but his reply to Standing and Pratt qualified as eloquent.

"Now, I am glad to say we have a white man for a coach, but we have no white man on the team when we are on the gridiron," Pierce declared. "Therefore, I say if the Indian can do this, why can he not as well handle the team, and handle the financial part? If he can do so well in this game, I believe in time he can do most anything."

Pierce would soon prove his assertion. By 1901, he was a head coach in his own right, first at a high school in Buffalo, New York, then successively at the University of Buffalo, Kenyon College, and the Sherman Institute in California.

What the Carlisle players did on the field, they considered their own. From that night on, self-governance was to be a continual issue for the Indians—and for the man who was about to become famous as their next head coach.

In 1898, the Indians had a desultory and unimproved record of 5-4 under yet another former Yalie, John A. Hall. The Indians were clearly tired of the Yale influence. It was time to look in an entirely new direction. Carlisle still aspired to beat the Big Four; "we only need a little more time and coaching to surpass them," Frank Cayou asserted.[7]

Pratt decided to hire a full-time athletic director, someone who would be more dedicated to, and compatible with, the Indians' ambitions. For advice, he turned to the ultimate expert: Walter Camp. Who, he asked Camp, was the very best young coach in the United States? If possible, Pratt intended to hire him.

Camp had just the man. He was a young newcomer and a relative outsider, but in just two seasons as a head coach at Cornell, he had developed a reputation for creativity. His name was Glenn Scobey

"Pop" Warner, and he would spend the better part of the next thirteen years on the Carlisle campus, with one significant interruption.

A FIGHT in a mud puddle was the making of Warner. He could tell you the very day it happened; it was the day he went from being the butt of the joke and became the town bully. It was the day the fat kid got even.

His nickname in the farm community of Springville, New York, was "Butter." He was a big, ungainly boy, with rolls of fat around his gut and hips, which made a broad target for slingshots, bean shooters, and snowballs. He lumbered around the playing fields of Springville in a pair of football pants his mother made for him from the legs of old farm overalls. He was a figure of fun, perennially picked on, until one intolerable day when, as he walked home from school, a boy pulled Warner's cap from his head, threw it in a mud puddle, and stomped on it.

Warner's temper, pent up from hundreds of humiliations, finally broke. He charged the bully with his fists flailing and knocked his tormentor to the ground. The realization that he could turn his bulk to his advantage was a seminal moment. Warner began seeking out fights and winning them. The battle, he always said, "showed me a new way of looking at life."[8]

A stint in the West as a teenager solidified his fat into muscle. Warner's family joined the land rush of the late 1880s, staking out a cattle ranch in Wichita Falls, Texas, near the Oklahoma border and not far from Fort Sill. The pastures were so huge that it took Warner ten hours to ride from one end to the other. Warner and his younger brother, Bill, helped their father break the prairie soil, clear brush, herd cattle, and plant wheat.

In Texas, Warner discovered he liked to gamble. He went to work as a tinsmith apprentice, only to wager away the first $20 he earned. It was the first of a series of lifelong bets by a man with an appetite for winning that was as large as his appetite for food. But antes weren't just about easy money to Warner; they were about using his wits. They were less a matter of risk than judgment. They were about being right.

Warner thought his cow pony could outrun a local mustang and bet his entire salary on a match race. But he failed to factor in the weight of the jockey—himself, at almost 200 pounds. The pony tore along the ground, back bowed from the effort of carrying Warner's load, and lost. Instead of being chastened by the outcome, however, he merely accepted it as a lesson in math. From then on, Warner was a habitual speculator.[9]

In the summer of 1892, on the pretext of visiting relatives in Springville, he spent a week wagering on the Grand Circuit harness races in Buffalo. When he went up $50, he took the roll of bills in his pocket as evidence that he was born to be a horseplayer. He followed the circuit when it moved on to Rochester—where he lost not only his winnings but his entire stake, "many of the animals I bet on not even having the sportsmanship to finish," he recalled. On his way out of the park, he made one last desperate effort to recoup his losses, and wound up with nothing in his pocket but his ticket to Springville.

Warner was afraid to admit to his father what he had done with his money, and looked for an excuse not to return home. He found one at Cornell University, in nearby Ithaca. He wrote his father that he had decided to enter Cornell law school, and asked for help with his expenses. His father responded with a check for $100. Back in the chips, he boarded a train for Ithaca.

On Warner's first day on campus, he was drawn to the football field, where he watched practice. He had been standing on the sideline for about fifteen minutes when Carl Johanson, Cornell's captain, noticed his size and build, and walked over and asked him what he weighed.

"Two hundred and fifteen pounds," Warner answered.

"Fine," Johanson said. "Get on a suit right away. We need a left guard."

"Wait a minute, I don't know anything about the game at all."

"Never mind," Johanson said. "All you've got to do is keep them from going through you and spoiling the play when we've got the ball, and when they've got the ball, knock the tar out of your man and tackle the runner. Perfectly simple."[10]

Warner earned the nickname "Pop" for the fact that he was the oldest freshman on the team and because, as he put it, "There has to be a Pop on every team." His physique was suited to the straight-ahead mass plunges of the era, and he played like the school boxing champion he was, with wild headlong swings. He became a team captain.

Warner supplemented his pocket money by painting and selling watercolors. These were the days a man wasn't just one thing—he was a football player and an artist, a sportsman and an inventor, a cowboy and a tinsmith. They were also the days when a man was unafraid to tinker. Warner began to apply his creative sensibility to the game. He saw a fascinating abstraction when he looked at a field, one that was open to improvisation.

One afternoon the Cornell coach, Marshall Newell, went on a scouting trip and left Warner in charge of the team. Warner's first act was to draw up a new play. Today it seems a fairly elementary piece of misdirection, but considering the plodding style of the era, it was a bold trial: all of the running backs faked a run around the left end, while the quarterback kept the ball and ran right. That weekend in a game against Williams College, Warner put himself at quarterback and called the play. It was good for a twenty-five-yard gain—but he was such an inexperienced runner that he fumbled when he was finally tackled.[11]

Warner graduated from Cornell in 1894 and took a brief stab at the law, opening an office in Buffalo. But his passion for games made legal work seem "pretty tame," and he quickly decided to try to make a full-time living at coaching. The problem was that profession didn't really exist yet, at least, not formally or respectably. Football was a launching point into other professions—an Ivy hero could expect to be rewarded with a position in the New York financial markets. But football was not a job in itself.

It had long been the accepted system at Ivy League schools for football to be overseen by graduate or undergraduate committees, such as the one Woodrow "Tommy" Wilson served on at Princeton in 1879. The amateur sensibility of the era was so strong that overt coaching on the sidelines was expressly forbidden.[12]

But by the mid-1890s, there was a movement toward specialized leadership. In 1891, Amos Alonzo Stagg was hired at the University of Chicago, for a professor's salary. In 1893, a Harvard captain named J. H. Sears wrote an article for *Harper's Weekly* entitled "Modern

Coaching of Modern Football," in which he argued that football had become too complex to be handled by undergrads: "The game of American football, as time goes on, is coming to represent more of science, of skill, of careful forethought, and theoretic and practical study, than any other American game." Players needed a detached, mature adult to tutor them in this sporting equivalent of calculus, Sears asserted, offering as evidence the fact that teams required blackboards.

The notion of paying coaches, however, was still controversial. Even Sears maintained that football must remain free of "the professional element." This led to a laughable charade.[13]

At Yale, Camp had become widely acknowledged as "general chief" of the football program, overseeing a small army of alum advisors. But he presided over the practices at Yale under the guise of casual recreational advisor. Camp worked as an executive at the New Haven Clock Company, but every afternoon he somehow found time to wander over to the Yale practice field. Camp would slip in unobtrusively through a back door of the locker room, "exactly as though he had wandered in by mistake and was surprised to find an entire football eleven occupying the premises," the journalist Richard Harding Davis mockingly observed in *Harper's Weekly*. "He stood modestly out of sight and suggested . . . quite as though it was a matter of which he could not be expected to know much, that the ends seemed to him to be bending back in a half circle and that as this tended to shut in rather than assist the backs, it would be perhaps a good thing if . . ."[14]

But Warner had no such self-consciousness. In 1895, he abandoned the law in order to coach not one but two teams for pay. Western schools had begun to look to easterners to teach them the game, and some of those schools for the first time offered salaries. Warner received an offer from Iowa State (then called Iowa Agricultural College) of a flat fee of $150 for five weeks of work. Meanwhile, the University of Georgia offered him $34 a week for the entire season. Warner accepted both; he would coach Iowa State in the preseason, and Georgia in the regular season.

Warner went west, where once again his "youthful gambling spirit" ran rampant. He accepted an offer for a money game between his Iowa State team and a squad of all-stars in Butte, Montana. Butte, he found, was "one of the wildest, wide open roughneck sporting towns in the United States." Mining went on twenty-four hours a day, and the saloons were open around the clock. The town never closed.

Warner bet his entire salary that Iowa State could beat the local team, made up of miners and roustabouts. But once again, he failed to take a crucial factor into account: the home field advantage. "My judgment regarding the athletic ability of both teams was sound," Warner maintained. "However, I had not figured on the condition of the Butte playing field, the officials, and several other distractions."[15]

Instead of a sward, the game was played on a patch of bare earth; the fumes from the ore smelters in town were so toxic they prevented anything from growing. The hometown cheerleaders were a cadre of whiskey-breathed, bearded men with gun belts at their waists, who celebrated every gain by Butte with fusillades from their six-shooters.

"By way of soothing our nerves still more," Warner related, "we found that the referee didn't mean to let us win." When Warner's team threatened to score, the ref blew the whistle and called the play back. Finally, Warner threatened to withdraw his squad from the field. The official calmly informed him that if he did, he would forfeit their appearance fee, including their train fare home. Iowa State went down to defeat, 13-10. From then on, Warner "always made sure I knew a lot more about my competition before betting on one of my teams."[16]

At Iowa State and Georgia, Warner helped to establish his new profession. He and a small handful of other pioneers, working in the West free of the conventions of eastern football, began to extemporize and experiment with different methods. Men such as Warner, Amos Alonzo Stagg at the University of Chicago, and John Heisman at Auburn University collectively devised many of the recognizable features of the modern game. Heisman was responsible for the center snap—previously the ball was rolled along the ground—as well as the audible "hike" signal and the scoreboard. Stagg put numbers on players' jerseys and fooled the opposition with ruses such as the fake punt; he also invented the baseball batting cage. Warner toyed with the spiral, the screen pass, and the tackling dummy.

Warner also experimented with fitness, diet, training, and motivational techniques. He rousted the Bulldogs at 6 A.M. for five-mile runs, and locked them in their dormitory at night. He was an authoritarian who backed up his words with physical force, and he was still fit enough to scrimmage with the Bulldogs, though he gave it up when he broke the collarbone of one of his own players. He shouted, swore, and made a sarcastic example out of his star runner, who liked to draw attention to himself by feigning injury whenever female undergraduates watched practice.

"Wait a minute," Warner said. "Don't you see that we are over near the girls? Give the ball to our good-looking halfback. It's time for him to break his leg again."

In his second year at Georgia, Warner transformed the Bulldogs into an unbeaten 4-0 team, and his success was noticed at Cornell. At the end of the season, his alma mater invited him back, offering a stipend of $800. Warner accepted. He kept the Iowa State job, however, commuting to Ames each summer for five years.

But the job of coach was still aggravatingly undefined at Cornell. Alumni tended to meddle in the affairs of the team and offer unsolicited advice. Warner was frustrated by the interference, and by his lack of control over his players. On game day, the most helpless man on the field was the head coach, forbidden to do anything but stand on the sideline and watch with his hands in his pockets as players called their own signals, and often thought they knew better than he did. After a loss to Princeton, when his quarterback countermanded his orders, Warner was so frustrated that he locked himself in a dressing room and wept.

In two seasons as Cornell's head coach, Warner went 15-5-1. But he feuded with his own players, assistant coaches, and alumni. By the end of 1898, he and his alma mater were mutually discontented, and he looked elsewhere for a job.

When Warner received an overture from Pratt to become the athletic director at Carlisle, he was intrigued. Cornell had beaten Carlisle that season, 23-6, but Warner saw enough in the Indian players to believe he could win with them. To make matters more inviting, Pratt offered him $1,200, an almost unheard-of amount for a coach.

Warner accepted, but not just because of the money. "The Indian boys appealed to my football imagination," he said. As it turned out, it was a meeting of minds.

ON A September day in 1899, Warner stood on Carlisle's practice field and scrutinized a collection of rail-thin and less-than-animated players. His first impression of his new team made his heart drop into his shoes. They were "listless and scrawny, many looking as if they had been drawn through a knothole," he remembered. After practice, Warner went straight to Pratt's office.

"The squad ought to be trying for beds in a hospital rather than places on the football team," he complained.

Pratt smiled and explained that the boys had just returned from doing hard labor as part of the Carlisle "outing" program. "They have been on farms all summer," Pratt said, "and these Pennsylvania farmers insist on getting their money's worth. The youngsters will soon begin to pick up weight, so don't worry."[17] But it was an empty promise. Over the next thirteen years, Warner would have just one Carlisle team that averaged more than 170 pounds per player.

The first practices went slowly. A number of the players didn't speak English, and when Warner wanted them to do something, he had to point with his cigarette and gesture. In addition to the language barrier, there were other difficulties and misunderstandings. On his arrival at Carlisle, Warner admitted later, "I had all the prejudices of the average white." Among them was the idea that Indians were lazy. "Back in the days when Daniel Boone was my hero, I used to read that Indians always quit if they didn't win a fight at the very outset," Warner admitted.[18]

The Indians understood enough English to know profanity when they heard it. Warner was an incorrigible cusser, and the field rang with his invective and insults. "Having been coached by some rather hard boiled gents during my days as a player, I took a fairly extensive vocabulary with me to Carlisle, and made full use of it," Warner recalled.[19]

The Indians were so offended by the verbal abuse that after absorbing a few days of it, some of the best players abruptly turned in their practice suits. Warner, alarmed, convened a team meeting and apologized with all the sincerity he could muster. "I told them that I meant nothing personal toward them by my outrages of profanity and swearing at them and that this was being done simply to impress certain things more forcibly upon them," Warner remembered. "I then concluded our meeting by telling them that in the future I would tone down my swearing and cussing at them."[20]

Gradually, coach and players got better acquainted with each other. The Indians had a mordant locker room wit that Warner began to enjoy. They gave each other acerbic Indian nicknames. One boy was Running Nose. Another, who a habit of eating pie with his knife, was known as Sword Swallower. Still another was Heap Big Talk.

Each month, in keeping with school policy, the players wrote home, and it was Warner's job to supervise and inspect their letters. He read their missives curiously, and some of them made such an impression on him that he kept copies.

One boy, a scrub, wrote to his mother:

> I have been played in football. I played on second team here at Carlisle. I used to play at left halfback and could do better there but they put in the right end I have a hard time trying to ketch who got the ball, but sometimes I get a chance to ketch him. Sometimes I have to throw myself down when they come around on my side and they all fall on top of me. But as school book say, genius capacity for taking infinite pain.

Another wrote:

> We had a hard time playing football last Saturday. We play with Quaker team at Philadelphia. They were pretty good play and heap much bigger but we beat him anyhow us Indian boy side. We too slick for him. Maybe white men better with cannon and guns but Indian just as good in brains to think with.[21]

As Warner got to know his players, he found he had something in common with them: audacity. Warner was brimming with fresh theories, and the Indians were open to the most experimental of them. Best of all, Warner was pleased to note, they were fast and observant learners. No sooner would he draw something up on a piece of paper than the players made his pencil marks come alive on the field. He only had to show them something once, and they would do it. "After a week or so of keen-eyed watching, with every movement noted and observed, these beginners would turn and do the thing as though they had been trained to do it their whole lives," he remarked.[22]

Since the Indians lacked size, they would by necessity have to be a team of deception and quickness. Warner began to think about new techniques to emphasize their speed and agility over strength. He invented the body block: the standard method of blocking was with the shoulder, but Warner taught the flyweight Indians to leave the ground entirely, half rolling as they used the length of their body to cut the opponent down at the knees. When the Indians blocked a man this way, he stayed blocked. Quick, low line charges would become their hallmark, a style so distinctive opponents termed it "Indianizing."

Next, he came up with the crouching start. The normal position for a running back was upright, with his feet apart, hands on knees. But it occurred to Warner that a runner could fire more quickly from a coiled position. He had the Carlisle backs crouch over the ground and push off one or both hands for a faster start.

Carlisle opened the season impressively, with four straight victories. The Indians' low, aggressive line charges frustrated their heavier opponents, who didn't take it well. In the midst of a game, Warner watched from the sidelines as one of his players engaged in an earnest conversation with a referee. When the player jogged off the field, Warner asked, "What was the trouble? What were you saying?"

"Well," the boy explained, "other fellows use much vile language all through the first half and I tell the referee such bad words very distasteful to us Carlisle boys, and we leave the game unless profanity and blasphemy brought to full stop."[23]

But the Indians' sportsmanship was pushed to its limits, Warner found, by the cheap-shot tactics used by some of their opponents, who thought nothing of slugging them viciously. The tall, stolid Bemus Pierce was a favorite mark of the opposition, and calmly withstood all sorts of fouls and mistreatment. "Trying to cripple his two hundred pounds of bone and muscle was about as profitable as smashing a concrete pillar, and for the most part he merely grinned when they bashed him," according to Warner.

One afternoon, however, Pierce had enough. After absorbing three or four punches and gouges from an opposing player, Pierce said, "Do that again and you're going to be sorry." His tone must have been unconvincing, because the player tried it once more. Pierce unfurled a long right hand and felled him with one punch. "When he came to his mates were digging him out of the ground and hunting for stray pieces," Warner remembered.

"Now play clean," Pierce said softly, "or I'll send you to the hospital."[24]

On another occasion, Pierce laid out an opponent, and as he stood over him, he politely informed him, "White man hit Indian ten times. Indian hit paleface once. We're quits."[25]

On October 14, 1899, Carlisle met Pennsylvania, a team that featured three all-Americans, including a future Hall of Fame guard named Truxton Hare. Penn had beaten Carlisle by an average of 24 points in their previous meetings, but the heavier Quakers weren't prepared for the speed with which these Warner-coached Indians jumped off the lines.

A signal would be called, and before the Quakers could react, the Indians would lunge. Frank Hudson gave Carlisle a 5-0 lead with an elegant drop kick between the uprights, and the Indians never trailed on their way to a 16-5 victory. It was the first time they had ever beaten a member of the Big Four.[26]

Carlisle went on to an 8-2 season, their only losses coming to the number one and two teams in the country, Princeton and Harvard, respectively. Before the Harvard kickoff, the Indians suffered a boorish display by a Crimson secret society called the Dickey, which ran on the field and gave a mocking dance in Indian costumes. The Indians replied by throwing the biggest scare of the season into the Crimson, taking a 10-0 lead at halftime. After that, "The Crimson players quit looking bored," Warner reflected. But Carlisle lost, 22-10.[27]

On Thanksgiving Day, Carlisle met Columbia at the Polo Grounds and set out "to prove to the patronizing sportswriters that [Carlisle] wasn't a fluke," Warner said. The Indians put on a virtuoso exhibition of their new techniques and formations, including a baffling new line shift they employed for the first time: the entire team moved to one side of the center. On a signal, the unbalanced line surged forward, followed by a ball carrier.

Carlisle's Isaac Seneca vaulted out of his crouched, three-point stance, ripping off gains of twenty-five and thirty yards. He scored twice, while Hudson kicked four goals. The final score was 42-0, and Columbia's players retreated to their dressing room with shame written all over their faces.

The Indians were rewarded with a number four national ranking from no less an eminence than Walter Camp. In addition, Camp named Isaac Seneca a first-team all-American at running back, the only man on the squad who didn't attend one of the major Ivy schools. Martin Wheelock was a second-teamer at tackle, and Hudson a third-teamer at quarterback. It was as much honor as Warner could hope for.

But the Indians weren't finished playing yet. Another postseason invitation came in: the best team in the West was the University of California, unbeaten at 7-0-1. Cal's manager, Jerry Muma, was tired of hearing how superior eastern football was, and he invited Carlisle to play Cal in an East-West matchup in San Francisco on Christmas Day.

Carlisle accepted. It would be another first—the record for the farthest a team had yet traveled to play a football game. The boys would lose time from school, but the education they received from traveling would be worth it, Pratt believed. He instructed Warner to make sure that the players were energetic sightseers, and prepared reports on their travels to deliver to the student body when they returned.

On the train trip to the coast, Warner kept the players in shape by making them exercise at whistle-stops. One afternoon, Warner sat on a bench outside a station, watching the boys throw a ball around in their red sweaters with the monogrammed old-gold letters. A whiskered citizen paused to ask who they were and where they were going. Warner explained that they were headed to San Francisco to play the mighty Californians.

"Well, they are going a darned long way to get the hell kicked out of them," the old man replied.[28]

Carlisle's willingness to travel anywhere earned the Indians the nickname "Nomads of the Gridiron." Pratt saw an opportunity in such far-flung games: the team was becoming a national ambassador. He included in the travel party Carlisle's medical director, Dr. Carlos Montezuma, a special protégé of his. Montezuma was a Yavapai Apache with an extraordinary story: as a boy he had been captured by Pima Indians and sold to a traveling photographer, who raised him in New York and Chicago. He had received a medical degree from Northwestern and was becoming an influential public lecturer on Indian affairs while working at Carlisle. His main purpose on the trip to California was not to attend to the players but to remind the public that there were larger issues at stake than just football.

Montezuma wrote an editorial in the *San Francisco Examiner* explaining the real mission of the Indian players. "Truly, we are an All American team," he wrote. "We have come to the Pacific Coast not to exhibit our so-called savagery nor to show the so-called physical powers of the Indian, but for a nobler and higher purpose, to demonstrate what education means to the Indians when given under the same conditions and with the same environment enjoyed by the white boy."

The real motive of the Carlisle football team, Montezuma averred, was nothing less than "a determination to contradict misconceptions of centuries . . . though it must be done by use of the pigskin."[29]

On Christmas Day, fifteen thousand fans came to San Francisco's Sixteenth and Folsom Streets field simply to watch a game, one intriguingly billed as the "East-West Championship." Unfortunately, the westerners had gone to extreme lengths to secure their home field advantage: they had covered it with slow, thick sand. Next, Cal presented the game ball. It was a weighty, roundish thing that looked like a large squash. Between the sand and the heavy ball, Cal meant to negate the Indians' speed and Hudson's dropkicks. Warner and the Indians protested, but as the visitors, they had no choice but to accept. The players nicknamed the ball "the California pumpkin."[30]

All afternoon, they crawled through the sand. Hudson missed every kick he tried, and finally retired with a sore leg. The Indians scored just once—on a safety. But they proved to be the only points for either side in the boggy sand, and Carlisle won its ninth and final game of the season, 2-0.[31]

As the Indians made their way home via the rails, they stopped to visit other Indian academies. Carlisle's influence had resulted in a burgeoning of off-reservation schools. (By 1902, there were twenty-four similar institutions across the country, campuses that teemed with 21,568 Indian students.) One of them was the Haskell Institute, a school in Lawrence, Kansas, a set of gray stone buildings with a similar military-industrial curriculum.[32]

On January 12, Carlisle visited Haskell, where the student body turned out for a dress parade and a breakfast in their honor. Among the students in the dining hall, there was one boy who gazed with particular awe at Bemus Pierce and the famous all-Americans Seneca, Wheelock, and Hudson.

He was a woebegone, hooded-eyed boy, and he was infected with the football craze that had taken over the Haskell campus. Boys played it in their work jeans and boots, chasing a homemade ball, a stocking stuffed with grass and tied at both ends. Among the most dedicated was the twelve-year-old Jim Thorpe.[33]

By THE fall of 1900, Pratt was growing weary. Carlisle was an immensely needful institution of 1,218 students from seventy-six tribes, some of whom behaved tiresomely, as boarding students will. Pratt was sixty years old, and the constant care of so many pupils and the maintenance of such a large campus would strain any man's abilities, much less those of an aging one. His correspondence that autumn reflects his fatigue.

Six pupils died, five from tuberculosis and one from pneumonia. Several pairs of uniform trousers had to be burned because they were exposed to diphtheria.

Enormous amounts of supplies had to be ordered to keep the school running efficiently and cleanly. The laundry was an industrial-sized operation powered by electric motors, a constant tumbling of washers and centrifugal wringers that consumed 1,400 pounds of liquid soap, 600 pounds of starch, and 14,000 pounds of laundry soap a year.

In the kitchens, student cooks stirred huge pots full of cereals and stews. Just to start the term, Pratt ordered 5,000 pounds of bacon, 9,000 pounds of beans, 190,000 pounds of beef, 180,000 pounds of flour, 4,000 pounds of hominy, 6,000 pounds of rolled oats, and 14,000 pounds of dried fruit.

Clothing wore out quickly. Students went through 800 pairs of overalls, 100 girls' coats, 600 boys' undershirts, and 60 dozen men's collars.

Boilers broke and steam drums needed maintenance.

Seven hundred and seventy-five desks needed refinishing. Two hundred and fifty mattresses and pillows were moth-eaten and had to be replaced. Textbooks became tattered: he ordered new copies of *Higgins' Young Folks History of the United States* and *Fry's Complete Geographies.*[34]

Then there were the supplies needed for the trade shops: 2,000 tons of soft coal, 400 pounds of nails, 60 pounds of rivets, 300 gallons of linseed oil, 10,000 feet of white pine boards, and tons of cement, plaster, iron, glass, and tin. Not to mention the braces, drills, vises, caps, nozzles, valves, loops, eyelets, plates, reaches, nuts, shackles, clips, bolts, sockets, poles, props, tips, buckles, bits, bands, screws, shears, shovels, steps, and springs he had to remember to order.

He was swamped by correspondence. The government pestered him for paperwork on the smallest matters, down to the feed for his cavalry horses. Letters came in from tradesmen seeking payment. Concerned or unhappy parents wrote, begging for children to be sent home, while reservation agents pestered him to accept more students.

Students pulled pranks, and they broke rules. They got sick, and sometimes they got pregnant. They drank, smoked, and ran away.

Boys went to a local market and bought bottles of vanilla extract, which was 75 percent alcohol, to try to get a high. The town was full of taverns, and barkeeps ignored Pratt's edict not to sell drinks to students. Pratt's method of dealing with these pupils was a stint in the old stone guardhouse on a diet of bread and water. Passers-by could sometimes hear the moans coming from inside.[35]

One night, a party of incorrigibles went on a soused rampage. They got hold of some firearms, which they took to the athletic field, where they engaged in some "Wild West shooting." When school disciplinarian W. G. Thompson appeared, they drunkenly threatened to kill him.

Pratt may have been aging, but he was still a fearsome figure with a physique of 230 pounds. The physician Charles Eastman and his wife, Elaine Goodale Eastman, were residing at Carlisle that year, and watched from the teachers' balcony as Pratt dealt forcefully with the affair. He mustered the student officers into a brigade, overcame the intoxicated hoodlums, and physically hauled them away to the guardhouse. "They were too limp to use their feet but they still could swear," Goodale Eastman recalled. They carried on their riot behind the guardhouse walls.[36]

The stress told on Pratt. For relief, he snuck cigarettes. Sometimes, when he was in Philadelphia on business, he slipped off to indulge a secret taste for burlesque. He frequented Carnacross and Dixie's nightly minstrel performances, shouting with laughter.[37]

It was no wonder Pratt sometimes felt like playing hooky. Runaways were another constant problem at the school. In 1901, forty-five boys deserted the campus and had to be chased down.[38] Once, two boys made it as far as Ohio before Pratt had them picked up and returned. When they arrived back at campus, the boys were brought to his office.

"James, what made you run away?" he asked one of them.

The boy's lip quivered. "I didn't get enough to eat."

Pratt turned to the other boy. "John what made you run away?"

"I just wanted you to know I wasn't stuck on your durned old school!"

"I am not greatly stuck on it myself," Pratt replied wearily. "I have been here much longer than you and am perhaps more tired of it than you are, but the Government says I must stay and makes it my duty to keep you here until you know enough to be of some use. I shall have to stick to it and hold onto you until you graduate. Both of you report to the disciplinarian. Clean up and begin where you left off."[39]

Yet, after nearly a quarter of a century as Carlisle's superintendent, Pratt managed to retain a warmth and sympathy for his students. Elaine Goodale Eastman recalled Pratt's care for a young student who faltered during the performance of a voice solo at Carlisle's 1900 commencement ceremony. The gymnasium was packed with three thousand spectators, and the boy, overwhelmed by the occasion, stood silent. Pratt went to the reticent singer, took his hand, and stood holding it until the reassured boy began to sing "with a voice of uncanny beauty," according to Goodale-Eastman—a sound made all the more affecting by the presence of the craggy, uniformed man at his side.[40]

Pratt never tired of his students. Rather, what wore him down was bureaucracy. He found a single political meddler more difficult to deal with than the most incorrigible students. "I can handle my school and its affairs after a fashion but my Board of Trustees are quite beyond my capacity," he once remarked.[41]

He chafed at oversight from, and railed at, the inefficiency of the Bureau of Indian Affairs. Supplies he requisitioned from the government were invariably late in coming or didn't arrive at all. On September 13, 1900, he wrote to the commissioner, irate that twenty-one thousand pounds of freight he needed to begin the school term was six weeks late. Among the items badly lacking were suspenders. Pratt had ordered a thousand pairs. Just two hundred were delivered.

To a certain extent, Pratt was becoming worn out by his own disposition. As early as 1885, he despaired of his ability to tolerate the foolishness of his superiors. "If we continue to move on this mountain of ignorance like a headless rabble it will continue to laugh at and baffle us. . . . I am getting quite uncertain of my own stick-to-it, if weakness and ignorance is to manage for us much longer," he wrote in a letter to a friend.[42]

Chronic bigotry and dismissive politicians frustrated him. The notion of Indian intellectual equality was still far from accepted: in 1897, the incoming superintendent of Indian schools, Estelle Reel, all but declared Indian pupils inferior and urged deemphasis of academics at the government schools. The *Washington Post* summarized her beliefs:

> The boys should be taught stock-raising and farming . . . and given a sufficient knowledge of tools to enable them to mend their wagons and farm implements and shoe their horses, and the girls should be trained in the art of practical housekeeping. There was no point, Reel said, in educating the Indian in subjects "for which, in all probability, he will have no use in later life."[43]

Political opponents continually charged that Carlisle was a waste of funds and questioned its effectiveness. On one occasion, a senator berated Pratt as a "swindler" and called Carlisle a "farce" and "twaddle."[44]

Pratt found criticism of Carlisle intolerable. He was susceptible to feelings of persecution, and believed that some of his more unruly pupils were sent to Carlisle by agents seeking to harm the school. He obsessively catalogued negative or false stories in the press, and counted no fewer than twenty erroneous reports about Carlisle students over five years. "There has seemed to be a syndicate of fabricators, moved by a common purpose to disparage results and manufacture prejudice," he asserted. When the *Philadelphia North American* printed a false potboiler that alleged a Carlisle student named White Buffalo had committed a triple murder, Pratt sued for criminal libel, and won a correction.[45]

Pratt grew increasingly irascible, and bickered with his superiors over petty issues. At times, he almost *tried* to be fired. He wrote to a friend at one point, "I cannot quit of myself, and I seem unable to make the other fellows kick me out."[46]

He made a fatal enemy of the ambitious young Theodore Roosevelt. Between 1889 and 1895, Roosevelt had labored as a Civil Service commissioner to create a merit system to replace the old system of political spoils. But Pratt belittled the Civil Service as "a bundle of inefficiency and hindrance." He was downright insubordinate on the subject, flatly refusing to let the Indian office tell him whom to hire, "knowing that it might lead to a court martial and thus give me a chance to expose the rottenness of the Civil Service methods."

Pratt added, "There is no more conspicuous and inveterate office seeker in the country than Teddy Roosevelt."[47] But in 1899, the inveterate office seeker became the hero of San Juan Heights, and in 1900, he rose to the vice presidency under McKinley.

The tension between Pratt and Roosevelt may have been personal. Both men were autocratic and hugely energetic, but they were also dead opposites. Pratt was the strapping son of a proletarian; Roosevelt was a privileged, striving heir. Pratt spent eight years in the West in a cavalry saddle; Roosevelt ranched as a hobby on western jaunts. Pratt was a lifelong soldier who fought gallantly in two wars; Roosevelt spent one valorous week in a uniform tailored by Brooks Brothers. When Roosevelt led the Rough Riders up Kettle Hill, Pratt's old unit, the Tenth Cavalry, aided him. Pratt may have felt Roosevelt never gave the Tenth proper credit. Roosevelt, on the other hand, may have felt Pratt should have served with his unit.

Pratt's military colleagues continued to resent his absence from active duty, especially as the Tenth saw action in Cuba during the Spanish-American War and then in the Philippines. A letter from the Secretary of War to the Interior on June 7, 1901, remarked that Pratt had been on detached service for twenty-three years and eight months, "a length of service away from troops quite unprecedented in the history of the Army." The officer insisted Pratt was needed with his regiment and asked whether "you cannot now arrange to dispense with his further services at the Indian School at Carlisle."

But W. A. Jones, the commissioner of Indian affairs, replied to the Secretary of War that Carlisle and Pratt were inseparable. "It is the creation of Colonel Pratt and he has stamped his individuality upon every branch of it to such an extent that it has become practically a part of himself and himself a part of the school."[48]

Somehow, Pratt kept his job, surviving the reformers, meddlers, commissioners, cabinet officers, and his own frustrations. By the turn of the century, he was something of an eminence, capable of cowing his critics. He had cultivated a number of wealthy patrons, and been twice promoted. As he aged, he tended toward hauteur. Pratt would ride into Carlisle in a phaeton with a two-horse team and a driver wearing a blue coat and a high silk hat. He would purposely stop at a busy corner on High Street, where he could be seen by the most prominent townspeople, who would gather around the carriage eager for his conversation.[49]

Among those who watched Pratt go to and fro was a well-bred town girl named Marianne Moore, who would grow up to teach at Carlisle before she became one of America's leading poets. Moore remembered, "Both General Pratt and his wife were very substantial and imposing. They were romantic figures, always dashing up with their horse and carriage, and they were intelligent and cultural. But General Pratt was so monumental no one could dare approach him to tell him one approved of the work he was doing."[50]

In Roosevelt, however, Pratt encountered someone more monumental than he. With the assassination of McKinley in September of 1901, Roosevelt became president, and Pratt suddenly found himself at the mercy of the inveterate officer seeker.

As the new century began, political sentiment was turning hard against off-reservation schools. In 1901, the commissioner of Indian affairs claimed in his annual report that despite $40 million spent to educate Indian youths, the average Indian "is little, if any, nearer the goal of independence than he was 30 years ago." Roosevelt, though socially conscious, was a firm believer in the superiority of his race and the weakness of all others, and seems to have regarded American Indians primarily as artifacts to be collected and preserved.[51]

Pratt scrambled to work his way into the good graces of the new administration. On October 11, 1901, he wrote the new president an earnest five-and-a-half-page disquisition on all that needed to be done in Indian affairs, and Carlisle's critical role. Above all, he wrote, the Indian must be absorbed "far more speedily" into society. He closed with a personal note, saying, "I believe in your Strenuous Life."

Roosevelt didn't respond. Instead, Pratt received an impersonal index-sized card from an aide, acknowledging receipt of the letter.[52] It was the first of a series of snubs. When the young president and the aging officer finally met in person and spoke about Carlisle, it wasn't the sort of conversation Pratt had in mind.

Instead, Roosevelt greeted him by saying, "Hello Pratt! How's football?"[53]

Pratt was deeply offended. Over a span of twenty-five years, including his frontier years, he had served under seven previous commanders in chief: Grant, Rutherford Hayes, James Garfield, Chester Arthur, Grover Cleveland, Benjamin Harrison, Cleveland again, and William McKinley. All of them had at least pretended to listen politely to his ideas. But this cocksure, bawling man, who boasted that Kettle Hill was a "bully fight," had no use for his opinions.

Pratt's son-in-law, Dr. Robert McCombs, remembered, "When a man's whole life has been passionately devoted to a great idea, that sort of treatment hurts." And when a man had spent as much time in Washington as Pratt had, he recognized the insult for what it was. His days were numbered under Roosevelt.[54]

8

DODGES AND DECEPTIONS

F OOTBALL AND CARLISLE had become indivisible. A fifteen-
year-old new boy named Albert Exendine was summoned to
meet Pratt and stood at attention as the superintendent looked
him up and down. "Ex," as his friends called him, was a promising six
feet and 160 pounds. Pratt said, "Do you play football, baseball?"

Exendine replied that he played some baseball but he didn't really
know about football.

"You'll learn, you'll learn," Pratt said.[1]

Exendine had never so much as held an oval ball before arriving on
campus, but it seemed that every male student at Carlisle was required
to play some form of the game. The message of "team" seemed inextri-
cably bound up with the school's jingo tribal-smashing mission. Ex
attended an assembly for new students, and seventy years later, he
could still recall the stentorian words of the school founder: "Remember this," Pratt said. "You are no longer Comanche, Kiowa, Sioux or
Apache—you are of one student body. You are Carlisle Indians."[2]

The campus boiled with competitive energy. The old intramural
system flourished, and in addition, Pop Warner had instituted an
ambitious junior varsity nicknamed the Hotshots. The field house
and gymnasium were hives of constant training: athletes hefted

dumbbells, pulled on rowing machines, or scrimmaged in the grass. The routine of work, study, and football was underscored each week by Pratt's ringing addresses. "Begin immediately . . . take hold of the work that lies next you . . . work for all you can get but WORK," he said. "Work for nothing rather than not work."[3] Or, "My son, observe the postage stamp. Its usefulness depends upon its ability to stick to one thing until it gets there."[4]

Exendine was ripe for the Carlisle doctrine. To him, the school provided a doorway, offering opportunity and an exit. Ex was yet another product of allotment, born in 1884 in a remote northern corner of Indian Territory to a stern, diligent Cherokee, William Jasper Exendine, and his wife, Amaline, a Delaware. The Exendine ranch lay in the rolling, thickly wooded country close to the Kansas border, near what is now Bartlesville, Oklahoma, a place so isolated there wasn't a neighbor for ten miles.[5] But with allotment in 1890, the Exendines moved south to Anadarko to take up a 160-acre plot, on which they had to support six children. In his boyhood, Anadarko was barely yet a town, just a tented city in a cornfield with stacks of raw lumber and half-built structures on the edge of the Kiowa, Comanche, and Apache reservation. His father was resourceful, opening a general store and a post office. He even did a stint as a deputy marshal.[6]

Exendine was in school at the local Presbyterian mission one afternoon when he saw a poster that announced, "Students Wanted for Carlisle School." But Ex was too afraid of his imposing father to ask for permission to go, and he found himself working unhappily in a hayfield when his best friend, a Cheyenne named Joe Tremp, came by in a buggy to say goodbye, en route to Carlisle. Ex enviously told Tremp to write. He would show the letters to his father and hope to win him over that way.

It took a few months for Exendine to overcome his father's reluctance—five years seemed too long a time to send away a son. But just before the century turned, he won his father's consent and boarded a train for Carlisle. It was his first excursion outside of Indian Territory, and as the rail car passed through Kansas City, he stared at a handsome three-story house with a hog in the front yard, tied to a chain and grazing on the lawn. It was as though wilderness and society met right there. Ex wondered what the dwellers in those tall brick homes did for a living, and it struck him that Indians had formerly "owned, hunted, and stomp danced on that very ground." He told himself, "This is civilization, and the way Indians must learn to live." But he wondered if they would. "I was going to find out at Carlisle," he remembered.[7]

On arriving in Carlisle, Exendine caught a streetcar to the gates of the school. As he walked into the boys' dorm, a smartly dressed officer asked him, "New student?" Ex replied yes, and asked if Joe Tremp was around. The officer called upstairs, "Joe, some fellow from Oklahoma to see you!" Ex could hear Joe's feet hit the floor and thump down the stairs. Joe took Exendine upstairs and taught him his first marching steps and bugle commands.

Exendine was too self-conscious to try out for varsity football in his first year. Instead, he played intramurals, first for the bakers' team, as Ben American Horse once had, and then for the blacksmiths. He was a well-built athlete but a crude one, and intramural coaches kept hollering at him, "Get down! Get lower!"

He enrolled in the outing program and spent a summer digging potatoes for a wealthy farmer. A group of Princeton professors came up to help harvest, and Exendine listened, fascinated, as they discussed immigration laws. His intellect was fired, and he joined the debate society and decided to be a lawyer. He developed a more confident demeanor, one that seemed bookish and manly at the same time, with a habit of standing with his hands clasped behind his back.

In August, Exendine mustered the confidence to approach Warner and ask if he could try out for the varsity. The coach regarded him brusquely.

"How much do you weigh?"

When Exendine told him he weighed 165 pounds, Warner replied, "You should have come out last year."

Warner turned Exendine over to his beefy younger brother Bill, a captain at Cornell, who had volunteered to help to coach the Indians. Bill weighed 270 pounds, and the first time Exendine tried to block him, he got thrown over backward. But Exendine rose from the ground and went at the big collegian again. He charged, over and over under the hot sun, until, slowly, he began to move the larger man with his shoulder.

When they finished, both men were soaked in sweat. Bill walked over and said something quietly to Pop. The next day, Exendine was in uniform.[8]

Carlisle's system of filling football rosters resembled the old British naval system of impressments. The Indians were perennially short-handed, and they had to cull an eleven from just a couple of hundred fit male students, most of whom, like Exendine, had vastly less experience than their collegiate counterparts. Their ranks were so thin that the captain of the 1900 team, a Chippewa from Minnesota named Ed Rogers, had to play three different positions. Harvard, Princeton, or Yale, meanwhile, could pick and choose from enrollments of four thousand to five thousand college men. Mark Twain attended the Yale-Princeton game in the fall of 1900 and observed, "The Yale team could lick a Spanish Army." The author was amazed at the size and bulk of the players, whom he compared to "granite, like the rocks of Connecticut." (It was Twain's first time at a football game, and he was less than enthused by the experience, as he stamped his feet and huddled in his greatcoat to keep warm. "This beats croquet," he pronounced.)[9]

To bolster Carlisle's roster, Pratt and Warner resorted to recruiting. Then, as now, the practice of enrolling students purely for the purpose of playing football was regarded as ethically questionable—and it was also rampant. According to Caspar Whitney, the Columbia team of 1899 was "nothing short of an offense against college sport," with four adult ringers brought in strictly to strengthen the roster, two of whom were in business and one of whom had already played quarterback at Wesleyan as well as coached.[10]

Pratt delicately queried the reservations, looking for likely football candidates. "Have you not a small number of exceptionally good boys and girls to send to Carlisle?" he wrote one agent. "They should be in good health and of good character, and advanced at least to the fourth grade, although I do not make that last a condition. Incidentally, if you should by chance have a sturdy young man anxious for an education who is especially swift of foot or qualified for athletics, send him and help Carlisle compete with the great universities on those lines and to now and then overcome the best."[11]

But the search for players didn't necessarily pay off. John Walletsic, twenty, arrived at Carlisle from Oregon to play fullback in November of 1900. But while Walletsic was an avid athlete—he was also a high jumper on the track team—he was a reluctant pupil who bolted from campus every chance he got. He played just one season at Carlisle before he ran away in the summer of 1901 to join the Ringling Brothers circus. Pratt debated whether to send Warner after him, but finally decided the young man was "not worth the powder."[12] Walletsic went on to become a successful horse wrangler on the rodeo circuit, and it was said he could high-jump five feet even in a pair of boots and chaps. Sadly, he committed suicide by taking strychnine in 1914 after a drinking spree.[13]

Recruiting made the image-conscious Pratt uneasy. He worried that Warner's loose definition of the term "student" could harm Carlisle's reputation, and tried to rein in his coach. The relationship between Pratt and Warner became a tug-of-war: Warner would find players and ask Pratt to admit them, and Pratt would wrestle with his conscience and the best interests of the school.

He wrote to Warner in the summer of 1901, "I believe that in some way we shall be able to make up a good football team without resorting to the duplicity so common in the football field and I want this year to be the abandonment of the system at this school . . . we carry the seeds of failure all the time by resorting to questionable methods of inducing football players to come here especially for football. Within the limits of right, I will give no end of leeway."[14]

On another occasion, he told Warner, "Let our team rest upon the merits of the actual students . . . you will find material here to your liking and can get on with what we have."[15]

But Warner was realistic: Carlisle was not like other colleges or universities. It defied easy classification. It wasn't a university or a college, but a training school with a bastardized academic curriculum that extended only to the rough equivalent of eleventh grade. As late as 1886, Pratt reported that more than half of Carlisle's students had no previous education when they arrived, and only six entered above third grade. They were often in less than robust health, and English was still a second language—a number of the football players spoke it only brokenly.

Most Carlisle pupils didn't "graduate," as the term is conventionally understood. The general age of enrollment was fourteen, and some stayed in school as long as ten or twelve years, depending on their education level. Between 1899 and 1904, Carlisle would issue thirty to forty-five degrees a year, but graduation merely equipped them for entry to a prep school or regular university. Debates about the "eligibility" of its football players were therefore senseless; Carlisle simply wasn't a school like other schools. It was first and last a social experiment.[16]

All that notwithstanding, the Carlisle football teams weren't much different from the teams they faced. The players were in their late teens and early twenties, college-age men. If there was a difference, it was that they played against teams that were invariably bigger, wealthier, better educated, and more privileged.

The Indians' lack of wherewithal led to a losing season in 1901. That November, a small, beat-up squad traveled to Detroit for a forbidding matchup with Michigan's "Point a Minute" team, the sensation of the West, noted for its hectic style under imaginative head coach Fielding "Hurry Up" Yost. As the Indians checked into the Hotel Cadillac, a reporter from the *Detroit Free Press* was taken aback at how young and diminutive they were, "some of them apparently just out of knickerbockers."

When one of the Indians walked to the front desk and began writing a list of names in the register, the clerk looked at him with astonishment.

"You aren't the Carlisle Indians, are you?"

"Yep."

"You aren't a football eleven? Where's your ribbons, and war whoops, and tomahawks?"

According to the *Free Press*, "The Indian just smiled and continued to write in a hand that would be a credit to a bank clerk."

The Indians were so badly depleted by injuries that only four players were starting in their regular positions. "Our team is badly cut up," Warner warned the reporter. When he expressed surprise at their youth, Warner explained. "We are greatly hampered by the age of the students. The average age of students entering the great universities is 18 or 19 years, and our average entrance age is only 16. . . . Then, too, they are absolutely untaught when they arrive. They have to be taught to read in many instances, and when they leave the school, they have not received the education which the average high school scholar has. Of course, this is a big hindrance to them. But they make good players."[17]

The Indians would be even more shorthanded on game day. One of Warner's recruits was a twenty-year-old Stockbridge from Gresham, Wisconsin, named Louis Leroy. But Leroy was only a halfhearted team-mate—he really aspired to baseball's big leagues. Leroy would stroke his arm and tell the other players, "Now this here is a ten thousand dol-lar arm." He had already run off once, jumping off a train in Lancaster, Pennsylvania, in hopes of playing in the local baseball league. Leroy knew Warner would follow him, and sure enough the coach showed up at the clubhouse and asked if an Indian ballplayer had by any chance signed on. No, was the reply, but there was a new Italian pitcher.

Warner knocked on the door of Leroy's room at a nearby boarding-house. "Come along with me kid," he said, pulling Leroy into the hall-way. "You're going back to Carlisle. Your summer play-days are over."[18]

Back at Carlisle, Warner tossed Leroy in the guardhouse. Leroy responded by attacking the guard who brought him his meal. Leroy hit him with the heel of his shoe, broke out of the cell, and tried to hide in a haystack. He spent the rest of the summer in the dank cell, and was finally released in September, just in time for football practice.

Leroy affected remorse and was a steady performer for the Indians at halfback until they reached Detroit, when, at lunchtime on the day of the game, Warner discovered he was missing. Worse, Carlisle's other halfback, Edward DeMarr, another Wisconsin recruit who had enrolled only three months earlier to play football, had gone with him. Carlisle's backfield had deserted on the morning of their biggest game, a fact Warner struggled to explain tactfully to the press. The two had "evidently tired of the discipline," he said.

A beleaguered Warner appealed to Yost to cut the game short, given his lack of players, but Yost refused. Carlisle was manhandled, 22-0, as the Michigan students paid their respects to Carlisle by singing:

One little, two little, three little Injuns
Four little, five little, six little Injuns
Seven little, eight little, nine little Injuns
Leven little Injun boys . . .

We got a—we got a—we got a drubbing
We got a—we got a—we got a drubbing
We got a—we got a—we got a drubbing
We got it in the neck.

The game was distinguished only by the presence of the Chinese ambassador, Wu Ting Fang. Minister Wu was in town to give a speech at the University of Michigan, and he attended the game in blue-hued embroidered silks, a conical cap, and black silk slippers. His escort was a student guide, who gamely tried to explain football to him as he watched the action.

After the first collision on the field, Minister Wu asked, "They are not dead yet?"

"Oh no, see they are getting up again."

"Marvelous tenacity of life. How many sudden deaths would it require to postpone the game?"[19]

Carlisle went on to finish the season with a 5-7-1 record. The following summer, Warner was in upstate New York visiting family when he heard that Leroy was playing baseball for Buffalo in the Eastern League. Warner decided to pay a visit to the young man who had left him in the lurch. Warner strode into the dugout and whacked Leroy on the shoulder. The startled ballplayer drew back.

"Come over here for a minute," Warner said.

"Where to?" Leroy said warily.

"Back to Carlisle," Warner said.

Leroy blanched. But Warner burst out laughing and told him

he was only kidding. He left the young man in the dugout. Leroy actually made it to the majors and played for the New York Highlanders in 1905 and 1906. Warner wished him well, and never saw him again.[20]

To WARNER'S surprise, players seemed to spring all but unbidden from the small, chronically underfed, ordinary-seeming student body. As the Indians continued to make do with what they had, a grudging physical toughness became their hallmark. In 1902, Warner said, "Gameness was a marked characteristic of every Carlisle boy."[21]

A short but stout 165-pound Alaskan named Nikifer Shouchuk fashioned himself into a center. Shouchuk arrived on campus barely able to understand English, and Warner had to make sure he understood the play signals. He summoned Shouchuk and asked him, "Nik, what do you do on 15-25-36?"

"Me run," he said. "Yes siree, Mister Pop. Me run most fast."

Shouchuk wasn't a decorated player, but he managed to hold his own against the best in the country. During a game against Harvard, Crimson captain Carl Marshall berated his own center. "A big fellow like you," he said, "weighing twice as much as that little Indian, and letting him carry you around on his back all afternoon!"[22]

Nobody exemplified toughness more than Exendine, who made the '02 varsity, though he was still learning the game, by bulling his way around the field. "I didn't know what a football was until I went to Carlisle, but I was a mean son of a gun," he remembered. "Those were the days of push, drag and slug football. I would get the ball and just stand there, pumping my knees while other fellows pushed me into the line."[23]

Ex became Carlisle's most reliable and hard-hitting tackler, and he took it personally when an opposing player got by him. One afternoon in practice, he was humiliated when a Carlisle running back named "Bull" Williams ran him over and kneed him in the stomach. Ex said hotly, "Try my side of the line again." Williams obliged. As he dove through the line, Ex stepped aside and delivered a right hand to Williams' face. Williams dropped to the ground, out cold.

That evening after practice Williams knocked at the door of Ex's dormitory room. Ex was sitting in his room, feeling penitent and reading the Bible. A passage said, "Be not hasty in thy spirit to be angry, for anger resteth in the bosom of a fool."

As he opened the door, Ex nervously cocked his hand, half expecting Williams to swing at him. Instead, Williams surprised Ex by extending his hand, and apologized for kneeing him, explaining it wasn't the Carlisle way. The two men shook. Ex was shamed by the encounter and wouldn't strike an opponent again. "It taught me never to slug," he said.[24]

Another of the most rugged Carlisle players that year was Antonio Lubo, a full-blooded Mission Indian who arrived at Carlisle in 1898 and would stay ten years. Lubo was such a physically attacking player that he was nicknamed "The Wolf," and his deceptive good looks cloaked a deep tolerance for pain. He played through the season with only one good arm, after he developed a tubercular condition in his wrist that required surgery to remove a large amount of diseased bone. Lubo refused to quit the team. Instead, he devised a leather protector that covered his arm from fingertip to elbow, and played the entire season without complaint.

That same season, veteran lineman Martin Wheelock came down with pleurisy, just before the Cornell game. Wheelock protested when Warner ordered him to report to the school hospital.

"No, no!" he cried. "Pop, it's nothing at all. I only got a little pleurisy. Please don't keep me out of the game."

"But you can't run, Martin," Warner said.

"Change me from guard to center," Wheelock suggested. "Then I won't have to run."

Carlisle's reserves were so thin that Warner actually did as Wheelock suggested. The game was personally important to Warner, who wanted bragging rights over his younger brother and his alma mater. The night before the game, the two brothers met up, and the younger Warner asked the elder coach how his team was.

"So-so," Pop Warner said, shrugging. "I've got a sick lad at center and a one-armed chap at guard."

"Say," Bill said. "We don't want to play a bunch of cripples."

"Don't worry, old boy," Warner replied. "You'll find 'em lively enough."[25]

The Indians were further motivated by a chance remark they overheard in the hotel lobby the evening before the game. While they milled around, another guest said loudly, "Well, those Indians sure can draw a crowd but they can't play much football."[26]

Cornell learned different. Bill Warner found himself driven into the turf all day by the one-armed Lubo, while the wheezing Wheelock buried the Cornell center and also kicked a crucial goal from the field. The Indians won, 10-6. "The play of the two cripples was the outstanding feature of the game," Warner noted delightedly.

After the game, the young Bill said ruefully to Warner, "Thank the Lord those boys weren't feeling well."[27]

The victory over Cornell was a turning point for Carlisle, which finished the season 8-3. So often, the Indians had come close to beating an Ivy powerhouse, only to wind up on the wrong end of the score. For once, they had a genuine victory to celebrate, not just a moral one. Back at Carlisle, students burst into the streets in their nightshirts and paraded through the town.

An ebullient Pratt addressed the school and took the opportunity to remind them of how far they had come in the public estimation. Had Indians taken to the streets a few years earlier, the residents of Carlisle "would have been badly scared," Pratt said. "The women would have run down . . . and locked the cellar doors and the men would have got their guns ready to shoot." But now, "our friends and neighbors, the white people, join in our rejoicing when we succeed even though those we overcome are of their own race."

In Pratt's view, beating a white team at its own game meant that Carlisle had somehow erased its own Indianness. That was the ultimate goal, to Pratt: for the players to become indistinguishable from their white opponents.

"We put aside Indian thoughts, and Indian ways, Indian dress and Indian speech," Pratt shouted that night. "We DON'T want to hold on to anything INDIAN!"[28]

But Pratt was wrong. The Carlisle players hadn't put aside Indian thoughts, far from it, and neither had anyone else. At the end of the

1902 season, the Indians went to Washington, D.C., for a game against Georgetown. Afterward, they were invited to the White House. Roosevelt was curious to meet them.

The president congratulated them on their record, and chatted about his alma mater, Harvard. Then, Roosevelt did something that must have frustrated Pratt. As each player was introduced to him individually, "the President spoke a pleasant word and asked him about his tribe, or some famous Indian leader," the *Washington Post* reported.[29]

It was impossible to forget who the Carlisle players were and where they had come from. They were named, after all, the Carlisle Indians. Their presence on the football field presented an unmistakable shadow play, for players and spectators alike, of the old frontier battles. Football was a game, of course, not a fight for survival. Nevertheless, it was a fight, and the Carlisle players intended to win.

"On the athletic field where the struggle was man to man, they felt that the Indian had his first even break," Warner observed, "and the record proves they took full advantage of it."[30]

In 1903, Carlisle fashioned a unique solution to its problems. Other teams continued to plow predictably ahead, carrying the ball upfield with bruising strength. But Warner and the Indians decided to do something totally different that season. They became the first team in history to *hide* the ball.

As usual, Carlisle lacked the numbers and the poundage to play the game straight up. In late August, just as Warner was about to return from his vacation to start practice, Pratt wrote with typical bad news. "Arthur Bonnicastle, William Hole in the Day, and George Johnson have run away; Felix Highrock has been sent home on account of consumption and Hiram Runnells has been expelled," Pratt informed him.[31]

Warner resignedly went to work with what was left of his squad. Three of the twenty-four men on the Carlisle team had never even played football before. Fully half the members had only played the game for two or three seasons. On hand to assist, however, was Bemus Pierce, who had returned to campus to serve as Warner's assistant coach.[32]

"There is a great scarcity of heavy material, and indications are that the team will be even lighter in weight than last year," reported the school newspaper, the *Red Man and Helper*, "but there is said to be a good fighting spirit among the candidates and the team may be able to prove the old saying that 'victory is not always to the strong but to the active, the vigilant, and the brave.'"[33]

Carlisle had one great weapon: quarterback and team captain Jimmie Johnson, a team veteran with five years' experience. Johnson was a Stockbridge from Wisconsin who weighed all of 140 pounds, and he looked like a changeling, with a small, triangular, brooding face. He was so slender that his football pants billowed around him. But he had a superb head for strategy, and he not only mastered Warner's schemes and innovations but added to them with his decision making on the field.

The Indians had always favored shifty, quick-firing plays, to neutralize superior force. But now they were more deceptive than ever. Warner installed crisscrosses, feints, and a piece of razzle-dazzle called a double pass: Johnson would turn and toss the ball to a halfback sweeping laterally, who then tossed it back to the quick-footed quarterback. In Johnson's hands, the shifting Carlisle lines looked like a shuffling deck of cards.

As the practices wore on, the Indians strained even Warner's enthusiasm for a ploy. Anything went, so long as there wasn't a rule against it. There was no artifice, con, contrivance, dupe, trap, or double cross the team didn't want to run. Trick plays were what they loved best. "Nothing delighted them more than to outsmart the palefaces," Warner remembered.[34]

One afternoon, just to keep his players interested during a scrimmage, Warner introduced the Indians to a play he had dreamed up as a young Cornell coach. It was called the "hunchback" or "hidden-ball" trick, and it was more of a stunt than a play. There was something about it, in fact, that had a touch of irreverence.

The play required every man on the team to fill a role, and it also required a sewing machine. Warner enlisted the help of Carlisle's tailor, Mose Blumenthal, who owned the men's clothing store in town.

Warner had Blumenthal sew elastic bands into the waists of two or three players' jerseys. Among those he selected was that of Charles Dillon, one of their larger players, a Sioux lineman who stood nearly six feet and weighed 190 pounds. Dillon was a perfect choice for the trick play: although he was a guard in the Carlisle line, he had scathing foot speed, able to run the hundred-yard dash in ten seconds.

Once the jersey was doctored, Warner instructed Dillon to wear the shirt untucked, so the opposition would get used to seeing it that way.

The play was designed for a kickoff. As the ball descended into the arms of quarterback Johnson, the other players would huddle around him, facing outward. Hidden from view, Johnson would slip the ball up the back of Dillon's jersey. It was Exendine's job to pull out Dillon's elastic waist. The huddle would then split apart, leaving the opposing team with no idea where the ball had gone.

The Indians were enraptured by the play and wanted to use it right away. But Warner restrained them: the play was risky, and he wasn't even sure it was entirely legal or sporting. He had only tried it once, in an obscure game between Cornell and Penn State. And the truth was, Warner was a little ashamed to rely on tricks instead of the more conventional power game. "Neither the Indian boys nor myself considered the hidden ball play to be strictly legitimate," he said later.[35]

But Warner believed the play was good for one thing: it would punish any team that took the Indians lightly. And there was one team in particular that had a tendency to do so—Harvard.

Carlisle had developed something of a rivalry with Harvard, and though the Indians had never beaten the Crimson, they always gave them a game. The Indians both admired and resented the Crimson, in equal amounts. They loved to sarcastically mimic the Harvard accent; even players who could barely speak English would drawl the broad Harvard *a*. But Harvard was also the Indians' idea of collegiate perfection, and they labeled any excellent performance, whether on the field or in the classroom, as "Harvard style."[36]

By the time Carlisle checked into the Copley Square Hotel in Boston on October 30, 1902, the team had a 5-1 record and a growing reputation for guile. The Boston correspondent for the *New York World* reported on the eve of the game, "As usual, the Indians will probably spring some startling trick plays upon the Crimson team. . . .

If the Indians once get fairly started . . . there is no telling where they will stop."[37]

But Harvard seemed to view the game as a mere scrimmage. As the Indians lounged in the lobby of the hotel and read the reports in local papers, it was obvious that the Crimson players took a victory for granted. Harvard's committee of graduate coaches seemed far more preoccupied by their next opponents, Columbia and Yale, than by Carlisle, especially a vociferous former Crimson fullback named Percy Haughton, class of '98, who hollered during practice, "Yale will rush you way down the field before you wake up!" What Carlisle might do did not seem to concern him.[38]

On the day of the game, a near-capacity crowd of twelve thousand filled Soldier Field, but the size of the crowd had less to do with Harvard's opponent than it did with the nostalgic occasion: it was the last game scheduled to be played there. The new, thirty-five-thousand-seat Harvard Stadium, a steel-reinforced concrete structure that was the first of its kind, and mammoth for its day, was to open two weeks later—just in time for the Yale game. Soldier Field was to be demolished.

As the Indians warmed up, the stadium hummed with anticipation of an easy victory. The Indians were visibly dwarfed by the Crimson. Their heaviest player was the center Shouchuk at 165 pounds, while two Harvard linemen checked in at 215. The Indians' uniforms even seemed too big for them. Tightly cinched belts held up their baggy knee pants. Heavy flannel pads sewn into their sweaters at the shoulders and elbows, and ribbed socks, added only a little substance to their slight figures.

But as the game began, Johnson directed the Indians in lightning line charges, and the Crimson defense ripped like paper. The Indians constantly shifted and realigned, tossing the ball back and forth. Johnson would fake a run to the outside only to hand the ball to Exendine, coming around from the end. The Indians moved all the way to the Harvard eighteen-yard line, where Johnson kicked a field goal that arced straight through the uprights.

Trick plays worried the Crimson throughout the first half. Johnson bluffed them on punt returns, holding his arms out as if he was going to wait for the ball, only to snatch it out of the air on a dead run. Harvard was scoreless as the first half ended.[39]

Warner was emboldened. In the locker room, as he went over second-half strategy, he called the play his team had been waiting for all season. On the kickoff, he said, run the hunchback trick.

Johnson led the Indians back onto the field. The referee, Mike Thompson, raised his arm and asked the Indians if they were ready. Johnson nodded and glanced at Dillon. The two men dropped back a little deeper than usual, to the five-yard line. A Harvard kicker sent the ball into the air.

Johnson and the rest of the Indians gazed upward and followed the long, lazy flight of the ball. It was a perfect kick.

"Instantly we realized the kick was made to order," Exendine recalled. "We raced back to form a wedge for Jimmie and Dillon."

Johnson gathered the ball in, and the Indians formed a wall in front of the quarterback. Ducking behind the cluster of teammates, Exendine pulled out the back of Dillon's jersey. Johnson slipped the ball beneath it.

Johnson yelled, "Go!"

The Indians scattered. Each player hugged his stomach, as if he held the ball. The Harvard players bore down on them.

As the Crimson slowed, looking for the ball, Dillon ran straight through them and up the field, his arms swinging freely. After thirty yards, Dillon was alone and in the clear.

Johnson, meanwhile, ran for the sidelines with his arms doubled over his midsection, as if he had the ball. A Harvard man launched himself at Johnson, who tripped. As Johnson went down, another Crimson player fell on top of him, and then another, and then another. "I guess the whole Harvard team hit me," Johnson said later. The crowd roared. But Johnson was empty-handed.[40]

Suddenly, a roar swept the stadium. Dillon continued to lope in a straight line toward the opposite goal. The hump beneath his sweater had become obvious. The roar deepened: Dillon was the ball carrier.

While everyone in the stands knew it, not a single Harvard player seemed to realize what was happening. The Crimson were still chasing the Carlisle backs and slamming them to the turf. Carl Marshall, the Harvard team captain, had been playing safety on the kickoff, and as Dillon came toward him, Marshall, thinking he was a blocker, stepped neatly out of the way and let him go by.

Spectators gasped, screamed, and pointed to Dillon as he galloped closer and closer to the end zone. And as the Harvard players still scuttled around wildly, looking for the ball, the crowd began to shriek with laughter.

Finally, Marshall understood what was happening. The Harvard man wheeled and chased vainly after Dillon for the last several yards.

Dillon tumbled across the end line, exhausted. The rest of the Indians raced to join him. Johnson jerked the ball out of Dillon's sweater and triumphantly placed it on the turf for the touchdown. Soldier Field measured 110 yards, and Dillon had just sprinted 103 yards, untouched.

On the Harvard sideline, the players were fuming. Harvard coach John Cranston violently protested to Thompson, the official. But Warner had taken the precaution of warning Thompson that his team might attempt the play, and the referee had watched carefully as it unfolded. He signaled a touchdown.

A celebration erupted on the Carlisle sideline. The Indians had just outwitted and embarrassed the foremost university in the country— Carlisle style—and taken an 11-0 lead. "I don't think any one thing ever gave them greater joy," Warner said later.[41]

But the game was far from over. The Crimson were incensed, and the game from then on was a mauling. Time after time, the measuring sticks were called for. Harvard's superior depth and size began to tell. The Indians "looked like children against the Harvard giants," Warner remembered.

The Crimson flooded the field with fresh players, while the Indian starters were on the brink of exhaustion. Harvard bulled its way over the line for a touchdown. To Warner, watching helplessly from the sideline, it seemed that "every Indian was out on his feet." Harvard scored again, and went ahead, 12-11.[42]

There was one last chance: Harvard fumbled at its own forty, and Carlisle got the ball. Johnson took over and directed the Indians to the fifteen-yard line, with a few seconds to go. Johnson made one last dash at the center of the line—but he was met by the full force of the

Crimson line and fumbled. Harvard took over as time expired, to preserve the 12-11 victory.[43]

"For once however there was no mourning after a loss," Warner
remembered. The final score only slightly dampened the Indians' joy
over the hidden-ball trick. On the trip home, the players relived the
play over and over again.[44]

The Indians had lost again, but the trick made headlines across the
country. The *New York Times* called it "one of the most spectacular,
unforeseen and unique expedients ever used against a member of the
big four." The *New York World* ran an exhaustive series of follow-up
stories explaining and diagramming the play. "It was decidedly the feature of the game and will undoubtedly give rise to a vast deal of discussion." Which it did—lasting for days. At Harvard, Franklin Delano
Roosevelt, class of '04, the president of the *Crimson* newspaper and
former captain of the freshman team, railed at the embarrassment.[45]

For the first time, the Indians were credited with intelligence. The
Carlisle school paper excerpted praise for them from all over the
country, including this comment from the *Norfolk Landmark:* "More
strategy was displayed by the Indians in this contest than has been
displayed by any of the big four teams this year. The standard of education at Harvard and the rest seems to be falling. Think of the reflection on scholarship when a lot of lightweight Indians make monkeys
of the great leaders at football!"[46]

The *World*'s leading sportswriter was Charles Chadwick, a former
Yale star, who like so many sportswriters had often written patroniz-
ingly of the Indians. In 1899 he declared, "The redskins are always
easily open to a surprise of any kind." Now a repentant Chadwick
joined the admiring chorus: the Indians had not only intellect but wit.

"The poor Indian, so often sized up as deficient in headwork, has
at last earned the right to be considered as something more than a
tireless, clumsy piece of football mechanism," Chadwick wrote. "He
is now to be regarded as a person of craft. He has added his quota to
the history of strategic football. But where, outside of the columns of
the Harvard Lampoon or the Yale Record, would anyone hope to see
such a delightful combination of football with hide and seek, such a
burlesque of strategy put forth in all earnestness?"[47]

But the play was controversial, too, and some football experts were disapproving. Coaches discussed whether the play was permissible. At the University of Chicago, Stagg termed it "parlor magic."[48] Camp decided that while it was clever and technically legal—barely—it was a bad precedent. "Its success is sure to result in imitation unless a rule is passed to cover it," the *World* noted. In fact, it would be outlawed.

As the controversy went on, there was one person at Carlisle for whom the play lost some of its luster: Warner. The head coach became defensive, especially against charges that the play was not real football or somehow not aboveboard. "We have two or three tricks and Dillon's is one," he bridled. "It may not be straight out football but it is strategy that works very well and no rule covers it. . . . There is nothing in the rules to prevent the play."[49]

For Warner, the hidden-ball play was a curiously defining event, one that exposed a fracture in his personality. The trick was the ultimate expression of a rogue and an outsider who took pleasure in mocking Harvard's pretensions. But in the aftermath, a less secure Warner emerged. The gambler in him had an impulse for bending rules, yet the Cornell social climber clearly wanted the regard of the Ivy establishment.

With the hidden-ball trick, Warner struck on a compromised ethic, one that he hoped allowed him to be innovative and respectable at the same time: if a rule didn't exist, then it was impossible to break it. "There is nothing in the rules to prevent it" was his battle cry.

But as the play continued to draw national attention, he grew increasingly self-conscious about it and suggested it was somehow beneath him. "It can hardly be considered varsity football, but I think it is all right for the Indians to use," he said, loftily. "Harvard was caught napping. It's a trick that can only be used every once in a great while and it pleased the Indians to get away with it."[50]

Even thirty years later, Warner was still ambivalent about the play. In a memoir he wrote for *Collier's Weekly*, he said, "We never considered it a strictly legitimate play and only employed it against Harvard as a good joke on the haughty Crimson players." On another occasion later in his life he remarked, "In a way I'm glad that Harvard was able to come back to win because I never liked to win a game on a fluke, although the hidden ball play was within the rules at that time."[51]

But the trick was a significant breakthrough for the Indians, a group of young men with little hope of social acceptance in white America, and within whom there must have dwelled a complicated mix of ambitions and frustrations. It was difficult if not impossible for the Carlisle players to escape the larger, depressing context of Indian affairs. Even if they wanted to, they couldn't. If there was any doubt of that, a tragic event reminded them of their position on the Monday morning after the game.

The same newspaper editions that carried accounts of their escapade also carried a horrifying front-page headline: "Whites in Battle with Indians," the *New York World* reported.[52] A former Carlisle student named Charlie Smith had been ambushed and mortally wounded by a sheriff's posse, at a place called Lightning Creek in Wyoming.

The event roiled the Carlisle campus. Charlie Smith, also known as Eagle Feather or Red Hawk, was a well-regarded, hardworking foreman at the Pine Ridge agency, a "peaceable and useful man." There is at least one indication that he may have played football at Carlisle from 1899 to 1900. The *Washington Post* of November 4, 1903, identified the leader of the Sioux party as "Eagle Feather, who . . . is a highly intelligent Indian, a graduate of Carlisle College, where he played on the football team."[53]

Smith and another former Carlisle student, a blacksmith named William Brown, along with their wives and several friends, had left Pine Ridge to go on a hunting trip in the last week of October. The party of nine men and a dozen women and children was traveling home along Lightning Creek, near Gillette, Wyoming, when a county sheriff named W. H. Miller and his posse accosted them and tried to arrest them on phony charges of violating game laws, probably in order to strip their wagons of meat and gear. Smith, the leader of the party, had been careful to observe all laws and was having none of it. "I know your duty as well as you do, and what they expect of you, but you can't take me," Smith told Miller.

The next day, the sheriff and his men opened fire from a grove of trees, cutting down a boy named Peter White Elk. The Sioux fought back, and in the firefight, Miller was killed and a deputy was wounded. Six Sioux were slain, including Smith, who was shot through the knees while running for his rifle, and bled to death. His wife was shot through the chest.[54]

Wyoming governor Fenimore Chatterton declared the shooting a hostile uprising and tried to put the Sioux on trial for murder. But the agent at Pine Ridge, Major J. R. Brennan, intervened and demanded a U.S. attorney be sent out to protect the rights of the accused. At a hearing, the charges were dismissed for lack of evidence, much to Chatterton's ire.[55]

The emotions of the football players on the subject of Lightning Creek aren't recorded, but it consumed the school newspaper into December, and the reaction of one former student, Clarence Three Stars, was well documented, and probably reflective of the rest of the Carlisle community. Clarence, the boy Pratt had once braced, was still living at Pine Ridge, where he worked as a schoolteacher and clerk. He had spoken with the survivors, and on November 30, 1903, he wrote an outraged letter to Carlisle faculty member Edgar Allen.

Lightning Creek was no hostile outbreak, he informed the Carlisle teacher; rather, it was "a pale-faced uprising." As for the slain Sioux, "William and Charlie were out in Wyoming on a pleasure trip, namely to hunt wild game, just the same as President Roosevelt does; the only difference is that no one ambuscades Roosevelt." Clarence added bitterly, "If it was a general fight the whites would never have escaped, not a single one."[56]

This was the context in which the Carlisle football team played out the rest of their 1903 schedule. With Lightning Creek as a backdrop, the Carlisle Indians did not lose a game for the rest of the season. They finished with an 11-2-1 record, the school's best ever, and Jimmie Johnson was named all-American at quarterback.

There was a distinct tension on the Indian team as the season drew to a close. Johnson, their all-American and team captain, openly quarreled with Warner while on a three-game road trip to the West. On the morning of a game against Utah on December 19, Warner suddenly benched Johnson. Warner didn't publicly specify the reason except to say that his quarterback had become "temperamental."[57]

Johnson may have been resentful or tired. Carlisle was competing a fourteen-game slate, a nearly unheard-of number of games in those brutal days, and for a light team with few substitutes it was especially onerous. But an equally likely explanation for the trouble between quarterback and coach is that Johnson may have wanted to play ball one way and Warner wanted him to play another.

The Indians beat Utah anyway, 22-0, with reserve Joe Baker at quarterback, and continued on to San Francisco, where they had a date with a team of local all-stars. A host of Californian newspaper writers were eager to interview Johnson and see him work his famous sleight of hand. But Johnson and Warner were still feuding. "Of course, this vast publicity build-up also served to widen the recent strain that had developed between Johnson and me," Warner remembered.[58]

An hour before kickoff, Warner pulled Johnson into a corner of the locker room, told him he'd be the starter, and sternly launched into a set of game instructions. But Johnson was still simmering. He burst out, "Listen Pop, I don't care if I never play in one of your ball games!"

Warner immediately turned to Baker and assigned him to start. But the other players had overheard, and they began to lobby on behalf of Johnson; they wanted their all-American on the field with them. Warner said, "I couldn't play a player whose heart wouldn't be in the game."

Johnson replied, "If the other boys want me to play, I will."

Warner, recognizing he had a near mutiny on his hands, chose to take that as an apology. He relented and assigned Johnson the start. Johnson played brilliantly. One of the referees, a former Harvard fullback named W. T. Reid Jr., said later, "Carlisle played the fastest football that has ever been seen on this coast."[59]

The *New York Times* remarked, "Their average weight is 164, exactly twenty pounds lighter to a man than Harvard or Princeton but they have fairly outplayed and outwitted every eleven tackled so far this season."[60]

Matters between Warner and Johnson didn't end there, however. The Indians finished their season with a visit to the Sherman Institute in Riverside, California, a game in which Johnson's play calling consisted almost exclusively of trick plays. The Indians were more concerned with "trying to see if they could succeed in pulling off more gadget, or hocus pocus plays" than with winning, Warner remembered. They left the field with just a 12-6 victory. Writing thirty years later, Warner recalled, "Normally, I would have gotten upset at this kind of performance," but he asserts that he was lenient, realizing it was the end of a long season.[61]

In fact, at the time, Warner was angry, and so was Johnson. On returning to Carlisle, the quarterback went to Pratt to complain about Warner's treatment of him. Warner, livid, in turn suggested Johnson should be whipped or demoted, and demanded Pratt convene a disciplinary hearing.

But Pratt was inclined to side with Johnson and decided to ignore the incident. The young man was a bright student and a popular campus leader. He was taking college courses at nearby Dickinson and was scheduled to enter Northwestern University after he graduated. He would go on to get his degree from Northwestern and become a prosperous dentist, and over the years would be repeatedly held up as a model Carlisle graduate.

Warner was beside himself at Pratt's reluctance to reprimand Johnson. Furthermore, he let Pratt know, he was feeling unappreciated. Cornell had made him an overture, inviting him back as head coach. Warner was weighing whether to accept, he petulantly informed Pratt.

But if Warner thought he could leverage Pratt by threatening to leave, he was mistaken.

The old soldier wrote him a letter, in a tone stiff with dignity and disapproval.

> Dear Mr. Warner,
>
> We do not agree as to the methods and duties of Colonel Pratt, nor as to the manner of treating young people as mature as James Johnson. James is 25 years old, rather far removed, as you must admit, from the childhood stage. He has gone considerably beyond Carlisle, has been for several years in Dickinson College, and as you know is now well advanced in the college-proper; so that the point you suggest that he should have been told that he had been served right or that he ought to have been whipped and sent back is hardly applicable. James Johnson was captain of the team and as captain there were not only no complaints against him, but he has received special credit and notice from the press and the football world. For me to admit that he should be treated

as a child would be exceedingly inconsistent. He stood next to you as an official in the football aggregation. That again advises me that he is entitled to consideration. You intimate that he came to me whining. This is not in accord with my own views of what he did. I listened to you and I listened to him . . . he reached home before you did and insisted upon making a statement. . . .

You do not seem satisfied with my statement, and having heard various things that it is alleged James Johnson has said, you insist upon an aggressive settlement. . . . I am sorry to say that to me it has assumed the aspect of a personal quarrel, and my experience in such things warns me that it would be extremely difficult to settle it amicably on the lines you propose. . . .

I feel I cannot be mistaken in this and shall regret to adopt the course you urge, particularly if you stay here. To have your conduct and reputation resting in the hands of the members of the team who will feel that they can talk about you freely and can bring an issue and put you on trial will surely work injury. Some may speak for you, some may speak against you. In the profession you have chosen you are at the top and are too big to come within the pale of such bickerings as you plan to inaugurate.

I regret exceedingly that it seems to you there has not been sufficient appreciation of your efforts. I have certainly myself on all occasions claimed I had the best coach in the country and have been especially proud of the exploits of the team this year. With a light team you have accomplished results that entitle you to greatest credit. I thought that had been expressed and you understood it.

If for the sake of higher reward or because of loyalty to your own university you leave, I acquiesce; but if it can be avoided by me it shall not be an enforced leaving as the result of an inquiry into acts committed under momentary anger and resultant pro and con alleged statements arising therefrom.

In writing to you this frankly, I override my judgment a little as to just the temper in which I should meet your instructions and allegations aimed at me personally. Your friend, RH Pratt.[62]

Amid all of this emotional turmoil, Warner, Johnson, and Pratt had to attend the annual banquet together in honor of Carlisle's season. In the school gymnasium, tables were laid with linen, china, and silver, and decorated with candles and floral arrangements in the team colors. The meal was kingly by boarding-school standards: creamed oysters, roast turkey, ham, asparagus sprigs, cheese straws, beaten biscuits, and scoops of ice cream in red and old gold, shaped as footballs, as well as peanuts, celery, pickles, olives, and boxes of bonbons. Johnson crisply marched the team into the banquet hall and delivered a speech entitled "My Experience as Captain." Warner gave a toast entitled "Five Seasons with the Indians," while Pratt's speech was "Has Football at Carlisle Been a Success?"[63]

Soon afterward, Warner resigned. It was a move he would be quickly sorry for. When he calmed down, he found he missed coaching the Indians and wasn't as happy at his alma mater. It wouldn't be long before he returned to Carlisle.[64]

WARNER'S DECISION to leave Carlisle coincided with the arrival of a new student: Jim Thorpe. The sixteen-year-old Thorpe, who set foot on campus on February 6, 1904, was a narrow shouldered boy with shy eyes and an uncertain mouth. He was slight and guileless. Carlisle voice and piano teacher Verna Whistler described him: "He had an open face, an honest look, eyes wide apart, a picture of frankness but not brilliance. He would trust anybody."[65]

He was yet another child of removal and allotment, born into the rank stewpot of Indian Territory. The Sauk and Fox tribe was originally Algonquin stock from the Great Lakes but had been expelled by western expansion from Illinois to Wisconsin to Kansas. Finally, they were allowed to come to rest on a narrow, seventeen-mile-wide rectangle cut by rivers in what is now northern Oklahoma.

He and his twin brother, Charles, had been born three months after the Dawes Allotment Act passed, on May 22, 1887. His mother saw a beam of sunlight fall on a path to their cabin, and named him Wa-Tho-Huch.[66]

Allotment would cost the Sauk and Fox 78 percent of their reservation to white settlers. As Thorpe grew up, the Sauk and Fox were in transition, with half the tribe still clad in blankets and living in traditional bark houses. The Thorpes, however, were a literate family and lived year-round in a timber house on the banks of the Canadian river, where they worked a living from their 160-acre parcel of land.

Thorpe's father, Hiram, was a rowdy, horse trader, and bootlegger, while his mother, Charlotte Vieux, was Kickapoo-Potowatomie and French Catholic, and as refined as one could be in Indian Territory, educated by Jesuits and fluent in three languages. Thorpe had some of each parent in him, but Hiram's influence won out by the sheer size and force of his personality. Hiram was over six feet tall and weighed 225 pounds, with exaggeratedly villainous good looks. He wore a black hat over black hair, a kerchief around his neck, and a six shot on his hip. In his large right hand, he tended to carry a long cigar. For drunken sport, he shot out the lanterns of neighboring farms.

Hiram fathered at least nineteen children by five women and was in and out of the house. "It was said that he liked to keep a matching team and two women at all times," his granddaughter wrote of him. But he had more allegiance to Charlotte than to his other wives while she was alive. She bore him eleven children, only five of whom survived to adulthood. She herself did not see forty.[67]

Hiram frequented Keokuk Falls, a stagecoach boomtown with a red-light district that featured seven famous "deadly saloons." The stage driver liked to announce as he pulled in, "Stay for half an hour and see a man killed." Hiram would get drunk and pass out in the front yard of the justice of the peace. Or he would ride home along the wagon road, shooting out the lights of the homesteads along the way.

Keokuk Falls was so awash in booze that even the pigs got drunk. A distillery on the edge of town dumped its waste mash behind the building, and free-ranging hogs would eat it, then sidle down the main street and take liberties with the pedestrians. Alcohol was illegal on the reservation, but whiskey peddlers hid booze in hollowed-out wagon axles. Hiram didn't bother to acknowledge the law, and simply sold drink in gallon jugs out of the back of his wagon.[68]

The Thorpes were fairly prosperous by local standards, and their land was an abundant provider, studded with heavy elm, oak, cottonwood and pecan trees, and floored with grasses to feed the horses Hiram bred.

They planted corn, hay, squash, beans, melons, and cabbage and raised hogs, chickens, and cattle. One of Jim's responsibilities was to help fill the larder, and by the age of five he could wield a shotgun, with which he hunted deer, turkey, rabbits, pheasant, and squirrel. He made traps out of cornstalks to catch quail, fished for catfish and bass in the river, and collected blackberries from the thick bushes.[69]

As a father, Hiram seems to have been an interesting combination of affectionate and abusive. He beat his children liberally, but he also tied a rope to a tree that hung over the riverbank so they could swing on it, and encouraged them in foot racing and wrestling. He taught his sons to become expert in the handling of guns, horses, and dogs, and passed on an enormous physical vitality. Thorpe always remembered a certain hunting trip when they killed so many deer that the horses couldn't carry the whole load. Hiram threw one deer over each shoulder and walked the twenty miles home.

To a certain extent, Hiram's back-alley toughness was a requirement for survival in Indian Territory. As a stockman, he was constant prey to the white cattle thieves and other outlaws who plagued the region. Each spring, cattle thieves congregated in the area to raid, driving off Indian stock for their annual roundups. At night the Thorpes' cattle and horses had to be corralled, and one of Jim's chores was to help with the herding. He shared his father's touch with horses, and was an experienced hand with a lasso by the age of ten.

Thorpe would have been just as happy to hunt and handle horses for the rest of his life, but his parents, both of whom were educated, insisted he go to school. In 1893, after his sixth birthday, he and Charles were enrolled in the Quaker-run agency boarding school—an event at which he rebelled furiously. He hated the shut-in, rigid routine of school; the boys wore restricting dark suits with vests and hats, and when they weren't smothering in class, they did field chores. He became a chronic runaway, and not even repeated whippings from Hiram could keep him in school. One afternoon a neighbor watched the truant wagon go by, with shrieks coming from the back. Thorpe was lying in the bottom of the wagon, red-faced and howling with rage.[70]

A teacher labeled him "incorrigible" and noted that he didn't do anything in class except kill flies with a rubber band. He was an ungovernable boy, and, at least when he was very young, he was also a comical one. Once his mother gave him a coin. His elder brother Frank asked, "Why don't I get one?" Thorpe replied, "Because you can't do this." With that, he farted and turned a somersault.[71]

When he was ten, however, grief subdued him. A typhoid epidemic hit the school, and Charlie was stricken. So many children were sick that the infirmary nurse could barely care for them all, and Charlie steadily worsened, eventually contracting pneumonia. His parents were summoned, but at about 5 A.M. on the morning after they arrived, he died. Thorpe never recovered from losing his brother; it appears to have made him permanently withdrawn.

Nothing, however, could make him stay in school. He refused to return after Charlie's death, despite repeated whippings from Hiram. According to Thorpe's daughter Grace, "Hiram finally tired of beating him and asked the Indian Agency to send him so far away he would not find his way home again." He was packed off to Haskell, in Lawrence, Kansas, three hundred miles away, where he learned to march and play football.

Thorpe ran away from Haskell, too. When word reached him in the summer of 1901 that Hiram had been wounded in a hunting accident, he walked off campus in the work clothes he was wearing and hopped freight cars, hiked, and hitched rides on wagons for two weeks until he reached home, where he discovered that his father was fine but that his mother was pregnant again. This time Hiram whipped him so badly that he bolted to Texas.

Thorpe was just fourteen, but he found work on the Texas cattle ranges, breaking horses and mending fence lines. He earned enough to buy his own team of horses, which he drove back home after several months, in late 1902, this time to learn that Charlotte had died from childbirth complications.

This time, Hiram let him stay home for a while. Thorpe went to a public school three miles from home and helped care for his three younger siblings. However, by December 1903 Hiram had remarried, and he was again seeking a place for his son in a boarding school, probably at the insistence of his new wife. The agency received a letter asking that on behalf of Thorpe it "make rangements to Send of to school some ware."[72]

Thorpe arrived at Carlisle a brooding teenager who stood just five foot five and weighed a waiflike 115 pounds. A notation in his student record read, "Deserter." But if Thorpe was tempted to go home again, his motivation died just a few weeks after he arrived. On April 24, 1904, word reached him that his father had been killed by blood poisoning, probably from snakebite. Hiram was just fifty-two when he died. Now there was nothing to go home to except a raft of smaller siblings, who were also scattered in boarding schools.[73]

With nowhere else to go, the orphaned Thorpe settled into the regimen and routine of Carlisle. He would reside there for the better part of the next seven years, with one interruption. He lived in a dormitory where he shared a room, sparsely furnished with a wardrobe and washstand, with three other boys. He entered the outing system, and was sent to a farm on the Susquehanna River. A Carlisle outing could be a pleasant experience—some students were treated like family, and some, like Exendine, even found them enlightening—or not. Just as often, the students were used as hired hands for low, even slavish wages. Thorpe earned just a miserable $5 a month for cleaning house, and was made to eat away from the family, in the kitchen.[74]

He played football for a trade shop team, the tailors, and like most of the athletic-minded males on campus, he yearned to play for the varsity. But when he asked to try out for the squad, Carlisle's athletic trainer, Wallace Denny, told him, "You're too little. Come around later."[75]

As Thorpe mourned the loss of his father, the Carlisle student body mourned the loss of the school's father and founder, Pratt, who was finally forced to resign in June 1904. Pratt's list of enemies in Washington had steadily lengthened over twenty-five years to include various and sundry senators, officials, Indian agents, and anyone else who could be characterized as a federal bureaucrat. Leading the list, however, was Roosevelt.

Early in 1903, Pratt, by then sixty-two, had applied for a promotion to brigadier. Roosevelt did not look with favor on the request, and in fact was irritated by it. The president refused the promotion on the grounds that Pratt had spent so many years on detached duty instead of serving in a military capacity. He also went a step further and summarily placed Pratt on the retired list. It was another graceless insult, and it was also pointless—Pratt was eventually granted the promotion by an act of Congress elevating Civil War officers.

Pratt understood that his career at Carlisle was at an end. In October 1903, he traveled to Indian Territory for a reunion with his old Fort Marion students and former scouts, "to do honor to the memories of the past." When he came back, he intentionally hastened his own firing. Pratt had never stopped railing against government policy—"I would blow the reservations to pieces"—but now he publicly turned on the entire Indian Bureau.

On May 9, 1904, in a speech to the New York Ministers Conference, Pratt thundered, "I believe that nothing better could happen to the Indians than the complete destruction of the Bureau. . . . Better, far better, for the Indians had there never been a Bureau."[76]

This was too much for Secretary of the Interior E. A. Hitchcock, who demanded an explanation. Pratt refused to furnish one. An agent was dispatched to investigate whether Pratt had spoken "in a derogatory way of the President of the United States, the Secretary of the Interior, and the Indian office." On June 11, 1904, Pratt was relieved as superintendent of Carlisle by a special order from the War Department, effective at the end of the month.

The reaction to Pratt's firing was mixed. "The old soldier told the truth," the *Albany Express* said, while the *Catholic Watchman* called him "an honest lunatic." But a *Washington Post* editorial best summed up Pratt and the behavior that led to his professional demise.[77]

> Because everybody could not share his crude enthusiasms, Pratt became soured on most of the elements in civilized life that were struggling as hard as he, but by different paths, to reach the solution of the Indian problem. The authorities of the Indian Office and Department of the Interior, who were interested in seeing the Indian advanced but could not accept Pratt's cure-all as the one remedy for the difficulties in their way, aroused his special

animosity and he lost few opportunities to condemn the government he was serving, and the superior whose official orders he
was bound as a good soldier to obey.[78]

But Pratt did not leave Carlisle without one final defiant gesture.
Shortly before his fatal speech to the ministers in New York, in what
was his last significant act as superintendent, Pratt searched for a successor for Pop Warner. And he did not look among white men.

Pratt decided to name an Indian as head coach. He well knew that if
he didn't take such a step, no one would. Throughout the spring, Carlisle
players and former players had urged him to consider one of their own
for the job. Pratt did even better, naming three former Carlisle players:
Ed Rogers as head coach, assisted by Bemus Pierce and Frank Hudson.

Each man brought something to the staff. Rogers was the most polished of the three, a particularly bright student, and a favorite of
Pratt's. He was a Chippewa from the lumber region of Minnesota and
a devoted student who believed that without Carlisle his only future
would have been to saw, haul, and drive logs. He had entered Carlisle
at the age of eighteen in 1894 and was still a new student when Pratt
paused one day to examine him during a tour of inspection. As Rogers
stood at attention, Pratt asked him why he had come to Carlisle. "I
came to learn something, sir," he said. Pratt was pleased with the
answer, and Rogers meant it. After graduating from Carlisle, Rogers
went on to the University of Minnesota, where he had captained the
football team in 1903 while earning his law degree.

Bemus Pierce brought leadership: he commanded the loyalty and
affection of the entire school, and Pratt probably would have named
him head coach but for the fact that he still spoke in somewhat broken English. Hudson, the famed dropkicker, was named for his acuity
and business sense. He had gone from Carlisle to play at the University of Pittsburgh, where he studied accounting, and was employed as
head bookkeeper at the Pittsburgh Deposit Bank.

Pratt gave the Carlisle players what they wanted and believed they
had earned: self-governance. Their own graduates would coach them
just as the Ivy schools were coached by alumni. Their victories would
no longer be attributed to white men. "Carlisle will be entitled to all

the glory for the victories our team achieves under the leadership and instruction of these former Carlisle students," the *Red Man and Helper* announced.[79]

In the sports pages, the appointment of Indians as head coaches was greeted with shock. "Never before have the redskins been trusted to do the brain work incident to the planning of a football season, and in the past their victories have undoubtedly been due to the careful coaching of such men as Glenn S. Warner, Cornell, and Bull, Hickok and McCormick, of Yale," the *Washington Post* wrote.[80]

On June 30, 1904, Pratt took his leave of Carlisle. His immediate replacement was a military officer named Major William Mercer, a functionary with little energy for taking on superiors or for lobbying on behalf of the school. Pratt's effectiveness as an administrator, if not an educator, would be seen in the coming years as Carlisle slowly but surely deteriorated under his less competent successors.

With Pratt's resignation came debate about his legacy. The *Post* declared that Pratt's grand experiment, "admirable as it appears on paper, proved about as flat a failure in practice as any fad ever invented in the modern world." In 1905, however, a survey of 296 Carlisle graduates showed that 124 had entered government service, and 47 were employed off the reservations. As Pratt's friend and fellow teacher Elaine Goodale Eastman remarked, "This does not look like failure."

In fact, Pratt's legacy was decidedly mixed. His methods were obviously devastating to a culture, and he consistently failed to recognize the full scope of problems his students faced in entering American society. But he also risked his career to fight for them, and he was respected and even beloved by many them. More than one referred to him as a "foster father," and believed he had been the making of them.

Not long before he left the school, Pratt was asked whether he was proud of what he had done at Carlisle. His reply was self-effacing. "I don't feel particularly proud of it, for the reason that seventy millions of intelligent Christian people ought to have cured the whole question years ago," he said.[81]

Pratt's departure from Carlisle was a relief to the exhausted old officer. He no longer had to push his shoulder against an all but immovable wheel. "Father thought all he had to do was prove the success of Carlisle," his eldest daughter remarked. "At the end of ten years he began to see what he was up against." In retirement, Pratt and Anna Laura traveled widely, often visiting former students, and he launched a second career as a lecturer and writer on Indian issues. Sometimes, he made solitary, unannounced visits to Carlisle, strolling quietly across the grounds by himself.[82]

Whatever one felt about Pratt, he had built Carlisle into a flagship. The school had become so symbolic, in fact, that in the spring of 1905, Theodore Roosevelt invited the student body to march at his inauguration. Roosevelt also invited a half dozen of the greatest living Indian chiefs, including American Horse, to march at the head of the parade in full tribal costume. Roosevelt, the cowboy imperial hero, would preside over a procession of Indian icons of the Old West, followed by the modern ideals of Indian youth and reeducation.

Commissioner of Indian Affairs Francis Leupp explained what the significance of the display was to Roosevelt. Each of the old leaders, Leupp said, was "a thoroughly typical specimen of the old time hostile Indian, whom civilization can never reach—whose very being seems opposed to its influence. But on the other hand, each recognizes that the only chance of survival lies in the adoption of the younger generation of the ways of the white man."[83]

On a raw spring day in March, Carlisle hosted the illustrious delegation of chiefs as they traveled on their way to Washington. American Horse and Hollow Horn Bear of the Sioux, Quanah Parker of the Comanches, Geronimo of the Apaches, Little Plume of the Blackfeet, and Buckskin Charlie of the Utes spent a night on campus visiting the students. It was a testament to how removed Carlisle pupils such as Thorpe were from these renowned men that the school paper had to run biographies of them, explaining who they were and to which tribes they belonged.

That evening the tribal leaders spoke to a student body that included the young Thorpe. Their faces were aged and weathered, and their words were at once despairing and grand.

"You are here to study, to learn the ways of the white man," Geronimo said. "Do it well. . . . Do as you are told all the time and you won't get hungry."

American Horse was by now sixty-six years old, a man visibly of two worlds, in braids and store-bought clothes. Black hair streamed from a cattleman's hat, and his broad chest pulled at the sharp lapels of his coat, vest, and watch chain. He had been sending children to Carlisle and visiting its grounds for twenty-five years. He addressed the Carlisle students with warmth and suggested he consider them his own.

"Now my grandchildren," he began. "I came to see you all and I shake hands with you with all my heart. I do not wish to go back and tell you what I have come through. I am made by the almighty God the same as any other being, but still I have been through a great many bad things."

American Horse related how he had sent his children to Carlisle in the first class, and the shock of his first visit. He was having a similar experience all these years later. He observed that he hardly recognized the pupils before him as Indians. "You all look like white people," he said. "I do not know any of you, you look so well."[84]

On the morning of the inaugural, the Carlisle students and the tribal leaders rode a train to Washington. On the White House lawn, American Horse, Geronimo, and their fellow chiefs posed for photographer Edward Curtis. The ponies on which they rode were painted, and so were their faces.[85]

It was a day of intense sunshine but a constant north wind that made flags blow straight out on their poles and caused ladies to hold their hats. The Indian leaders rode down Pennsylvania Avenue, resplendent as their long ceremonial feather bonnets waved and brushed the haunches of their horses. Marching in their wake was a brigade of 350 Carlisle students, young men martial in blue uniforms, their capes dashingly turned back at the shoulder and snapping in the wind. "This is an admirable contrast," Roosevelt said on the viewing stand. "First the chiefs, in their native costumes, and then these boys from Carlisle."[86]

At their front, carrying a whipping flag, was Carlisle's ardent young color sergeant, Albert Exendine. He thrilled as he marched stiffly down the avenue—he thought President Roosevelt was the second most charismatic man he'd ever met.

The first was Richard Henry Pratt.

9

EXPERIMENTS IN FLIGHT

T HE INDIANS PRACTICED so enthusiastically under their new head coaches that they tore apart the tackling dummy. It had to be carried off the field for repair, a limp, frayed casualty. Fifty-four men turned up for tryouts, and any student crossing the quadrangle who looked tall enough or wide enough was hustled to the field "to see if there is any football in him, or not," Ed Rogers said. Even so, the roster was light as usual. "A nervy lot of little men," Rogers termed his team.[1]

Nerve was called for, because 1904 was among the dirtiest and most violent college football seasons ever played. There were twenty-one fatalities and more than two hundred serious injuries across the nation, including fractured collarbones, splintered legs, dislocated shoulders, and concussed heads. At Harvard, only one player made it through the entire schedule unhurt.[2]

In a game unsurpassed for foul play and bloodshed, Bucknell wore metal face guards and gored the Indians. *The Carlisle Arrow,* the latest incarnation of the school newspaper, labeled the Bucknell game "the roughest that we have ever participated in with any team during the ten years we have been playing football."

It began when a Bucknell player tackled a Carlisle player, threw one arm around his neck, and with his free arm deliberately punched him several times in the face. As the Indians lay on the ground after the play ended, their opponents clubbed them with the metal-edged headgear. Somehow, the Indians held their tempers—they were later praised for their restraint by the local Williamsport paper—and survived to win, 10-6. But they were so battered afterward that they couldn't practice for an entire week.

"There is not one man on the team who does not bear some mark of remembrance of that contest," Rogers said disgustedly.[3]

At Harvard, there was no repeat of the hidden-ball play. Instead, the Crimson completely closed Charlie Dillon's eye for him, and sent a half dozen Indian players off the field with injuries or fatigue, as Carlisle went down to defeat, 12-0. "Harvard simply wore us out with her ponderous attack," Rogers said.[4]

The Indians gave almost as good as they got, judging by their respectable 9-2 record. But the season left the new superintendent discontented. Mercer was a balding, mustachioed bureaucrat whose uniform tunic was stretched by an expanding waistline. He tended toward apathy and perhaps even corruption—he would depart the school abruptly in 1908 with a hint of financial impropriety—and he does not seem to have done much at Carlisle. But Mercer recognized what an asset football was, financially and politically, and he seized control of it. He attended virtually every game, and by the end of the season, the Indians' experiment in self-determination was over. He dismissed Rogers, and went in search of a white coach. Mercer "was strongly in favor of placing a white man where an Indian could do as good work," according to Bemus Pierce.[5]

Mercer demonstrated his utter lack of feel for the place with a totally unsuitable hire: George Woodruff, a Skull and Bones Yale alum who as a head coach in the late 1890s at Penn had devised one of the most archetypal and bruising mass plays, a diabolically injurious thing called "guards back." Woodruff took over at Carlisle for the 1905 season, with another Yale man named Ralph Kinney assisting him. The disconsolate Rogers went home to Minnesota, where he embarked on a career in law and politics.

The Indians were a predictable disappointment under Woodruff.

Their once-marvelous offense, formerly a maze of men going in different directions, became ordinary. They looked and played just like any other team, and their record showed it. They were 10-5 and lost every significant game, and more important, they lost their uniqueness. Their only real fun came in a 36-0 defeat of crosstown rival Dickinson. Before kickoff, a couple of Dickinson students dressed as cowboys and Indians and pantomimed a fight. Carlisle students answered by presenting a wheelchair that contained a gaunt, wasted dummy in a Dickinson sweater, shot full of arrows. Every time the Indians scored, they fired another arrow into the dummy.

Even the *New York Times* complained that the Indians were no longer entertaining. "Their style of game was altogether different from that used by Carlisle teams in years past, being directed at the tackles and the centre, and not at the ends. . . . Coach Woodruff explained this by saying that as long as his team found it was able to gain through the line, there was no need of its trying anything else, but this does not alter the fact that the Indians no longer play the game that used to be so distinctly and exclusively their own."[6]

On the same day that Carlisle was losing in such plodding fashion to the Crimson, the President's son, Theodore Roosevelt Jr., was playing football for Harvard's freshman team. The boy was twice laid out on the field with injuries, and at one point he was prone on the field for three full minutes. When the young Roosevelt finally rose, his team captain said, "If you feel like it, go at them again." He did. The boy's pluck finally resulted in a broken nose against Yale when he was kicked in the face. It was said the Yalies had intentionally gone at him.[7]

The president was getting fed up with the brutal mass play, which threatened to ruin a game he enjoyed and believed in. Roosevelt had often defended football from its critics. "Of all the games, I personally like football the best, and I would rather see my boys play it than see them play any other. I have no patience with people who declaim against it."[8]

The president's personal vigor was antic. He lost the vision in one eye in a boxing match, broke his nose and his arm chasing hounds, fractured his ribs in a cattle roundup, was knocked cold in polo, and once jumped from a horse to stab a cougar to death. "Don't flinch, don't foul, and hit the line hard," he liked to say. He periodically left the White House to go on fruitless hunting trips for black bears, to a rising tide of national hilarity that resulted in the production of a souvenir called the "teddy bear."

But the lack of governance in football had become indefensible. In the 1905 season there were another eighteen deaths and 149 serious injuries reported. An outcry against the game swept the country. Even John L. Sullivan, the famed boxer, said: "Football! There's murder in that game. Sparring! It doesn't compare in roughness or danger with football. In sparring, you know what you are doing. You know what your opponent is trying to do, and he's right there in front of you, and there's only one. But in football, say, there's twenty one people trying to do you."[9]

Newspaper photos of football men with bloodied and mangled features repulsed readers. Professor Shailer Mathews of Chicago's divinity school railed against "a social obsession—a boy-killing, education prostituting, gladiatorial sport. It teaches virility and courage, but so does war. I do not know what should take its place, but the new game should not require the services of a physician, the maintenance of a hospital, and the celebration of funerals."[10]

Reformers equated the game with vice as well as violence. A president of the University of Illinois, Andrew Draper, asserted that football encouraged "loafing, gambling and drinking!" In June 1905, an investigative series by Henry Beach Needham of the muckraking *McClure's* exposed the Ivy League as rife with professionalism and corruption. It charged that J. J. Hogan, the all-American captain of Yale, was a twenty-five-year-old who entered Exeter at the advanced age of twenty-three and was living in college on commissions from the American Tobacco Company. A Princeton player was supported by income from a baseball concession. Andrew Smith managed to play for both Penn State and Penn, in the same season, and Penn used ringers from Middlebury, Colorado, and Lafayette. At Harvard, a number of Crimson played semipro baseball under assumed names. A Princeton player confessed he had explicit instructions from his coaches to single out the other side's best player and injure him in the first five minutes. The only schools that played the game honestly, according to *McClure's*, were Army and Navy.

Roosevelt recognized the game was in full-blown crisis. In the first week of October 1905, he summoned representatives from Harvard, Princeton, and Yale to lunch at the White House and impressed on them that without urgent reform, the game would soon be prohibited on most campuses. On October 12 Walter Camp issued a statement: "At a meeting with the president of the United States, it was agreed that we consider an honorable obligation exists to carry out in letter and in spirit the rules of the game of foot-ball, relating to roughness, holding and foul play."[11]

A movement to abolish it had already gained momentum. Schools all over the country were considering dropping the sport, led by Harvard, where the game's old critic, president Charles Eliot, declared it on probation. At the end of the 1905 season, Columbia acted unilaterally and banned it, while Northwestern suspended it and California and Stanford temporarily substituted rugby for it.

In late December, representatives of twenty-eight major colleges met and formed a new governing organization, called the National Intercollegiate Football Conference, charging a new seven-member rules committee with developing a safer, cleaner sport.[12]

Over some heated objections from Walter Camp, they instituted a half dozen crucial rule changes that the current audience would recognize. Mass plays were forbidden. Teams now had to move ten yards for a first down, instead of just five yards, which took the emphasis off pure strength in the center of the field. Most experimental of all, the forward pass was legalized, though with an inhibitor: a team that tried to throw and failed would be penalized 15 yards.

Previously, there had been no necessity for anything but the "slam bang method of attack," as Warner put it. "The stronger team usually was able to smash and grind the ball downfield in short, steady gains until they had finally crossed the goal line." With the reforms, it was hoped that the game would be safer and more "open," with an emphasis on using the entire field.[13]

At Carlisle, Mercer used the name of reform to make changes, welcome and unwelcome. He removed the prim old Victorian schoolteacher, W. G. Thompson, from his job as disciplinarian and went in search of another white coach. It appears he was unsuccessful in trying to lure Fielding "Hurry Up" Yost away from Michigan; a report that he had vainly pursued Yost made it into the newspapers.

Left with no choice, for the time being Mercer named Bemus Pierce to an interim position, with Frank Hudson, who was also employed as the school's financial clerk, as his assistant. But even then, Mercer had his eye on another coach for the school.[14]

That Pierce's appointment was just temporary became clear when an "advisor" turned up at Carlisle practices in September '06: none other than Pop Warner. He was there at the invitation of Mercer, to consult with the Indians on how to adapt to the rewritten rulebook. But it's also probable that Warner was there to discuss returning as Carlisle's head coach, because he would resume the position by Christmas.[15]

Warner spent a full week on campus, watching the Indians practice. As always, he and the Carlisle players fired each other's imaginations. In the harness shop, Warner devised something called a "bucking strap" to teach proper techniques in blocking and tackling. Meanwhile, on the field, Warner and the Indians experimented with the forward pass.

"It may be basketball, but it's in the rules, so let's try it," Warner said.

Warner learned as much as the players did, and what he learned intrigued him: the Indians could throw the ball. A couple of fellows could even fling it forty yards in the air. And Albert Exendine could catch it.[16]

It was a team worth returning to Carlisle for, Warner decided.

IN THE meantime, the Indians played under their Indian coaches for one last season. In November 1906, they traveled to Minneapolis for a game against the unbeaten team of the West, the University of Minnesota, and posters went up all over the region, announcing their arrival. A meager-boned boy in tattered overalls stared at a flyer that said, "Carlisle Indians," and determined to go and see them.

Gus Welch, a fourteen-year-old Chippewa from the lake country of Spooner, Wisconsin, was enthralled by the idea of playing for Carlisle, although the only football he'd ever kicked was a homemade one, a swatch of cowhide stuffed with grass and sewn with buckskin thongs.

Welch himself looked like the furthest thing from a player. In fact, he appeared tubercular. He was a thin-faced, jug-eared, lank-haired boy with a sharp sense that he could be struck by infirmity at any time. Tuberculosis had wiped out almost his entire family, and everyone kept waiting for him to succumb.

He was an orphan. His father, an Irishman named James Welch, was killed in a logging accident when he was a small child. His mother, Wawiens, was a daughter of Kewanzee, chief of the Lac Courte Oreilles band. Wawiens refused to live on a reservation, because she didn't believe in segregating herself or her eight children; instead, she sold her allotment to buy a farm and a rambling ranch house, where she raised her family. "You've got to live with the white people. You might as well grow up with them," she said. But before Welch was ten, most of his family was dead, as a plague of tuberculosis took his mother, three brothers, and two sisters in the space of five years.[17]

Welch and his younger brother Jimmy went to live with their ancient grandmother, Chemamanon, the wife of Kewanzee. Born in 1797, she would live through presidencies ranging from George Washington to Woodrow Wilson. Chemananon was still gliding across the lakes in a canoe as she neared the age of 100, and she supported Gus by trapping and taught him to how to survive in the wilderness.[18]

Welch hunted, trapped, and went to work driving for a livery stable, in order to stay outdoors as much as possible in hopes of avoiding the dreaded tuberculosis. He and his grandmother would take furs and hides to Duluth to sell, which is where he saw the advertisement for the Carlisle game.[19]

When Gus shot a timber wolf and collected $20 in bounty money, he bought his train ticket to Minneapolis. He boarded the train in his threadbare, mismatching clothes, the only ones he owned. When he reached Minneapolis, he asked around until he found out where the Carlisle team was staying. In the lobby of the hotel, he stared at the trim athletes, so dapper in their travel suits. There was Albert Exendine, the team captain, exuding glamour, with curly dark hair swept back in waves. Gus shyly asked if there were any Chippewas on the team.

The Carlisle players befriended the thin boy. "I was just a ragamuffin wearing odd pieces of cast off clothing," he remembered. They arranged for a cot to be set up in one of their hotel rooms for him, so he could stay with them. They fed him and took him with them to practice and on strolls through Minneapolis, looking in shop windows and buying peanuts or sweets. At a men's clothing store, Welch stared at the sharply cut suits of fine woolen fabrics, twills, and worsteds. A blue serge suit caught his eye, but it cost $15, and he had only enough money left to get home.

For a few days, Welch regained a sense of family. The Carlisle team was a large, roughhousing brotherhood. They entertained themselves with card games and played something they called "Indian Counting," a semifraternal hazing rite that required a player to bend over, close his eyes, and take a smack in the rear. He then rose, turned around and gazed at his teammates' faces, and tried to guess who had hit him from their expressions.[20]

Younger players were teased with pranks. A favorite trick they played on a boy who had never been in a hotel before was to pour olive oil on bread, and then ask him if he didn't want some syrup. The veterans stole the clothes of the younger players and locked them out of rooms. They hid the silverware at the dinner table and left fake messages in the lobby. They told them to leave their shoes in the hotel hall for shining and then mismatched them, or removed or knotted the laces.[21]

On November 16, Carlisle met Minnesota before a crowd of about twenty thousand that included hundreds of reservation dwellers; like Welch, they had come from all over the region to see a team of Indians, coached by Indians. Carlisle was playing out an uneven season under Bemus Pierce and had lost three games, including an upset to inferior Penn State. But the Indians overwhelmed Minnesota, 17-0, as quarterback Archie Libby kicked three field goals. The victory convinced the eastern experts to rank Carlisle fifth in the country at the season's end, with a 9-3 record.

After the game, Welch had a few hours to kill before it was time to board his train for the eighty-five-mile trip back to Wisconsin. The Indian players took him back to the clothing store, and Welch again looked longingly at the blue serge suit.

The players told him it was already his. They had chipped in and bought it for him. The suit was boxed up and placed in his hands, and he accepted it with a catch in his throat.

"I got on the train crying," Welch remembered. Aboard the railcar, with tears streaming down his face, he told the Carlisle boys goodbye. They promised him they would write.[22]

P OP WARNER agreed to return as the Indians' head coach on December 1, 1906, in the midst of the noise and pomp of the Army-Navy football game. The contest was held at Philadelphia's Franklin Field, and Albert Exendine was standing on the sideline, listening to the uplifting strains of a new anthem debuted that afternoon by the Navy band, called "Anchors Aweigh!," when his old coach clapped him on the back and said hello.

Word had gotten around that Warner was unhappy at Cornell, and Exendine asked if he was considering coming back to the Indian school.

"You have coaches," Warner replied.

"They aren't coaches," Ex said.

Warner's studied casualness on the subject was deceiving. In fact, he was anxious to leave Cornell. Despite a successful 21-8-2 record in three seasons, he had again fought with the school's meddlesome graduates over control of the team. "Off the field, I began to run into a lot of friction with certain alumni over my handling and the direction of the Cornell football program," Warner admitted.[23]

By the end of the afternoon, Warner and Mercer—the superintendent was also at the game, primping with a cane and a corsage—had reached a deal. As Ex left the field to catch a train, Warner said, "I want you to meet the new football coach."[24]

Warner's summary replacement of Bemus Pierce as Carlisle's coach occasioned an explanation in the *Arrow*, the official mouthpiece of the school administration. Despite praising Pierce for the job he had done and observing that the Indians "rank among the first money teams," Mercer made it clear he didn't believe the Indian coaches were capable of managing the program.

"With him [Warner] to direct their efforts our teams will be relieved of all handicaps so far as efficient instruction and manage-ment is necessary to success," the *Arrow* said. The story stressed the previous coaches had "a lack of these qualifications." Mercer couldn't have been any clearer: Indians were handicapped.[25]

There may have been another issue at work, too. The decision to bring back Warner that December coincided with a hushed scandal involving Carlisle's finances. On December 3, two days after the Army-Navy game, a federal auditor concluded that Frank Hudson, employed as the school's chief bookkeeper, was responsible for a shortage of $1,410.62 in the Carlisle student accounts. Carlisle oper-ated as a bank for pupils, who deposited their earnings from outings or money from home and could only withdraw sums with express permission from school authorities. The investigator found that Hud-son had misappropriated the money in small amounts of petty cash over the course of a year. Oddly, Hudson did not seem to deny it or offer an explanation, nor does he seem to have been prosecuted. Instead, Mercer filed an insurance claim to recoup the funds, claim-ing Hudson "defaulted." That Mercer allowed Hudson unfettered access to petty cash without checking the daily accounts defies belief, but possibly Mercer was that lazy. Hudson left Carlisle after the '06 season and appears to have gone into banking or advertising in Philadelphia. In 1914, the great dropkicker would apply for the Carlisle head-coaching job, citing his employment at the school in 1905–1906, a strange thing to do if he was guilty of embezzling. The event reflected just as poorly on Mercer and may have had something to do with his short term as superintendent. In any case, by the end of December Pop Warner was in charge as athletic director.[26]

Warner was pleased to be back in the company of athletes whose capabilities clearly fascinated him—and still bewildered him, too. That spring, Warner met the athlete who would amaze yet confound him more than any other. Seemingly out of nowhere came that unac-countable great, Jim Thorpe.

On a late-April afternoon, the seventeen-year-old Thorpe ambled along across the upper end of the athletic field with some friends, on his way to play in a football match between trade schools. Even at a saunter, the young Thorpe possessed a physical ease that caused the sportswriting legend Grantland Rice to remark that he moved "like a breeze."[27]

Thorpe stopped to watch the track team practice the high jump. The bar was set at five foot nine inches, and nobody in the school had ever cleared that height, not even Carlisle's track captain, Albert Exendine. Body after body jackknifed through the air, but with each leap, the bar clattered to the cinder track. Everyone knocked it down.

"Can I try?" Thorpe asked.

Thorpe was dressed in overalls, a work shirt, and a pair of borrowed gym shoes. The varsity boys laughed at him and told him to go ahead. They stood around and waited for Thorpe to crash into the apparatus.

Thorpe took a couple of practice strides toward the bar, and then took off and scissored his body over the bar. As the track boys stared at him, agape, Thorpe laughed and strolled away, rejoining his friends.

Among those who watched Thorpe's jump at track practice was a student named Harry Achenbald. He went straight to Pop Warner to report what happened. The next morning, Warner summoned Thorpe.

"Have I done anything wrong?" Thorpe asked.

"Son, you've only broken the school record in the high jump. That's all."

"I didn't think it was very high," Thorpe said. "I think I can do better in a track suit."

Warner put an arm around the boy and told him that wouldn't be a problem. That afternoon he exchanged his overalls for a uniform and was on the team.[28]

After eighteen months at Carlisle, Thorpe had grown almost five inches. A couple of hard-laboring summers in the outing system— including a stint in the guardhouse for running away from another country home where he was paid just $8 a month—had helped him put on thirty pounds. By that spring day in 1907 when he cleared the high bar, his weight was up to 145, and he had worked his way onto the football scrub team, called the Hotshots.[29]

Warner turned his new prodigy over to Exendine for athletic tutoring. Exendine held most of the Carlisle records in track and field, but he had nothing to teach the skinny teen who moved like a breeze. It took only one meet for Thorpe to break all of Exendine's marks.

"Before Jim hit Carlisle, I was quite the athlete around there," Exendine remembered. "I held the college records in the broad jump and the high jump, the shot put, and the hammer, and several other track and field events, and I was captain of the football team. But it took Jim just one day to break all my records. We went to a dual meet together and he won everything."[30]

In August 1907, as fall football practices began, Thorpe pleaded with Warner for a chance to try out for the varsity. Warner was reluctant; Thorpe's build struck him as too "scrawny" for football and he didn't want his best track prospect to get hurt. But the boy pestered him so tirelessly that he relented.

"All right," Warner said irritably. "If this is what you want, go out there and give my varsity boys a little tackling practice. And believe me, that's all you'll be to them."[31]

As Thorpe walked out onto the field he thought, "If I have to lick all these men to play football, now is when I start."[32]

Warner tossed the ball at Thorpe and ordered an open-field drill. About thirty or forty players were scattered around the field. Thorpe began to sprint, cutting and weaving through them.

Thorpe ran through the entire varsity "like they were old maids," Warner remembered. Some of them he outran; others he faked out and left facedown in the turf. Standing on the sideline, Warner was furious at his defense, but he caught his breath at Thorpe's performance. After he crossed the goal line, Thorpe skipped back to Warner and tossed him the football.

"I gave them some good practice, right Pop?"

One of Warner's assistants said, joking, "You're supposed to let them tackle you, Jim. You weren't supposed to run through them."

"Nobody's going to tackle Jim," he said.

Warner was goaded by Thorpe's cockiness. He slapped the ball in Thorpe's middle. "Well let's see if you can do it again, kid."

Thorpe cheerfully went back onto the field, while Warner had a loud word with his varsity. "This isn't a track meet! Who does this kid think he is? Hit him so hard that he doesn't get up and try it again! Hit, hit, hit!"

Thorpe ran through the entire defense a second time. Once more, he tossed the ball to Warner, who stood there cussing both Thorpe and his defense. When Warner finally calmed down, he said to trainer Wallace Denny, "He certainly is a wild Indian, isn't he?"

Years later, Warner wrote, "Jim's performance at practice that afternoon on the Carlisle varsity playing field was an exhibition of athletic talent that I had never before witnessed, nor was I ever to again see anything similar which might compare to it."[33]

In 1907, football went airborne, and so did the world. Hot-air balloons rose and floated through the sky, causing strange accidents. A French aeronaut named Eugene Godet took off in an "airship" from Jamestown, Virginia, struck a water tower and damaged his propeller, and blew around aimlessly over the Atlantic before a gust sent him back to land. A balloon full of amateurs in France was lost off the coast of Bordeaux, swept to sea by wind and fog. They were last seen drifting toward the Bay of Biscay.[34]

Heavier-than-air machines struggled awkwardly off the ground: the Wright brothers, pioneers of gas-powered flight, struggled to refine their winged design and keep it aloft. At Issy les Moulineaux in early October, Henri Farman, born in Paris to English parents, hurtled into the air above a parade ground and electrified all of France by performing the first banked turn and flying in a circle.[35]

It seemed like the whole world was fascinated with acceleration, in any form. The first crude versions of the Maytag washer and Hoover vacuum appeared. The *Lusitania* and *Mauretania* ocean liners were launched, and set speed records as 324 men shoveled a thousand tons of coal a day into their furnaces. The *New York World* mocked playwright George Bernard Shaw for his timidity in learning to drive. "His nerve," the paper reported, "is not evenly distributed." Shaw's instructor revealed, "He is afraid of the machine. He crawls and crawls."[36]

At Carlisle, Pop Warner ripped around campus in his new motorcar. It must have put him in a fast mood, because the Carlisle Indians of 1907 would be the most dynamic team in college football, as they pioneered an elegant, high-speed new invention called the passing game. The Indians were about to take off.

In popular histories, the first use of the forward pass on a major collegiate stage tends to be wrongly ascribed to Notre Dame in 1913, and the tandem of Gus Dorais and Knute Rockne. In fact, the Indians were the first team to throw the ball deeply and regularly downfield, in 1907.[37]

Up until 1906, if a player threw the ball at all, he pitched it underhanded, sidearmed it, or lobbed it through the air end over end. Though the pass was legalized that season, almost none of the major teams in the East dared to use it. It was simply too unfamiliar and awkward. Even Warner, after his week spent "advising" the Indians before the '06 season, believed the pass was "good for gains at times, but not at all regularly."[38]

Though it's difficult to imagine now, the concept of a spiral was not an obvious one then. Two men seem to have hit on the idea at about the same time: Warner, who realized that throwing the ball point first would present less surface to the air and make it travel farther, and a coach named Eddie Cochems at St. Louis University, who decided that holding the ball by the laces offered the most secure grip.

The first downfield, overhand spiral was completed on September 5, 1906, when St. Louis quarterback Bradbury Robinson threw to teammate Jack Schneider in an obscure game against Carroll College. A more notable pass was recorded when Wesleyan completed one against Yale on October 3. Carlisle may deserve partial credit for that throw: Wesleyan's coach, Howard R. "Bosey" Reiter, claimed he learned how to throw a spiral from an unidentified Carlisle Indian *in 1903*, when Reiter coached the semipro Philadelphia Football Athletics and an Indian was on the team. The only other significant pass that season was thrown by Yale, which gained a first down that led to victory over Harvard, when Paul Veeder threw thirty yards to Bob Forbes.[39]

By the start of the '07 campaign, most major teams still considered the pass too exotic and unsound, and refused to practice it. But as Warner watched the Indians work out in the fall of '07, he found that they had already become "deadly accurate" in the long pass. The squad that gathered on the practice field that September was Carlisle's most talented ever, so rich in ability that Warner considered it "about as perfect a football machine as I ever sent on the field." They put his imagination to work.[40]

The Indians were led at quarterback by Frank Mount Pleasant, a nine-teen-year-old Tuscarora-Iroquois chief's son from just outside of Niagara Falls with deceptive looks. Mount Pleasant only weighed somewhere between 130 and 140 pounds, and his student card said he had a "weak heart." He was so finely built that Warner nearly dismissed him from the football team, considering him "too light and frail" for the game. "He was always begging, however, and finally, thinking his speed might be useful, I gave him a chance," Warner remembered. As it turned out, you didn't dare judge Mount Pleasant by his appearance. Games came as naturally to him "as breathing," Warner discovered. He was a springy, dodging runner with surprising leg strength, a good punter, and, most unexpected of all, a great passer who could set his feet and fling the ball fifty yards downfield, on target.[41]

He was also an accomplished pianist and an Olympic long jumper, and he would soon enter Dickinson Law School. This oddly talented young man, so in tune with himself, nonplussed Warner, who found him to be "a handsome, careless lad." To top it off, he was modest almost to the point of taciturnity about his talent. "As a man, Mount Pleasant is a frank, open-hearted gentleman, quiet and courteous," an acquaintance once wrote. "To meet Mt. Pleasant is to like him; to know him is to admire him; to live in the same little world with him is to appreciate his sterling qualities and his noble nature."[42]

Mount Pleasant wasn't the only member of the squad who could throw. So could Pete Hauser, a burly twenty-one-year-old Cheyenne from Oklahoma, who lined up at fullback. For targets, they had two tall, fleet veteran ends in Exendine and William Gardner, a Chippewa from Turtle Mountain, North Dakota. Both had recently graduated but remained on campus while they took courses at Dickinson Law.[43]

Warner's pencil strokes seemed to flicker as he drew up a new offense to take advantage of their versatility. Camp would dub the new scheme "the Carlisle formation," but later it would be known as the "single wing" for its wing-shaped appearance. Whatever it was called, it was a bolt of inspiration. It was predicated on one small move: Warner shifted a halfback out wide, to outflank the opposing tackle, forming something that looked like a wing. But it opened up a world of possibilities.

Its beauty lay in its many options and disguises. They could show one thing and then do another. They could line up as if to punt—and then throw. No one could know whether the Indians were going to run, throw, or kick out of the formation.

For added measure, on pass plays Warner taught his quarterbacks to sprint out a few yards to their left or their right, buying more time to throw. The rest of the players flooded downfield and knocked down any opponent who might be able to intercept or bat away the pass.

The players loved it. "How the Indians did take to it!" Warner remembered. "Light on their feet as professional dancers, and every one amazingly skillful with his hands, the redskins pirouetted in and out until the receiver was well down the field, and then they shot the ball like a bullet."[44]

Carlisle roared off to a 6-0 start. On October 26, they went to Philadelphia to face unbeaten Penn, ranked fourth in the nation, on Franklin Field before a crowd of 22,800. No team all season had crossed Penn's goal line.

On just the second play of the game, Hauser whipped a forty-yard forward pass over the middle that Gardner caught on a dead run.

There are three or four signal moments in the evolution of football, and this was one of them. Imagine the excitement of the crowd that day—and the confusion of the defenders—if all they had ever seen was a densely packed, scrum-like game. Suddenly, the center snapped the ball three yards deep to a man who was a powerful runner, a dead-eye passer, and a great kicker. The play must have felt like an electric charge.

"It will be talked of often this year," the *Philadelphia North American* said. "No such puny little pass as Penn makes, but a lordly throw, a hurl that went farther than many a kick."

It was the sporting equivalent of the Wright brothers taking off at Kitty Hawk. And it utterly baffled the Quakers. From that moment on, the Indians threw all over the field.

"The forward pass was child's play," the *New York Herald* reported, "they tried it on the first down, on the second down, on the third down—any down and in any emergency—and it was seldom that they did not make something with it. . . . They wriggled out of tackles and made ten and fifteen yards when any ordinary football players would have been satisfied with one yard."[45]

To the panicked Quakers, the Carlisle receivers came at them like a stampede. At the start of a play, every man shot downfield. Some decoyed the defensive backs and others hit the safeties. Penn's all-American fullback, William "Big Bill" Hollenback, described what it was like: "I'd see the ball sailing in my direction. And at the same time came the thundering of what appeared to be a tribe of Indians racing full tilt in my direction. When this gang hit you, they just simply wiped you out, and you lost all other interest in the football contest."[46]

There was one other significant event that day: Jim Thorpe's debut. In the first half, Carlisle's veteran starting halfback, Albert Payne, wrenched his knee. Thorpe finally had his chance, and he raced onto the field. He was so excited that the first time Carlisle called his number, he ran in the opposite direction from his blockers and was buried under a pile of tacklers. But on the next play, he ran forty-five yards.[47]

The Indians completed eight of sixteen passes—even Thorpe threw one—and outgained Penn by 402 yards to 76. The Quakers were so confused by the Indians' fakes and feints that they "finally reached a point where the players ran in circles emitting wild yawps," Warner remembered. Carlisle won, 26-6.[48]

The ease of Carlisle's victory over Penn startled and discomfited football traditionalists. The *New York Times* reported that the Indians' explosive use of the pass "put all the coaches at the large universities at sea." Clearly, the Indians were miles ahead of any other team. Unsurprisingly, the competition did not congratulate them for it, but resented them. In the past, the Indians had been a novelty act, a plucky little team that played over their heads. But now they were a powerful and undefeated machine, and they had made an opponent look slow and stupid.

The Indians frustrated their opponents to the point of lashing out. At one point during Carlisle's unbeaten streak, Pete Hauser had to be helped off the field. As he came to the sideline, Warner asked him what happened.

"Same old thing. They kneed me."

"Know who it was?" Warner demanded.

Hauser nodded. "Yep."

"Well, what did you do?" Warner said. "Didn't you say anything?"

"Sure, I said something," Hauser replied. "I said, 'Who's the savage now?'"[49]

To the relief of the football establishment, the Indians finally encountered an opponent they couldn't beat: bad weather. On November 2, the Indians met Princeton at the Polo Grounds in New York under a drab, swollen sky. By the time the game got under way, it had been raining for ten hours and the gridiron was an expanse of mud. Umbrellas looked like blossoms among the twenty-two thousand on hand. Ribbons, streamers, and garlands wilted while Mount Pleasant and Hauser could barely grip the sodden ball, much less throw. Their formations were useless, and Princeton's superior weight told in the slop. The Tigers won decisively, 16-0. Afterward, official Mike Thompson needed an hour to comb all the mud from his hair. To make matters worse, the Princeton fans serenaded Carlisle with a ditty:

Mr. Indian, he is American
Mr. Indian, he is all right
For he used to be
In North America
When society
Was out of sight
As a potentate
Of Yankee real estate
He is just as great
As any man
He may have beaten dear old Penn
But he can't do a thing to the Princeton men
Poor Mr. Indian![50]

But the following Saturday, the Indians had a summery, glass-blue sky to play under. It was perfect weather for the game that was annually the emotional high point of their season: Harvard. The Crimson were the last of the Big Four teams the Indians would play and, as always, somehow the most meaningful.

In ten previous meetings, the Indians had never beaten Harvard. They had only come close. But this time, they were convinced they had the superior team, and the loss to Princeton a week earlier had only made them hungrier for revenge. Thirty thousand people made a wall of colors around the field at Harvard Stadium, which was firm and green. The Indians bounded up and down it excitedly in their pregame warm-ups, chanting, "Remember last week!"

Back at Carlisle, the student body was massed at the athletic field, sitting in the grandstand, waiting for bulletins that were carried to the campus by wire and then posted on a large chalkboard.

The game wasn't seven minutes old when Mount Pleasant struck Exendine with a forty-five-yard pass that the end gathered in at Harvard's three-yard line. From then on, the Crimson didn't know where to look.

"Only when a redskin shot out of the hopeless maze . . . could it be told with any degree of certainty just where the attack was directed," the *Boston Herald* reported.

The Indians scored three more times that afternoon, each play set up with spectacular pieces of misdirection. Albert Payne started around end as if to run—but pulled up short and heaved a scoring pass all the way back across the field to Antonio Lubo. Then Hauser caught a thirty-one-yard pass from Mount Pleasant.

Last but not least, Mount Pleasant wove through the entire Harvard defense on an eighty-yard punt return. As Crimson players sprawled in his wake, "I saw only goal posts in front of me. I made for them," he said afterward with typical modesty.

As it became apparent that the Indians were going to win, the mood in the stadium grew ugly. Some of the angrier fans among the thirty thousand flooded the field and delayed the game. When the officials got the crowd cleared, Harvard's Waldo Pierce, a 205-pound guard, jumped on Exendine from behind and hit him in the jaw. Pierce was thrown out. One of the Indians replied by hitting Harvard captain Bartol Parker so hard that he had to be helped off the field. Mount Pleasant and Lubo strode up the Carlisle lines, roaring, "Remember last Saturday, remember last Saturday!"[51]

The final score was 23-15. On the Carlisle campus, each time a score was posted on the chalkboard, the students went into a frantic celebration. When the victory was finally announced—the first over Harvard in school history—they erupted into pure pandemonium. As night fell, they paraded into town in their nightshirts. Residents of the village stood on their doorsteps and cheered as the Carlisle band led a snake dance from one end of town to the other.

At the head of the impromptu parade, students dressed as hospital attendants carried a stretcher. Lying on the stretcher was a dummy in a crimson sweater, with a large H on the chest.[52]

The players, meanwhile, celebrated with a jubilant if weary dinner at the Copley Square Hotel, while they waited for the eight o'clock train to take them home. Several of them visibly limped, according to the *Boston Herald*.[53]

From Boston to New York, Carlisle's victory was front-page news. "Crimson Hopelessly Baffled by Brilliant Tactics of Redskins," a headline announced. The racial motif was still there—"There may be temperamental defects in the Indian makeup, but Carlisle showed very few of them," the *Boston Herald* remarked—but at least praise and the word *brilliant* preceded it.

The Crimson, meanwhile, were mortified by losing to Carlisle. They had also lost one-sided games to Dartmouth and Yale that season, and it was more than some could bear. Interior Secretary James Garfield seized on Harvard's football misfortunes to gibe at President Roosevelt. Perhaps, he suggested, Harvard should schedule Vassar.

"I behaved with what dignity I could," Roosevelt said later, "under the distressing conditions."[54]

But the real story wasn't that a team of Indians had beaten Harvard. It was that the Indians were the "Masters of the 'New Football.'" They had invented a whole new brand of game. Carlisle football, mixing the run, pass, and kick with elements of surprise, was the game of the future. The traditional powers would cling to their old tactics at their peril.

CROWDS THRONGED to stadiums to see what the Indians might try next. They became the biggest box office team in the country: by the year's end they would take in $45,000 in ticket sales.[55]

Warner was as energetic a promoter as he was a coach. He pumped up the gate receipts by hiring a press agent in Carlisle named Hugh Miller to place stories in the New York, Philadelphia, Chicago, and Pittsburgh papers. Warner bought Miller a camera and came to his office almost daily with proposed story ideas or bulletins. Finally, Warner decided it took too much time to make the trip into town, and instead hired a young stringer named Arthur Martin to come out to Carlisle each day and report on the Indians. Gradually, the reporter evolved into the coach's personal secretary.[56]

The Indians' already loaded schedule ended with a flourish: they embarked on a road trip to meet the best team in the west, Chicago. Amos Alonzo Stagg's team was unbeaten and laying claim to the national championship, with a scheme just as creative as Carlisle's and an all-American running back named Wally Steffen, dubbed "The Wizard of the West" for his miraculous open-field jaunts.

First, the Indians revisited Minneapolis where once again fans from surrounding regions or nearby reservations came to see them play. Gus Welch, the ragamuffin boy with the blue serge suit, had stayed in touch with his idols by mail, and they introduced him to Warner and arranged for an impromptu tryout for the team. Welch announced that he could kick farther than some of the boys practicing, and proceeded to prove it: a real ball felt lighter to him than the old buckskin-and-grass balls he was used to kicking. Welch did well enough to make an impression on Warner, who urged him to enroll at Carlisle.[57]

But it was a costly trip: while Carlisle gained a prospect in Welch, it lost a player in Mount Pleasant. The quarterback broke his thumb in the midst of a 12-10 defeat of Minnesota, though not before throwing two long scoring passes. Chicago's Stagg and three of his players scouted the entire game from the bleachers.

With Mount Pleasant out, Carlisle's chance of beating Chicago was significantly diminished. Warner wrote a despondent bulletin for the *Carlisle Arrow*.

> We had a hard fight to win from Minnesota and the victory cost
> us dearly, in that Mt. Pleasant broke a bone in his thumb and hurt
> his hip so badly that he can't get into the game Saturday except

through a miracle. With him out of the game, you realize how we are crippled as so much has depended upon him. Exendine also has a bad injury to his side but may be able to play. Coach Stagg and three of his men saw us play on Saturday and the game was so hard we had to show everything we had, and have had no time to get anything new ready. We have not seen Chicago play at all, but I hear they are one of the best teams in the west and the best Chicago ever had. They are expected to win and it will take the very best efforts on our part to win. I think the boys will win but with Frank out of the game, it looks pretty blue.[58]

Carlisle arrived at the Del Prado Hotel in Chicago to find that the local newspapers unanimously predicted a large victory by Stagg's team. "Sports writers refused to concede that poor Lo had a chance," Warner remembered. But the Indians still had some wherewithal, and nothing affronted them like being underestimated. Mount Pleasant's backup was Mike Balenti, a bright Cheyenne student and a capable quarterback. And they still had Exendine. At a pregame banquet at Lake Forest College, Lubo remarked, "We lost the Princeton game by overconfidence, but we will not lose the Chicago game on this account."[59]

The Indians passed the time in Chicago by dining at the States restaurant and attending the La Salle Theater. When they rose on the morning of the game, they were encouraged to see perfectly crisp football weather. At Marshall Field, the turf was covered by hay to keep it dry, and workers raked it away to reveal a brilliant green rectangle as spectators began filing into the bleachers.[60]

By kickoff, the stands were packed to capacity with twenty-seven thousand onlookers, awash in Chicago's maroon colors. People jammed together on extra standing-room platforms that had been erected behind each end zone, giving the stadium an amphitheater quality. Still thousands more fringed the sidelines, peering through wire netting. Carlisle's share of the gate was $16,960, a scarcely believable sum for a single game.[61]

From the opening kick, Carlisle defied the predictions of a rout. The first time Chicago's Steffen gathered in the ball, Exendine and Gardner hit him, one from each side. Exendine rose and stood over

Steffen's prone figure. "Huh," he said. "Wizard of the West." He turned away contemptuously.[62]

It was a contest between two of the strongest and most innovative teams in the country—and an impasse. Each time Steffen took a step, it seemed the Indian end was there to spear him. There would be no open-field runs.

But Carlisle couldn't make any progress, either, unable to connect on its long passes over the middle. All game long Stagg assigned two and three men to shadow Exendine. Whenever he tried to run downfield, they hit him. "They would wait until I almost had the ball," he remembered, "and then chop me down."[63]

Chicago tried small, short passes to the sidelines, with no effect. The Indians settled for a pair of field goals by Hauser.

But early in the second half, Exendine noticed that the Chicago scrubs were crowding the sideline. It gave him an idea. In the huddle, Exendine told Hauser, "Hold the ball as long as you can." Hauser understood and nodded. They went into formation.

As the ball was snapped, Exendine took off down the sideline. Once again, two Chicago players converged on him and hit him. Exendine let them knock him out of bounds. As Exendine stumbled off the field, the Chicago players stopped and turned back to the play.

Using the Chicago players crowded along the sideline as a shield, Exendine circled the bench—and started running again.

Behind the line of scrimmage, Hauser launched the ball forty yards downfield. Exendine darted back onto the field, all alone near the Chicago goal.

For a moment, it was a frozen scene in a staged drama. The ball hung in the air, a tantalizing possibility. Could Exendine reach it? Would he catch it or drop it? Defenders wheeled and stared downfield. Spectators, watching from the stands, found that the breath had died in their collective throats.[64]

The spiraling ball seemed to defy physics. What made it stay up? When would it come down? In that long moment, twenty-seven thousand spectators, mashed together on benches and crammed on platforms, may have felt their loyalty to the home team evaporate, in the grip of a powerful new emotion. They may have noticed something they never had before: that a ball traveling through space traces a profoundly elegant path. They may have realized something else: that it was beautiful.

The ball struck its human target. Exendine caught the pass, all alone, and trotted over the Chicago goal line.

The stadium exploded in sound and motion. On the Chicago sideline, coaches and players screamed with outrage. On the field, the referee signaled the score. But in the stands, the spectators marveled. The crowd "held its breath in amazement for a time, then stifled its local pride, and turned loose its enthusiasm, and cheered for the Indians," the *Chicago Daily Tribune* reported.

It was the game-breaker; the rest was just anticlimax. The final score was 18-4 for Carlisle.

The long pass had arrived in Chicago, although by a circuitous and out-of-bounds route. The Indians, declared the *Tribune*, had given "such an exhibition of its possibilities as will not soon be forgotten in that vast throng."[65]

ON THE morning after the game, Warner and the Indians awoke to a nasty surprise. The *Chicago Daily Tribune* carried a scathing editorial by Carlos Montezuma, the former school physician, accusing them of "professionalism." Montezuma charged that Carlisle's feats that season had come under "false colors." Only about one-third of the players were real students, he claimed; the rest shirked class and were no more than "hired outsiders."[66]

W. G. Thompson, the former Carlisle disciplinarian and football manager, had put Montezuma up to the editorial. Thompson was one of many of the Carlisle old guard who had been forced out during the wholesale changes made by Mercer, and he was embittered. He wrote Montezuma, who also resented the changes at the school as an old Pratt ally, a long and inflammatory letter.

> *My Dear Doctor,*
>
> *As you are probably aware, I am no longer at the Carlisle School. All, or nearly all, those who served under General Pratt have left one way or another. As you know I have been a strong*

advocate of clean sport, and as the present Supt. and also the coach care only to win and at any price, I failed to dovetail in their schemes as well as I could have. The school has degenerated into a school of professional athletics, where everything—the welfare of the individual as well as that of the community—must step aside to gratify the desire of major Mercer and "Pop" Warner (the coach) to win, and create a large account to use as they wish, without supervision from Washington. When an official was there from Washington about a year ago, the athletic finances were not inspected, the Supt. making a fight against it, claiming he should not have to account for such money, etc. An inspection of the athletic finances would have shown some undesirable conditions—conditions that might have reflected upon the School's management very much.

You will recall that when I introduced football in 1894, that I required the boys that took part to be pretty good boys, and the team was made up of boys who were bona fide students, and who, when away on trips, not only behaved properly, but took active part in church and YMCA meetings wherever they were. You also know that not a penny was ever paid to a player. But all this has changed! The discipline of the school has so degenerated (caused very much thru the loafers brought to and kept at Carlisle for athletics) that not long ago the ministers of Carlisle were on the point of petitioning the authorities at Washington but were held off by a prominent divine who is one of the chaplains of the school. The disciplinarian has at different times received orders not to permit punishments to interfere with the student athletic duties—athletic "duties" above everything![67]

Thompson suggested Montezuma publish an indictment of the football program—knowing full well that the mood in the press was turning against Carlisle. The *Tribune* editorial was typical of a punitive tone that had crept into the press coverage of the Indians that season. Montezuma's editorial was just one salvo, though a damaging one, coming as it did from an old ally and prominent intellectual.

In early November, the *New York Herald* had done a feature story on the Indians that made similar insinuations. "The reason assigned for the overwhelming success of the Indian footballists by a local authority is that they are months or years better equipped physically than their college opponents, and that they have the highest type of professional coaching back of them. Football has been reduced to a science at Carlisle."

The story mentioned Carlisle's blocking sleds and their new athletic dorm, as if they were unsavory professional elements. "It has been said in Carlisle that those who make up the local eleven have caught from their coaches not only the true meaning of the new game of football but have gone so far beyond it as to have nullified the intentions of the rule makers," the piece concluded.[68]

Most of the charges against Carlisle were exaggerated. Warner responded swiftly to Montezuma, with an accounting of the roster showing that fifty-two of the fifty-four players were full-time students. Five of them, including Exendine, Gardner, and Mount Pleasant, were taking special college prep or law courses at Dickinson, simply because Carlisle didn't offer such classes. He did acknowledge that the center, Shouchuk, was no longer a student but an employee.[69]

"Of necessity, the eligibility rules for athletes at Carlisle cannot exactly coincide with those of the universities, as conditions here are entirely different," Warner said. But he added, "They are as fine a body of young men morally, of correct habits and gentlemanly demeanor as anybody, school boy, or university student athletes in the country. The school is proud of them and of their character."

The accusations against Carlisle could have been made against any school, then or now. The topics of eligibility and compensation were hardly unique to the Indians. It was difficult to see how Mount Pleasant, age nineteen, Thorpe, nineteen, Hauser, twenty-one, or Exendine, twenty-three, differed greatly from their opponents in a year when five of the men Walter Camp named to his all-American team were twenty-three or older.

Yet only the Indians suffered such heated discussion about their legitimacy. The treatment of the Indians in the popular press had shifted over time: first, they were curios, and next, they were "Poor Lo," an interesting racial foil for superior Ivies. But in 1907 they defeated four nationally ranked teams, including Penn and Harvard, and demanded serious consideration as the best team in the country. At this point the press, with the help of the axe-grinding Montezuma, turned on them and began to ask whether they belonged in the college ranks. Were they a "real" college team?[70]

So long as the Indians lost to the Ivies, they were considered a legitimate opponent. But now that they'd won, they were suddenly illegitimate. It smacked of another equation. As one of the Carlisle players said to Warner, "You outnumbered us, and you had the press agents. When the white man won it was always a battle. When we won it was a massacre."[71]

The punishment of the Indians for their temerity came from all sides. The *New York Sun* ranked them just fourth in the season-end rankings, behind Penn, the team they had destroyed. Camp did not include a single Indian on his first team of all-Americans. Princeton refused to schedule them for the following season. Warner was disgusted with the whole debate and the bigotry of the press, and he said so publicly.

"If Carlisle's methods are not liked, no institution is compelled to compete with the Indians; but when they do compete and the Indian comes out on top, it is mighty poor sportsmanship for the supporters of beaten institutions and some of the $10 a week molders of public opinion to come out in the papers and belittle and throw mud at the visitors," he said.[72]

Balanced observers understood that the attacks on Carlisle were unfair and more than a little soreheaded. The *Washington Post* wrote a season-ending editorial suggesting that Carlisle's "humiliating" defeat of Penn had provoked much of the criticism. "But for that, no charge of professionalism would ever have been made against the red men." Members of the press "took the defeat of their pet team to heart, and in their anxiety to get even are overstepping the line a trifle."

But some observers were magnanimous about the Carlisle season of '07, recognizing that it was a breakthrough, a history-making advance in the way the game was played. Football would be a much faster and more elegant contest from then on. One of them was Yale head coach William F. Knox, who wrote a wrapup of the season for *Harper's Weekly*. Knox could perhaps afford to be generous, since Yale had gone undefeated that season without playing Carlisle. He praised the Indians for irrevocably altering the game.

"There is no doubt that of all the teams of the year the Indians are far and away ahead of every one in that particular department of the game," Knox wrote. "The great value of their pass as a scoring medium has been its great distance and accuracy. Like a shot they shoot from Hauser's hand straight as a die twenty, thirty, forty yards down the field, where, in the majority of cases, an Indian is on hand to receive the ball. They work it beautifully. . . . The Indians have had a harder schedule than any team in the country, and they have done marvelously well. The game of this year owes to them more than to any other new developments of the forward pass, and for that reason alone, by showing the fuller possibilities of this pass, deserve much commendation."[73]

But perhaps the best and most gratifying defense of all came from the elite Caspar Whitney. Writing in *Outing* magazine, Whitney suggested they were the equals of any team in the country.

"It seems to me the forward pass has unlimited possibilities in the way of clever and skilled development," Whitney wrote. "The 1907 record of the Carlisle Indian School team is certainly a remarkable one. They seemed to be on a train most of the season and as travel is very fatiguing, their succession of victories over the strongest elevens in the country was therefore the more notable. It may be said without implied criticism that the Indians are naturally less bound by eligibility rules than other college teams. Carlisle's game was conceived under new rules and was played brilliantly from first to last as a team, as well as individually, especially with regard to the spectacular performers Houser [sic], Exendine and Mount Pleasant. They used the forward pass successfully as well as more persistently than any other team of the year. Had they been prepared for one big final game like Yale, Princeton, and Harvard, no one can say for certainty who would be number one on the list."[74]

10

ADVANCES AND RETREATS

Pop Warner's routine at Carlisle was the same every Monday morning. He summoned his assistant coaches and his scouts into his study, where he fit his bulk into a chair, lit a Turkish Trophy cigarette, and started scheming against the opposition. "Now, how would you break that up?" he'd ask. Warner wouldn't strike another match. He'd chain-smoke through the morning and into the afternoon, the ashes dropping and the haze wreathing upward, while he thought.[1]

When Warner got tired of thinking, he went into his workshop. He believed that a man who used his head for a living should also work with his hands, in order to balance his life. If Warner wasn't in his study or on the football field, he could be found pottering and dabbling in his workshop. Anything at all might come out of his tool fetish: on one occasion, he invented a machine to smooth the wood floor at Carlisle's athletic clubhouse. It looked like an old cotton gin. "All are invited to come and see the wonderful invention," the *Carlisle Arrow* announced.[2]

He carved a golf club out of an old broken wooden bedpost. He made his own cherry cordial, grinding the pits. He jury-rigged so many devices for practicing football drills, sleds, harnesses, mannequins, and dummies that Illinois coach Bob Zuppke would say of him, "Pop Warner has all kinds of gadgets for his boys to use in developing fundamentals without personal contact, and I don't think he will ever be satisfied until he invents a robot player which will yell 'ouch' when tackled."[3]

Warner's head and his hands worked together. When his mind perceived a difficulty or a quandary, his fingers itched to draw or hammer out a solution. His tactile sense led him to invent modern shoulder pads. There was no garment heavier than an old wool football uniform when it got wet—players made their own pads out of felt and papier-mâché, and when the thickly stuffed sweater-jerseys grew heavy with perspiration or soggy in the rain, they were dead weight. The ribbed moleskin football pants were especially unwieldy, rattling with rattan or cane strips under the fabric to protect against bruises.

Warner looked for a material that could bend to the body and yet shield it. One day when he was buying a pair of shoes in town, a salesman handed him a shoehorn. As soon as Warner fingered it, he knew it was what he had been looking for. He found out where the shoehorn was manufactured, and sat down and drew a series of thigh and shoulder patterns. When the products arrived, he soaked them in hot water, bent them into the shapes he wanted, waterproofed them with varnish, and lined them with felt.[4]

As he neared forty years of age, Warner had grown into a man of abundant creativity—and contradictions. There was still a hint of the rogue opportunist about him, but he had acquired polish. His thick light hair was parted and smoothed straight down the middle, and his beefy neck was fairly well hidden under a high, elegantly starched white collar. A Windsor knot was tucked neatly into a tweed suit. The insecure young bully had turned into a formidable man.

He still had an appetite. In the afternoons, Warner liked to wander to the nearby Flickinger family store and bakery, where he sat in the kitchen and ate apple pie with butter. He wasn't a big drinker, but he liked his cocktails, and his trainer, Wallace Denny, kept a bottle handy for those cold afternoons when Warner desired it. "Wally, hand me my cough medicine!" he'd say.[5]

He had not lost his taste for a wager or an easy dollar. He frequented the local stocks and bonds office, and the local bookie, too, sometimes betting hundreds of dollars on Carlisle's games.[6] He was still an operator, merely a more savvy one. Among other things, Warner came up with a canned goods scheme. The government wouldn't pay for the school to requisition athletic equipment, but it would pay for canned goods. So, Warner went into the canned goods business: He acquired an interest in the Springfield Canning Company, and got Carlisle to order its goods from his warehouse. Warner used the profits to buy the equipment he wanted.[7]

Warner's huge presence pervaded the Indian school's campus. He overshadowed even the superintendent—not a difficult thing to do given the weaklings who held the position after Pratt. At the conclusion of the 1907 season, Major Mercer announced he was stepping down, claiming to be worn out by his duties. "Though in good personal health, I find the daily annoying responsibilities all more than I can stand, and I am advised that a few months leave of absence would be of benefit," he announced in the December 27 edition of the *Carlisle Arrow*.

Mercer's replacement was an unimpressive, nonmilitary man, Moses Friedman, a bureaucratic climber who had risen fast in the Indian Bureau. Friedman was just thirty-four, but he had already served as assistant superintendent at the Haskell Institute. He was the slender, good-looking son of a German Jewish immigrant, educated at the University of Cincinnati, and he had married well.[8]

His wife, Mary Buford, was from an old Kentucky family with heroes on both sides in the Civil War. She was the daughter of General John Buford, a Union savior at Gettysburg, and a cousin of the Confederate raider Basil Duke. Mary Buford was an attractive woman who scandalized the more conservative faculty members and students by using makeup and powder, playing peekaboo behind the porch pillars with her husband, and hosting suffragist events.[9] She must have been a catch for Friedman, whose good head of hair and pleasant smile were accompanied by a wan personality. Like Mercer, Friedman doesn't seem to have brought much to the campus in the way of competence or caring. He was certainly no match for a thousand or so energetically rebellious adolescents, or for the bold influence of Warner.

The enormous profits Warner had brought in from the 1907 season paid for a building project that included a new print shop and an art studio, an overhaul of the dining hall, and new electrical wiring in the dormitories. Last but not least, $3,400 went into building a two-story, white-shingled cottage for Warner and his wife. Their home sat on the lower edge of campus, near the Letort Spring and the school vegetable gardens.

Some of the profits went to the players, too. Warner was silent on that tricky subject at the end of 1907, but he had indeed paid his players. As the Indians became such a huge box office draw, it had only seemed right to give them a small cut. Mostly players received small amounts of $10 and $15 at a time, but some of them had received loans, or larger cash bonuses. Exendine, for one, received $200 in that year.[10]

Arthur Martin, Warner's secretary, observed, "Yes, the boys felt they'd earned it, so Pop turned it over to them."[11]

As far as the Indians were concerned, the payouts from Warner were just one more negotiation with authority. Whatever they earned from football was perfectly in keeping with the adamant dictates of the school that they be wage earners. It was also yet another limited allowance. They were accustomed to school authorities and federal agents strictly controlling their access to money, even the funds they earned from low-paying outing jobs. Every dime had to be pulled from the pocket of a government agent with an itemized list of what they wanted the money for, as if they couldn't be trusted. In 1907, Thorpe wrote the Sauk and Fox agent, requesting $50 to buy a suit, a hat, a watch, an overcoat, and a pair of shoes. He was denied.[12]

Warner seems to have genuinely sympathized with his players on this account. For years, Warner kept a copy of a letter from one student complaining of his plight in the outing program, earning slave wages.

> Now I am going to write you this day and inform you how I like my place. First of all matters I would say earnestly I don't like it. I think the trouble is I am too big for him because he told me right before my face, he said he rather have a small boy so he can give him six or seven dollars a month for his labor. This was when I first came to this place, and ever since he has had the

same opinion and I thought to myself sometimes as I was here
with him like a great defileth or endless defileth.

Another thing he can't give me higher wages, he wouldn't do
it for any man, and yet he wants me to work on two farms and
he only gives me ten dollars a month. Gracious life, a woman
gets more than ten dollars a month for housekeeping. I would
rather be a housekeeper than work on two farms for ten dollars
a month.[13]

But Warner also understood that if the rest of the collegiate world
knew about the cash bonuses to players, they would find Carlisle
guilty as charged of "professionalism." He soon decided the practice
was either improper, risky, or bad policy, because he discontinued
cash rewards after the end of the 1908 season. Instead, he opened an
account in town at Mose Blumenthal's clothing store, where players
were allowed to charge items.[14]

Football profits also paid for the remodeling of the old infirmary
into a new dormitory solely for athletes. It was their personal king-
dom, an airy, gracious white Victorian building with a wraparound
porch and tall windows looking out onto the quadrangle. It had reading rooms, pool tables, and, most important, its own kitchen. Life
inside the building was privileged, primarily because the football
players got vastly better victuals. While regular students were fed a
diet of tasteless oatmeal with no milk or sugar, beans, hominy, rice,
infrequent meat, and watery gravy, the football boys were the envy of
campus for their heaping plates of beef and potatoes, along with milk
and butter. Friends begged invitations for breakfast on weekends,
when the players cooked huge batches of pancakes.

Warner's influence was heard and felt as much as it was seen on
campus. On the practice field, he bellowed and gestured with his cigarette. When he was pleased he swatted his players on the back, and
when he was displeased he kicked them in the backside. At the chalkboard, he lectured them. "There is no system of play that substitutes
for knocking an opponent down. When you hit, hit hard."

On the field, he cussed them: "You god-damn bonehead!" or "I'll
knock your block off!"

But, oddly, Warner could also be heard leading the school songs. He was an amateur composer who fashioned a loving Carlisle anthem:

Nestling 'neath the mountains blue,
Old Carlisle, our fair Carlisle,
We ne're can pay our debts to you,
Old Carlisle, our fair Carlisle.
While the years roll swiftly by,
In our thought thou'rt always nigh,
To honor thee we'll ever try.
Old Carlisle, our dear Carlisle.

All your precepts we hold dear,
Old Carlisle, our fair Carlisle,
The world we'll face without a fear,
Old Carlisle, our fair Carlisle.
Rememb'ring thee we'll never fail,
We'll weather every storm and gale,
While on life's troubled sea we sail,
Old Carlisle, our dear Carlisle.[15]

On another occasion, Warner decided the Carlisle rooting section needed better cheers. He wrote a ditty for the students to chant when his team was on the field:

'Taint no use to stand and whine
When they're coming through the line
Hitch your trousers up and climb
Keep a goin'.

On the football field, Warner needed all the creativity he could muster. The seasons from 1908 to 1910 were difficult ones for Carlisle, as they were for other teams around the country. The game was regressing into a violent grind.

★   ★   ★

FAMILIAR PLAYERS left, and new ones came in. Carlisle lost much of its brilliance as Mount Pleasant, Exendine, and Gardner graduated to Dickinson Law School. Everything seemed harder. "No rooters followed us, we had no cheer leaders and no old grads to bellow encouragement, so that the Indian boys played in an alien and oftentimes hostile atmosphere," Warner remembered. On one occasion, they walked onto a field to hear thirty thousand people chanting the fight song of the home team.

A lineman named Man Afraid of a Bear turned to Warner ruefully and said, "Good thing this isn't a singing contest, hey Pop?"[16]

Carlisle cadged out a 10-2-1 record on the strength of Thorpe's running and Warner's ruses. With such an elusive personality as Thorpe in the backfield, the Indians were more than ever a team of feints and misdirection. Warner hadn't lost his penchant for trickery—and he didn't restrict his feints to the field, either.

Before the Indians met Syracuse, Warner declared that his team was riddled with injuries. As the Indians took the field, they wore heavy bandages around their heads, hands, and various limbs. They hobbled through their pregame warmup, audibly groaning. But as soon as the ball went up, they sprinted down the field.[17]

Confusing Syracuse even more was the fact that the Indians wore leather patches in the exact shape and color of footballs sewn onto the fronts of their jerseys. On each snap, the entire Carlisle backfield clutched at the front of their sweaters and doubled over, as if they had the ball. To the Syracuse defenders, it looked like an entire team of ball carriers. They didn't know which one to chase.

But sitting in the stands was a scout for Carlisle's next opponent, Harvard. Assistant coach Harry von Kersburg returned to Cambridge and reported the stunt to the Crimson's new head coach, Percy Haughton, and told him to beware of it.[18]

Haughton called his team together and offered a varsity letter to anyone who could devise a way to counter the Indians' trick. Players and coaches studied the rulebook and came up with outlandish plots, with no luck. Finally, a newspaperman suggested the perfect solution to Haughton, who cheerfully awaited Carlisle's arrival, confident that he could outsmart Warner.

On the afternoon of November 7, 1908, Haughton and Warner met on the field before the game to choose the game ball. Haughton had his team manager, Dick Eggleston, haul out a dozen balls for inspection.

All of them were dyed crimson. They perfectly matched the color of the Harvard jerseys.

"You can't do that!" Warner said.

"Glenn, there is nothing in the rules against it," Haughton replied archly.

After a fairly heated argument, Haughton and Warner came to an agreement: Haughton would use an unpainted ball if Carlisle removed the imitation footballs from their jerseys. Harvard won, 17-0.

It was the beginning of a fascinating rivalry. Haughton and Warner could hardly have been more different as people or as coaches. Haughton derided Carlisle's style of football as "whiff whaff." He was an arrogant Groton and Harvard grad with an affinity for the power game, if not outright brutality. He had made all-American at tackle in the punchy, bloody days of 1895, and even then earned a reputation as a bitter competitor. As captain of the Harvard baseball team in 1899, he threw dirt in the Yale catcher's face.[19]

Haughton was working as a bond salesman in 1908 when Harvard's alumni turned to him as head coach. The Crimson had lost twenty of the last twenty-eight games with Yale, and the previous season of humiliation had turned the slogan "Fight fiercely, Harvard!" into an intolerable joke. Haughton was hired to put pugnacity back into the program, which he immediately did. The Crimson went 9-0-1 in '08, and would go unbeaten for thirty-nine games between 1911 and 1915.

Haughton was a martinet, a hard-line disciplinarian who made a direct connection between football and military leadership. The first thing he did at Harvard was hire Ernest "Pot" Graves, the West Pointer, as his line coach. Graves was a commissioned lieutenant of engineers, and Haughton needed special permission from the Army to borrow him. Haughton sent a plea to Teddy Roosevelt, who in turn sent an emissary with a note to his secretary of war, William Howard Taft:

"Dear Mr. Secretary, I was a Harvard man before I was a politician. Please do what these gentlemen want."[20]

Haughton demoted players to the scrubs if he caught them looking away during a lecture. He installed military hand signals for calling plays. He instilled a sense of soldierly pomp in the Crimson. He would dress forty or fifty players for a game and drill them in pregame warm-ups just to intimidate opponents.

He labeled the week of the Yale game "joy week," and tied a toy bulldog mascot behind his car and dragged it along the highway. He grabbed a Harvard student manager who happened to be standing in his path on the field and tossed him aside, screaming, "Out of the way, damn you!" He shouted at a player, "The trouble with you is that you perspire! I want men who sweat!"

When the player collapsed from his exertions, Haughton screamed, "Haul him off! This is no field hospital!"[21]

It was Haughton who was as responsible as anyone for the trend back to brute force in college football in 1909. In a way, the Indians were also responsible: schools so feared the forward pass that they began to move defenders off the line in order to protect against large gains. With the weakening of the defensive front line, some coaches, led by Haughton at Harvard, turned once again to mass wedge plays.

In the '09 season, Haughton debuted a terrible new flying wedge assault called "barnyard football." It entailed concentrating the entire force of the Crimson on a single "salient" in the line. Every available player interlocked and hit the line at a dead run and either pushed, pulled, or hurled the ball carrier downfield.

There were fourteen fatalities that autumn. One of them came in a fraught game between Harvard and Army, when West Point cadet Alexis Eugene "Ici" Byrne, son of a police chief and Civil War veteran, died trying to defend against the barnyard formation. As the Crimson's line barged downfield, Byrne dove headfirst into the pile. When the heap of men was peeled away, Byrne did not get up. "I can't move," he said. His neck was broken, and he was paralyzed. He died shortly after reveille Sunday morning, leaving the corps so heartsick that they canceled the rest of their season.

Just a week earlier, Navy's quarterback, Earl Wilson, had suffered a spinal injury in a game that eventually cost him his life. On November 15, a fullback for Virginia named Archer Christian died in a game against Georgetown.

The deaths led to yet another reform movement. In a series of meetings from February to May of 1910, the rules committee once more overhauled the game. Wedge formations were permanently abolished, as was any form of interlocking interference or pushing and pulling. At least seven men were required on the line of scrimmage, so as to prevent mass momentum plays, and no one was allowed to hurl the ball carrier forward, effectively outlawing the barnyard. Last but not least, restrictions on the use of the forward pass were removed. The devout hope was that teams would finally use the whole field and stop killing each other.[22]

CARLISLE TRUDGED through the violence of '09 without its best player. Thorpe's footloose nature had gotten the better of him, and he had bolted from school again. "Ran," a notation in his record said.

In June 1909, Thorpe was waiting unenthusiastically on the train platform at the Cumberland Valley depot for a ride to his summer outing job when he struck up a conversation with two of his teammates, Joe Libby and Jesse Young Deer. They were not headed to farms; they were going to North Carolina to play baseball, they told him. Thorpe was intrigued—he wanted to be a ballplayer. During his summer outings, he would go off by himself and find a tree, walk off the distance to a pitcher's mound, and hurl walnuts at a knothole.

On an impulse, Thorpe joined his schoolmates. The trio boarded a train for Rocky Mount, a tobacco and mill crossroads of about 7,500 on the Carolina coastal plains, where Thorpe signed on to play third base for $15 a week. He found a room in a small hotel, walking distance from the diamond and an easy stroll to the local taverns as well.[23]

Thorpe would be remembered in Rocky Mount for his kindnesses to local kids and his quarrelsomeness in the local bars. Like his father, liquor made him cantankerous, and after a few orange blossoms he wanted to take on all comers. One evening in Rocky Mount, when a local sheriff tried to arrest Thorpe for drunkenness, he turned the officer upside down and dumped him headfirst into an iron garbage can.

Among Thorpe's family, the legend still circulates that after this incident, when a barkeeper called the police, they responded they'd have to send ten men to quiet him down.[24]

Thorpe had promised Warner he would return to Carlisle after the summer. But August came, and Thorpe didn't. Instead, he decided he was done with school and went back to Oklahoma, where he lived with family and hunted for days at a time, running miles at the heels of his dogs.

Thorpe wasn't the only player who left campus that year. In February 1909, the *Washington Post* reported that more than half of Carlisle's starters were gone from school and being sought by officials. Fullback Albert Payne told a reporter that half a dozen players had skipped campus in rebellion over an unspecified disciplinary issue. "I was in the same fix and will not be back to play," Payne said. "The men broke the rules, and when an effort was made to punish them they walked out. The superintendent is hunting them, but he will not get them." Friedman denied the story and insisted Payne had been dismissed for "intemperance."[25]

One reason for the rash of runaways may have been Warner's effort to reform his program. Early in '09, Warner ceased paying the players. At about the same time, he dropped baseball as a varsity sport, citing a desire not to encourage "summer professionalism." Finally, Warner sent press agent Hugh Miller a letter and a check for $50, in exchange for muting his coverage of the team. The charges of professionalism had apparently chastened Warner. So had the fact that the Ivies were reluctant to schedule the Indians. Harvard and Princeton each temporarily dropped Carlisle for that season of 1909, the Crimson interrupting a series that had lasted for eleven consecutive years.[26]

"We wish at this time to make a few suggestions with reference to your handling of the athletic news of the school," Warner's letter to Miller said. "We feel that the time has come when Carlisle should adopt a more conservative policy in regard to her football team, because of the fact that at the present time there is so much said about commercialism in athletics. If Carlisle is to hold her place upon the schedules of the best teams in the country, we feel there should be no effort made to advertise or try to force publication of news of

our football team. We feel that there has been a little too much sen-
sationalism in connection with the football news sent out from
Carlisle, and by flooding the newspapers with pictures, the impression has been gained that news matter has been sent out more for
advertising purposes than as news items."[27]

There wasn't much to sensationalize, as Carlisle struggled through
back-to-back seasons of 8-3-1 in 1909 and 8-6 in 1910. The highlight
of '09 was a 32-0 victory over St. Louis, in which the Indians completed ten of thirteen passes. Watching the game from the stands was
Thorpe, who must have had second thoughts about leaving school or
else missed his teammates, because he traveled to Cincinnati to see
the contest. He turned up at Carlisle a few weeks later for Christmas
and to ring in the New Year. But if Warner hoped Thorpe would remain
on campus, he was disappointed. Thorpe went back to Oklahoma,
and to North Carolina for another summer of baseball.

The 1910 roster was one of Carlisle's less illustrious. Rather, it featured a player who was notorious. Asa Sweetcorn was a Sisseton
Sioux from South Dakota, and surely the most ungovernable player
the Indians ever had. He was an enormous, brawling, swilling man
who wore size twenty-one collars and was said to be able to ram his
head through a wooden door in a liquored-up stupor.

Sweetcorn had trouble getting down into a lineman's crouch, and
one afternoon Warner came up behind him and administered a hard
kick to Sweetcorn's rear, to force him into the proper position. Sweetcorn barked in pain and rose up to face Warner. "Thanks," he said.
"Now I can get down. You just busted a boil that was hurting me."

On another occasion, a referee named Dr. Forest E. Craver had to
warn Sweetcorn he would throw him out of the game if he didn't stop
swinging his fists so wildly. Sweetcorn continued to throw punches,
and finally, Craver called time and ordered Sweetcorn off the field.

"What did I do?" Sweetcorn asked.

"Slugging," Craver replied.

"Did you see me?" Sweetcorn asked.

"Out," Craver said.

"Did you see blood?" Sweetcorn asked.

"Out," Craver said again.

"When I slug them you see blood," Sweetcorn said, and walked off the field.[28]

Finally, Warner had enough. At the end of the season, the Carlisle team was to attend the Army-Navy game in Philadelphia. Warner told the players to dress in their best, and when Sweetcorn showed up for the train looking slovenly, Warner decided to leave him at home. Sweetcorn got staggering drunk and shot up the Cumberland Valley rail station. He was arrested and thrown into the local jail, making him the subject of a one-liner that swept around campus: "Did you hear about Sweetcorn? He's in the can."

Sweetcorn was shipped home, where he achieved near-mythic, if tragic, status. He was arrested forty times for intoxication, and had an ear bitten off in a wrestling match, occasioning another joke about his name in the local paper: "Chews Sweetcorn Ear in Winter."[29]

Warner didn't miss Sweetcorn, but he continued to miss Thorpe. As it happened, Thorpe missed Carlisle. He was at loose ends, having soured on summer-league ball after the team he played for in Fayetteville folded. He was bumming around Oklahoma when he ran into Exendine, who had finished Dickinson Law and was home to check on his family and property, on the main street of Anadarko. The two men shook hands and exchanged news, and Thorpe told his old friend that he was finished with minor-league ball.

"Why don't you go back to Carlisle?" Ex asked.

"They wouldn't want me there now."

"You bet they would."[30]

At about the same time, Warner sat down and wrote a letter coaxing his old protégé back for the 1911 season. As a lure, he dangled the possibility that Thorpe could make the 1912 Olympic team if he trained hard.[31]

Thorpe was quickly readmitted to Carlisle. That fall he was back on campus, where his new roommate in the spacious athletic dormitory was Carlisle's quarterback—a spare young man named Gus Welch.

Gus, the former ragamuffin, was at last a football player at Carlisle. In September 1908, Welch's grandmother had put him on a train east along with his younger brother, James, handing them a jug of water and some food for the trip. The boys walked through the Pullman cars and stared into the compartments. Welch asked a conductor, "Where do we sleep?"

The conductor said, "Do you have a reservation?"

"No, our mother sold it," Gus replied. "We live with our grand-mother."[32]

Three years later, Welch was president of the Carlisle student body. He had grown into a twenty-year-old with a narrow, solemn face and an outthrust chin that gave him a confident air. He kept his black hair closely cropped and combed straight back from his forehead, which gave him a look of added seriousness.

Welch was another one of those students who considered Carlisle a self-defining opportunity, and he intended to make the most of it. At five foot eight, he was 155 pounds of concentrated fury. As a member of the track team, he regularly finished second only to Thorpe in sprints and hurdling events. When Warner told him he could move into the special quarters for varsity athletes, he was so overcome that Warner had to tell him twice before he believed it.[33]

Welch regularly made the honor roll. He was earnest about his leadership position on campus, especially when it came to the younger boys, whom he constantly urged out of doors and taught to bat or throw. He hadn't forgotten his family's tuberculosis-ridden history, and he was acutely aware of the health issues at the school.

Once, Warner found Welch rummaging around in the gymnasium for cast-off equipment. Warner asked him what he was doing. Welch replied that he was looking for secondhand bats and balls to give to the younger students.

"We want those kids to grow up to be big and take the lesson of health with them when they go back home," Welch said. "Now that we're no longer people of the chase, poor physical condition is the curse of the Indian. A game of some kind is our one chance against tuberculosis."[34]

Welch was as highly regarded by the Carlisle faculty as he was by his peers. He was a particular favorite of the willowy young poet Marianne Moore, who as a new teacher found herself grateful to him for helping to maintain discipline in her classes. Moore remembered Welch as one of the most resolutely dedicated students, "oh, so tenacious."

Moore was barely out of school herself, a 1909 graduate of Bryn Mawr and the well-bred granddaughter of the minister of the First Kirkwood Presbyterian Church in town. Moore had a frail, Victorian appearance, tiny-waisted and long-skirted, with ruffled shirtfronts. But underneath her ruffles, she was sporty. She rode her bicycle to campus every day, and she was a baseball and football fan. As a villager, she had been reared on the stirring success of the Indian school teams. "We were just proud of them," she said. "The whole town was."

Moore had returned from Bryn Mawr and was taking courses at the local business college when Friedman hired her in 1911 to run Carlisle's "commercial" department, a course of study in which students learned how to handle their business affairs. She taught arithmetic, typing, stenography, and commercial law (a class in contracts so they wouldn't be cheated when they went home). Initially there was some concern that Moore might be too delicate to handle a class of thirty Indian students. But the athletes set an example and protected her from the occasional rowdy or recalcitrant student. "I found them incomparable in cooperativeness, courtesy, earnestness as students—also friends and invaluable in aiding me to preserve discipline in my part of the building—a rather serious matter at times," she remembered.[35]

The solicitousness of the athletes may have had something to do with Moore's sensitivity toward them. On Memorial Day, Moore took her class out to the Indian cemetery to tend to the graves of the children who had died at the school. Moore, Welch, Thorpe, and the rest of the pupils spent the afternoon cutting the grass around the tiny headstones. When they finished, Moore chaperoned them to a holiday circus performance. Toward the end of the day, rain threatened. "Miss Moore, may I carry your parasol?" Thorpe said chivalrously.[36]

Thorpe had returned to Carlisle that fall more mature, with a superbly proportioned 180-pound physique, over which he seemed to have gained absolute command. There was no kinetic movement that he didn't perform gracefully. He could run a hundred yards in ten seconds, throw a sixteen-pound shot forty-eight feet, and leap six feet one inch in the high jump. In addition to his world-class ability in football, baseball, and track, he led the school in basketball, lacrosse, hockey, handball, and tennis. And that didn't count dancing or billiards. When he made a good shot, he would celebrate by leaping over the pool table, landing with his feet together.[37]

But Thorpe was perplexing. He was curiously sleepy-eyed, and his movements never seemed urgent. Nobody could quite figure him out. "A strange, whimsical fellow," Exendine called him.[38]

Warner was stymied by Thorpe's temperament. His practice habits, to Warner, bespoke laziness. Exendine recalled that Warner thought Thorpe was "inclined to loaf and be a bit careless. This drove Warner almost to distraction." Warner continually lost his patience with Thorpe in practice and would hector him, but Thorpe would just say, "I'm satisfied."[39]

Warner then would explode, shouting, "I tell you what to do, and you start a debate!"[40]

Even though Thorpe had the strength of a bull, it was only with difficulty that Warner could persuade him to hit the center of the line. "Oh hell, Pop," Thorpe would say. "What's the use of going through 'em when I can run around 'em?"[41]

Warner and Thorpe were two singular, headstrong men, and they took the full measure of each other. For one thing, neither could intimidate the other. Thorpe was mule-headed and proud, and he had no physical fear. He believed he could overcome anything, which made him careless about his ability. "In addition to having every needed physical asset, Thorpe had a rare spirit," Warner told sportswriter Grantland Rice. "Nothing bothered Jim. When he was 'right,' the sheer joy of playing carried him through. When he wasn't, he showed it. For that, I used to call him 'a lazy Indian' to his face. I'll admit it, though it didn't bother him. . . . Thorpe only gave it on certain occasions. It was difficult to know if Jim was laughing with you, or at you."[42]

Interestingly, Thorpe tended to agree with Warner's estimation. "He never knew how hard I was going to try," Thorpe said. "Maybe he was right. I played for fun. I always have, ever since I was a kid." Thorpe put it even more succinctly on another occasion to Rice. "I played with the heart of an amateur—for the pure hell of it."[43]

For Thorpe, games were an escape; he was far more comfortable in the physical world than in society, where he was shy and lacking in social skills. His parental relationships had been taken from him early, and he was fundamentally a loner who competed for his own stakes and no one else's.[44]

But beneath the seeming carelessness, something burned. Thorpe's teammates noticed an almost taunting quality to his running. Exendine, who spent more time coaching Thorpe than anyone but Warner, understood that Thorpe enjoyed making opponents look silly. "Now, Thorpe had speed and plenty of strength," Exendine remarked. "But he was a master at deception in his running. He'd come straight up to a man, then fake him one way ever so slightly, then go the other. He'd hit him a kind of glancing blow which knocked him more off balance than flat as a pancake."[45]

There were times when Thorpe would seek out a defender and take him on just for the sport of it. If one man remained between him and the goal, he'd purposely go at him. "Thorpe did one thing I've never seen another football player do, nor have I ever been able to teach another one to do it," Exendine remembered. "When he'd get loose and head for the goal he took a devilish delight in upsetting the safety man. He'd run at him instead of away from him. When he'd get a few yards in front of him, running full tilt mind you, he'd begin to feint with his shoulders, eyes and legs, until the anxious fellow was in a fearful state of indecision. Then he'd charge right for the man, with his head and shoulders down and his legs far out of reach. When they met, Thorpe would somehow manage to deal him an awful blow with his hip. I've seen him spin them almost completely around in the air."[46]

Thorpe had yet another peculiar trait: when he was angry, he laughed. Once, during a fight with a teammate, Thorpe took a blow on the chin. Thorpe barked out loud—and then whirled and delivered a punch to his opponent, opening a cut that required nine stitches. The worst thing one could do was hit him unnecessarily. Thorpe would just stand with his hands on his hips, snicker, and then run right over the poor soul who'd struck him. "Just before he was about to tear somebody apart, he always laughed," Exendine said.

Early in the 1911 season, it became obvious that the two roommates with the disparate temperaments, Welch and Thorpe, were complementary talents and the soul of the team. Their partnership had an improvisational quality. As Welch took the field in the season opener against Lebanon Valley College for his first start at quarterback, he was nervous. He turned to Thorpe to go over his assignment on the first play. "What do I do if I miss my block on the end on 48?" he asked Thorpe.

Thorpe said, "Just keep on running, but keep out of my way."

Welch missed the first block, and a second one, too. But he kept on running, with Thorpe behind him. Thorpe gave the safety a head fake and raced into the end zone with Welch leading him. They went to a 53-0 victory.[47]

Welch was a natural field general who could twist a defense entirely around with his play calling. Thorpe was a game breaker who alternately feinted or muscled opponents. In the second game of the season, against Muhlenberg College, a player who tried to tackle Thorpe head-on left the field with a broken collarbone.

Around them, the rest of the team was an assortment of role players. Stancil "Possum" Powell, a durable, barreling fullback, was from Cherokee, North Carolina. Alex Arcasa was a quiet Colville from the Northwest who served as a versatile all-purpose halfback and an able passer. Elmer Busch, a 192-pound lineman, was a lumbering, easygoing twenty-year-old Pomo from Potter Valley, California.

One of the oldest and oddest members of the team was lineman William "Lone Star" Dietz, a twenty-seven-year-old student-teacher in the art department who claimed to be part Sioux, but whose origins were in fact murky. According to Dietz, he was born on the Rosebud reservation, the son of an Oglala named Julia One Star and a German engineer, but was raised by whites in Wisconsin. Recent scholarly examination of his story suggests he may have fabricated at least parts of his background, and it's impossible to know whether he was in fact part Sioux. He went to small colleges in St. Paul, Minnesota, and Wichita, Kansas, where he showed talent as both a ballplayer and an artist, before arriving at Carlisle to play football and to court the school's art instructor, Angel DeCora, whom he married. Dietz drew many of the illustrations that decorated Carlisle school publications.[48]

Carlisle opened the 1911 season with eight consecutive victories, six of them shutouts. The Indians beat Pitt 17-0 and Lafayette 19-0 on successive weekends. When Thorpe suffered a sprained knee and wrenched ankle that kept him on the sidelines for a game against Pennsylvania, the Indians proved they weren't a one-man team. Welch broke the game open on a ninety-five-yard punt return, for a 16-0 victory.

That brought the Indians to the inevitable big game: Harvard. The 1911 edition of their meeting would be a classic, included in collections and anthologies as one of the greatest games ever.

In the days leading up to the game, Warner and Haughton played cat and mouse. Their rivalrous maneuverings enlivened the papers even in a busy news week: Count Zeppelin flew his dirigible over the Kaiser's palace, Mrs. Reginald Vanderbilt introduced the turkey trot at a dinner party at her Newport estate, and Enrico Caruso arrived from Europe and denied he had become engaged. "Bah!" he said.[49]

Haughton made news when he suggested that he might not use his starters against Carlisle. It seemed he preferred to save them for Dartmouth and Yale, more important upcoming contests. This may have been a ruse: it was a typical Haughton strategy to wear an opponent out with the second team, and then use his starters to mop up.

Warner publicly ignored Haughton's arrogance, while in secret he devised a new play to make the Crimson look silly. It was a little something called the reverse.[50]

Warner also devoted his time to trying to heal the leg of his star player. Thorpe was still hobbling around campus on crutches. In hopes that Thorpe would at least be able to kick the ball, Warner went into his workshop and contrived a combination of wrap and plaster cast to stabilize Thorpe's leg. It ran from his toes to above his knee.

Game day arrived, and thirty thousand people jammed into Harvard Stadium, beside the Charles River. As the Indians jogged into the gigantic horseshoe of steel and concrete, the thousands of fans roared, and colored pennants rippled across the steep bleachers. The field was a rich and soft green, freshly lined with chalk. A Carlisle end named Henry Roberts thought, "No one could get hurt here." Thorpe, with his wrapped leg, was more than usually quiet. But it was a sign of determination, not pain. In the first half, he kicked field goals of 13 and 43 yards.[51]

Welch waited until early in the second half to unveil the reverse—and caught Harvard completely unaware. He handed off to teammate Alex Arcasa, who ran to the outside—and then handed off to Thorpe, sprinting in the opposite direction. Thorpe raced for twenty yards before he was stopped at the forty. It was the key play in a drive that resulted in their only touchdown of the day.

Welch burned the Crimson on the reverse over and over, and at the end of the third quarter, Thorpe kicked a third field goal of thirty-seven yards. The Indians led, 15-9.

But during the two-minute time-out before the start of the next quarter, there was a flurry of activity on the Harvard sideline. A fresh collection of players pulled off their warm-up sweaters and sprinted onto the field. They were the Harvard starters, including all-American halfback Percy Wendell. The crowd erupted.

On the Carlisle side, the Indians' starters were exhausted, bent double trying to catch their breath. Almost to a man, they experienced a sinking sensation as they watched the excited Crimson players jump up and down on the field.

The fresh Harvard starters blocked a Thorpe punt, and lineman Bob Storer retrieved it and ran it in for a touchdown. It seemed impossible that Carlisle could hang on.

"Most of the fellows, I guess, believed that we were beaten," Thorpe remembered. "Somehow, I never thought so."[52]

But if the Indians' morale flagged, Thorpe restored it. He told Welch to give him the ball. "Get out of my way," he told his teammates. "I mean to do some real running."[53]

It was the combination of Welch's strategy and Thorpe's kicking leg that made the difference. As time ran down, the Indians worked the ball to Harvard's forty-eight-yard line, where they faced fourth down. The Indians started to line up in a punt formation. But Welch studied the situation and turned to Thorpe. Why not try a field goal? he suggested.

Thorpe said angrily, "Who in the hell heard of a place kick from here? Let's punt the ball."

Welch insisted. He pointed out that a placekick was as good as a punt, and they might even get lucky with it and score. For a brief moment Welch and the other Indians argued back and forth. "I'm the quarterback," Welch said, and he was calling for the field goal.[54]

It was a now-or-never moment. Thorpe nodded. "My leg was pretty sore," he remembered, "but I think the soreness sort of helped me, because it made me more deliberate. I was pretty tired. All the other boys were the same."

Thorpe took a couple of extra paces backward while his holder, Arcasa, kneeled to take the snap. The line surged. Arcasa caught the snap, and placed it in the grass.

Thorpe strode forward and drove his leg into the ball. It rose and tumbled end over end. Years later, Thorpe recounted the kick:

> As long as I live, I will never forget that moment. . . . There I stood in the center of the field, the biggest crowd I had ever seen watching us, with the score tied, and the game depending on the accuracy of my kick. I was tired enough so that all of my muscles were relaxed. I had confidence, and I wasn't worried. The ball came back square and true, and I swung my leg with all the power and force that I had, and knew, as it left my toe, that it was headed straight for the crossbar and was sure to go over.
>
> The Harvard tackles came through, but they got there a little too late, and though they blocked my sight of the ball, I got the thrill of that moment. Just before the crowd started to yell, I was sure the three points had been made, and that Carlisle had beaten Harvard. Nothing else mattered. . . . When the gun was fired and we knew that we had beaten Harvard, the champions of the East, a feeling of pride that none of us has ever lost came over all of us, from Warner to the water boy.[55]

As the ball settled over the goalposts and bounced several yards into the Harvard end zone, for the 18-15 lead that represented the final score, Thorpe buckled. He was so enervated that "my legs seemed to give way after that play, and I could hardly walk back for the kickoff." Although there were still a few minutes left in the game,

he signaled to Warner. As he hobbled off the field, the Harvard crowd
rose to its feet in a standing ovation.

As the final minutes ticked down, a mass celebration began on the
Carlisle sideline, with players clutching at each other. As Henry
Roberts came to the jubilant sideline, a Harvard lineman stopped
him, to shake his hand. Tears were streaming down his face.[56]

It was a short-lived celebration. The victory over Harvard left the
Indians in a strange state, overconfident and yet sore and lethargic.
They lost the very next week, to an inferior Syracuse team.

Welch had injured his back against the Crimson and did not dress
for the game, and Thorpe was distracted and still limping. The field
at Archbold Stadium was ankle deep in slush from a freezing rain, and
after just a few minutes, the entire team was shivering and plastered
in mud. Thorpe missed a crucial extra point and let a punt go over his
head. Warner pleaded with him. "Where's your sense Jim?" he said.
"Don't you see that speed isn't getting you anything on this slippery
ground? For heaven's sake, use your weight."[57]

Welch put on a uniform and ran onto the field, and Thorpe scored
a bulldozing touchdown. But it was too late—they lost 12-11, to ruin
their perfect season. Warner believed the Harvard game had gone to
their heads and given them "an exaggerated idea of what they could
do themselves."[58]

The Indians never quite recovered their form, though they finished
with two more victories for an 11-1 record. To Warner, it was yet
another instance of Thorpe's baffling carelessness.

With the football season over, Warner and Thorpe moved inside to
the gymnasium, to train for the Summer Olympics in Stockholm. But
to Warner's deep frustration, there were times when Thorpe wasn't
even sure he wanted to go to the Olympics. He had never completely
lost his love for baseball, and he seemed more interested in the idea
of playing in the majors than in Olympic medals. "What's the use of
bothering with all this stuff?" Thorpe would say in the midst of a
track workout. "There's nothing in it."[59]

After a meet that spring, as the Carlisle team rode a train back to
campus, Warner was furious to see Thorpe strolling through the cars

smoking a big cigar. Warner called him over, jerked him into a seat, and lectured him on his duty to his school and to himself. After a while, Thorpe heaved a sigh. "Oh, all right then," he said, "but I'd rather play baseball."

Warner never entirely reconciled himself to Thorpe's casual outlook. But he gradually accepted that Thorpe had his own inner ear when it came to training. He was fundamentally fit from a lifetime spent outdoors, and believed that overwork would only harm him. "More athletes are hurt by going stale than by dissipating," Thorpe declared.[60]

Anyway, it was hard to argue with Thorpe's results. In the late spring of 1912, Warner took Thorpe, Welch, and half a dozen other Carlisle athletes to Lafayette for a meet. The Lafayette coach was skeptical as he surveyed Warner and his squad of eight men.

"Where's your team?"

"Right here," Warner said, smacking Thorpe on the shoulder.

"You'd better call off the meet. We have a squad of fifty."

"We'll try to make a contest out of it," Warner said.

Thorpe took first place in six events.

Thorpe was a grown man and an Olympian, and yet he still didn't have access to his own income as he prepared to leave for Stockholm. He wrote to the Sauk and Fox agent, Horace Johnson, asking to withdraw expense money for the trip. "Please send me $100 from my account. Will need same this summer in taking trip to Sweden with Olympic team."

Johnson refused. "I have to advise that I cannot conscientiously recommend to the Indian office that this be done," he wrote. It was the agent's conviction that Thorpe should stay at home and find a job or farm. "He has now reached the age, when, instead of gallivanting around the country, he should be at work on his allotment, or in some other location."[61]

Thorpe sailed for Stockholm with empty pockets, which must have made the *Finland* of the Red Star line, on which he sailed, seem even more luxurious. He joined an Olympic team that included a West Pointer named George Patton, competing in the pentathlon, and a Hawaiian swimmer named Duke Kahanamoku. Also on the team was his fellow Carlisle student Lewis Tewanima, a distance runner with an extraordinary story. He was one of a dozen Hopi students who had arrived at Carlisle from the mesas of Arizona practically as prisoners because of their tribes' refusal to accept white education. They impressed Warner as "a wild looking bunch with their long hair, huge earrings and furtive eyes." Tewanima watched Warner train the track team with the intentness of a hawk, and one afternoon he asked for a track suit. He was a tiny, emaciated man of 110 pounds, and he hardly looked able to stand, much less run.

"What for?" Warner said. "You're not big enough to do anything."

"Me run fast good," he said. "All Hopis run good."[62]

Tewanima had grown up chasing rabbits as a child and once ran 120 miles to Winslow just to see the trains. Tewanima became America's greatest distance runner despite the fact that he had never run an oval. Once he lost track of his lap count, and Warner had to remind him he wasn't at the finish line.[63]

Thorpe spent his time in transit training on a cork track laid on the ship's deck or napping in a hammock. According to one story, his penchant for saving himself appalled the head trainer for the Olympic squad, Mike Murphy, who also coached the Yale track team. According to Grantland Rice, who heard the details from American marathoner Johnny Hayes, one morning Murphy went looking for Thorpe and found him swinging in the hammock, while Warner lounged in a deck chair getting some sun.

"Glenn, I've seen some queer birds in my day, but your Indian beats all. I don't see him do anything. Except sleep," Murphy said.

"Mike, don't worry," Warner said. "All those two-for-a-nickel events you've got lined up for Thorpe won't bother him. He's in shape, what with football, lacrosse, baseball and track back to back at school, how could he be out of shape? This sleeping is the best training ever for Jim."[64]

The episode, true or not, created the myth that Thorpe never worked out, as did another supposed exchange aboard the *Finland*. Newspaperman Francis Albertanti of the *New York Evening Mail* was also aboard the liner, and one afternoon he noticed Thorpe relaxing in a deck chair.

"What are you doing, Jim, thinking of your Uncle Sitting Bull?"

"No, I'm practicing the long jump," Thorpe said. "I've just jumped 23 feet, eight inches. I think that will win it."[65]

In fact, Thorpe trained hard during the ten-day trip on the liner, keeping warm as he pounded around the track in a turtleneck, cardigan, and knickers. He was in peak condition, as his performances showed in those "two-for-a-nickel" events. Thorpe won four of the five pentathlon events. He was third in the javelin. After pocketing his first gold medal in a rout, he relaxed for six days before the start of the ten-event decathlon. During the break, he watched Tewanima take the silver in the ten thousand meters behind Finland's Hannes Kolehmainen.

Thorpe set a record in the decathlon that would stand for sixteen years. He took firsts in the fifteen hundred meters (in a blistering time of 4:40.1), the hundred-meter hurdles, the shot put, and the high jump. With each victory the Stockholm crowds cheered louder and louder. "Isn't he a horse?" became a common refrain among spectators. Thorpe's point total of 8,412.96 was almost seven hundred points better than what the runner-up, Sweden's Hugo Wieslander, could put together.

The decathlon concluded on the final day of the Games, when Thorpe had his famous exchange with King Gustav of Sweden. Thorpe walked to the medal podium, neatly attired in blazer and necktie with a white panama hat held over his heart. King Gustav, splendid in top hat and swallowtail coat, a walking stick hung on his arm, presented him with the gold medal and a wreath, as well as a bronze bust of himself and a jeweled chalice of gold and silver in the shape of a Viking ship offered to the decathlon champion by the Czar of Russia. As Gustav and Thorpe shook hands, Gustav said, "Sir, you are the greatest athlete in the world."

"Thanks, King."

That evening, ebullient and released from training, Thorpe toured the bars of Stockholm, sampling Swedish beer and punch. Late that night he returned to the *Finland*, which was docked in Stockholm harbor, roaring drunk. Thorpe was "more than a little cheered," Warner reported, and he pranced and leaped about the ship, yelling, "I'm a horse! I'm a horse!"[66]

When the athletes arrived back in New York, a million people lined the parade route along Fifth Avenue. While other Olympians rode together in a caravan, Thorpe was intensely uncomfortable alone in an open car, followed by his gleaming trophies, which were topped by a fluttering Carlisle pennant. As the throngs applauded, Thorpe sat frozen "in embarrassed silence," according to the *Boston Post*. He pulled his Panama hat over his eyes, chewed gum, dug his fingernails into his knees, and barely lifted his chin. He became animated just once, as he passed the reviewing stand and recognized James E. Sullivan, head of the Amateur Athletic Union.[67]

The constant ceremonies were intolerable to Thorpe. Back at Carlisle, he and Tewanima were cheered as they rode through the streets in a horse-drawn carriage to the Dickinson athletic field, where he had to sit and listen to droning speeches. Moses Friedman read a letter from President Taft that said, "You have set a high standard of physical development which is only attained by right living and right thinking." Thorpe's own speech was brief and taut. "You have shown us a splendid time and we are grateful for it." Then there was a dinner at the Elks Club, and more speeches. Finally, Thorpe had enough, and slipped out to a bar. Warner had to send Arthur Martin after him. The only enjoyable part of the whole affair was the dance in the school gymnasium. Thorpe could finally unwind, and he danced until well after midnight.[68]

Thorpe's modesty was not an affectation. He was genuinely discomfited by his fame and took pains to remain a regular student. Two days after he returned to campus, an awestruck young Sioux student named James Garvie said to him, "I saw a picture of you," and asked Thorpe if he could have a copy of the photograph. Thorpe said, "I'll get you that one." A few days later, Thorpe walked over to Garvie's room himself and presented it to him. He also remained gently attentive to the school's youngest boy, Dick Kaseeta, a Chiricahua Apache orphan who had come to the school at age six in 1907. Thorpe carried Kaseeta on his shoulders, and the boy called him Uncle Jim.[69]

As the attention finally died down, Thorpe considered his future and sorted through an array of financial offers. Promoter C. C. Pyle offered him $10,000 to go on a baseball exhibition tour, and Thorpe was tempted to accept. But Warner fended off Pyle and all the other hucksters "with their own personal version of exploiting Jim's new-found national popularity." He intended to keep Thorpe at Carlisle, to exploit him for one more season of big football gate receipts.

Warner and Thorpe talked it over. Another all-American season would give him more negotiating leverage, Warner argued. "I pulled Jim aside and told him that with the anticipated large gate ticket sales at Carlisle football games for the season, along with a fine performance by him that season and his recent Olympic victories, there was little doubt his market value would substantially increase by season's end."[70]

Warner also appealed to Thorpe's competitive nature. Thorpe could help the Indians take revenge on Syracuse if he came back, Warner pointed out. Also, he could help them beat Pittsburgh—the coach at Pitt, Colonel Joe Thompson, had been a member of the Olympic staff and had taunted Warner and Thorpe throughout the Games.

But what made up Thorpe's mind was the prospect of helping the Indians gain a victory they would cherish more than any other, over a team that had recently become one of the most powerful in the country. It was a team that Thorpe personally viewed as the Indians' "greatest rival."[71]

Army.

11

THE REAL ALL AMERICANS

RIBAL LAND THEFTS were a standing source of jokes on a foot-ball team that fought for every yard. The Carlisle Indians had a saying when they were on the end of a bad call from a referee: "What's the use of crying about a few inches, when the white man has taken the whole country?"[1]

The 1912 Indians were a team of rampant high spirits and collective banter. It wasn't unheard-of on the Carlisle campus to find the dairy cows locked in the gym, or a pig in a bag hung from the school flagpole. Unsuspecting students, standing at attention with their hands behind their back in the dining hall, might discover they were holding a hot potato, suddenly thrust on them by Thorpe.

A few years earlier, James Garvie was standing at attention and saying grace before a meal in the dining hall one afternoon when he felt something slipped into his hand. He squeezed it—and a soft prune exploded.

"Who is that guy?" Garvie asked.

"That's Jim Thorpe who played that trick on you," the reply was. "That won't be the last one either."[2]

Laughter was their glue, and often as not, their humor was based in a shared subversive drollery about their Indianness. On the practice

field, Welch kidded around that they didn't need all those complicated plays. All they needed was one sound, fundamental strategy:
"When you see a white man with the ball, get him. When your man
has the ball, knock down every white man you see."[3]

To a certain extent, Carlisle's brand of humor reflected a broader
sensibility that was blooming among tribal intellectuals. The previous autumn, a new organization called the Society of American Indians had convened for the first time. It was made up of about fifty
prominent members of the intelligentsia who would gather annually
from 1911 to 1923 to exchange views on issues collectively con-
fronting their tribes. Among them were Dr. Charles Eastman, Dr.
Carlos Montezuma, and Carlisle's art teacher, Angel DeCora. The
organization was heavily influenced by the Carlisle philosophy, but it
also gave birth to pan-Indianism, the notion of an intertribal movement that stressed solidarity as a way to cope with white hegemony.

Although the society tended to be conservative and serious-
minded, some of its members possessed an incendiary wit. The society printed a quarterly magazine in which lampoons occasionally
appeared, including this bull's-eye caricature that echoed the experiences of a number of Carlisle's players, from Delos Lone Wolf to anyone who'd ever played against Harvard:

Me workum on my farm. Wearum overalls. My boy come long
home. Been way gov'ment school. Putum on overalls help ol'
man plow um fields. Boston man come along in smell-bad-snort-
wagon. . . . Boston man him say, say 'um his wife-woman,
"really, aborigines laboring! Most extraordinary!" Boston-heap-
talk-man yell 'um, "Aw! Come here my good fellow." My boy he
go see um. Heap-talk-Boston-man say um, "You got farm no?
You been Carlisle? You no go back to blanket? You paint face?
You got heap squaw? You civilize, sure, eh? You get drunk all the
time, no? You Carlisle failure, no? You got cough inside? You got
high blood pressure? Me your friend. Understand me? I do you
heap of good. Believe me! Have a cigarette, no?"

My boy, he stan' heap straight. Face hard, eye flash black fire.
Him talk um pale face dictionary silly. Him say 'um, "Stranger,

I perceive you are afflicted with hallucinations concerning the present status of the portion of our country's population you are wont to designate Indians. In all probability a practitioner of psychopathic therapeutics would diagnose your evidently microscopic intellect as due to some phase of cerebrocardiac neurosis producing paralsthesis and dyaethesis, if not atropathy of the entire cerebral tissue. As for your questions couched in stilted English, I have no inclination to answer them. May Cerberus bite you when you reach the Styx. Good day, sir."

Boston man heap sick, yell, "Maimie fetch the smelling salts!" Me say 'um, very anxious, "Boy you kill um Boson talk man, no?" Boy say, "No, Dad, I told him he was crazy and go to blazes."[4]

The members of Carlisle's football team were themselves a pan-Indian movement. They took pride in their cohesion and in the fact that so many disparate characters from so many different tribes, regions, and circumstances could form such a brilliant whole. They were a close-knit group who would remain friends all their lives, serve as best men at each other's weddings, and have numerous reunions. A decade later, in 1922, they would even attempt to reconstitute themselves in a barnstorming professional football team called the Oorang Indians. The team featured seven former Carlisle players, led by Thorpe, and was an entertaining version of what they had been in their youth.

The Indians of 1912 were exquisitely—and sardonically—aware that they were "making a record for their race," as Pratt put it. But their way of doing so was to literally set a record: they became the highest-scoring team in the country.

Over the first four games of the season, the Indians averaged almost fifty points an outing. Crack timing and cutting-edge stratagems, as usual, were their stock in trade. In the hands of the rapid-fire play caller Welch, the Indians operated a hurry-up offense that kept opponents continually off balance and out of breath. The Indians hardly huddled—they would just line up and run a series of plays at lightning speed as Welch reeled off audible signals or used hand gestures to make adjustments. Some of the gestures he used were Indian signs.[5]

The Indians were improved by the addition of two wildly talented new reserves in the backfield, recently promoted from the Hotshots. Pete Calac was a Mission Indian from California who'd lost much of his family to typhoid fever and who rode the Union Pacific to Carlisle when he was just a 113-pound boy. Joe Guyon was a mortally shy nineteen-year-old from the White Earth Agency in Minnesota who rivaled Thorpe in broken-field ability. "Splendidly developed," his enrollment card said. His heart was judged by the school physician to be "best I ever examined." Guyon would make all-American in 1913, but he stayed at Carlisle for just two seasons before enrolling at Georgia Tech in 1916, where he became an all-American again under John Heisman.

The Indians experienced just one early-season hitch, in a game against Washington and Jefferson that they had trouble taking seriously. Thorpe was unfocused and missed three field goals, while Welch indulged in overly flamboyant signals that aggravated Warner. "The team's play calling of fancy end runs and daring passes sapped them of their energy in the hot weather," Warner observed. As he stalked the sideline in mounting frustration, the Indians fumbled around, and the game ended in a scoreless tie.

The team had a stopover in Pittsburgh on the way home, and Thorpe and Welch, moping over the game, decided to go to a saloon down the street from the train station. After about an hour Welch rejoined the team for dinner, but Thorpe stayed at the bar. Warner, irate, went after Thorpe and hustled him out of the saloon and into the street, where Thorpe resisted and "created a lot of excitement by his shouting and loud talking," Warner remembered. As a crowd of onlookers gathered, Warner manhandled Thorpe into a local hotel lobby, then out the back door and to the train station. The next morning the Pittsburgh papers were full of sensational accounts of the incident, reporting that Warner and Thorpe had traded punches.

The following day at Carlisle, Warner shamed a hung-over Thorpe with a lecture about his public stature and threatened to throw him off the team. "Thorpe, you've got to behave yourself. You owe it to the public as well as your school. The Olympic Games have made you into a public figure and you've got to shoulder the responsibility." He showed Thorpe a story from a Pittsburgh paper accusing Warner of knocking out "the world famous Jim Thorpe in a street fight." Thorpe apologized to his team and settled down for the rest of the season.[6]

The Indians blew out Syracuse 33-0, Pittsburgh 45-8, and Georgetown 34-20. During the trip to Washington, Thorpe took Welch to the home of his Oklahoma representative, Charles David Carter, one of the first congressmen from the new state and a leader of the Chickasaw nation. Carter would serve for twenty years on Capitol Hill, but of more interest to Thorpe and Welch was the fact that he had an attractive daughter named Julia, whom Welch soon began dating.

The Indians became so cocksure that they teased their opponents with their signal calling in a 34-14 victory over Lehigh. The game was such a romp that they began to announce their plays ahead of time. Welch, Thorpe, and Arcasa would arrange themselves in the backfield, and then one of them would yell, "What about going around right end this time?" They would race around the right end.

"Left tackle now, eh?" Thorpe would holler, and they would slash through the left tackle despite the fact that the whole Lehigh team was there waiting.[7]

Lineman William Garlow, a Tuscarora from New York, rivaled Welch as the most intellectual member of the squad. Garlow reduced his teammates, and the Lehigh players, to paroxysms of laughter with a riff he delivered whenever the Indians crossed the goal line.

"Gentlemen," Garlow would say, his voice full of sympathy, "this hurts me as much as it does you, but I'm afraid the ball is over. Nobody regrets it more than we do. If there was any way of correcting this error on our part, we should be glad to do it. But there is not the slightest doubt about the condition that confronts us here. It's a touchdown. We should much prefer that this were happening to somebody else but the facts are clear and you will very soon see that the little pellet is resting very securely behind the white line. We regret it, I am sure you regret it, and I hope that nothing happening here will spoil what for us had been a very pleasant afternoon."[8]

The Lehigh victory gave the Indians a 10-0-1 record. But that's when the joking stopped. The following week, they were going to West Point for what promised to be the fight of their careers.

Football, Caspar Whitney once observed, "is a mimic battlefield, on which the players must reconnoiter, skirmish, advance, attack, and retreat in good order."[9]

THE GAME had come to West Point relatively late. For years, play was constricted by a uniform code that forbade cadets from unbuttoning their tunics or removing their crisp gray trousers, even when engaged in outdoor recreation. The regulations were finally relaxed one day in 1888, when Lieutenant Colonel Hamilton Hawkins was walking by the barracks and saw two cadets trying to toss a ball back and forth in their stiff, high-necked coats.

"Have you young gentlemen white shirts on?"

"Yes sir."

"Then," Colonel Hawkins said, "I authorize you to lay aside your jackets."[10]

With uniform regulations relaxed, the cadets entered intercollegiate athletics in 1890 with a football game against Navy. They caught up with the top teams in the East quickly: by 1912, they were in the midst of a four-year stretch in which they built a record of 28-5-1. In 1914, they would be undefeated and untied.

But there was still something a touch archaic about the cadets. The accepted treatment for a sprained knee or ankle on the Army sideline was a glass of whiskey. Just that spring an outgoing all-American tackle, Robert McGowan Littlejohn, had challenged a man to a duel. Littlejohn was on horseback in the streets of Highland Falls when he encountered a motorcar and his startled horse shied toward some ladies. The driver yelled at Littlejohn, "If you don't know how to ride, you had better go back to the post and stay there instead of putting life and limb in danger here."

Littlejohn replied, "It would be well for you, sir, to attend to your own business. If you will only mind your own affairs, I shall be able to take care of mine."

Later, Littlejohn sent a note to the driver: "Permit me to say that I regret extremely the rules of the United States Military Academy do not permit me to dismount in the streets of Highland Falls. If they did, allow me to assure you there would be no necessity of addressing you now. However there are other opportunities, and it will give me great pleasure to meet you on any Wednesday or Saturday afternoon."[11]

The brand of football played by the Army team of 1912 was old-fashioned, and so was the man who coached it. To Pot Graves, football was not so much a game as an exercise in sheer violence. "Pot was a supreme proponent of designed butchery," said lineman John McEwan. "And he was right. Football is not a game. You can't get anywhere in it by going out and exuding an aroma of good fellowship."

Graves' motto was "Carry the fight to the opponent and keep it there all afternoon." The slogan was written on the bulletin board before every Army game, and he looked for men who would play that way.[12]

Alexander Weyand was a 200-pound sophomore and a tireless one-man wrecking crew at tackle. In 1911, he personally sent two Yale men to the sidelines, one with a broken collarbone and one with a knee injury. He played thirty-seven straight games without a breather, and he was also the academy's wrestling champion.

Leland Swarts Devore was Army's huge captain: The six-foot-six tackle and five-year letterman from Wheeling, West Virginia, was nicknamed "Big Un," with a stolid, meaty face.

In the backfield, there were four future World War II generals. The eventual three-star commander of the U.S. Second Corps, Geoffrey Keyes (class of '13), was possibly the most admired man in his senior class, a letterman in lacrosse and track, and winner of the academy tennis championship in doubles. The *Howitzer* yearbook said of him, "Our first inclination in taking up this subject is to bootlick." Yearling halfbacks Leland Hobbs and Vernon Prichard were future major generals, Hobbs as commander of the Thirtieth Infantry in Europe and Prichard as commander of the First Armored. Both belonged to the class of 1915, which would become known at the Academy as "the class the stars fell on" because it produced fifty-eight generals from a class of 164 members, including the five-stars Omar N. Bradley and Dwight D. Eisenhower.

Eisenhower worked his way into the varsity backfield that season with pure perseverance. As a plebe he weighed just 155 pounds and was relegated to the junior varsity as "too light." But he spent a year in the gym relentlessly strengthening his body until he put on twenty pounds of muscle. In West Point's first practice game that fall, he finally attracted the attention of Graves. Eisenhower ran some post-game laps around the field and was trotting toward the locker room when Graves called out, "Eisenhower!" The yearling ran back, saluted, and said, "Yes, sir."

"Where did you get those pants?" Graves asked. Eisenhower's scrub pants were too large for him and bagged around his ankles.

"From the manager."

"Look at those shoes. Can't you get anything better than that?"

"I am just wearing what was issued."

Graves turned to a team manager. "Get this man completely out-fitted with new and proper fitting equipment." Eisenhower understood from the gesture that Graves had just elevated him to the varsity. He was so thrilled that he barely heard the rest of the conversation.

Eisenhower had just average speed, but he was a hard charger who loved to hit and be hit, and he was a critical factor in victories over Rutgers and Colgate that season. "I so loved the fierce bodily contact of football that I suppose my enthusiasm made up somewhat for my lack of size," he recalled. He was so combative a player that in one game, an opponent protested to the referee.

"Watch that man," the opposing player said.

The ref replied, "Why, has he slugged you or roughed you up in any way?"

"No. But he is going to."[13]

For both Army and Carlisle, the game had national implications. The cadets had lost just once all season, to Yale, 6-0, when Devore was injured and unable to play. Eisenhower almost single-handedly pulled that game out, carrying the ball on almost every play in a seventy-yard drive before they finally stalled on a penalty. But the cadets had bounced back on the strength of the best defense in the country, surrendering just thirteen points in four games. With a victory over Carlisle, they would still have hope of consideration for the number one spot in the year-end rankings.

For the Indians, the emotional and practical stakes were obvious.

From an immediate standpoint, the game represented their continual fight for respect. Though they were clearly the best offense in the land, commentators continued to mark them with an asterisk, as if they were something less than a real college team, and suggested they had run up their extravagant scores against weaker competition. A defeat of gritty Army, combined with their run of victories over Pitt, Syracuse, and Lehigh, would end all argument and establish them as the front-runner for the mantle of best team in the country.

Then there was the longer view. For Welch, the game couldn't help but recall "the real war out in the West." It was a theme that Warner harped on as he prepared them for the game, referring to their forefathers. Warner paid special attention to Thorpe. "He was primed for that battle," Warner remembered. "He and I had planned it ever since our trip to Stockholm and, when the time came to deliver, Thorpe was there."[14]

The day of the game was blustery and overcast. Kickoff was scheduled for three in the afternoon, under a sky that was as gray as the Hudson River. The entire palette of day seemed to be in West Point's colors. Heavy clouds were banked up in the sky. As the cadets entered the stadium in dress parade, their tunic capes spread over their shoulders, blowing in a cold, gray mist that came across the field. The Indians huddled on their sidelines underneath their scarlet blankets, trying to keep warm.[15]

Carlisle won the toss and chose the north goal, and the game began with the stiff wind at their backs. As the kick from Devore went up, the wind played with the ball, and Thorpe bobbled it momentarily before he brought it to the twenty-eight-yard line. The rest of the offense came onto the field.

What happened next was football history. Gus Welch called the first play, and in that moment, the "double wing" made its debut. The formation, which Warner had designed and reserved expressly for Army, was another radical departure: both halfbacks shifted closer to the line of scrimmage, just outside of the defensive tackles. The formation infinitely multiplied the Indians' options for trick plays. Anything and everything could happen. Thorpe, Arcasa, and Welch were never still, constantly shifting; they might run, fake, reverse, pitch, block, catch passes, or throw them. It was kaleidoscopic. The offense was thoroughly modern, and it would be enduringly effective and influential.

"Football began to have the sweep of a prairie fire," Warner observed.[16]

It played havoc with Army—and electrified the crowd. The Indians sheared off huge chunks of yardage: Thorpe on a crisscross around the end for fifteen, Thorpe off tackle for twenty.

"The shifting, puzzling, and dazzling attack of the Carlisle Indians had the Cadets bordering on a panic," the New York Tribune observed. "After a few minutes of play none of the Army men seemed to know just where the ball was going or who had it."

Army scored first, when Leland Hobbs broke loose around the right end for a touchdown. But Prichard missed the extra point, and the Indians countered immediately with a blitzkrieg of a scoring drive to take the lead.

The cadets tried vainly to defend with a seven-man line, as Eisenhower and his partner at linebacker, Charles Benedict, double-teamed Thorpe. It didn't matter. "Starting like a streak, he shot through the line, scattering tacklers to all sides of him," the Tribune reported. "It was just before he was tackled or hit that Thorpe displayed his hardest running, and more than once it took half a dozen men to drag him to earth."

On one play as Thorpe broke through, Ike and Benedict both hit him at the same time, one high and one low. Thorpe lay on the field for a long count. Carlisle called time, as Thorpe was unable to get up. Finally, referee J. A. Evans announced that play had to resume, although Thorpe was not yet recovered.

Devore said sarcastically, "Nell's bells, Mr. Referee, we don't stand on technicalities at West Point, give him all the time he wants."

Thorpe, revived, didn't appreciate being patronized by Devore. For the rest of the half he and Arcasa ran expressly at the large lineman. When Thorpe didn't carry the ball, he tore huge holes in the Army line with his blocks—one of which sprang center Joe Bergie for Carlisle's first score. Thorpe kicked the extra point, for a 7-6 lead.

On play after play, the Indians showed up Devore with the double wing. "The boast of their line was actually made to look absurd," Warner remembered. Just after the second-half kickoff, Devore finally lost his temper. As Guyon lay on the field, Devore took a running start and stamped on Guyon's back. The crowd hissed, and Devore was thrown out of the game.

The Indians responded by further embarrassing the cadets. Thorpe caught a punt at his own forty-five-yard line, and Calac and Welch opened the field before him with leveling blocks. Thorpe snatched the ball from the air and began dodging and zigzagging. He worked his way through the entire team and crossed the goal line, for a fifty-five-yard touchdown. But it was nullified by a holding penalty.

This time Keyes was careful to punt away from Thorpe. The Indians scored anyway. They moved downfield in just seven plays, Arcasa crossing the goal easily, and Thorpe kicked the extra point for a 14-6 lead.

From then on, the Indians totally outplayed the cadets. Thorpe put on his greatest single performance as a college player, dodging and hurdling out of the wingback. He ripped off runs of twenty yards as if they were commonplace. "It was like trying to clutch a shadow," the New York Times observed. His runs set up three touchdowns by Arcasa, whose scoring was merely the finishing touch.

Once, when Eisenhower and Benedict seemed to have Thorpe cornered, he stopped short. The two men crashed head-on, and Thorpe galloped past them. The Army coaches decided the linebackers were done for the day, and brought them to the sideline. It was one of the last games Eisenhower would play. In the very next week, he sprained his knee against Tufts. When he reinjured it while vaulting on a horse in the riding ring, he was forced to give up football.

Thorpe made one last spectacular play, a circus catch of forty yards on a pass from Welch in which he jumped two feet off the ground and made a twisting aerial move to snare the ball while surrounded by cadets.

By the late afternoon "the Cadets had been shown up as no other West Point team has been in many years," the New York Times wrote. "The Indians simply outclassed the Cadets as they might be expected to outclass a prep school." The final score was 27-6, and it could have been much worse: Carlisle did not give up a first down in the second half, and had the ball four more times on the Army five-yard line without scoring.

It was only Army's fourth loss in nineteen games, and it shocked the public, "which had firmly believed that the big Army team had passed the stage where such a thing might happen," the *New York Times* commented. "But the unexpected did happen, and its materialization was effected by the wards of the Nation that distinctly places the Carlisle team among the great elevens of the year."

The Carlisle team, joyous, spent, bruised, and damp from showers, boarded a train for the trip home. As they seated themselves in the rail car, a gentleman with a distinguished silver mustache boarded the train and took a seat with them. Walter Camp introduced himself and congratulated the Carlisle Indians on their victory.

All the way to New York, the Indians and the eminence of the game chatted. They quizzed each other and exchanged thoughts and opinions on strategy. Naturally, the Indians wanted to know his opinion of their offense. Camp greatly admired the team, he replied, but he didn't understand their lightning style.

"Your quarterback calls plays too fast," Camp said. "He doesn't study the defense."

Thorpe replied for the Indians that speed was the whole point. "Mister Camp," he said, "how can he study the defense when there isn't any defense?"[17]

The conversation with Camp must have seemed like the ultimate validation. The headlines the following day shouted their victory: "Army Eleven in a Rout." The *New York Times* rewarded them with arguably the highest public compliment they had ever received: the Indians were "one of the most spectacular aggregations of football players, especially in the backfield, ever assembled." As a whole, Carlisle played "the most perfect brand of football ever seen in America."[18]

In the end, it was just a football victory, and one-sided at that. Nevertheless, every member of the team, including Thorpe and Welch, considered it the most satisfying game they ever won. "The rattling of the bones," Welch called it.[19]

* * *

THE ARMY game was the closing of a chapter. The sad postscript to the 1912 season is well known: a scandal engulfed Thorpe, and Carlisle with him.

The immediate aftermath was an anticlimax: the Indians, brimming with overconfidence, lost the very next week to Penn, 34-26. The defeat was "due entirely to carelessness," Warner believed. Thorpe saw a deep pass coming toward his man, Quaker end Lon Jourdet, but he let the ball go, thinking it was out of reach. Jourdet made a stunning catch, and Penn went on to score—and win. Warner was beside himself. In his opinion, Thorpe could have knocked the ball down if he'd tried. After the game, he asked Thorpe about it.

"I didn't think he could get it," Thorpe replied.[20]

It was the beginning of a terrible period for Thorpe. He was in love with a Carlisle student named Iva Miller, but her parents forbade the marriage and she went home to California. Warner was in an awful mood and issued an edict that any player who missed an assignment had to receive a blow from every man on the team. Lastly, Thorpe was dogged by worry that his past as a semipro baseball player might be exposed in the press.

With a week off before the final game of the season against Brown, Warner took the team to Worcester, Massachusetts, to work out and rest. As the Indians practiced, some locals came out to observe them, including a minor-league manager named Charles Glancy, who had spent time in baseball's Carolina League. As Glancy was standing on the sidelines one afternoon, Thorpe jogged by, and Glancy recognized him. Glancy mentioned to a reporter from the *Worcester Telegram* that he knew Thorpe from the semipro league. It was a bombshell for the journalist: it meant Thorpe had been a professional when he competed in the Olympics, and could be stripped of his medals.[21]

That week, a curious story hit the news wires: "Athlete Thorpe to Quit Indian School," the story said. A brooding Thorpe suddenly announced to reporters that he was finished with school and wanted out of the public eye. "The only reason Thorpe gives for quitting the Indian School is that of an absolute dislike of notoriety and utter abhorrence of the public gaze which his athletic prowess has brought him," the story said.[22]

Thorpe crowned his Carlisle career with another epic performance, accounting for virtually all of Carlisle's points in a 32-0 defeat of Brown. Three touchdowns gave him a season total of twenty-five and an all-time collegiate record of 198 points. But Thorpe was unhappy. According to his friend and fellow Olympian Charley Paddock, "It was about this time too that Thorpe was beginning to hear rumors in regard to his amateur status. He was harried and worried when he went to Providence for his last college battle."[23]

On January 25, the story broke: Thorpe had played pro ball in North Carolina. While scores of college athletes played in the leagues, they had used assumed names. Thorpe, believing he was finished with Carlisle, had used his real name as he collected about $15 a week over two summers in 1909 and 1910.

Thorpe initially tried to deny the story, but reporters from the major newspapers quickly found his name listed in the records of the Carolina League. Warner and Superintendent Friedman professed shock and ignorance, protesting they'd had no idea Thorpe had played semi-pro ball, a position that now seems absurd. Warner advised Thorpe to throw himself on the mercy of the Amateur Athletic Union, and drafted a letter of confession for Thorpe to sign, which Thorpe copied over in the athletic dorm one afternoon. "I hope I will be excused partly by the fact that I was simply an Indian schoolboy and I did not know all about such things," Thorpe announced. "In fact I did not know I was going wrong because I was doing what I knew several other college men had done." Nevertheless, the AAU demanded the return of his medals and trophies. On January 28, the New York *Herald Tribune* reported, "Olympic Hero to Be Stripped of His Honors."[24]

Thorpe said to Warner, "I don't understand, Pop. What's that two months of baseball got to do with all the jumping and running and field-work I did in Stockholm? I never got paid for any of that, did I?"

Warner had no adequate reply. All he could do was try to swallow his own sense of guilt as he denied any knowledge of Thorpe's status. Years later he said, "I made the statement then and I make it now, that it was a brutal business."[25]

For the rest of his life, Thorpe was outwardly stoic about the loss of his medals. But the hurt was evident in a remark he made to Henry Flickinger, the Carlisle village boy who sold pies at the athletic field and became a good friend: "Hen, I didn't have too much, and now I don't have the medals."[26]

With his amateur status lost, there was nothing for Thorpe to do but play baseball. It was Warner's suspicion that the scandal was the work of a baseball scout who wanted to force Thorpe out of school and into the majors. If so, it worked. Warner notified teams that Thorpe was available to the highest bidder. Thorpe signed with John McGraw and the New York Giants for $5,000 a year, and officially left school.

The Carlisle football team was angered and disheartened by Thorpe's disgrace. To Thorpe's teammates, it seemed that he had taken the fall alone, with no one to defend him, while the two men who should have stood by him, Warner and Friedman, had affected ignorance and went uncensured. There was deep discontent with Warner in the locker room, even as the Indians went on to a 10-1-1 record in 1913.

In a game against an inferior Dartmouth team, the Indians trailed by 10-0 in the first half. A frustrated Warner turned to Al Exendine, who was working as his assistant coach. "You talk to them," he said shortly. Warner stayed outside the locker room while Exendine made the halftime speech. The Indians went on to a 35-10 victory.[27]

Warner had reason to be anxious about the Dartmouth game: he had $300 on the outcome. Shortly before the Indians retook the field, in an attempt to motivate them, Warner told them about the wager and offered them a cut if they prevailed. "If each of you wants to earn $5 apiece to have a little fun when we stop off in New York on the trip home, all you have to do is win this game," he said. At least some of the Indians found Warner's remark offensive, and it would come back to haunt him.[28]

By November 1913, the Carlisle students were in open rebellion against both Friedman and Warner. A group of 276 pupils signed a petition and sent it to the Secretary of the Interior, calling for an investigation into the conditions and management of the school. The ringleader who organized the petition was Carlisle's student body president, Gus Welch.

At the same time, students also filed complaints with the Indian Rights Association. The IRA forwarded a ten-page document to the Commissioner of Indian Affairs containing dozens of student allegations "reflecting seriously upon the moral atmosphere of the school." They charged that Friedman was unfit, that corporal punishment was used excessively, and that Friedman and Warner skimmed from the athletic fund.

The students were at least partly motivated by their anger over Thorpe's predicament. A pupil named Fred Bruce, who lived in the athletic dorm, wrote an affidavit to the IRA accusing Warner and Friedman of being complicit in Thorpe's ball playing. "I am sure that if you take up James Thorpe's case that it will be proven to you that Mr. Friedman and Mr. Warner knew that James Thorpe was paid and that it was for base ball before he went to Stockholm to win victory in the Olympic Games," Bruce wrote. "I am just writing this letter to show you how when an Indian is in trouble that they will have him shoulder all the blame and keep themselves clear. I say that is rotten business. I am yours truly, Fred Bruce, Indian from Montana."[29]

A four-member joint congressional committee launched an investigation of Carlisle. Sitting on the panel was Representative David Carter of Oklahoma, the father of Welch's girlfriend, Julia. An investigator named E. B. Linnen was assigned to make a surprise inspection of the school.

Linnen found the campus in disrepair and the students contemptuous of Friedman and Warner to the point of open hostility. Among their grievances were that the crockery was chipped and there weren't enough cups, plates, towels, or linens. Meals consisted of unsweetened oatmeal, a slice of bread, gravy, and rice and beans. There was butter just once a week, and a chronic shortage of bread, milk, and syrup.

Wallace Denny, who served as a school disciplinarian, described the hunger and the tension in the dining room for the committee: "I walked around the dining room, all over the dining room, and we are short of grub, we are short of bread; everybody would be asking for bread . . . they tell the students there is no more bread in the dining room and we know there is plenty of it in the bakery shop . . . They are dissatisfied and kind of unruly. I don't say they are bad, but they are hungry, and it is a mighty hard thing to please them."

A dozen members of the faculty testified before the panel, as did several students, to Friedman's mismanagement. He was said to lack "any human side of fatherly interest in the welfare of this student body." He rarely visited classrooms or residence halls, and when he did, students threw shoes at him and called him "pork dodger." Pupils were punished with hard labor or beatings. A girl who refused to go into the outing program was whipped with a piece of wood and punched in the face by the bandmaster, Claude Stauffer.

Faculty complained that Warner had become the real authority on campus. Four boys who refused to play in the band were taken to the guardhouse and whipped in the presence of Warner. Warner had struck players, kicked one, taken a switch to another, and told yet another, "I'll knock your block off!"

Most damning of all, Welch testified against his head coach. Warner was "a man with no principle," Welch stated. Other players added that Warner "used the worst cursing and swearing that he could use," and that they had seen him in hotel lobbies pocketing the "rake off" from selling extra tickets to games. They also testified to his gambling, and recounted his heavy betting on the Dartmouth game.[30]

The committee delved into the Carlisle Athletic Association finances and Warner's business dealings, looking for evidence of misappropriation. They found none. However, they did find that Carlisle's enormous football profits had paid for anything and everything on campus. The athletic association had as much as $25,000 in its treasury at its peak, so much that it invested in Northern Pacific and Reading Railroad bonds. William H. Miller, Carlisle's financial clerk, testified that the athletic fund was "a cure for all diseases" on the Carlisle grounds.

The committee became preoccupied by the question of to whom exactly the money belonged. Was it the government's? The school's? Were the players entitled to some of it? Warner's payments to players were detailed: all told, over the 1907 and 1908 seasons, he had given the thirty or so of them a total of $9,233, about $300 each.

Representative Carter asked, "Who does it belong to? Can you say?"

Miller replied, "No sir, I cannot."

Committee chairman Joe T. Robinson then interrupted to make a point: "As a matter of fact, it is earned by the pupils in the school?"

To which Miller answered, "Yes, sir."

As the hearings continued, they increasingly focused on the outsized role of athletics on the Carlisle campus. At the heart of the matter were ethical issues that the NCAA continues to agonize over today, without satisfactory answers. To what extent was football an enhancement, and to what extent did it interfere with student life? Should a coach be the highest-paid and most powerful employee on campus? Is he a teacher, or should he be purely concerned with winning? Were players—who put in exhausting physical labor in addition to their classwork—entitled to special treatment? The academic performance of Carlisle's football players tended to be excellent, and many of them went on to success in professional life. Did they deserve some kind of compensation in return for the huge profits, credit, and rich enjoyment they gave to Carlisle?

When it was Warner's turn to testify, he defended himself vehemently. He pointed out that football profits had paid for a new printing office, business department, heating system, lights for the dorms, and remodeling of the dining hall. As far as he was concerned, the only problem at Carlisle was a lack of discipline. "Instead of running the large boys quarters and telling the boys what they should do and what they should not do, they have allowed the boys to run them and tell them what they shall do and shall not do. . . . It seems to me that if the large boys are going to run that school up there and run the disciplinarian, it is time a change was made."[31]

In the end, the committee found no evidence of criminal wrongdoing by Warner. Nevertheless, he was irreparably damaged by the hearings. It was clear he had lost the respect of his players and had behaved less than ethically, and the committee recommended that he resign.

The investigation resulted in wholesale reform at Carlisle. Friedman stepped down in September 1914. He was charged with embezzling petty sums from the school (mainly for traveling to football games at government expense) but was eventually acquitted, and disappeared from public view, teaching at vocational schools. His replacement was an earnest young man charged with restoring Carlisle's prestige, Oscar Lipps.[32]

Warner stubbornly refused to quit, and he remained on campus to coach through the 1914 season. But it quickly became apparent that his position was untenable. A number of the players on his team had testified against him, and the rest were disaffected. Guyon left school, and Welch declined to rejoin the team.

The Indians lost to every significant opponent they played that year. In the tenth game of a miserable 4-7-1 season, which included a five-game losing streak, they met a powerful new dynasty: Notre Dame. The Fighting Irish were the current crowd favorites, thanks to their sensational use of the forward pass. In 1913, the tandem of quarterback Gus Dorais and end Knute Rockne had combined for five touchdowns in a dramatic upset over Army, 35-13. The press greeted the victory as if no team had ever used the aerial game on a national stage before, an error perpetuated to this day.

Welch had remained on campus preparing to enter Dickinson Law School, and he was so eager to defend Carlisle's football honor against Notre Dame that he returned to the squad for the game. He and Warner somehow buried their ill feelings, and he traveled to Chicago for the November 14 contest, to suit up at quarterback. It was a vain attempt to help the team, and he almost killed himself.

The Indians were slaughtered, 48-6. The Fighting Irish were led by a massive fullback named Ray Eichenlaub, and late in the game, as Eichenlaub burst through the middle of the line, Welch charged up and tried to stop him. Eichenlaub's knee met Welch's face.

Welch collapsed in a heap on the field, with a fractured skull and cheekbone. He was rushed by ambulance to Mercy Hospital, where for four days his condition was in doubt. As the hospital issued daily bulletins on his health, someone on the Carlisle team mailed a cryptic postcard to Julia Carter in Washington: "Gus Welch is badly hurt it is liable to stay with him for life. We lost after he went out."[33]

Slowly, Welch recovered. As he did, he fought to get out of bed against the advice of his doctors. The once-sickly boy must have been horrified at being in the hospital, because after just a week, he announced his intention to leave, alarming his physician, Dr. W. E.

Morgan, who wrote to Superintendent Lipps and asked him to intervene. "Like all young bloods who want to be stoical and laugh injuries to scorn he insists he is going to get up. Now it won't do at all to give him a loose rein. He not only sustained a fracture of the cheek bone (which he feels), but he had also a fracture of the base of the skull in front (which he don't feel) . . . which require absolute rest to ensure a future without invalidism, such as epilepsy, paralysis, deafness or loss of sight, anyone of which might develop in after years from recklessness or negligence at this time."[34]

Just four days later, Welch disobeyed doctor's orders and left the hospital. He stayed with a friend in Chicago for one night, and then made his way back to campus. "I am sorry to say that our patient Gus Welch deliberately kicked over the traces today and in spite of all advice to the contrary, left his bed and dressed himself, declaring he would assume all responsibility," Morgan wrote to Lipps. "Under these circumstances he passes out of my care and I do not care to be further responsible for him. I've done my best for him and I hope he will have no further trouble but if he does, he alone will be to blame." On November 30, Welch arrived back on campus, but his collegiate football playing was over.

The loss to Notre Dame effectively marked the end of Carlisle's heyday. At the end of the season, Warner tendered his resignation. He had an offer to become the new head coach at Pittsburgh, and he accepted it. On February 15, 1915, Warner took his official leave of Carlisle at a farewell banquet. Despite everything, Warner departed with regret. While his relationship with the school had often been tempestuous, he had an abiding affection for the place, and respect for the players. "They never gloated, they never whined, and no matter how bitter the contest, they played cheerfully, squarely, and cleanly," he remarked.[35]

Warner went on to a far more illustrious career after Carlisle, so much so that his early years there became almost forgotten. At Pittsburgh, he went undefeated four times between 1915 and 1920. At Stanford, he coached another unbeaten team and won a Rose Bowl victory in 1926–1927. He spent his last few years at Temple before finally retiring in 1938, with a record of 341-118-33.

But while Warner had greater success at other schools and continued to innovate, he never again drew up plays with quite such reckless flights of imagination as he had at Carlisle. Much of his later work was a refinement of his first experiments there. When he set down his memoirs as an aging legend, his tumultuous heyday with the Indians was what he dwelled on. "The experiences that stand out most vividly in my memory are those connected with the Indian lads," he wrote.[36]

The Indians were never the same without Warner, either. His replacement for the 1915 season was a Texas A&M graduate named Victor M. Kelley, but Kelley was unable to reforge the team. He left after just one season with a 3-6-2 record. In 1917, the Indians played their final season, under a physical instruction teacher named Deed Harris. It was a 2-7 nightmare, in which they lost 98-0 to a Georgia Tech team starring Joe Guyon.

The squad disbanded. Carlisle's football history was complete.

MUCH IN the long story of Carlisle was depressing. The history of the school was one of tribal capitulation, cultural destruction, and endless racial axe grinding. Carlisle's football record, therefore, is all the more striking: between 1911 and 1913, the Indians won thirty-eight football games while losing only three. It was a triumph amid so many other crushing kinds of defeat.

The numbers alone didn't fully express what the Indians accomplished. They were unique. Nobody before or since has played the way they did. Somehow, out of the uniformed, shorn, catechized student body came a team that was absolutely unmistakable. Not even Pop Warner was in command of that process—he was the first to ruefully admit how often the Indians played the game in their own way. The Indians' contributions to the game were original, and the game belonged as much to them as to anyone.

"Whenever I see one of those All America teams," Warner said, "I cannot help but think what an eleven could have been selected from those *real* All Americans who blazed such a trail of glory."[37]

The exploits of the Indians on the football field mirrored an epic transition all Carlisle students participated in: while a new American game was being born, the country's past was dying. The Indians first took up football against a backdrop of frontier cavalry battles. They finished playing the game on the eve of a new, mechanized world war—one in which ten thousand Native Americans served with the American Expeditionary Force. Among them were several hundred Carlisle students, including Gus Welch.

In April 1917, the United States entered the Great War, and Welch enlisted. He had slowly healed from his terrible injuries, but it had been a hard couple of years. Migraine headaches and poverty slowed his progress through law school.

Welch worked as an assistant disciplinarian at Carlisle for $20 a month. He borrowed from acquaintances, stole tips from tables in restaurants to make ends meet, and dodged creditors who wrote to the school seeking payment. He earned cash by playing for the Canton Bulldogs in the fledgling professional football league from 1915 to 1917. In one game, Welch dashed by a former Notre Damer named Charles Bachman as he raced for a sixty-five-yard touchdown. Bachman had been on the field the day Welch fractured his skull. "Pretty good for a dead Indian," Bachman thought as Welch ran by.[38]

In April 1917, Welch was well enough to enter officer training school at Fort Niagara. The entire student body at Carlisle waited anxiously to see if he would get a commission. Under the strain of boot camp, Welch began to have symptoms from his old head injury. He wrote to Carlisle's new superintendent, John Francis Jr.: "The shock received from the rifle fire causes me to have severe headache, while shooting the pain almost blinds me. My record on the range has been very good, although I have been working against a big handicap. I have said nothing to my officer."

Francis replied, "I do hope it is merely a matter which will wear off in a few days. . . . I am quite sure you would give a splendid account of yourself on the firing line and it would be a shame for a man of your splendid physical equipment to be barred on a technicality."[39]

Welch won his commission as a second lieutenant, despite the migraines and some missteps while he learned to drill a company of men. "One of these days I will get excited and will mix some principles of Indian warfare with our drill regulations, and no doubt I will have a great combination," he joked in another letter.

His superiors thought enough of him to place him in a special program at Harvard Barracks. There, he studied for three weeks under French officers, drilling in the same stadium where he had watched Thorpe's field goal flutter through the uprights. There was nothing to win at Harvard this time except a promotion.

"I have done my best, keeping in mind that I am a Carlisle man," Gus wrote. "I also had to remember that I was the only Redskin in camp, and of course my errors would naturally look larger than the other fellows'."[40]

On June 13, 1918, Welch made captain. The announcement of his promotion was made at Carlisle's fortieth commencement, to cheers. But after Harvard, Welch was put in charge of regimental recreation at Camp Meade in Maryland, to his frustration. He was impatient with the duty and wanted to get into the war.

Welch found a way to get to France. Like Pratt before him, he volunteered to join a company of all-black troops, a hastily organized new regiment that was about to be sent overseas. The 808th Pioneers were the forerunners of combat engineers, sent to do the dirty work of clearing the way for major offensives, and the Army needed officers who would lead them.

The 808th was organized in July 1918 out of 81 officers and 2,721 enlisted men and given just one month of training before it was shipped out, singing, "Goodbye Broadway, Hello France." Welch commanded a company of about 250, many of whom had been drafted just four or six weeks earlier, but he considered them "fine soldiers." Their insignia was a pick, shovel, and rifle.[41]

The Meuse-Argonne offensive began at 5:30 A.M. on September 26 with a barrage of 2,700 guns and lasted for forty-seven days. The Pioneers cleared the way for an offensive involving 850,000 men, scrambling with their Enfield rifles through a maze of barbed wire and machine gun pits. They were engulfed by rolling banks of smoke, poison gas, and the smell of cordite, and dodged shells that blasted great holes in the earth. It rained, creating a sucking mud, and what few roads there were became choked with wounded soldiers and stalled traffic. Ammunition couldn't move in, and the injured couldn't move out.

The 808th worked under close fire, cutting wire, removing obstacles, and restoring the shelled roads and bridges. They ran communication lines to the front, dug trenches, loaded and unloaded ammo, and pushed up supplies. At one point, the 808th had to build a light railway well within range of enemy fire. To cope with the fear and stress, they sang as they worked. One officer reported, "We cannot understand their makeup, for under the hardest conditions they hold themselves together and are able to raise a song."[42]

An anonymous poet wrote a tribute to those thankless battalions.

They sleep in pup tents in the cold, and work in mud and mire
They fill up shell holes in the roads most always under Fire;
Far o'er the lines, the scout plane goes, directing the Barrage,
Just as the zero hour draws near, or just before the charge,
As o'er the top the dough boy goes, to put the Hun to tears,
But who went out and cut the wire? (THE HUSKY PIONEERS)

They bury beaucoup heroes, and carry beaucoup shells
From every dump on every front, the kind of work that tells,
A heavy pack on every back, on every truck in France
They never won the Croix de Guerre—they never had the chance,
And as the heavy trucks whirled by, they worked to calm their fears,
Who was it made the road so smooth?
(THE SAME OLD PIONEERS)[43]

There were fourteen regiments of Pioneers sent to France, and seven of them were entitled to wear combat ribbons. Two were decorated, and one of those was the 808th.

The armistice came in November 1919, but the 808th remained in France for several more months, doing jobs that no one else was willing to. In June, Welch finally came home wearing combat ribbons, twice decorated, and carrying letters of commendation.[44]

Welch arrived stateside to find Carlisle closed. In August 1918, the school had been shuttered and the campus converted to a hospital for the wounded returning from France.

Carlisle had become an anachronism, a lingering reminder of the blunt old frontier-driven policies, directed against tribes that were regarded as enemies. Forcibly educating children was what the U.S. government did to Indians instead of making war on them. The school, especially in its early days, was a bloodless attempt at extinction, in which pencils and slates were wielded instead of gunstocks. Even later, as a more gradual exercise in assimilation, it was a vivid illustration of the difficulty the country had in swallowing people whole.[45]

An Indian commissioner named William Jones once observed that the government's decades-long attempts to "civilize" the tribes had failed through a series of "well-meant mistakes." It was a neat phrase that surely described Carlisle. Like so many other federal experiments regarding the Indians, what in 1879 was seen as a creative solution had come to seem wrongheaded.

Increasingly, Washington policy makers questioned Carlisle's basic premise. Humanitarians argued that removing children from their homes was cruel and counterproductive. Still others believed that Carlisle created false expectations and that it ill-equipped students for the grim realities of life back home. Beginning in 1905, Roosevelt's Indian commissioner, Francis Leupp, was the first to recommend that off-reservation boarding schools be deemphasized. Better that children should be educated closer to home, he asserted. "It is a great mistake to start the little ones in the path of civilization by snapping all the ties of affection between them and their parents, and teaching them to despise the aged and nonprogressive members of their families," he said.[46]

Over the next decade government support for Carlisle steadily declined. One by one, federal boarding institutions for Native Americans began to close. Slowly but surely, efforts to educate Indian children were redirected toward the American public school system. By 1920, there were 30,858 Indian children in public schools.[47]

In the forty years of Carlisle's existence, an estimated 8,500 students passed through its halls. Its results as a social and educational experiment were equivocal. Only 741 pupils actually received Carlisle degrees, though scores of alumnae went on to graduate from public high schools. As a training school, it was an undeniable success: the federal Indian agencies were full of Carlisle graduates working as teachers, clerks, interpreters, police, lawyers, blacksmiths, farmers, bakers, and tailors. But the school took an undeniable personal toll on students: it razed their personal histories, sundered families, and obliterated their languages, faiths, and traditions.[48]

Not surprisingly, students had wildly divergent views of their Carlisle experience. Some, like Plenty Horses, bitterly resented the place and wanted to wipe all marks of it from their character. To others, their association with Carlisle was a source of tremendous pride. Jim Thorpe and Iva Miller, who finally married, remembered Carlisle with affection and believed it offered a decent education, and sent all of their children to government boarding schools. Albert Exendine, who would send a son off to Dartmouth, was deeply grateful to the school and believed its closing "set back Indian education 100 years."[49]

Ironically, if there was one person who wholeheartedly approved of the shuttering of the school, it was Pratt. The school founder never believed Carlisle should be permanent. The separation of the races in the classroom was to him a necessary but strictly temporary evil. Public schools were the emblem of American opportunity, and that was where he aspired to see his students. He once said to them, "If I were sure you would fall into the public schools I would burn these buildings tonight!"[50]

On the day Carlisle shut down, Pratt, by then seventy-seven, was invited to make one last visit to the grounds. All of the classrooms and departments closed at three-thirty. The student battalion marched in dress parade to the train depot, where they stood at attention as the band played a march. As Pratt stepped from the train, his old friends, former students, and faculty closed in around him, offering affection and congratulations. They escorted him to campus, where he stood under a spreading old walnut tree in the center of campus, a favorite old shady spot of his, and gazed around.

That evening Pratt addressed the entire student body and faculty, and as he spoke, there was still an urgent ring in his quavering, elderly voice.

"The thing for you to think about all the time is to be a complete individual," he said. "Don't lean on anybody else! Don't allow anyone to compel you to lean on anybody else! . . . I do want to see Indians filling big places. I'm holding on to life with all my might and main, hoping that before I pass away it will come about that there will be no Indian schools in this country—that every Indian is his own man and her own woman."[51]

For Pratt, the statement contained a gentle insight. The sweeping generalizations he had tried to enact at Carlisle had been undone by the irrepressible behaviors of the individual pupils. They broke out of the dorms and sailed on the lawns in their nightshirts. They set things on fire, shot the place up, studied, read, fought, cried, and courted. Some of them yearned to enter American society, and others fiercely resisted it. And some of them played football. Pratt had set out to destroy the old tribal identities at Carlisle. But the students of the school redefined themselves in a blazing and prideful new way.

EPILOGUE

T HE CARLISLE INDIANS reside in spine-cracked old annuals, dusty as Plutarch. Their football feats are largely forgotten or obscured, and they have been consigned to that bin of trivia, yesteryear. But the ghostly outlines of the campus are still discernible on its grounds, now the U.S. Army War College, just as its students' influence is still faintly felt in the modern game.

In the attic of the gymnasium, used today by American officers in residence to study battle problems, there are faded marks where students scratched their initials. On the edge of campus, rows of small white headstones mark the graves of pupils.

Long after Carlisle closed, the people connected to it continued to feel its trace marks, both for good and for ill.

American Horse: He never recovered financially from the destruction of his home and loss of his stock during the Ghost Dance war. He continued to travel to Washington on behalf of his people, including a visit in 1897 to insist on the return of the Black Hills, but it was fruitless. He finally died in 1910, having outlived some of his children and grandchildren.

Some of his descendants died of tuberculosis, some joined the Native American Church and took peyote, some ranched. His grandson Joe American Horse became an accomplished miler at the University of Nebraska and was twice elected president of the Oglala Lakota tribe, in 1982–1984 and 1986–1988. Joe American Horse remains active in land-use issues at Pine Ridge and is yet another extraordinary leader from an extraordinary family.

Ben American Horse lived the remainder of his life at Pine Ridge and worked as a police officer. He maintained his friendship with Buffalo Bill Cody to the end, and even worked as an interpreter on Cody's last and most ludicrous extravaganza, an attempt to film a reenactment of the Ghost Dance and Wounded Knee. It was a troubled, chaotic project and the film never saw the light of day.

Ben was active in tribal politics to the end of his life. He became known as an "old dealer," a traditionalist who believed in tribal councils and collective governance. He served as an alternate delegate to the Republican convention in 1944, and he traveled to Washington, D.C., in 1955, when he is supposed to have made a famous remark to Senator Alben Barkley, formerly Harry Truman's vice president. "Young man, let me give you a little advice," he said. "Be careful with your immigration laws. We were careless with ours."

The original American Horse allotment is down to just 20 acres from 320. But the foundation of the old house is still there.

Alex Arcasa: He became a mechanic for the railroad in Altoona, Pennsylvania.

Pete Calac: He went on to attend West Virginia Wesleyan and to play pro football with Thorpe for the Canton Bulldogs. He remained in Canton and became a police officer. Calac and Thorpe were great carousing buddies, and Grace Thorpe recalls that one night the two men jumped on top of the bar in a Canton watering hole and offered to fight the whole room. During World War II, Calac enlisted in the Ninety-first Division, and served in France and Belgium. He died in 1960.[1]

Frank Cayou: After graduating from the University of Illinois, he briefly enjoyed singing stardom, appearing on Broadway in a popular vaudeville revue under a stage name. In 1904 he became director of athletics at Wabash College, and from 1908 to 1913 he served as the football coach at Washington University at St. Louis. In January 1915, at the age of thirty-seven, he replied to an inquiry from Carlisle that he was married with two children. "I have tasted the bitter and the sweets and now I hope and believe I have arrived at the age of *genuine reason.* I have been a leader and counselor of men (*and they have not been Indians either*)."[2]

Leland Devore: On graduating from West Point, he was assigned to the Seventeenth Infantry and took part in the expedition that chased Pancho Villa. During the Great War, he was a chief motor transport officer and participated in the Meuse-Argonne offensive with distinction, becoming a lieutenant colonel by May 1919. He died at the age of fifty at Walter Reed Hospital after a long battle with cancer.[3]

Charlie Dillon: The man who hid the ball against Harvard in 1903 became a master blacksmith and a rancher in Montana. He married a fellow Carlisle graduate, Rose Laforg. In January of 1911 he replied to an inquiry from Carlisle: "I have a few head of horse and cattle and 480 acres of land five hundred dollars on hand. . . . Have nothing much of interest to tell of myself only I have plenty to eat plenty to wear and plenty of cash." At the age of fifty-one, he broke ground on a new ranch in Big Horn country. In September 1912 he was in Lodge Grass, Montana, where an agent wrote of him, "Has allotment and is a good man."

Dwight Eisenhower: As the supreme commander of the Allied forces in Europe during World War II, Eisenhower often looked for former football players to fill positions of command.

"I had occasion, because of my position, to be on the lookout for natural leaders," he remarked. "I noted with satisfaction how well ex-footballers seemed to fulfill leadership qualifications: among others, Bradley, Keyes, Patton, Simpson, Van Fleet, Harmon, Hobbs, Jouett, Patch and Prichard, and many others, measured up. I cannot recall a single ex-footballer with whom I came in contact who failed to meet every requirement. Personally, I think this was more than coincidental. I believe that football, almost more than any other sport, tends to instill into men the feeling that victory comes through hard—almost slavish—work, team play, self-confidence, and an enthusiasm that amounts to dedication."[4]

Albert Exendine: To the end of his life, he believed the closing of Carlisle "set Indian education back 100 years." He became a coach and an Indian activist, using his law degree to see that Indians didn't get swindled. He practiced law mainly in McAlester, Pawhuska, and Tulsa, Oklahoma, helping local residents seek cash settlements in claims against the government.

Exendine's coaching career was illustrious, and included winning tenures at Otterbein, Georgetown, Washington State, Occidental, Northeastern State, and Oklahoma State. He was renowned for his wide-open offensive attacks, for which his old mentor Warner scolded him: "Ex, you will become a good football coach if you remember that football is football, and not basketball."

In 1916, Exendine's Georgetown team scored more points than any team in the country. In 1936, while working as a lawyer in Oklahoma, he volunteered to coach an Anadarko high school team and led them to an unbeaten record as they scored 300 points to just 12 for the opposition.

Bud Wilkinson, the Hall of Famer who coached at the University of Oklahoma, said, "Ex knew more football than any men who ever stepped foot on Oklahoma soil. His mind was too far advanced in theories for most players to understand, and he knew offense better than any man who ever lived."[5]

William Gardner: After graduating from Dickinson Law School, he played some minor-league baseball and was admitted to the bar in Kentucky. For a time he worked as coach and athletic director at the University of the South in Sewanee, Tennessee. In November 1917, he received his captain's commission and served with the 338th Infantry. After the war he moved to Chicago, where there is some evidence he became an agent for Elliot Ness during Prohibition in the 1930s.

Percy Haughton: He volunteered in 1918, ever convinced of the connection between football and war. "Football is a miniature war game played under somewhat more civilized rules of conduct, in which the team becomes the military force of the school or university that it represents," he said. "Most of the combat principles of the Field Service Regulations of the U.S. Army are applicable to the modern game of football."[6]

Haughton was a commissioned major in chemical warfare service and mustered out six months later. He returned to coaching at Columbia in 1924 and had won four of five games when he suffered a heart attack during practice and died. He was just forty-eight.

Pete Hauser: The Cheyenne with the big passing arm returned to El Reno, Oklahoma, and took up an allotment. He was killed in a roadside accident while changing a tire near Pawhuska in the 1940s.

Frank Hudson: The legendary dropkicker faded from view. Not even his relatives saw him again. "Ever since he left home, he never came back," said his nephew, a Carlisle student named John Alonzo. "The reason he didn't return, he thought he'd do better outside the reservation. He realized there was nothing for him on the reservation."

A rumor circulated among his relatives back home that Hudson on one occasion played as a ringer for Penn, and helped the Quakers defeat Harvard with a forty-five-yard dropkick as time ran out.

Hudson's family believed he worked for Mellon Bank in Pittsburgh and then moved to Wycombe, Pennsylvania, where he retired as a farmer, living with two elderly Quaker ladies. A notation in his student record in 1910 says, "Farms on shares." Inquiries from his father went unanswered.

On November 24, 1917, Hudson apparently was in attendance in Philadelphia as Carlisle played its last football game, against Penn. The *Washington Times* reported, "Frank Hudson, peerless quarterback of the earlier Carlisle elevens, watched Pennsylvania defeat his old team Saturday at Philadelphia. After the game, he visited the Indians dressing room and congratulated the youngsters for their plucky performance against the heavier Quakers. Hudson is now in the advertising business in Philadelphia."[7]

Jacob Jamison: The hero of the 1896 Yale game returned to upstate New York and became a farmer, as well as a semipro football and baseball player who establishd his own league. In about 1916, Pratt visited him. "I was on Jakey's reservation making inquiries about my old students, and I found that he had established on his own property in New York a baseball and football park, where he trained Indians in both branches of sport and sent teams to travel the country thereabouts to make money. Two of his big lusty sons were on the teams, and I had a happy meeting with him and his players."[8]

Jimmie Johnson: The all-American quarterback and participant in the hidden-ball trick went on to captain Northwestern's team in 1907 while studying dentistry there. After receiving his degree, he stayed in Evanston for two seasons as an assistant coach to Maurice Conner. In 1909 he reconciled with Pop Warner and worked at Carlisle as an assistant coach for two seasons, and he took great pride in helping to develop Thorpe. He moved to Puerto Rico, where he practiced dentistry for the next thirty-six years. He died of cancer on January 18, 1942, at the Mayo Clinic in Rochester, Minnesota, at the age of just sixty-three.[9]

Vance McCormick: He served as mayor of Harrisburg, manager of Woodrow Wilson's 1916 reelection campaign, and publisher of the *Patriot* newspaper. In 1919, he was a member of the American delegation that went to Paris in the aftermath of World War I to negotiate the peace. He also served as director of the War Trade Board.

Frank Mount Pleasant: After graduating from Dickinson Law, Mount Pleasant coached at Franklin and Marshall and then Indiana Normal, where he built one of the great small-school records. During his three seasons, Indiana Normal went 23-4-1 and won state normal championships in 1912 and 1913, reeling off fifteen straight victories in one stretch, a school record that stood for over eighty years.

"As a coach he is ideal," the school paper wrote of him. "He is tact-ful but resourceful, a diplomat in handling men; pleasant and agree-able in his dealings with them, but rules with an iron hand when necessary."

Sometime during 1915, he returned home to New York when his father became seriously ill. According to Warner, Mount Pleasant also obtained an officer's commission in 1917 and served with distinction in France. His traces from then on are hard to follow. On April 12, 1937, not yet fifty, he was killed by a hit-and-run driver in Buffalo.

Bemus Pierce: The first great captain of Carlisle became an accom-plished football coach at Indian schools. He built dominant teams at Haskell and at the Sherman Institute in Riverside, California, where he coached until 1938 and also taught farming. He retired in Califor-nia and lived with his daughter.

Pierce always wanted to return to Carlisle as head coach but was never awarded the job. When Warner resigned in 1914, he tried once more, backed by a letter of recommendation from Pratt. "I feel confi-dent that I can do as good work as Warner for I have done it," Pierce wrote to Superintendent Lipps. "I feel that Carlisle owe me the favor for I help make her name in the football world." Lipps declined, hir-ing Victor M. Kelley instead.

Richard Henry Pratt: He remained a controversial crusader who fought for Indian citizenship to the end of his days. His energy never abated, and he rode his cavalry horse and played golf into his eighties.

As the years passed, he became less truculent. To charges that Carlisle failed to prepare his pupils to face conditions on their reser-vations, he replied that Harvard didn't prepare students to pick up rocks, either. Those who were capable of arguing with Pratt on equal terms tended to fare best with him. Some of his opponents even became his friends. He had a lively and warm correspondence with Anna L. Dawes, daughter of the senator. "We differ, you say, but is that not in itself strength?" he wrote to her on one occasion. "What a wishy-washy world this would be if all agreed! The clash of ideas is not weakness. Truth reaches its place when tussling with error."

In January 1921, he wrote to her again, "You know, my old friend, that there is in my mind and heart very little of material satisfaction with what I did, and there is very much regret that I did not do more."

A few days before he died, in February 1924, he broke down and wept in hopelessness that Indians had still not attained citizenship. He was failing, "and there still did not seem to be any hope for the red man," his eldest daughter said. Trying to comfort him, she said, "Father, maybe God has another and a better plan."

Pratt turned his head to the wall. "There is no better plan," he said.

They were his final words. His pallbearers were all Indians. His monument reads, "Erected in Loving Memory by His Students and Other Indians."[10]

Ed Rogers: In 1912, he was elected county attorney in Walker, Minnesota. He ran unsuccessfully for Congress but was voted a head of the Chippewa nation in 1913. In a letter to Carlisle on March 24, 1910, he wrote, "My home is located on the shore of Lake Leech upon a 60 foot bank. It is in the best part of town. The house is not a very sightly looking affair but I have it well furnished with the best of everything, such as parquet floors, electric lights, mahogany furniture, oriental rugs and grand piano. My law library comprises about 300 volumes of law books, I am the Village Recorder, on the health board, Deputy County Attorney, Deputy County Coroner, and have been appointed special census enumerator for the Leech Lake Indian Reservation. I give you the above facts as they may be of some value to you and also to show in a slight way how the Indian may hold the confidence of the people amongst whom he lives."

Lewis Tewanima: He returned to the mesas of Arizona, where he became a Hopi priest and lived to the age of ninety. He died in a fall from a cliff when he took a wrong turn on his way home from a religious ceremony.

Jim Thorpe: Champions are often created by dire need, some essential lack that drives them. Not even his family completely understood what internal forces of compression worked within Thorpe to create the world's greatest athlete.

"Dad, what sport did you like best?" his daughter Grace asked, decades later.

"I don't want to talk about that."

"Come on, everybody is always asking me."

"All right. I liked hunting and fishing the best."[11]

The reason, he explained, was that he could do them alone. Thorpe seems to have struggled all his life with a sense of isolation and personal tragedy. In 1918, he was devastated by another loss when his four-year-old son, James junior, died of influenza. Thorpe's recreational drinking became a full-blown problem, and it hastened the end of his marriage to his Carlisle sweetheart, Iva Miller, with whom he had three daughters, Grace, Gail, and Charlotte. His second marriage, to Freeda Kirkpatrick, with whom he had four sons, Jack, William, Carl, and Richard, also ended in divorce in 1941.

Thorpe never made the fortune from his athletic career that seemed promised to him. After a brief and disappointing baseball career he helped launch the National Football League, starring for the legendary Canton Bulldogs, with whom he won a championship in 1920. In 1922, Thorpe organized the Oorang Indians, a team made up almost entirely of his former teammates, including Guyon, Calac, Pierce, and others. They didn't win any championships but they were a crowd favorite, and their games were the occasions of raucous reunions among men who loved each other's company.

Thorpe vagabonded around the country, working promotional tours and giving exhibitions of dropkicking that, even as he grew older and developed a paunch, wowed spectators. His odd jobs and ill-fated business ventures included stints as an actor and wrestler.

For all of his problems, Thorpe was an affectionate and adored father, though frequently an absentee one as he sought to put money in his pocket and feed his offspring through the Depression. At one point, he took work as a security guard for the Ford Motor Company in Dearborn, so that his sons could live with him. His struggle with sobriety does not seem to have affected his family's or friends' feeling

NOTES

Prologue • Two Fields

1. *The Dickinsonian*, March 23, 1956. Clipping found in the Gus Welch Papers, Special Collections, McFarlin Library, University of Tulsa (henceforth Welch Papers).

2. "Indians to Battle with Soldiers," *New York Times*, November 9, 1912.

3. David Wallace Adams, "More Than a Game: The Carlisle Indians Take to the Gridiron, 1893–1917," *Western Historical Quarterly* 32, 1 (2001); W. Cameron Forbes, "The Football Coach's Relation to the Players," *Outing*, December 1900.

4. For a discussion of football's growth as part of a Victorian "cult of manliness," see Michael Oriard, *Reading Football: How the Popular Press Created an American Spectacle* (Chapel Hill: The University of North Carolina Press, 1991), 190.

5. Tim Cohane, *Gridiron Grenadiers: The Story of West Point Football* (New York: G. P. Putnam's Sons, 1948), 73.

6. Glenn S. Warner, "Indian Massacres," *Collier's*, October 17, 1931.

7. Alexander M. Weyand, *The Saga of American Football* (New York: The Macmillan Company, 1955), 101. "Babe" Weyand was a member of the 1912 West Point team and captained the 1915 squad. He personally corresponded with Warner, Thorpe, and other members of the Carlisle team for the material in his books.

8. Ibid., 101.

9. Warner, "Indian Massacres."

Chapter 1 • The Real Field

1. American Horse's role in the Fetterman battle and other biographical details are drawn from Richard E. Jensen, ed., *Voices of the American West*, vol. 1: *The Indian*

Interviews of Eli S. Ricker, 1903–1919 (Lincoln: University of Nebraska Press, 2005), 279–82, and from Elbert D. Belish, "American Horse (Wasechun-Tashunka): The Man Who Killed Fetterman," *Annals of Wyoming* 63, 2 (1991).

2. The battle description is based on the following sources: Dee Brown, *The Fetterman Massacre* (Lincoln: University of Nebraska Press, 1971); John D. McDermott, "Price of Arrogance: The Short and Controversial Life of William J. Fetterman," *Annals of Wyoming* 63, 2 (1991); Francis Carrington, *My Army Life and the Massacre at Fort Phil Kearny* (Lincoln: University of Nebraska Press, 2004); John G. Neihardt, *Black Elk Speaks* (Lincoln: University of Nebraska Press, 2004).

3. Carrington, *My Army Life*, 130.

4. Roy E. Appleman, "The Fetterman Fight," *Great Western Indian Fights* (Lincoln: University of Nebraska Press, 1966), 109–31.

5. Letter from William J. Fetterman to Dr. Charles Terry, November 26, 1866, reprinted in John D. McDermott, ed., "Documents Relating to the Fetterman Fight," *Annals of Wyoming* 63, 2 (1991).

6. For an explanation of the Tetons Sioux (Lakota) social structure, see Jeffrey Ostler, *The Plains Sioux and U.S. Colonialism from Lewis and Clark to Wounded Knee* (Cambridge: Cambridge University Press, 2004), 23. The Lakota are divided into seven *oyates*, or nations: Oglala, Brule, Minneconjou, Sans Arc, Two Kettles, Sihasapa, and Hunkpapa.

7. George E. Hyde, *Red Cloud's Folk* (Norman: University of Oklahoma Press, 1937), 63–69.

8. James H. Cook, *Fifty Years on the Old Frontier* (Norman: University of Oklahoma Press, 1980), 187.

9. Neihardt, *Black Elk Speaks*, 12.

10. *Carlisle Arrow*, March 5, 1905, quoting American Horse in a statement to Pine Ridge agent J. R. Brennan.

11. Neihardt, *Black Elk Speaks*, 12.

12. Belish, "American Horse."

13. American Horse told this story to two white men he befriended in his later years. Eli S. Ricker was a Nebraska judge who recognized that the Lakota versions of events were worth recording. He interviewed American Horse on the porch of James Cook's ranch at Agate Springs, in Sioux County, Nebraska, where American Horse and Red Cloud often camped in their declining years. Red Cloud seconded American Horse's version of events, though he may not have been present.

14. Neihardt, *Black Elk Speaks*, 9–12.

15. Letter from Horace D. Vankirk, Company C, Twenty-seventh Infantry, to his father, David Vankirk, reprinted in *Chicago Tribune*, February 27, 1867.

16. "The Indian Massacre," *Chicago Tribune*, January 16, 1867.

17. Interview with Joe American Horse, grandson of American Horse, Pine Ridge, South Dakota, August 29, 2006.

Chapter 2 • Pratt

1. Elaine Goodale Eastman, *Pratt: The Red Man's Moses* (Norman: University of Oklahoma Press, 1935), 17. Eastman was a schoolteacher, missionary, and author who briefly lived at the Carlisle School with her husband, Dr. Charles Eastman, a Santee Sioux and physician who was educated at Dartmouth. Elaine Goodale Eastman met Pratt in 1884 and remained friends with him until his death in 1924, despite deep differences of opinion.

2. Ibid., 13.

3. Ibid., 13.

4. Ibid., 14.

5. The account of Pratt's service is taken from his microfiche file in Letters Received by the Appointment, Commission and Personal Branch, Adjutant General's Office, 1871–1874, National Archives, and from Eastman, *Pratt*, 16–19.

6. Eastman, *Pratt*, 18.

7. Letter from R. H. Pratt to Anna Laura Mason, February 8, 1864, Richard Henry Pratt Papers, Western Americana Collection, Beinecke Rare Book and Manuscript Library, Yale University (henceforth Pratt Papers).

8. Eastman, *Pratt*, 188.

9. Thomas C. Leonard, "Red, White and Army Blue: Empathy and Anger in the American West," *American Quarterly* 26, 2 (1974): 176–90.

10. Robert M. Utley, *Frontiersman in Blue* (Lincoln: University of Nebraska Press, 1981).

11. Robert M. Utley, *Frontier Regulars* (Lincoln: University of Nebraska Press, 1981), 2–6.

12. Hugh Corwin, *The Kiowa Indians: Their History and Life Stories* (Lawton, 1958), 168.

13. Leonard, "Red, White and Army Blue."

14. Richard Henry Pratt, *Battlefield and Classroom: Four Decades with the American Indian* (Norman: University of Oklahoma Press, 2003), 4–5.

15. Ibid.

16. Ibid., 6.

17. Ibid., 269.

18. Anna Laura Pratt, "Memoirs of Army Frontier Life" (notes from a talk), Carlisle Collection, Military History Institute, Army History and Education Center, U.S. Army War College (henceforth AHEC), Carlisle, Pennsylvania, Box 16a.

19. Ibid.

20. Leonard, "Red, White and Army Blue," 180.

21. Anna Laura Pratt, *Memoirs*.

22. Leonard, "Red, White and Army Blue," 180.

23. Pratt, *Battlefield and Classroom*, 31.

24. Ibid., 31.

25. Richard N. Ellis, "The Humanitarian Generals," *Western Historical Quarterly* 3, 2 (1972): 169–78.

26. Leonard, "Red, White and Army Blue."

27. Letter from Frederick W. Benteen to the *St. Louis Democrat*, February 8, 1869, reprinted in Peter Cozzens, ed., *Eyewitnesses to the Indian Wars 1865–1890*, vol. 3: *Conquering the Southern Plains* (Mechanicsburg, 2003), 401–3.

28. Pratt, *Battlefield and Classroom*, 33.

29. Thomas Leonard, "Red White and Army Blue."

30. Leonard, "Red, White and Army Blue."

31. Pratt, *Battlefield and Classroom*, 101–2.

32. Ibid., 41.

33. Anna Laura Pratt, *Memoirs*.

34. The following account is based on W. S. Nye, *Carbine and Lance: The Story of Old Fort Sill* (Norman, 1969), 133–35; Pratt, *Battlefield and Classroom*, 41–45; Dee Broan, *Bury My Heart at Wounded Knee* (New York, 2000), 252–54.

35. Nye, *Carbine and Lance*, 135.

36. Brad D. Lookingbill, *War Dance at Fort Marion* (Norman, 2006), 51.

37. Pratt, *Battlefield and Classroom*, 45.

38. Ibid., 47–49.

39. Pratt's file in "Letters Received by the Appointment, Commission and Personal Branch, Adjutant General's Office, 1871–1874," National Archives.

40. Nye, *Carbine and Lance*, 200; Corwin, *Kiowa*, 172–75.

41. Excerpt of letter from Pratt, annotated by Mason Pratt, Carlisle Collection, AHEC, Box 16a.

Chapter 3 • Fort Marion: First Lessons

1. Brad D. Lookingbill, *War Dance at Fort Marion* (Norman: University of Oklahoma Press, 2006), 48.

2. David Wallace Adams, *Education for Extinction: American Indians and the Boarding School Experience, 1875–1928* (Lawrence: University of Kansas Press, 1995), 36.

3. Richard Henry Pratt, *Battlefield and Classroom: Four Decades with the American Indian* (Norman: University of Oklahoma Press, 1954), 113.

4. Ibid., 115.

5. Ibid., 123.

6. Pratt to Adjutant General, Pratt Papers; Lookingbill, *War Dance*, 64–69. Lookingbill's account of the war prisoners' experiences with Pratt is thorough and lyrical.

7. Pratt, *Battlefield and Classroom*, 118.

8. Sherman to Pratt, January 10, 1876, Pratt Papers.

9. Pratt, *Battlefield and Classroom*, 170.

10. Ibid., 150–51.

11. Ibid., 152.

12. Lookingbill, *War Dance*, 103.

13. Ibid., 108.

14. Undated letter from Mather to Pratt, Pratt Papers.

15. www.rootsweb.com/~flsag/saraannmather.htm.

16. Lookingbill, *War Dance*, 108–15.

17. Ibid., 108.

18. Pratt, *Battlefield and Classroom*, 157–58.

19. Reprinted in ibid., 162.

20. Reprinted in Adams, *Education for Extinction*, 46.

21. Pratt, *Battlefield and Classroom*, 138.

22. Lookingbill, *War Dance*, 162–63.

23. *The School News*, Carlisle Barracks, vol. 1, no. 7, December 1880.

24. W. S. Nye, *Carbine and Lance: The Story of Old Fort Sill* (Norman: University of Oklahoma Press, 1969), 253.

25. Elaine Goodale Eastman, *Pratt: The Red Man's Moses* (Norman: University of Oklahoma Press, 1935), 65.

26. Adams, *Education for Extinction*, 284.

27. Pratt's file, Letters Received by the Appointment, Commissioner and Personal Branch, Adjutant General's Office, 1871–1894, National Archives.

28. Richard N. Ellis, "The Humanitarian Generals," *Western Historical Quarterly* 3, 2 (1972).

29. Paul Tsait-Kope-ta to Pratt, December 16, 1881, Pratt Papers.

30. Undated letter from Mather to Pratt, probably summer of 1878, Pratt Papers.

31. Adams, *Education for Extinction*, 281.

32. Manimic to Pratt, January 26, 1880, Pratt Papers.

33. Nye, *Carbine and Lance*, 255.

Chapter 4 • Carlisle

1. Elaine Goodale Eastman, *Pratt: The Red Man's Moses* (Norman: University of Oklahoma Press, 1935), 208.

2. Richard Henry Pratt, *Battlefield and Classroom: Four Decades with the American Indian* (Norman: University of Oklahoma Press, 2003), 262. Pratt was also motivated partly out of fear that his career would be sidelined at Hampton. He informed the secretary of war that he would rather rejoin his regiment than remain there. "If you insist on my remaining in the Indian school work, give me 300 young Indians and a place in one of our best communities and let me prove it is easy to give Indian youth the English language, education and industries that it is imperative they have in preparation for citizenship" (216).

3. Ibid., 215.

4. Ibid., 220.

5. Mather to Pratt, August 10, 1879, Pratt Papers.

6. George E. Hyde, *Spotted Tail's Folk* (Norman: University of Oklahoma Press, 1974), 308–11.

7. Pratt, "Origin of the Carlisle Indian Industrial School, Its Progress and Difficulties Surmounted," Cumberland County Historical Society.

8. Peter Nabokov, ed., *Native American Testimony: A Chronicle of Indian-White Relations from Prophecy to the Present, 1492–1992* (New York: Penguin Books, 1991), xvii, 233.

9. Spotted Tail's children were Red Road, age eighteen; Stays at Home (William), eighteen; Talks with Bear (Oliver), fourteen; and Bugler (Max), twelve, as well as a grandson and granddaughter.

10. The naming of Indian children at Carlisle was problematic—family names and relationships were often misinterpreted, mistranslated, or assigned capriciously. While Pratt believed Robert was a son, Pine Ridge physician Charles Eastman refers to him as a nephew. Also, census records do not reflect a child named Maggie among American Horse's offspring; she too may have been a niece. He did have an elder daughter listed in census records as Millie. There are Carlisle student records for Guy, Robert, Ben, Joseph, Sophia, Lucy, and Alice American Horse, as well as Maggie. Distinctions between children and nephews and nieces are irrelevant, however. To a Lakota headman what was important was the *tiyospaye,* or extended family, for which he provided.

11. The account of the journey to Carlisle is taken from Luther Standing Bear, *My People the Sioux* (Lincoln: University of Nebraska Press, 1978), 128–34. He was a member of the first class at Carlisle. Also, from Pratt, "Origins."

12. Pratt, *Battlefield and Classroom*, 31.

13. Standing Bear, *My People*, 134.

14. Genevieve Bell, "Talking Stories Out of School," Ph.D. dissertation, Stanford University, 1998, 60–63.

15. *Eadle Keatah-Toh*, January 1880, Volume I, No.1.

16. Standing Bear, *My People*, 140.

17. Ibid., 141.

18. Pratt, *Battlefield and Classroom*, 232.

19. The first class was made up of eighty-four Lakota, fifty-two Cheyenne, Kiowa, and Pawnee, and eleven Apache. Statistics on Carlisle are taken from Bell, "Telling Stories Out of School," Ph.D. dissertation, Stanford University, 1998.

20. Pratt, *Battlefield and Classroom*, 335.

21. Standing Bear, *My People*, 143.

22. Ibid., 157.

23. Pratt, *Battlefield and Classroom*, 257.

24. Standing Bear, *My People*, 137.

25. For the best explanation of the effects of renaming in boarding schools, see David Wallace Adams, *Education for Extinction: American Indians and the Boarding School Experience, 1875–1928* (Lawrence, 1995), 108–10.

26. Eve Ball, *Indeh: An Apache Odyssey* (Norman: University of Oklahoma Press, 1988), 142–44.

27. Pratt, *Battlefield and Classroom*, 292.

28. Eastman, *Pratt*, 206. Adams, *Education for Extinction*, and Bell, "Telling Stories Out of School," also suggest the students surreptitiously preserved rituals.

29. Eastman, *Pratt*, 191.

30. Interview with Mrs. Ed (Verna) Whistler, DeWitt Clinton Smith Papers, Waidner-Spahr Library, Dickinson College, 34. Bell, "Telling Stories Out of School," notes that Plains sign language may have even had a coded cache at Carlisle.

31. Gertrude Simmons Bonnin, *Zitkala-Sa: American Indian Stories, Legends, and Other Writings* (New York, 2003), 88. For a particularly vivid explanation of how discordant and dislocating Carlisle must have seemed to Lakota children, see Adams, *Education for Extinction*, 112–14.

32. Luther Standing Bear, *Land of the Spotted Eagle* (Lincoln: University of Nebraska Press, 1978 [1933]), 38.

33. Bell, "Telling Stories Out of School," 142.

34. Charles F. Himes, "An Account of Illustrated Talks to Noted Indian Chiefs," paper read before the Hamilton Library Association, November 17, 1916, Cumberland County Historical Society.

35. Standing Bear, *My People*, 147–49.

36. Adams, *Education for Extinction*, 136.

37. Bell, "Telling Stories Out of School," 63.

38. Pratt, *Battlefield and Classroom*, 249.

39. Himes, "Account," 3; letter from William T. Sherman to Pratt, March 5, 1880, Pratt Papers.

40. Letter from Pratt to Rutherford B. Hayes, March 9, 1880, Pratt Papers.

41. Pratt, *Battlefield and Classroom*, 243.

42. Ibid., 275.

43. Eastman, *Pratt*, 209.

44. Ball, *Indeh*, 150; letter from Pratt to Mary I. Lewis, November 7, 1898, Pratt Papers.

45. Pratt, *Battlefield and Classroom*, 244.

46. Letter from Pratt to Dr. C. R. Agnew, December 22, 1883, Special Collections, Waidner-Spahr Library, Dickinson College.

47. Jeffrey Ostler, *The Plains Sioux and U.S. Colonialism from Lewis and Clark to Wounded Knee* (Cambridge, 2004), 157.

48. Standing Bear, *My People*, 159.

49. Adams, *Education for Extinction*, 126. Adams writes comprehensively about the various forms of Indian student resistance at boarding schools.

50. The account of the Sioux leaders' visit to Carlisle is drawn from George E. Hyde, *A Sioux Chronicle* (Norman, 1953), 53, as well as Wahnne C. Clark, "The Grand Celebration: An Indian Delegation to Washington," *Chronicles of Oklahoma* 66, 2 (1988). Pratt's own account of the incident is in *Battlefield and Classroom*, 235–38, but it's exactly that, his account.

51. Himes, "Account."

52. Clark, "Grand Celebration."

53. Pratt, *Battlefield and Classroom*, 238n.

54. Pratt claimed in *Battlefield and Classroom* that Spotted Tail had an ulterior motive: he wanted a pay raise for Tackett and removed his children only when Pratt refused to grant it. But the accusation is not supported and doesn't explain why the Lakota were unanimous in their objections to Carlisle's methods.

55. Adams, *Education for Extinction* 127.

56. Hyde, *Spotted Tail's Folk*, 332.

57. *Eadle Keatah Toh*, August 1881.

58. Ibid., April 1881.

59. Ibid., August 1880.

60. Letter from Pratt to Secretary of the Interior, December 6, 1880, Pratt Papers.

61. Letter from Pratt to White Thunder, December 15, 1880, Pratt Papers.

62. Adams, *Education for Extinction*, 129.

63. Eastman, *Pratt*, 231.

64. Letter from Pratt to Henry L. Dawes, April 4, 1881, Pratt papers.

65. Adams, *Education for Extinction*, 52; Eastman, *Pratt*, 220.

66. Kathleen Dalton, *Theodore Roosevelt: A Strenuous Life* (New York: Vintage Books, 2002), 44.

67. Eastman, *Pratt*, 217.

Chapter 5 • The Last Fight and First Games

1. A photo of American Horse's home is in Richard E. Jensen, R. Eli Paul, and John E. Carter, *Eyewitness at Wounded Knee* (Lincoln: University of Nebraska Press, 1991), 77.

2. *The Indian Helper*, February 27, 1891.

3. In 1905, in a speech to Carlisle students on one of his visits to campus, American Horse acknowledged his shifting opinion of the school in its early days. "We sent them to school, we sent them here. The following year we came down here and saw that they were not doing very well. Some of them took their children back home. I afterwards came here and saw the children and they were all doing nicely. They had plenty to eat and they all looked nice, and I thought that we ought to send all our children here." Yet he also complained that one of his sons had returned from Carlisle unable to find work. "I have one at home who served his time in school and went home. He could not get any work to do and all I could have him do was carry water for me."

4. Ben American Horse's conversation with his father was related by Darlene Rooks, niece and adopted daughter of Ben American Horse, interviewed October 5, 2006.

5. *The Indian Helper*, December 20, 1889.

6. Pratt often culled Carlisle students from defeated bands held as prisoners of war, who felt pressured by the government to send their children to school. In 1877, Pratt tried to recruit students for Hampton from the Nez Perce, who had led General Nelson

A. Miles on a thousand-mile chase before surrendering with Chief Joseph's magnificent words, "I will fight no more forever." For once, Pratt was rebuffed. Chief Joseph flatly refused to turn over any children. Richard Henry Pratt, *Battlefield and Classroom: Four Decades with the American Indian* (Norman: University of Oklahoma Press, 2003), 196.

7. Interview with Darlene Rooks, niece and adopted daughter of Ben American Horse, October 5, 2006.

8. Statistics on Carlisle's physical growth are from Genevieve Bell, "Telling Stories Out of School," Ph.D. dissertation, Stanford University, 1998, 63–65; those on Carlisle's academic growth are from Elaine Goodale Eastman, *Pratt: The Red Man's Moses* (Norman, 1935), 213. Given the level of illiteracy, it was ten years before Carlisle held its first commencement, in 1889. Graduates steadily increased in number. Between 1899 and 1904, Carlisle turned out between thirty and forty-five graduates a year, according to Eastman, 215.

9. Interviews with James Wardecker and Katherine Morehead, Cumberland County Historical Society oral history project.

10. Bell, "Telling Stories Out of School," 137.

11. *Eadle Keatah Toh*, January 1881.

12. Thomas J. Schlereth, *Victorian America: Transformations in Everyday Life, 1876–1915* (New York: HarperPerennial, 1991), 220.

13. Bell, "Telling Stories Out of School," 149.

14. Letter reprinted in September 1882 issue of *The School News*, Carlisle Barracks.

15. *The Indian Helper*, October 28, 1887; John S. Steckbeck, *Fabulous Redmen* (Harrisburg, PA: J. Horace McFarland Company, 1951), 18.

16. Pratt, *Battlefield and Classroom*, 317.

17. Alexander M. Weyand, *The Saga of American Football* (New York: The Macmillan Company, 1956), 3–4.

18. Tim Cohane, *The Yale Football Story* (New York: G. P. Putnam Son's, 1951), 32.

19. Ibid., 32.

20. Amos Alonzo Stagg and Wesley W. Stout, *Touchdown!* (New York: Longmans, Green and Company, 1927), 99–100.

21. Michael Oriard, *Reading Football: How the Popular Press Created an American Spectacle* (Chapel Hill, 1993).

22. Richard Harding Davis, "A Day with the Yale Team," *Harper's Weekly*, November 18, 1893.

23. Stagg and Stout, *Touchdown!*, 94.

24. Glenn S. Warner, "Battles of Brawn," *Collier's*, November 7, 1931.

25. Ibid.

26. Stagg and Stout, 206–7. Harry Beecher later helped popularize the game as a sportswriter and editor for William Randolph Hearst's *New York Evening Journal*.

27. Weyand, *The Saga of American Football*, 25; Stagg and Stout, 117; Jerome Karabel, *The Chosen: The Hidden History of Admission and Exclusion at Harvard, Yale and Princeton* (Boston, New York: Houghton-Mifflin Company, 2005), 43.

28. Richard Harding Davis, "The Thanksgiving Day Game," *Harper's Weekly*, December 9, 1893.

29. Robert M. Utley, *The Last Days of the Sioux Nation* (New Haven: Yale University Press, 2004), xviii. Turner delivered his paper to the American Historical Association on July 12, 1893.

30. James Trager, *The People's Chronology: A Year-by-Year Record of Human Events from Prehistory to the Present* (New York: Henry Holt and Company, 1994), xx.

31. Schlereth, *Victorian America*, 218.

32. David Wallace Adams, "More Than a Game: The Carlisle Indians Take to the Gridiron, 1893–1917," *Western Historical Quarterly* 32, 1 (2001). Oriard in *Reading Football* also observes that Camp, who became an executive at the New Haven Clock Company, saw connections between football and new businesses.

33. Arthur Martin oral history, Cumberland County Historical Society.

34. Steckbeck, *Fabulous Redmen*, 12. Steckbeck, a comprehensive and accurate compiler of Carlisle's football seasons, quotes Grant Cleaver, a former Dickinson player, who was on the field that day.

35. Pratt, *Battlefield and Classroom*, 317.

36. Eastman, *Pratt*, 210.

37. James Mooney, *The Ghost Dance Religion and Wounded Knee* (New York: Dover Publications, 1973 [1896]), 900.

38. David H. Miller, *Ghost Dance* (New York: Duell, Sloan and Pearce, 1959), 127. Miller was a painter and writer who was personally acquainted with the sons of American Horse.

39. Elbert D. Belish, "American Horse (Wasechun-Tashunka): The Man Who Killed Fetterman," *Annals of Wyoming* 63, 2 (1991).

40. Jeffrey Ostler, *The Plains Sioux and U.S. Colonialism from Lewis and Clark to Wounded Knee* (Cambridge, 2004), 238; Belish, "American Horse."

41. Belish, "The Man Who Killed Fetterman."

42. Letter from Pratt to American Horse, November 11, 1890, Pratt Papers.

43. Ostler, *Plains Sioux*, 294.

44. Ibid., 301–5.

45. Belish, "The Man Who Killed Fetterman."

46. *The Indian Helper*, December 5, 1890.

47. Pratt always denied that Carlisle students were involved in any trouble, ever. On January 7, 1891, he wrote J. W. Leeds of Philadelphia, "Seven covers the number we have been able to hear about and they have all been led by parental and family pressure." He raised the number to twelve in a statement to the *Washington Post*, January 28, 1891.

48. Interview with Joe American Horse.

49. Letters from Pratt to Elaine Goodale Eastman, January 15 and January 21, 1891, Pratt Papers.

50. Letter from Pratt to William G. Fisher, January 16, 1891, Pratt Papers.

51. David Graham Phillips, "Chiefs Visit," *Harper's Weekly*, February 21, 1891.

52. Mooney, *Ghost Dance Religion*, 887.

53. An account of the Carlisle visit appeared in the *Washington Post* on February 16, 1891.

54. *The Indian Helper*, Feb. 27, 1891.

55. Robert Utley, "The Ordeal of Plenty Horses," *American Heritage Magazine* 26, 1 (1974). Details of the murder of Casey are from the *Washington Post*, "Plenty Horses Plea," April 28, 1891.

56. "What Plenty Horses Says," *New York World*, April 25, 1891.

57. "Lieut. Casey's Slayer," *New York World*, April 26, 1891.

58. "Trial of Plenty Horses," *New York World*, May 27, 1891; "It Was War," *New York World*, May 28, 1891; "Plenty Horses Free," *New York World*, May 29, 1891.

59. "Plenty Horses Happy, American Horse Pleads for His Race," *New York World*, May 30, 1891.

60. Utley, "Ordeal."

61. Eastman, *Pratt*, 155.

62. Letter from Matlock to Pratt, September 29, 1892, Pratt Papers.

63. Carlisle Student Records, Data Concerning Former Students, ca. 1898, National Archives, Record Group 75, entry 1331.

64. Pratt, *Battlefield and Classroom*, 296.

65. Eastman, *Pratt*, 213.

66. Letter from Pratt to Abram Vail, December 10, 1896, and letter from Pratt to J. Powlas, September 4, 1896, Pratt papers.

67. Army was captained by Dennis Mahan Michie, who would later die at San Juan, Cuba.

68. Pratt, *Battlefield and Classroom*, 316–18.

69. Ibid., 318.

70. Cohane, *Yale Football Story*, 87–88.

71. Letter from Vance McCormick to the Military History Institute, June 3, 1938, Army History and Education Center, Carlisle Barracks, Carlisle Indian School Collection box MCIS 32. McCormick responded to an inquiry from the MHI.

72. Ibid.

73. Ibid.

74. Cohane, *The Yale Football Story*, 90.

75. Ibid.

76. Letter from Pratt to W. W. Wotherspoon, November 21, 1894, Pratt Papers.

77. "Lo, The Poor Indians," *Washington Post*, November 25, 1894.

78. Interview with Joe American Horse, July 28, 2006. Also, interview with American Horse in Richard R. Jensen, ed., *Voices of the American West*, vol. 1: *The Indian Interviews of Eli S. Ricker, 1903–1919* (Lincoln, 2005), 284. Also, interview with Darlene Rooks, adopted daughter of Ben American Horse, October 2006.

79. *Indian Helper*, March 4, 1892.

80. Interview with Joe American Horse.

81. Interview with Darlene Rooks.

82. Carlisle Indian School student file 1827, National Archives, Record Group 75, Entry 1327.

Chapter 6 • Cheats and Swindles

1. John Rickards Betts, "The Technological Revolution and the Rise of Sport, 1850–1900," in Steven A. Riess, ed., *The American Sporting Experience: A Historical Anthology of Sport in America* (New York: Human Kinetics Publishing, 1984), 141–57, and Thomas J. Schlereth, *Victorian America: Transformations in Everyday Life, 1876–1915* (New York: HarperPerennial, 1991), 209.

2. *New York World*, November 5, 10, and 25, 1896.

3. Ibid., November 29, 1895.

4. *The Red Man*, December 1895.

5. *Indian Helper*, October 25, 1895.

6. Ibid., December 6, 1895.

7. Hugh D. Corwin, *The Kiowa Indians: Their History and Life Stories* (Lawton, 1958), 178.

8. Peter Nabokov, ed., *Native American Testimony: A Chronicle of Indian-White Relations from Prophecy to the Present, 1492–2000* (Penguin Books, 1991), 233.

9. Ibid., 246; Jack Newcombe, *The Best of the Athletic Boys* (New York: Doubleday, 1975), 33–36.

10. Blue Clark, *Lone Wolf v. Hitchcock, Treaty Rights and Indian Law at the End of the Nineteenth Century* (Lincoln: University of Nebraska Press, 1999).

11. Satank's son, Joshua Given, played a conspicuous role as a government interpreter and aroused such hostility from his own people that he had to be protected by a guard.

12. Corwin, *Kiowa*, 177.

13. *Indian Helper*, January 21, 1896.

14. The ages of the players are approximate, and are taken from their student files (which are frequently incomplete) in the National Archives. The ages were often guessed at.

15. Letter from Pratt to John H. Bradbury, October 22, 1896, Pratt Papers.

16. *New York World*, October 25, 1896.

17. Details of the game are from *New York World*, October 25, 1896, and *New York Journal*, October 25, 1896.

18. Richard Henry Pratt, *Battlefield and Classroom: Four Decades with the American Indian* (Norman: University of Oklahoma Press, 2003), 319.

19. Quoted from David Wallace Adams, "More Than a Game: The Carlisle Indians Take to the Gridiron, 1893–1917," *Western Historical Quarterly* 32, 1 (2001).

20. Letter from Pratt to Andrew Freedman of the New York baseball club, November 3, 1896, Pratt Papers.

21. Letter from Pratt to J. H. Spears, October 28, 1896, Pratt Papers.

22. *New York World*, November 1 and 8, 1896.

23. Caspar Whitney, "Amateur Sport," *Harper's Weekly*, November 14, 1896.

24. Editorial, *Harper's Weekly*, November 14, 1896.

25. Letter from Pratt to Abram Vail, December 10, 1896, Pratt Papers.

26. *Outing*, December 1896.

27. "Two Curable Evils," *New York Times*, November 23, 1897.

28. In 1889, Amos Alonzo Stagg of Yale made Camp's all-American team at the grizzled age of twenty-seven.

29. Letter from Pratt to C. E. Patterson, December 17, 1896, Pratt Papers.

30. "Ready for the Game," *Chicago Tribune*, December 19, 1896.

31. Letter from Pratt to Edward C. Mann, December 4, 1896, Pratt Papers.

32. Telegrams to Bemus Pierce, W. G. Thompson, December 19, 1896, Pratt Papers.

33. Game details are from "Indians Get the Scalps," *Chicago Daily*, December 20, 1896.

34. Letter from Pratt to Luzena Chouteau, January 7, 1897, Pratt Papers.

35. Letter from Pratt to Henry S. Penfield, January 6, 1897, Pratt Papers.

36. Caspar Whitney, "Amateur Sport," *Harper's Weekly*, January 23, 1897.

37. "Fun over the Indian Bill, Proficiency of Carlisle in Football Proof of Culture," *Washington Post*, January 27, 1897.

38. Corwin, *Kiowa*, 179.

39. *Indian Helper*, March 6, 1896.

40. "Data Concerning Former Students," Record Group 75, Entry 1331, National Archives; Corwin, *Kiowa*, 179. According to Corwin, Delos Lone Wolf's children were Mary Reynolds Lone Wolf, Hazel Lucille, Margaret Belle, Esther, Celia, and the Reverend Theodore R. Lonewolf.

41. Letter from Pratt to Delos Lone Wolf, October 24, 1898, Pratt Papers.

42. Blue Clark, *Lone Wolf v. Hitchcock*, 66.

43. Ibid., 60.

44. Frederick E. Hoxie, "Exploring a Cultural Borderland," *Journal of American History* 79, 3 (1992).

45. Clark, *Lone Wolf v. Hitchcock*, 71; Tim Garrison, "The Nadir of American Sovereignty," *Reviews in American History* 24, 2 (1996).

46. *Red Man and Helper*, February 27, 1903.

Chapter 7 • Not a Parlor Game

1. *Indian Helper*, June 24, 1898.

2. Glenn S. Warner, "The Indian Massacres," *Collier's*, October 17, 1931. Also, interview with John Alonzo, January 1977, DeWitt Clinton Smith III Papers, "Interviews with Former Carlisle Personnel and Students," Special Collections, Waidner-Spahr Library, Dickinson College.

3. Description of Carlisle locker room taken from *Washington Post*, April 8, 1906.

4. *Washington Post*, November 14, 1897.

5. Walter Camp, "The Football Season," *Harper's Weekly*, October 30, 1897.

6. Account of the banquet is from *The Red Man*, January 1898.

7. Ibid.

8. Glenn S. Warner, *Pop Warner, Football's Greatest Teacher*, ed. Michael J. Bynum (Langhorne, PA: Gridiron Football Properties, 1993), 5. Warner wrote two autobiographical accounts, one for *Collier's* in 1931 and one for the Christy Walsh Syndicate in 1929. Both were no doubt ghost-written. The Bynum-edited book is based on the Walsh material, which is more detailed. Walsh and Warner were good friends, and Walsh knew Warner's mind and his opinions as well as anyone. Bynum has edited the series into a single volume.

9. Bynum, *Pop Warner*, 41.

10. Glenn S. Warner, "Battles of Brawn," *Collier's*, November 7, 1931.

11. Bynum, *Pop Warner*, 54–55.

12. Sideline coaching wouldn't be fully sanctioned until 1967.

13. J. H. Sears, "Modern Coaching of Modern Football," *Harper's Weekly*, November 11, 1893.

14. Richard Harding Davis, "A Day with the Yale Team," *Harper's Weekly*, November 18, 1893.

15. Warner, "Battles of Brawn"; Bynum, *Pop Warner*, 62.

16. Bynum, *Pop Warner*, 62.

17. Glenn S. Warner, "Indian Massacres," *Collier's*, October 17, 1931.

18. Glenn S. Warner, "Heap Big Run Most Fast," *Collier's*, October 25, 1931.

19. Warner, "Indian Massacres."

20. Bynum, *Pop Warner*, 85.

21. Warner, "Heap Big Run Most Fast."

22. Warner, "Indian Massacres."

23. Warner, "Heap Big Run Most Fast."

24. Warner, "Heap Big Run Most Fast."

25. John S. Steckbeck, *Fabulous Redmen* (Harrisburg, 1951), 27.

26. Scoring was still rugby-like: a field goal counted for five points, a touchdown also for five points, a safety for two points, and a kicked point after for one point.

27. E. S. Martin, "The Busy World," *Harper's Weekly*, November 18, 1899; Warner, "Indian Massacres."

28. Warner, "Indian Massacres."

29. *The Red Man*, January, 1900.

30. Jack Newcombe, *The Best of the Athletic Boys* (New York: Doubleday, 1975), 56.

31. *New York World*, December 26, 1899.

32. David Wallace Adams, *Education for Extinction: American Indians and the Boarding School Experience, 1875–1928* (Lawrence: University of Kansas Press, 1995), 26, 56–57.

33. Newcombe, *Best of the Athletic Boys*, 55.

34. The details and statistics of Carlisle's operation in 1900–1901 are taken from

Pratt's correspondence in "Letters Sent," Record Group 75, entry 1323, National Archives. In particular, see Pratt to Commissioner of Indian Affairs, September 13, 1901, and Pratt to Commissioner of Indian Affairs, January 30, 1901.

35. Henry Flickinger interview, Cumberland County Historical Society oral history project.

36. Elaine Goodale Eastman, *Pratt: The Red Man's Moses* (Norman: University of Oklahoma Press, 1935), 210.

37. Richard Henry Pratt, *Battlefield and Classroom: Four Decades with the American Indian* (Norman: University of Oklahoma Press, 2003), 332.

38. According to Genevieve Bell, "Telling Stories Out of School," Ph.D. dissertation, Stanford University, 1998, 210–12, at least 1,850 students ran away over the life of the school.

39. Pratt, *Battlefield and Classroom*, 309.

40. Eastman, *Pratt*, 219.

41. Letter from Pratt to Dr. C. R. Agnew, June 2, 1884, Carlisle Collection, Waidner-Spahr Library, Special Collections, Dickinson College.

42. Letter from Pratt to Dr. C. R. Agnew, March 21, 1885, Waidner-Spahr Library, Special Collections, Dickinson College.

43. "Educating the Indian," *Washington Post*, December 26, 1900.

44. Pratt, *Battlefield and Classroom* 287.

45. Eastman, *Pratt*, 234–5.

46. Letter from Pratt to General John Eaton, January 29, 1897.

47. Letter from Pratt to Mrs. Charles Russell Lowell, January 29, 1897, Pratt Papers; Eastman, *Pratt*, 255.

48. Pratt's file, Letters Received by the Appointment, Commission and Personal Branch, Adjutant General's Office, 1871–1874, National Archives.

49. Arthur Martin, oral history project, Cumberland County Historical Society.

50. Robert Cantwell, "The Poet, the Bums, and the Legendary Redmen," *Sports Illustrated*, February 15, 1960, 74–84.

51. Adams, *Education for Extinction*, 307.

52. Letter from Pratt to Theodore Roosevelt, October 11, 1901, Pratt Papers.

53. Eastman, *Pratt*, 261.

54. Ibid., 261.

Chapter 8 • Dodges and Deceptions

1. Jack Newcombe, *The Best of the Athletic Boys* (New York: Doubleday, 1975), 79.

2. Biographical details are from an interview with Albert Exendine by Mac Bartlett, state editor of *Tulsa Tribune*, for the Cimarron Valley Historical Society, excerpted in the *Tulsa Tribune*, August 11, 1971, clipping found in the Exendine Papers, Special Collections, McFarlin Library, University of Tulsa (henceforth Exendine Papers). Also, included in the Exendine Papers is a brief biography provided by his wife, Grace Exendine.

3. David Wallace Adams, *Education for Extinction: American Indians and the Boarding School Experience, 1875–1928* (Lawrence: University of Kansas Press, 1995), 275.

4. *Indian Helper*, October 4, 1895.

5. In 1905, Phillips Petroleum would be founded in Bartlesville.

6. Bartlett interview of Exendine, in the *Tulsa Tribune*, August 11, 1971, Exendine Papers.

7. Ibid.

8. Newcombe, *Best of the Athletic Boys*, 79.

9. *New York World*, November 18, 1900.

10. Caspar Whitney, "Amateur Sport," *Harper's Weekly*, October 21, 1899.

11. Newcombe, *Best of the Athletic Boys*, 64.

12. Letter from Pratt to Warner, August 8, 1901, Pratt Papers.

13. Genevieve Bell, "Telling Stories Out of School," Ph.D. dissertation, Stanford University, 1998, 337.

14. Letter from Pratt to Warner, July 1, 1901, Pratt Papers.

15. Letter from Pratt to Warner, August 23, 1901, Pratt Papers.

16. Elaine Goodale Eastman, *Pratt: The Red Man's Moses* (Norman: University of Oklahoma Press, 1935), 215.

17. "Fierce Gridiron Battle Today," *Detroit Free Press*, November 2, 1901.

18. Glenn S. Warner, *Pop Warner, Football's Greatest Teacher*, ed. Michael J. Bynum (New York, 1993), 96.

19. "Four Scalps from Carlisle for Michigan's Gridiron Warriors," *Detroit Free Press*, November 3, 1901.

20. Warner, *Pop Warner*, 96–100; Newcombe, *Best of the Athletic Boys*, 100.

21. Warner, "Heap Big Run Most Fast."

22. Glenn S. Warner, "Heap Big Run Most Fast," *Collier's*, October 24, 1931.

23. Exendine Papers.

24. *Tulsa Tribune*, August 11, 1971.

25. Warner, "Heap Big Run Most Fast."

26. John S. Steckbeck, *Fabulous Redmen* (Harrisburg, PA: J. Horace McFarland Company, 1951), 64.

27. Warner, "Heap Big Run Most Fast."

28. *Red Man and Helper*, October 24, 1902. Adams, in *Education for Extinction*, 186, points out that Pratt made an "ironic miscalculation." Indians and whites in a football game couldn't help but evoke the old clichéd tomahawk and scalping images. Newspapers were full of it whenever they played.

29. "Indians at White House," *Washington Post*, November 29, 1902.

30. Glenn S. Warner, "The Indian Massacres," *Collier's*, October 17, 1931.

31. Letter from Pratt to Warner, August 20, 1903, Pratt Papers.

32. *Red Man and Helper*, January 8, 1903.

33. *Red Man and Helper*, September 11, 1903.

34. Warner, "Indian Massacres."

35. Bynum, *Pop Warner*, 105.

36. Warner, "Heap Big Run Most Fast."

37. *New York World*, October 31, 1903.

38. *New York World*, October 30, 1903.

39. Newcombe, *Best of the Athletic Boys*, 87–89.

40. "A Famous Old Carlisle Star and Coach Dies," obituary of Jimmie Johnson, *Chicago Daily Tribune*, January 19, 1942.

41. Warner, "Indian Massacres."

42. Ibid.

43. "Harvard 12, Indians 11," *New York Times*, November 1, 1903.

44. Warner, "Indian Massacres."

45. *New York World*, November 1, 1903.

46. *Red Man and Helper*, November 13, 1903.

47. *New York World*, November 30, 1899, and November 2, 1903.

48. Amos Alonzo Stagg and Wesley W. Stout, *Touchdown!* (New York: Longmans, Green and Company, 1927), 134.

49. *New York World*, November 2, 1903.

50. As quoted in Newcombe, *Best of the Athletic Boys*, 88–89.

51. Warner, *Pop Warner*, 107.

52. *New York World*, November 2, 1903.

53. In Steckbeck, *Fabulous Redmen*, an appendix shows a Smith on the team in those years. The description of Charlie Smith–Eagle Feather is from Philip J. Deloria, *Indians in Unexpected Places* (Lawrence: University of Kansas Press, 2004), 16–17.

54. Deloria, *Indians* (Lawrence, 2004), 18–19.

55. *New York World*, November 6, 1903.

56. Letter from Clarence Three Stars to Edgar Allen, November 30, 1903, Pratt Papers.

57. Bynum, *Pop Warner*, 108–11.

58. Ibid.

59. *Red Man and Helper*, January 8, 1903.

60. *New York Times*, November 22, 1903.

61. Bynum, *Pop Warner*, 110.

62. Letter from Pratt to Warner, February 1, 1904, Pratt Papers.

63. *Red Man and Helper*, January 29, 1904.

64. Bynum, *Pop Warner*, 111–12.

65. Unmarked, undated clipping, Welch Papers.

66. Biographical details are from Grace Thorpe, "The Jim Thorpe Family, Part II," *Chronicles of Oklahoma* 59, 2.

67. Ibid.; Newcombe, *Best of the Athletic Boys*, 27–29.

68. Thorpe, "The Jim Thorpe Family, Part II."

69. Thorpe, "The Jim Thorpe Family, Part II."

70. Ibid.

71. Newcombe, *Best of the Athletic Boys*, 44.

72. Thorpe, "The Jim Thorpe Family, Part II."

73. Thorpe's student file #1783, Record Group 75, entry 1237, National Archives.

74. Newcombe, *Best of the Athletic Boys,* 72.

75. Alexander M. Weyand, *Football's Immortals* (New York: The Macmillan Company, 1962), 183. The conversation with Denny was related by Thorpe himself in the *Arlington Daily,* January 5, 1950.

76. Adams, *Education for Extinction,* 323.

77. As quoted in Eastman, *Pratt,* 262.

78. "The Change at Carlisle," *Washington Post,* June 13, 1904.

79. *Red Man and Helper,* March 11, 1904.

80. "Indians to Coach Eleven," *Washington Post,* September 11, 1904.

81. Eastman, *Pratt,* 250, 264.

82. Ibid., 237, 253, 264–65.

83. "Savage Indian Chiefs," *Washington Post,* March 5, 1905.

84. *The Arrow,* March 9, 1905.

85. "Roosevelt Hero of Brilliant Day," *New York Times,* March 5, 1905; "Oath and Address," *Washington Post,* March 5, 1905.

86. *The Arrow,* March 9, 1905.

Chapter 9 • Experiments in Flight

1. *The Arrow,* September 8 and 29, 1904.

2. John Hammond Moore, "Football's Ugly Decades, 1893–1913," *Smithsonian Journal of History,* fall 1967, 49–68.

3. *The Arrow,* October 13 and 20, 1904.

4. *The Arrow,* October 27, 1904.

5. Pierce's #1647, Record Group 75, entry 1327, National Archives.

6. *New York Times,* November 5, 1905.

7. *New York World,* November 5, 1905.

8. John S. Watterson III, "Political Football: Theodore Roosevelt, Woodrow Wilson, and the Gridiron Reform Movement," *Presidential Studies Quarterly,* summer 1995, 555; and Edmund Morris, *Theodore Rex* (New York: Modern Library, 2001), 6–8.

9. Alexander M. Weyand, *The Saga of American Football* (New York: The Macmillan Company, 1955), 148–56; Tim Cohane, *The Yale Football Story* (New York: G. P. Putnam's Sons, 1951), 150–51.

10. Moore, "Football's Ugly Decades," 49–68.

11. Ibid.

12. This organization would eventually evolve into today's governing body, the NCAA.

13. Glenn S. Warner, *Pop Warner, Football's Greatest Teacher,* ed. Michael J. Bynum (Langhorne, PA: Gridiron Football Properties), 118.

14. "Pierce to Coach Indians," *Washington Post,* February 3, 1906.

15. Bynum, *Pop Warner,* 112.

16. Allison Danzig, *Oh, How They Played the Game* (New York: The Macmillan Company, 1971), 177–88. Danzig chronicles the development of the forward pass with first-person accounts from the principals.

17. *The News of Lynchburg, Virginia*, September 19, 1954, feature story on Gus Welch.

18. *Bedford* (Virginia) *Bulletin*, October 9, 1952.

19. *Richmond Times-Dispatch*, February 12, 1928; Jack Newcombe, *The Best of the Athletic Boys* (New York: Doubleday, 1975), 67.

20. Newcombe, *Best of the Athletic Boys*, 119.

21. Glenn S. Warner, "Heap Big Run Most Fast," *Collier's*, October 24, 1931; Arthur Martin interview, oral history project, Cumberland County Historical Society.

22. Details of Welch's meeting with the Indians are from *The News of Lynchburg, Virginia*, September 19, 1954, and the *Richmond Times-Dispatch*, February 12, 1928. Welch gave slightly conflicting accounts of the encounter. In the *News*, he assigns the date of his meeting with the Indians to 1906 and says he was fourteen. However, in the *Times-Dispatch* he suggests it was 1907. Newcombe in his biography of Jim Thorpe, *Best of the Athletic Boys*, assigns it to the 1907 season but does not explain why. The Indians played Minnesota in both 1906 and 1907. Welch states that Carlisle "trounced" Minnesota in the game, which could only refer to the '06 season. In 1907, the Indians would win by just two points. It seems reasonable that Welch stayed with the Indians on both occasions.

23. Bynum, *Pop Warner*, 112.

24. Newcombe, *Best of the Athletic Boys*, 94–95.

25. *The Arrow*, December 21, 1906.

26. Hudson's student file in the National Archives (5305) contains a letter from the investigator stating that the shortage resulted from "small abstractions from the cash in his hands from time to time during the last year." The file also contains a "surety in bond" that Mercer took out in Hudson's name with U.S. Fidelity and Guaranty in Baltimore. When the funds went missing, Mercer filed a claim stating that Hudson "defaulted in his accounts to me as Superintendent of this school to the sum of $1410.62."

27. Grantland Rice, *The Tumult and the Shouting* (New York: Dell Publishing, 1954), 206.

28. Bynum, *Pop Warner*, 118–19.

29. Newcombe, *Best of the Athletic Boys*, 98–100.

30. "Jim and Exie Meet Once More," *Muskogee Daily Phoenix*, May 12, 1929. The piece is notable for the recollections of each other by Thorpe and Exendine during a reunion in Oklahoma.

31. Bynum, *Pop Warner*, 119.

32. Thorpe's recollection in the *Arlington Daily*, January 5, 1950.

33. Bynum, *Pop Warner*, 119–22.

34. "Airship Runs Wild," *New York Herald*, October 3, 1907; *New York Herald*, October 25, 1907.

35. *New York Herald*, October 26, 1907.

36. *New York World,* November 3, 1907; Trager, *A People's Chronology,* 715–21.

37. Knute Rockne always declined credit for the pass, and named Warner, Eddie Cochems at St. Louis, and Stagg at Chicago as the real pioneers.

38. *Washington Post,* September 6, 1906.

39. Danzig, *Oh, How They Played the Game,* 177–88.

40. Danzig, ibid., noted that Knute Rockne of Notre Dame always disclaimed the credit he was wrongly given for the pass, and named Cochems, Warner, and Stagg as deserving of it, in that precise order.

41. Bob Fulton, "A Frank, Open Hearted Gentleman," *Indiana University of Pennsylvania Magazine* 10, 3. Mount Pleasant would place sixth in the long jump and triple jump in the 1908 Olympics, despite a strained ligament. Shortly after the Games, when he was healthy again, Mount Pleasant beat the Olympic long jump champion Frank Irons in a meet in Paris and set the French record.

42. Glenn S. Warner, "Red Menaces," *Collier's,* October 31, 1931; Fulton, "Frank, Open Hearted Gentleman."

43. Newcombe, *Best of the Athletic Boys,* 110.

44. Warner, "The Indian Massacres," *Collier's,* October 17, 1931.

45. *New York Herald,* October 27, 1907.

46. Bynum, *Pop Warner,* 118.

47. Thorpe's recollection in the *Daily Oklahoman,* February 15, 1950.

48. Warner, "Indian Massacres."

49. Glenn S. Warner, "Heap Big Run Most Fast," *Collier's,* October 24, 1931.

50. *New York Herald, New York World,* and *New York Times,* November 3, 1903, and *New York Times,* November 12, 1907.

51. *New York Herald,* November 10, 1907; "Mt. Pleasant's Laconic Comment upon Victory," *Boston Herald,* November 10, 1907.

52. *Boston Herald,* November 10, 1907.

53. Ibid.

54. John S. Watterson III, "Political Football: Theodore Roosevelt, Woodrow Wilson, and the Gridiron Reform Movement," *Presidential Studies Quarterly,* summer 1995.

55. Carlisle Indian School Hearings Before the Joint Commission of the Congress of the United States, 63rd Congress, 2nd Sess., February 6, 7, 8 and March 25, 1914, Part II.

56. Interview with Arthur Martin, oral history project, Cumberland County Historical Society.

57. Newcombe, *Best of the Athletic Boys,* 67; *Richmond Times-Dispatch,* February 12, 1928.

58. Letter quoted in John S. Steckbeck, *Fabulous Redmen* (Harrisburg, 1951), 73.

59. Warner, "Indian Massacres"; "Maroons and Indians Ready," *Chicago Daily Tribune,* November 23, 1907.

60. Game details from "Carlisle Too Fast," *Washington Post,* November 24, 1907, and "Aborigines Win over Pale Faces," *Chicago Daily Tribune,* November 24, 1907.

61. *Chicago Daily Tribune,* November 23, 1907; Warner, "Indian Massacres."

62. John L. Johnson, "Albert Andrew Exendine: Carlisle Coach and Teacher," *Chronicles of Oklahoma* 43, 3.

63. Exendine's recollection in an undated clipping from the *Tulsa Tribune,* in Exendine Papers.

64. Johnson, "Albert Andrew Exendine."

65. Warner, "Indian Massacres."

66. "Carlisle's Athletic Policy Criticized by Dr. Montezuma," *Chicago Daily Tribune,* November 24, 1907.

67. Letter from Thompson to Montezuma. Photocopy in the Cumberland County Historical Society.

68. "Fast Indian Eleven," *New York Herald,* November 1, 1907. Warner's salary is from the Carlisle Indian School Hearings.

69. *The Carlisle Arrow,* December 13, 1907; "Warner Denies Charge, Claims Carlisle Indians Are Bonafide Students of School," *Washington Post,* December 6, 1907.

70. Ages of the all-American team members are from Weyand, *Saga of American Football,* who lists them in the appendix.

71. Warner, "Indian Massacres."

72. *The Carlisle Arrow,* December 20, 1907.

73. William F. Knox, "The New Football," *Harper's Weekly,* December 7, 1907.

74. Caspar Whitney, "The View-Point," *Outing,* December 1907.

Chapter 10 • Advances and Retreats

1. Arthur Martin interview, oral history project, Cumberland County Historical Society.

2. Edwin Pope, *Football's Greatest Coaches* (Atlanta: Tupper and Sons, 1955), 294–95. The wood lathing anecdote is from *The Carlisle Arrow,* February 19, 1909.

3. Allison Danzig, *Oh, How They Played the Game* (New York: The Macmillan Company, 1971), 341.

4. Ibid., 342.

5. Pope, *Football's Greatest Coaches,* 293.

6. Glenn S. Warner, *Pop Warner, Football's Greatest Teacher,* ed. Michael J. Bynum (New York, 1993), 151.

7. Pope, *Football's Greatest Coaches,* 294–95. In addition to being elegantly written, the profiles by Pope, a Hall of Fame sportswriter for the *Miami Herald,* have the advantage of being based on interviews and correspondence with former players of the coaches.

8. Genevieve Bell, "Telling Stories Out of School," Ph.D. dissertation, Stanford University, June 1998, 89.

9. Carlisle Indian School Hearings Before the Joint Commission of the Congress of the United States, 63rd Congress, 2nd Sess., February 6, 7, 8 and March 25, 1914, Part II.

10. Ibid. In 1907 and 1908, cash payments to player totaled $9,233. Also, Jack Newcombe, *The Best of the Athletic Boys* (New York: Doubleday, 1975), 121.

11. Arthur Martin interview, oral history project, Cumberland County Historical Society.

12. Newcombe, *Best of the Athletic Boys*, 103.

13. Glenn S. Warner, "Heap Big Run Most Fast," *Collier's*, October 24, 1931.

14. Carlisle Indian School Hearings.

15. John S. Steckbeck, *Fabulous Redmen* (Harrisburg, PA: J. Horace McFarland Company, 1951).

16. Warner, "Heap Big Run Most Fast."

17. Steckbeck, *Fabulous Redmen*, 75.

18. Pope, *Football's Greatest Coaches*, 107.

19. Ibid., 107–11.

20. Tim Cohane, *Gridiron Grenadiers: The Story of West Point Football* (New York: G. P. Putnam's Sons, 1948), 70.

21. Pope, *Football's Greatest Coaches*.

22. For an explanation of the 1910 rule changes and their causes and effects, see Parke H. Davis, *Football: The Intercollegiate Game* (New York: Charles Scribner's Sons, 1911), 112–14. Davis, Princeton class of 1893, was a member of the Intercollegiate Rules Committee and a terrible snob. He omits Carlisle from his account of football's evolution, particularly the use of the forward pass in 1907, acknowledging only Harvard, Princeton, and Yale. But his book contains useful explanations, as well as an appendix with notes and accounts of the rules committee meetings from 1876 to 1911.

23. Robert W. Wheeler, *Jim Thorpe, World's Greatest Athlete* (Norman: University of Oklahoma Press, 1979), 78.

24. Grantland Rice, *The Tumult and the Shouting* (New York: Dell Publishing, 1954), 204; interview with Grace Thorpe.

25. "Carlisle Players Desert," *Washington Post*, February 27, 1909.

26. Yale and Carlisle played only five times, and not at all after 1900. Princeton and Carlisle had only an intermittent series, playing just half a dozen games, and never met again after 1910. Carlisle and Harvard, however, played almost continuously from 1896 to 1915.

27. Letter from Warner and Friedman to Hugh Miller, January 22, 1909, Hugh Miller Collection, Cumberland County Historical Society.

28. Steckbeck, *Fabulous Redmen*, 103–4.

29. "South Dakota Sioux Attack Alcoholism," *New York Times*, July 17, 1970.

30. Exendine to the *Tulsa Tribune*, August 20, 1965; Newcombe, *Best of the Athletic Boys*, 148–49.

31. Warner always maintained that Thorpe played semipro ball without his knowledge, and denied any contact with Thorpe until he wrote to him in the summer of 1911. But according to Thorpe's grandson, Mike Koehler, Warner and Thorpe took a hunting trip together in 1909–10.

32. Welch's recollection from an undated and unmarked clipping, Welch Papers.

33. Newcombe, *Best of the Athletic Boys*, 153.

34. Warner, "Heap Big Run Most Fast."

35. Letter from Moore to John Steckbeck, March 9, 1952, Special Collections, Waidner-Spahr Library, Dickinson College.

36. Robert Cantwell, "The Poet, the Bums, and The Legendary Red Men," *Sports Illustrated*, February 15, 1960. Cantwell is one of the few people who realized that Moore was a sports fan, and interviewed her on the subject of Carlisle's glory days.

37. Newcombe, *Best of the Athletic Boys*, 224; "Jim Thorpe of Carlisle World's Most Remarkable All Around Athlete," *New York Evening World*, November 6, 1911.

38. *Washington Times-Herald*, March 26, 1940.

39. Undated clipping, *Washington Herald*, Exendine Papers.

40. Pope, *Football's Greatest Coaches*, 297.

41. Glenn S. Warner, "Here Come the Giants," *Collier's*, November 21, 1931.

42. Rice, *The Tumult and the Shouting*, 205. Rice quotes from a direct conversation with Warner.

43. Jim Thorpe, *Esquire*, September 1952; Rice, *The Tumult and the Shouting*, 202.

44. Interview with Thorpe's grandson, Mike Koehler.

45. Undated clipping from the *Tulsa Tribune*, in Exendine Papers.

46. Undated and unmarked clipping, Exendine Papers.

47. Welch handwritten notes, Welch Papers.

48. Linda Waggoner, "Reclaiming James One Star," five-part series for *Indian Country Today*, July 2–August 2, 2004. Waggoner, a professor at Sonoma State University, attempts to examine Dietz's claims.

49. *New York Herald*, November 3, 4, 8, and 9, 1911.

50. Alexander M. Weyand, *The Saga of American Football* (New York: The Macmillan Company, 1955), 100; Warner, "Heap Big Run Most Fast."

51. Newcombe, *Best of the Athletic Boys*, 165.

52. Charley Paddock, "Chief Bright Path," *Collier's*, October 12, 1929. Paddock won the gold medal in the hundred meters at the 1920 Olympics in Antwerp, after which he became a journalist. He was a friend of Thorpe's and wrote a five-part series about him for *Collier's*, which, though it contains some factual errors, has an intimacy most accounts of Thorpe lacked. Paddock enlisted in the Marines in 1942 and was killed in an airplane crash in 1943.

53. Warner, "Heap Big Run Most Fast."

54. Welch's handwritten notes, Welch Papers.

55. Paddock, "Chief Bright Path."

56. Newcombe, *Best of the Athletic Boys*, 167.

57. Game details from the *New York Herald*, November 19, 1911; Warner, "Here Come the Giants."

58. "Indians Get No Rest After Defeat," *New York Times*, November 21, 1911.

59. Glenn S. Warner, "Red Menaces," *Collier's*, October 31, 1931.

60. Paddock, "Chief Bright Path."

61. Newcombe, *Best of the Athletic Boys*.

62. Warner, "Red Menaces."

63. Undated clipping, Welch Papers.

64. Rice, *The Tumult and the Shouting*, 201–2.

65. Ibid.

66. Warner, "Red Menaces"; Bynum, *Pop Warner*, 135.

67. *Boston Post*, August 25, 1912.

68. Newcombe, *Best of the Athletic Boys*, 188–89.

69. James Garvie interview, Carlisle oral history project, Cumberland County Historical Society; unmarked clipping, Welch Papers.

70. Bynum, *Pop Warner*, 142.

71. Paddock, "Chief Bright Path."

Chapter 11 • The Real All Americans

1. Handwritten autobiographical notes by Welch, and also obituary of Welch in the *Bedford Bulletin Democrat*, February 5, 1970, Welch Papers.

2. Interview with James Garvie, oral history project, Cumberland County Historical Society.

3. Welch's handwritten notes, Welch Papers.

4. Excerpted from Peter Nabokov, ed., *Native American Testimony: A Chronicle of Indian-White Relations from Prophecy to the Present, 1492–1992* (New York: Penguin, 1991), 289–90.

5. Welch's handwritten autobiographical notes, Welch Papers.

6. Glenn S. Warner, *Pop Warner, Football's Greatest Teacher*, ed. Michael J. Bynum (Langhorne, PA: Gridiron Football Properties), 138.

7. Kyle Crichton, "Good King Jim," *Collier's*, November 14, 1942. Crichton played against Carlisle as a member of the Lehigh football team.

8. Ibid.

9. As quoted in David Wallace Adams, "More Than a Game: The Carlisle Indians Take to the Gridiron, 1893–1917," *Western Historical Quarterly* 32, 1 (2001).

10. Tim Cohane, *Gridiron Grenadiers: The Story of West Point Football* (New York: G. P. Putnam's Sons, 1948), 7–8.

11. Gene Schoor, *100 Years of Army Navy Football* (New York: Henry Holt and Company, 1989), 45. Littlejohn's duel is recounted in Cohane, *Gridiron Grenadiers*, 65.

12. Cohane, *Gridiron Grenadiers*, 74.

13. Schoor, *100 Years*, 47–48, cites a lengthy letter from Eisenhower to the author recounting his football career.

14. Welch as quoted in an unmarked clipping, Welch Papers; Warner as quoted in Charley Paddock, "Chief Bright Path," *Collier's*, October 19, 1929.

15. Game details from the *New York Tribune, New York Herald*, and *New York Times*, November 10, 1912, and Alexander M. Weyand, *Football's Immortals* (New York: The Macmillan Company, 1962), 183–86.

16. Alexander M. Weyand, *The Saga of American Football* (New York: The Macmil-

lan Company, 1956), 101. Allison Danzig, *Oh, How They Played the Game* (New York: The Macmillan Company, 1971), 346, cites a letter from Warner to the author describing the creation of the single and double wing offenses. "Defensive tackles had always been difficult to keep out of the offensive backfield because they generally played outside the offensive ends and therefore could not often be blocked on wide plays. I figured one back could be used to very good advantage by placing him in a position where he would outflank the opposing tackle and still be in position where he could run with the ball, as on reverse plays . . . in later years I carried it a step further."

17. Welch's reminiscence in the *Roanoke World News*, May 12, 1960.

18. *New York Times*, November 12, 1912.

19. Unmarked, undated clipping in Welch Papers.

20. Bynum, *Pop Warner*, 140; Weyand, *Football's Immortals*, 183.

21. Newcombe, *Best of the Athletic Boys*, 205.

22. *New York Times*, November 26, 1912.

23. Paddock, "Chief Bright Path."

24. *New York Tribune*, January 26, 28, and 29, 1913; letter from Fred Bruce to M. K. Sniffen, secretary of Indian Rights Association, November 18, 1913, Johnson Collection, Cumberland County Historical Society.

25. Glenn S. Warner, "Red Menaces," *Collier's*, October 31, 1931.

26. Henry Flickinger interview, Carlisle oral history project, Cumberland County Historical Society.

27. Exendine's recollection in the *Tulsa Tribune*, undated clipping, Exendine Papers.

28. Warner, *Pop Warner*, 147.

29. Letter from Fred Bruce to Indian Rights Association, November 18, 1913, Johnson Collection, Cumberland County Historical Society. Bruce's letter was unearthed by Genevieve Bell during research for her dissertation, "Telling Stories Out of School," Stanford University, 1998.

30. Details of investigation are from Carlisle Indian School Hearings before the Joint Commission of the Congress of the United States, 63rd Congress, 2nd sess., February 6, 7, 8, and March 25, 1914, Part II.

31. Ibid.

32. Bell, "Telling Stories Out of School," 97.

33. Postcard to Julia Carter Welch and letter from Charles Bachman to Julia Welch, October 12, 1976, Welch Papers. Bachman played for Notre Dame.

34. Letter from W. E. Morgan to Oscar Lipps, November 21, 1914, Welch's student file, no. 5234, National Archives.

35. Glenn S. Warner, "The Indian Massacres," *Collier's*, October 17, 1931.

36. Ibid.

37. Ibid.

38. Letter from Charles Bachman to Julia Welch, October 12, 1976, Welch Papers.

39. Correspondence in Welch's student file, no. 5234, National Archives.

40. Ibid.

41. Information on the Pioneers is from the Papers of Moses Thisted and from Thisted's *Pershing's Pioneers* (Hemet, California, 1981–82), Military History Institute, AHEC. Also from Arthur E. Barbeau and Florette Henri, *The Unknown Soldiers: Black American Troops in World War I* (Philadelphia: Temple University Press, 1995).

42. Barbeau and Henri, *Unknown Soldiers*, 105.

43. Found in papers of Moses Thisked, Military History Institute.

44. One of Welch's letters of commendation is in the Welch Papers. The other is referred to in handwritten notes by Julia Welch, Welch Papers.

45. For a discussion of the impact of Carlisle's policies as a form of tribal destruction, see the conclusion in David Wallace Adams, *Education for Extinction: American Indians and the Boarding School Experience, 1875–1928* (Lawrence: University of Kansas Press, 1995).

46. Ibid., 308, 318–19.

47. Ibid., 318–19.

48. For a numerical overview of Carlisle's students and their professions, see Bell, "Telling Stories Out of School," 331–40.

49. Thorpe's view of Carlisle is from an interview with Grace Thorpe. Exendine's view is expressed in the *Tulsa Tribune*, August 11, 1971.

50. Elaine Goodale Eastman, *Pratt: The Red Man's Moses* (Norman: University of Oklahoma Press, 1935), 66.

51. Ibid., 266.

Epilogue

1. Undated clipping from the *Carlisle Sentinel*, found by Barbara Landis of the Cumberland County Historical Society in the scrapbook of James Wardecker.

2. Student file 5299, National Archives.

3. *Assembly*, October 1942, obituary for Leland Swarts Devore.

4. Gene Schoor, *100 Years of Army Navy Football* (New York: Henry Holt and Company, 1989), 47–48.

5. *Daily Oklahoman*, February 15, 1950, feature story on Exendine.

6. Edwin Pope, *Football's Greatest Coaches* (Atlanta: Tupper and Sons, 1955), 113–14.

7. Student file 5305, National Archives; Luana Mangold interview, oral history project, Cumberland County Historical Society; interview with John Alonzo in Dewitt Clinton Smith Papers, Waidner Spahr Library, Dickinson College; *Washington Times*, November 26, 1917.

8. Richard Henry Pratt, *Battlefield and Classroom: Four Decades with the American Indian* (Norman: University of Oklahoma Press, 2003), 319.

9. "A Famous Old Carlisle Star and Coach Dies," *Chicago Tribune*, January 19, 1942.

10. Elaine Goodale Eastman, *Pratt: The Red Man's Moses* (Norman: University of Oklahoma Press, 1935), 266–70.

11. Interview with Grace Thorpe, June 15, 2006.

12. Letter from Thorpe to Welch, November 26, 1941, Welch Papers.

13. Charley Paddock, "Chief Bright Path," *Collier's*, October 4, 1929; interview with Grace Thorpe and Mike Koehler.

14. Pop Warner, "Heap Big Run Most Fast," *Collier's*, October 24, 1931.

15. Undated clipping in Gus Welch Papers.

16. Delos Lone Wolf's student file #5309, Record Group 75, entry 1327, National Archives.

17. Hertzberg, 145–50.

18. Nabokov, *Native American Testimony*, 266–67.

19. Blue Clark, *Lone Wolf v. Hitchcock, Treaty Rights and Indian Law at the End of the Nineteenth Century* (Lincoln: University of Nebraska Press, 1999), 96.

20. John R. Wunder, *The Kiowa* (New York: Chelsea House Publishers, 1989), 95.

21. Corwin, Hugh, "Delos K. Lone Wolf, Kiowa," *Chronicles of Oklahoma*, Vol. 39, No. 4, 433–38.

22. Obituary of Welch, *Washington Star*, January 30, 1970.

23. Letter from Willis Oglesby, Welch papers.

24. Obituary of Welch, *Washington Star*, January 30, 1970.